THE
EIGHTEENTH-CENTURY
CONSTITUTION
1688–1815

DOCUMENTS AND COMMENTARY

BY

E. NEVILLE WILLIAMS

Head of the History Side
Dulwich College

CAMBRIDGE
AT THE UNIVERSITY PRESS
1960

PUBLISHED BY

THE SYNDICS OF THE CAMBRIDGE UNIVERSITY PRESS

Bentley House, 200 Euston Road, London, N.W.1
American Branch: 32 East 57th Street, New York 22, N.Y.

©

CAMBRIDGE UNIVERSITY PRESS

1960

Printed in Great Britain by
Spottiswoode, Ballantyne and Co. Ltd
London and Colchester

THE
EIGHTEENTH-CENTURY
CONSTITUTION
1688–1815

Dedicated in gratitude to

BERT HOWARD

CONTENTS

CONTENTS

viii

CONTENTS

ix

CONTENTS

CONTENTS

CONTENTS

CONTENTS

A NOTE ON DATES

Till 1752 dates are given in the Old Style, except that (i) the year is taken to
begin on 1 January instead of on 25 March; and (ii) dates in documents are
given as they appear in the original, with a note where necessary.

PREFACE

Victorian historians assumed that the eighteenth-century political system was a dress rehearsal for their own polished performance, and condemned any divergencies they found as failures to come up to the demands of the script. Misinterpretation was the result; for the attribution to other people of our own aims and motives, customs and conventions is bound to lead to distortion. Irrelevant questions are asked and wrong answers are found; words are used with anachronistic meanings. During the last fifty years, however, much has been done to clarify the vision and rearrange the pattern. Patient labour by a generation of historians inspired by the genius of Sir Lewis Namier has given solid grounds for confirming what a minority of writers have been saying all along. It has been a question, in the main, of delineating the political structure of the period as it existed in the minds of the men who were involved in it. Political structure is not the whole story, of course, any more than psycho-analysis is biography; but both require the illumination that the others provide. This selection of documents attempts to give an idea of eighteenth-century institutions as they are seen by historians today. Much of the British constitution notoriously exists only in the minds of men, and it is hoped that this volume will enable some glimpses of it to be seen in the language men used from William III to William Pitt.

I am glad to count myself among the number of students who are fortunate enough to receive the warm interest and skilled guidance of Dr J. H. Plumb. I have also had the privilege of consulting Dr G. Kitson Clark, the distinguished scholar in constitutional history, for whose generous help I am most grateful. I wish to acknowledge my indebtedness also to the staff of the British Museum, the Public Record Office, the Leicester Museum, and the Library of the University of London; and to the Vicar of West Thurrock in Essex, who kindly allowed me to use his parish records. I must also record my appreciation of the efforts of my wife in transcribing and typing; a schoolmaster could not produce a work like this in his spare time without such help. And, finally, I wish to thank my colleagues, and also several generations of pupils from whose questions, pertinent and impertinent, I have learned so much.

E.N.W.

DULWICH
September 1959

ABBREVIATIONS

Add. MSS.	Additional Manuscripts, British Museum.
A.H.R.	*The American Historical Review.*
Atkinson	J. C. Atkinson, *North Riding Quarter Sessions Records*, 1892.
Barnes	S. J. Barnes, *Walthamstow in the 18th Century*, 1925–7.
Bulletin	*The Bulletin of the Institute of Historical Research.*
Burn	R. Burn, *The Justice of the Peace*, 21st ed., 1810.
C.H.J.	*The Cambridge Historical Journal.*
C.J.	*The House of Commons Journals.*
Corresp. George III	Sir J. Fortescue, *The Correspondence of George III*, 1927–8.
Cox	J. C. Cox, *Three Centuries of Derbyshire Annals*, 1890.
Econ. H.R.	*The Economic History Review.*
E.H.R.	*The English Historical Review.*
H.J.	*The Historical Journal.*
H.M.C.	Historical Manuscripts Commission.
J.M.H.	*The Journal of Modern History.*
L.J.	*The House of Lords Journals.*
L.Q.R.	*The Law Quarterly Review.*
P.D.	W. Cobbett, *Parliamentary Debates*, 1812–20.
P.H.	W. Cobbett, *The Parliamentary History of England*, 1806–12.
P.R.O.	Public Record Office.
P.S.Q.	*Political Science Quarterly.*
S.L.	D. Pickering (ed.), *The Statutes at Large from Magna Charta to . . . 1761; Continued* (to 1806), Cambridge, 1762–1806. Continued as *The Statutes of the United Kingdom.*
S.R.	*The Statutes of the Realm*, 1810– .
S.T.	T. B. Howell, *A Complete Collection of State Trials*, 1809–26.
T.R.H.S.	*Transactions of the Royal Historical Society.*

CHAPTER I

THE REVOLUTION

Sir William Blackstone, in typical eighteenth-century fashion, was fond of using mechanics to illustrate the working of the constitution in his day.[1] Possibly cybernetics would be a more suitable model; and, if the constitution is looked on as a self-regulating mechanism, then the seventeenth century was the period when it was 'hunting', when it was swinging wildly from one extreme to the other in search of equilibrium. At the start of the reign of James II a steadying can be observed, after the violent Country swing of the Exclusion period had outraged moderate opinion; but this was short-lived and a swing to the Court side was soon evident, so violent that not only the moderates but even the most fervent supporters of the crown began to take compensating action. Whigs and Tories, Anglicans and Dissenters combined to prevent a determined effort to convert the country into a Bourbon-type, Roman Catholic autocracy. The birth of a son to James in June 1688, which foreshadowed permanent success to this attempt, touched an extreme which triggered off action on the other side. At the end of that month, a committee of peers, four Whig and three Tory, despatched their invitation to William of Orange (1); and at the end of September the latter issued his declaration (2), in which may conveniently be found a summary of the misdeeds of his father-in-law and of his own motives in coming to England. He landed at Torbay on 5 November. On 11 December James left the capital on his first attempt at flight, and the interregnum had begun. The breach in the constitution was plugged the same day by the ancient counsellors of the crown, a group of spiritual and temporal peers who happened to be in the metropolis. They issued their declaration from Guildhall, resolving, since the king had 'withdrawn himself . . . in order to his departure out of this kingdom', to apply themselves to William, who had come to procure a free parliament (3). For the next few weeks the peers in their House took the necessary measures for governing the country on the civil side, while William dealt with military matters. On 23 December he called a meeting at St James's of members of Charles II's parliaments and the Lord Mayor, Aldermen and fifty Common Councillors of the City of London, to give him 'speedy advice' (4). This assembly, meeting on the 26th (and a separate meeting of the Lords in their House), asked William to take over the direction of affairs till a convention could be elected (5); and the letters ordering the election to take place went out on the 29th (6).

[1] See No. 24, p. 75.

This convention met on 22 January and proceeded to work out formulae which would decently cover the unpleasant rents in the fabric of the constitution, and to take steps to prevent the recurrence of Stuart extremism in the future. The first task was no simple one, for continuity had been broken in the two chief organs of government: the king had fled, and had burned many of the writs for the calling of parliament. It was now a question of stretching theory till it covered these facts, a problem complicated by the presence in the convention of several different opinions about how far and in which direction the stretching ought to be done. In the lower House, which contained many of the former enemies of Court extremism, it was not difficult to find a majority in favour of the proposition that James had 'abdicated the government' and that the throne was thereby 'vacant'; but in the House of Lords adherence to logic and the hereditary principle delayed acceptance of this formula for nearly two weeks. A few favoured recalling James upon conditions. Others were for regarding William as regent for him. The main body, however, wanted no more truck with him; but even these would only go so far as to assert that he had 'deserted' the throne, i.e. given up the exercise of his power, not 'abdicated'. And even if he had 'abdicated', it was said, in an hereditary monarchy the throne could never be 'vacant', for it was immediately filled with the heir. Everyone was agreed in regarding James's recently born son as suppositious, and therefore sticklers for hereditary descent, like many of the Tories, plumped for Mary as queen, with William as consort, or as regent. These various points of view, summarised by Reresby (**7**), emerge in the debates in both Houses and in the conferences between them in the early weeks of 1689 (**8**); but eventually the adherents of logical consistency had to retreat before practical reality, for Mary insisted on her husband being king, and William refused to be his 'wife's gentleman usher' (**9**). And so the throne became temporarily elective, and William and Mary became king and queen on 13 February, thus ending the interregnum (**10**). In this same document, the Bill of Rights, the particular ban on James and his son was made general by a clause which enacted that Roman Catholics and those married to Roman Catholics were 'for ever incapable to inherit, possess, or enjoy the crown and government of this realm'. All office-holders, members of parliament and clergy had to take the new oaths of allegiance to the new rulers, though at this stage no one was called upon to swear that they were 'rightful and lawful' sovereigns. Later in the reign, when the Assassination Plot and the recognition of the Pretender by Louis XIV had rallied the public more warmly to the new regime, this phrase appeared in the Association of 1696 and in the Oath of Abjuration of 1702. Thus both Whigs and Tories became wholesale Exclusionists, and it was a predominantly Tory parliament which passed the Act of Settlement, in which the hereditary descent was further tampered with (**21**). This measure excluded fifty-seven Roman Catholic heirs in favour of the Hanoverians, and imposed a number of restrictions on this new foreign dynasty. Sovereigns were hereafter to join in communion with the Church of England; and, without parliamentary consent, they were barred from involving this country in war on behalf of territories not belonging to the British crown. They were also forbidden to leave the country, though this clause was repealed for the benefit of George I in 1716. Similarly, foreigners were barred from the Privy Council and parliament, and were forbidden to hold any civil or military office, or receive any grants of land from the king.

Once the throne was filled, the convention could pull itself up by its own boot-laces, and in its first statute it 'declared, enacted, and adjudged' itself 'to be to all intents, constructions, and purposes whatsoever' the 'two houses of parliament' (**11**). And in the following year, the enactments of the convention were declared by the second parliament of the reign to be 'laws and statutes of this kingdom' (**16**).

The task of repairing the fabric of the constitution was thus completed—at the expense of the theory of Divine Right; indeed, at the expense of the consistency of all concerned. For, as David Ogg has pointed out,[1] if consistency had been pressed, the revolution could not have been bloodless. The men of 1688, however much they were revered in the centuries following, were not Founding Fathers enunciating general principles of constitutional law, but empiricists coping with practical difficulties. And in this same spirit they tackled the second problem mentioned above: that of settling 'the religion, laws and liberties of this kingdom, so that the same for the future might not be in danger again of being subverted.'[2] In other words, they regarded themselves not as revolutionaries demolishing the power of the crown, but as conservatives correcting revolutionary tendencies on the part of previous monarchs. And thus the revolution did not end the struggle between Court and Country, but merely ruled out of order certain weapons used by the former, leaving both sides free to forge new ones in the future.

The most dangerous weapons were those that directly attacked the position of parliament in the constitution; and the arrangements of 1688 and after were designed to guarantee, as far as verbal forms could guarantee, the crucial place which this institution had achieved in the struggles of the early part of the century. The Coronation Oath (**13**) contained a significant new phrase: the monarchs swore to govern according to 'the statutes in parliament agreed upon, and the laws and customs of the same'. This recognition of parliament's importance was reinforced by provisions to ensure its

---

[1] D. Ogg, *England in the Reigns of James II and William III* (Oxford, 1955), p. 211.
[2] Bill of Rights, p. 30.

independence. The elaborate arrangements of Charles II and James II to secure subservient parliaments by tampering with lord-lieutenants and J.P.s, and by remodelling the corporations (perhaps the most effective weapon of all, for the boroughs returned the majority of the M.P.s), dissolved in the events of 1688 and 1689. One of James's last acts was to proclaim the restoration of the charters. The House of Commons in the convention passed a bill having a similar effect, which contained the so-called Sacheverell Clause, calculated to swing too far in the opposition direction and place the boroughs permanently in the hands of the Whigs (**17**). However, the Lords could not agree that the *Quo Warranto* proceedings had been beyond the scope of the royal prerogative (and the judges were divided on this question), and so the bill was lost with the prorogation which came soon after. How far the borough constitutions changed in this period still awaits investigation, but what is clear is that it was from now on politically impossible for any government to attempt to control parliament by an open and general invasion of the rights of local authorities.[1] Further safeguards of the independence of parliament were provided by clauses in the Bill of Rights which laid down that 'the election of members of parliament ought to be free', and that 'freedom of speech . . . in parliament ought not to be impeached or questioned in any court or place out of parliament'.[2] The Act of Settlement went even further in this direction by its drastic provision (later modified[3]) excluding all placemen, which, though it would have prevented the full exploitation of another means of controlling parliament—'influence'—would also have made impossible the development of our present cabinet system.

Independence was illusory, however, unless parliament was called regularly, and further steps, some deliberate, others less so, were taken to ensure this. The Bill of Rights ordered that 'parliaments ought to be held frequently'[4]; and the Triennial Act of 1694 (**18**) laid down that a new parliament should be called within three years of the dissolution of the last, and that no parliament should last more than three years. But these statutes had less practical effect than the financial arrangements made by the post-Revolution parliaments to pay the vast expenses of the wars against Louis XIV, which, as a by-product, made annual sessions an absolute necessity for any monarch. As Burnet said, 'it was taken up as a general maxim, that a revenue for a certain and short term, was the best security that the nation could have for frequent parliaments'.[5] Appropriation became regular, public loans were guaranteed by statute, and more and more of public expenditure was brought into the realm of specific parliamentary grant, leaving, in the Act of 1697 (**19**),

---

[1] That this insulation of local government from central control also produced harmful effects may be seen in Chapter 4.

[2] Bill of Rights, p. 28.   [3] See No. **117** and p. **188**.   [4] Bill of Rights, p. 29.

[5] G. Burnet, *History of His Own Time* (Edinburgh, 1753), vol. IV, p. 61.

the Civil List, voted for life, responsible only for the civil administration and the royal household.

A firmer grip on finance gave parliament a surer hold on measures and men; and parliamentary influence over the executive was bound to grow as succeeding monarchs came to terms with this truth, as they gradually learned that a ministry and a policy could founder on the rock of supply. In the meantime, parliament was sharpening other weapons against ministers, soon to be rendered obsolete. Unsuccessful ministers were still treated as traitorous criminals instead of political failures, and the Act of Settlement contains a clause (later repealed) that attempted to pin them down by ordering that the government should be conducted in the Privy Council and that counsellors should sign their advice.[1] And, to prevent a repetition of the Stuart method of putting ministers beyond the reach of parliamentary attack, the same statute laid down that 'no pardon under the great seal of England be pleadable to an impeachment by the commons in parliament'.[2]

Another royal weapon destroyed by the Bill of Rights was the use of the dispensing and suspending powers in a manner that also encroached on the rights of parliament,[3] for such an extension of the prerogative had meant that monarchs could, in effect, alter the law without the concurrence of the two Houses. The power of the executive over the individual was limited in several other ways. The same statute enacted that 'excessive bail ought not to be required, nor excessive fines imposed; nor cruel and unusual punishments inflicted'[4]; that 'jurors ought to be impanelled'[4]; and that 'all grants and promises of fines and forfeitures of particular persons before conviction are illegal and void'.[5] Such courts as the 'commissioners for ecclesiastical causes' were declared to be 'illegal and pernicious'[6]; and the conduct of political trials was humanised, and the scales less weighted against the accused, by the Trial of Treasons Act of 1696 (20). The independence of the judiciary was ensured by the appointment of judges 'quamdiu se bene gesserint' laid down in the Act of Settlement,[7] though William had appointed them in this way from the beginning. These measures prevented for the future the use of Stuart techniques of overthrowing the law by legal forms and perverting justice by suborning the judges. They drew boundaries round the royal prerogative in areas where the frontiers had not before been clearly delineated, and brought it clearly within the scope of the common law. In addition, one undoubted prerogative was taken away from the crown at this time. The Bill of Rights stated 'that the raising or keeping a standing army within the kingdom in time of peace, unless it be with consent of parliament, is against law'.[8] Thus the final sanction of the State against the people depended from that time

[1] Act of Settlement, p. 59. [2] Ibid., p. 59. [3] Bill of Rights, p. 28.
[4] Ibid., pp. 28–9. [5] Ibid., p. 29. [6] Ibid., p. 28.
[7] Act of Settlement, p. 59. [8] Bill of Rights, p. 28.

forward on parliamentary enactment; and now that the army was theirs, and not the king's only, parliament was willing to give to the commanders the necessary means of disciplining the troops which they had resisted enacting before. The Mutiny Act of 1689 (12) was the first of a long series of Acts, passed at first for six months and then usually for twelve, which have gradually formulated the special code of military law.

The revolution was mounted, to use William's words, in order to 'preserve and maintain the established Laws, Liberties and Customs, and, above all, the Religion and Worship of God'.[1] We have seen how the first three aims were achieved, and it is now time to turn to the problem of the Church. The danger which threatened it in the days of James II was eliminated by the arrangements, already referred to, which prevented the throne being filled by a Roman Catholic or a monarch married to one. Monarchs had to make the declaration against transubstantiation, and in the new Coronation Oath swear to maintain 'the Protestant Reformed Religion established by law' (13). Later, in the Act of Settlement, it was ordered 'that whosoever shall hereafter come to the possession of this crown, shall join in communion with the Church of England, as by law established'.[2] With the Church thus safeguarded, something had to be done for the Protestant Dissenters, whose numbers made them a political force impossible to ignore, and whose loyalty to the 'laws, liberties and customs' in the face of royal blandishments in the previous reign cried out for reward. The furthest the Anglicans would go in this direction was to make the grudging concessions contained in the Toleration Act of 1689 (15), which, while it repealed not a single penal law, 'exempted their Majesties protestant subjects, dissenting from the Church of England', from the penalties of some of them, provided they took the new oaths of allegiance, and subscribed the old declaration against transubstantiation. Their ministers were allowed to hold services on subscription to most, though not all, of the Thirty-nine Articles. The Test and Corporation Acts were not among the statutes from which they were exempted; and thus, though they could now worship freely, they were still only second-class citizens.[3] Public opinion at that time would not stomach full equality: as Macaulay put it, the Toleration Act 'removed a vast mass of evil without shocking a vast mass of prejudice'.[4] Anything further would have been politically impossible, as those ministers found who tried to bring the Dissenters, or some of them, within the fold of the Church itself. As at the Restoration, an attempt was made at comprehension, but the measure was dropped owing to the opposition not only of the enemies, but also of the friends of religious liberty. The latter were suspicious that

[1] See p. 10. [2] Act of Settlement, p. 59.
[3] Though this theoretical position was substantially modified in practice: see Chapter 5, pp. 325–6. [4] History of England (1895), vol. I, p. 698.

comprehension, by drawing off the moderate Dissenters, would provide an excuse for cancelling toleration for the remainder.

The Dissenters were not the only group to take the new oaths. The Act which ordered all office-holders and members of parliament to take them, also imposed them on all the clergy (**14**). In spite of the fact that the oaths avoided referring to William and Mary as 'rightful and lawful' sovereigns, the Archbishop of Canterbury, five bishops and about four hundred of the lower clergy felt that they were inconsistent with their former oaths to James II, who was still living. These, the Non-jurors, as they were called, were deprived of their benefices; and in the ensuing controversy it became clear that in essence theirs was a protest against the central characteristic of the Revolution: the substitution of divine hereditary right by elective monarchy. Their defection, however, enabled the new regime to fill their places with clergy whose consciences were less tender and about whose political allegiance there was no doubt.[1]

By these measures, the Revolution Settlement extracted the poison from religious controversy, and on this count alone the events of 1688 deserve the epithet 'glorious'. When to this is added the other achievements, the preservation of the continuity of our institutions, the permanent entrenchment of parliament in the constitution, and the statutory guarantee of a number of vital individual liberties, we can be in no doubt about the prime importance of the Revolution in constitutional history. And we can appreciate this without falling into the error of regarding it as the birthplace of the Victorian system of government. We can savour the enthusiasms of the Whig historians without swallowing their anachronisms. Marlborough and Godolphin were a whole world away from Gladstone and Disraeli. Though the Revolution brought the monarchy down to human level, the Court was still the heart of British politics. As David Ogg puts it, 'it is one of the paradoxes of English history that the parliamentary constitution dates from an Act which diminished the royal power so little, and from the rule of a king whose prerogatives were so great'.[2] And these included the powers of calling and dissolving parliament, appointing ministers, vetoing legislation, and making war and peace. Halifax's note of William's conversations (**22**) show him to be a monarch of the seventeenth century, to a great extent at sea in the strange new world of annual sessions and political factions, and slow to see the importance of learning the new techniques of navigation which were not fully exploited till after his death. For the Revolution confirmed the establishment of a new centre of political power without demolishing the old, and the machinery for resolving deadlocks between the two was still primitive, as Godolphin's letter to William shows (**23**). But, though Locke

[1] See Chapter 5, pp. 326–7.
[2] D. Ogg, *England in the Reigns of James II and William III* (Oxford, 1955), p. 488.

provided them with theoretical foundations, the revolutionaries did not bind up the constitution in any philosophical strait-jacket, and this machinery could be perfected by practical men in the course of the period covered by these documents.

1. The invitation to William, 1688.

June 30, 1688

We have great satisfaction to find by 35, and since by Mons. Zulestein, that your Highness is so ready and willing to give us such assistances as they have related to us. We have great reason to believe, we shall be every day in a worse condition than we are, and less able to defend ourselves, and therefore we do earnestly wish we might be so happy as to find a remedy before it be too late for us to contribute to our own deliverance; but although these be our wishes, yet we will, by no means, put your Highness into any expectations which may misguide your own councils in this matter; so that the best advice we can give, is to inform your Highness truly both of the state of things here at this time, and of the difficulties which appear to us. As to the first, the people are so generally dissatisfied with the present conduct of the government, in relation to their religion, liberties and properties (all which have been greatly invaded) and they are in such expectation of their prospects being daily worse, that your Highness may be assured there are nineteen parts of twenty of the people throughout the kingdom who are desirous of a change; and who, we believe, would willingly contribute to it, if they had such a protection to countenance their rising, as would secure them from being destroyed, before they could get to be in a posture able to defend themselves; it is no less certain, that much the greatest part of the nobility and gentry are as much dissatisfied, although it be not safe to speak to many of them before hand; and there is no doubt but that some of the most considerable of them would venture themselves with your Highness at your first landing, whose interest would be able to draw great numbers to them, whenever they could protect them and the raising and drawing men together; and if such a strength could be landed as were able to defend itself and them, till they could be got together into some order, we make no question but that strength would quickly be increased to a number double to the army here, although their army should all remain firm to them; whereas we do upon very good grounds believe, that their army then would be very much divided among themselves; many of the officers being so discontented that they continue in their service only for a subsistence, (besides that, some of their minds are known already) and very many of the common soldiers so daily shew such an aversion to the Popish religion, that there is the greatest probability imaginable of great numbers of deserters which would come from them, should there be such an occasion; and amongst the seamen, it is almost certain, that there is not one in ten who would do them any service in such a war. Besides all this, we do much doubt, whether this present state of things will not yet be much changed to the worse before another year, by a great alteration which will probably be made both in the officers and soldiers of the army, and by such other changes as are not only to be expected from a packed parliament, but what the meeting of any parliament (in our present circumstances) may produce against those, who will be looked upon as principal obstructors of their proceedings there; it being taken for granted, that if things cannot then be carried to their wishes in a parliamentary way, other measures will be put in execution by more violent means; and although such proceedings will then heighten the discontents, yet such courses will probably be taken at that time, as will prevent all possible means of relieving ourselves.

These considerations make us of opinion, that this is a season in which we may more probably contribute to our own safeties than hereafter (although we must own to your Highness there are some judgments differing from ours in this particular) in so much that if the circumstances stand so with your Highness, that you believe you can get here time enough, in a condition to give assistances this year sufficient for a relief under these circumstances which have been now represented, we who subscribe this, will not fail to attend your Highness upon your landing, and to do all that lies in our power to prepare others to be in as much readiness as such an action is capable of, where there is so much danger in communicating an affair of such a nature, till it be near the time of its being made public. But as we have already told your Highness, we must also lay our difficulties before your Highness, which are chiefly, that we know not what alarum your preparations for this expedition may give, or what notice it will be necessary for you to give the States before hand, by either of which means their intelligence or suspicions here, may be such, as may cause us to be secured before your landing; and we must presume to inform your Highness, that your compliment upon the birth of the child (which not one in a thousand here believes to be the Queen's) hath done you some injury; the false

9

imposing of that upon the Princess and the nation, being not only an infinite exasperation of people's minds here, but being certainly one of the chief causes upon which the declarations of your entering the kingdom in a hostile manner, must be founded on your part, although many other reasons are to be given on ours. If, upon a due consideration of all these circumstances, your Highness shall think fit to venture upon the attempt, or at least to make such preparations for it as are necessary, (which we wish you may) there must be no more time lost, in letting us know your resolution concerning it, and in what time we may depend that all the preparations will be ready, as also whether your Highness does believe the preparations can be so managed as not to give them warning here, both to make them increase their force, and to secure those they shall suspect would join with you. We need not say any thing about ammunition, artillery, mortar pieces, spare arms, &c. because if you think fit to put any thing in execution, you will provide enough of these kinds, and will take care to bring some good engineers with you; and we have desired Mr. H. to consult you about all such matters, to whom we have communicated our thoughts in many particulars too tedious to have been written, and about which no certain resolutions can be taken, till we have heard again from your Highness.

| 25. | 24. | 27. | 29. | 31. | | 35. | 33. |
Sh[rewsbury]. Dev[onshire]. Danby. Lumley. [Bp. of] London. Russel. Sydney.

J. Dalrymple, *Memoirs of Great Britain and Ireland* (1783), vol. II, App. part I, p. 228.

2. William's declaration, 1688.

[30 Sept. 1688]

It is both certain and evident to all men, that the public peace and happiness of any state or kingdom cannot be preserved where the Laws, Liberties, and Customs, established by the lawful authority in it, are openly transgressed and annulled; more especially where the alteration of Religion is endeavoured, and that a religion, which is contrary to law, is endeavoured to be introduced; upon which those who are most immediately concerned in it are indispensably bound to endeavour to preserve and maintain the established Laws, Liberties and Customs, and, above all, the Religion and Worship of God, that is established among them; ... Upon these Grounds it is that we cannot any longer forbear to declare, that, to our great regret, we see, that those Counsellors, who have now the chief credit with the king, have overturned the Religion, Laws and Liberties of those realms, and subjected them, in all things relating to their Consciences, Liberties and Properties, to arbitrary Government; and that not only by secret and indirect ways, but in an open and undisguised manner.—Those evil Counsellors, for the advancing and colouring this with some plausible pretexts, did invent and set on foot the king's Dispensing Power; by virtue of which they pretend, that, according to law, he can suspend and dispense with the execution of the laws, that have been enacted by the authority of the king and parliament, for the security and happiness of the subject; and so have rendered those laws of no effect: . . . Those evil Counsellors, in order to the giving some credit to this strange and execrable maxim, have so conducted the matter, that they have obtained a Sentence from the Judges, declaring, that this Dispensing Power is a Right belonging to the crown; as if it were in the power of the Twelve Judges to offer up the Laws, Rights, and Liberties of the whole nation to the king, to be disposed of by him arbitrarily and at his pleasure, and expressly contrary to laws enacted for the security of the subjects. . . . It is also manifest and notorious, that, as his majesty was, upon his coming to the crown, received and acknowledged by all the subjects of England, Scotland, and Ireland, as their king, without the least opposition, though he made then open profession of the Popish Religion, so he did then promise and solemnly swear at his coronation, that he would maintain his subjects in the free enjoyment of their laws, rights, and liberties; and in particular, that he would maintain the Church of England, as it was established by law. It is likewise certain, that there have been, at divers and sundry times, several laws enacted for the preservation of those Rights and Liberties, and of the Protestant Religion; and, among other Securities, it has been enacted, That all persons whatsoever, that are advanced to any Ecclesiastical dignity, or to bear office in either University, as likewise all others that should be put in any employment civil or military, should declare, that they were not Papists, but were of the Protestant Religion, and that, by their taking of the Oaths of Allegiance and Supremacy, and the Test: yet those evil Counsellors have, in effect, annulled and abolished all those laws, both with relation to Ecclesiastical and Civil Employments. —In order to [sic] Ecclesiastical Dignities and Offices, they have not only without any colour of law, but against most express laws to the contrary, set up a Commission of a certain number of persons, to whom they have committed the cognisance and direction of all Ecclesiastical matters; in the which commission there has been, and still is, one of his Majesty's ministers of state, who makes now public profession of the Popish Religion; and who, at the time of his first professing it, declared that for a great while before he had believed that to be the only true Religion.... And those evil Counsellors take care to raise none to any Ecclesiastical Dignities but persons, that have no zeal for the Protestant Religion, and that now hide their unconcernedness for it under the specious pretence of moderation. The said Commissioners have suspended the bishop of London, only because he refused to obey an order, that was sent him to suspend a worthy divine, without so much as citing him before him to make his own defence, or observing the common forms of process. They have turned out a President chosen by the Fellows of Magdalen College, and afterwards all the fellows of that college, without so much as citing them before any court that could take legal cognisance of that affair, or obtaining any Sentence against them by a competent judge: ... and now those evil Counsellors have put the said College wholly into the hands of the Papists; though, as is above said, they are incapable of all such employments, both by the law of the land, and the statutes of the college. These commissioners have also cited before them all the chancellors and archdeacons of England, requiring them to certify to them the names of all such clergymen as have read the King's Declaration for Liberty of Conscience, and of such as have not read it, without considering that the reading of it was not injoined the Clergy by the Bishops, who are their Ordinaries. ... And, though there are many express laws against all Churches or Chapels for the exercise of the Popish Religion, and also against all Monasteries and Convents, and more particularly against the Order of the Jesuits; yet those evil Counsellors have procured Orders for the Building of several Churches and Chapels for the exercise of that Religion: they have also procured divers Monasteries to be erected; and, in contempt of the law, they have not only set up several Colleges of Jesuits in divers places, for corrupting of the youth, but have raised up one of the Order to be a privy counsellor, and a minister of state: ... They have also followed the same methods with relation to Civil affairs; for they have procured orders to examine all lords lieutenants, deputy lieutenants, sheriffs, justices of the peace, and also all others that were in any public employment, if they would concur with the king in the repeal of the Test and the Penal Laws: and all such whose consciences did not suffer them to comply with their designs, were turned out, and others were put in their places, who they believed would be more compliant to them in their designs. . . . They have also invaded the Privileges, and seized on the Charters of most of those Towns that have a right to be represented by their burgesses in parliament, and have secured Surrenders to be made of them; by which the magistrates in them have delivered up all their Rights and Privileges . . . to be disposed of at the pleasure of those evil Counsellors; who have thereupon placed new magistrates in those Towns, such as they can most entirely confide in; and in many of them they have put Popish magistrates, notwithstanding the incapacities under which the law has put them. . . . They have likewise disposed of all Military Employments in the same manner; for, though the laws have not only excluded Papists from all such employments but have, in particular, provided, that they should be disarmed; yet they, in contempt of those laws, have not only armed the Papists, but have likewise raised them up to the greatest military trusts, both by sea and land; and that, strangers as well as natives, and Irish as well as English; that so, by these means, they having rendered themselves masters both of the Affairs of the Church, of the Government of the Nation, and of the Course of Justice, and subjected them all to a despotic and arbitrary Power, they might be in a capacity to maintain and execute their wicked designs by the assistance of the Army, and thereby to enslave the nation. . . . And those evil Counsellors have endeavoured to make all men to apprehend the loss of their Lives, Liberties, Honours and Estates, if they should go about to preserve themselves from this oppression by Petitions, Representations, or other means authorized by law. Thus did they proceed with the archbishop of Canterbury, and the other bishops; who, having offered a most humble Petition to the king, in terms full of respect, and not exceeding the number limited by law, (in which they set forth, in short, the Reasons for which they could not obey that Order, which by the instigation of those evil Counsellors was sent them, requiring them to appoint their Clergy to read in their Churches the Declaration for Liberty of Conscience) were sent to prison, and afterwards brought to a Trial, as if they had been guilty of some enormous crime. They were not only obliged to defend themselves in that pursuit, but to appear before professed Papists, who had not taken the Test, and by consequence were men whose interest led them to condemn them; and the Judges that gave their opinions in their favours were thereupon turned out. . . . Both We ourselves, and

13

our dearest and most entirely beloved Consort the Princess, have endeavoured to signify in terms full of respect to the king, the just and deep regret which all these proceedings have given us; . . . but those evil Counsellors have put such ill constructions on those our good intentions, that they have endeavoured to alienate the king more and more from us, as if we had designed to disturb the happiness and quiet of the kingdom.—The last and great Remedy for all those evils is the calling of a Parliament, for securing the nation against the evil practices of those wicked Counsellors; but this could not be yet compassed, nor can it be easily brought about: for those men apprehending, that a lawful Parliament being once assembled, they would be brought to an account for all their open violations of law, and for their Plots and Conspiracies against the Protestant Religion, and the Lives and Liberties of the Subjects, they have endeavoured, under the specious pretence of Liberty of Conscience, first to sow divisions amongst Protestants, between those of the Church of England and the Dissenters; the design being laid, to engage Protestants that are all equally concerned to preserve themselves from Popish oppression, into mutual quarrellings, that so, by these, some advantages might be given to them to bring about their designs; and that, both in the Election of the Members of Parliament, and afterwards in the Parliament itself: for they see well that if all Protestants could enter into a mutual good understanding one with another, and concur together in the preserving of their Religion, it would not be possible for them to compass their wicked ends. They have also required all the persons in the several counties of England, that either were in any employment, or were in any considerable esteem, to declare beforehand, that they would concur in the Repeal of the Test and Penal Laws; and that they would give their voices in the Elections to Parliament only for such as would concur in it. Such as would not thus pre-engage themselves were turned out of all employments; and others who entered into those Engagements were put in their places, many of them being Papists. And, contrary to the Charters and Privileges of those Boroughs that have a right to send burgesses to parliament, they have ordered such Regulations to be made, as they thought fit and necessary for assuring themselves of all the members that are to be chosen by those Corporations: and by this means they hope to avoid that punishment which they have deserved; though it is apparent, that all acts made by Popish Magistrates are null and void of themselves: so that no parliament can be lawful, for which the elections and returns are made by Popish sheriffs and mayors of towns: and therefore as long as the authority and magistracy is in such hands, it is not possible to have any lawful parliament. . . . But, to crown all, there are great and violent presumptions inducing us to believe, that those evil Counsellors, in order to the carrying on of their ill designs, and to the gaining to themselves the more time for the effecting of them, for the encouraging of their complices, and for the discouraging of all good subjects, have published, that the Queen hath brought forth a Son; though there hath appeared, both during the Queen's pretended bigness, and in the manner in which the Birth was managed, so many just and visible grounds of suspicion, that not only we ourselves, but all the good subjects of those kingdoms, do vehemently suspect, that the pretended Prince of Wales was not born by the Queen. . . . And since our dearest and most entirely beloved Consort the Princess, and likewise ourselves, have so great an interest in this matter, and such a right, as all the world knows, to the Succession to the Crown; . . . and since the English nation has ever testified a most particular affection and esteem, both to our dearest Consort the Princess, and to ourselves; we cannot excuse ourselves from espousing their interests in a matter of such high consequence; and from contributing all that lies in us for the maintaining, both of the Protestant Religion, and of the Laws and Liberties of those kingdoms; and for the securing to them the continual enjoyment of all their just Rights: to the doing of which we are most earnestly solicited by a great many lords, both spiritual and temporal, and by many gentlemen, and other subjects of all ranks.—Therefore it is, that we have thought fit to go over to England, and to carry over with us a force sufficient, by the blessing of God, to defend us from the violence of those evil Counsellors; and we, being desirous that our intention in this may be rightly understood, have, for this end, prepared this Declaration, in which we have hitherto given a true account of the Reasons inducing us to it; so we now think fit to declare, that this our Expedition is intended for no other design, but to have a free and lawful Parliament assembled as soon as is possible; and that in order to this, all the late Charters, by which the elections of burgesses are limited contrary to the ancient custom, shall be considered as null and of no force; and likewise, all magistrates, who have been unjustly turned out, shall forthwith resume their former employments; as well as all the boroughs of England shall return again to their ancient Prescriptions and Charters; and more particularly, that the ancient Charter of the great and famous city of London, shall again be in force; and that the Writs for the members of Parliament shall be addressed to the proper officers, according to law and custom; that also none be suffered to choose or to be chosen members of parliament, but such as are qualified by law; and that the members of parliament being thus lawfully chosen, they shall meet and sit in full freedom, that so the two houses may concur in the preparing of such Laws as they, upon full and free debate, shall judge necessary and convenient, both for the confirming and executing the law concerning the Test, and such other laws as are necessary for the security and maintenance of the Protestant Religion; as likewise for making such Laws as may establish a good agreement between the Church of England and all Protestant Dissenters; as also, for the covering and securing of all such who would live peacable under the government, as becomes good subjects, from all persecution upon the account of their Religion, even Papists themselves not excepted; and for the doing of all other things, which the two houses of parliament shall find necessary for the peace, honour and safety of the nation, so that they may be in no more danger of the nation's falling at any time hereafter under arbitrary government. . . . We do, in the last place, invite and require all persons whatsoever, all the peers of the realm, both spiritual and temporal, all lords lieutenants, deputy lieutenants, and all gentlemen, citizens, and other commons of all ranks, to come and assist us, in order to the executing of this our Design, against all such as shall endeavour to oppose us, that so we may prevent all those miseries which must needs follow upon the nation's being kept under arbitrary government and slavery, and that all the violences and disorders, which may have overturned the whole Constitution of the English government, may be fully redressed, in a free and legal Parliament. . . .—Given under our hand and seal, at our court in the Hague, the 10th day of October [N.S.], in the year 1688. WILLIAM HENRY, Prince of Orange.

P.H., v, 1.

3. Declaration of the peers at Guildhall, 1688.

[11 Dec. 1688]

We doubt not but the world believes that in this great and dangerous conjuncture, we are heartily and zealously concerned for the Protestant Religion, the Laws of the land, and the Liberties and Properties of the subject. And we did reasonably hope, that the king having issued out his proclamation and writs for a Free Parliament, we might have rested secure under the expectation of that meeting: but his majesty having withdrawn himself, and, as we apprehend, in order to his departure out of this kingdom, by the pernicious councils of persons ill-affected to our nation and religion, we cannot, without being wanting to our duty, be silent under these calamities, wherein Popish councils, which so long prevailed, have miserably involved this realm. We do therefore unanimously resolve to apply ourselves to his highness the Prince of Orange, who, with so great kindness to these kingdoms, such vast expence, and so much hazard to his own person, has undertaken, by endeavouring to procure a Free Parliament, to rescue us, with as little effusion, as possible, of Christian blood, from the imminent dangers of Slavery and Popery.—And we do hereby declare, that we will, with our utmost endeavours, assist his highness in the obtaining such a parliament with all speed, wherein our Laws, our Liberties and Properties may be secured, and the Church of England in particular, with a due liberty to Protestant Dissenters; and in general, that the Protestant religion and interest over the whole world may be supported and encouraged, to the glory of God, the happiness of the established government in these kingdoms, and the advantage of all princes and states in Christendom, that may be herein concerned. In the mean time we will endeavour to preserve, as much as in us lies, the peace and security of these great and populous cities of London and Westminster, and the parts adjacent, by taking care to disarm all Papists, and secure all Jesuits and Romish priests, who are in or about the same. And if there be any thing more to be performed by us, for promoting his highness's generous intentions for the public good, we shall be ready to do it, as occasion shall require.

P.H., v, 20.

4. William summons an assembly, 1688.

[23 Dec. 1688]

Whereas the Necessity of Affairs do require speedy Advice; we do desire all such Persons as have served as Knights, Citizens or Burgesses in any of the Parliaments that were held during the Reign of the late King *Charles* the Second to meet us at *St. James's*, upon *Wednesday* the Six-and-twentieth of this instant *December* by Ten of the Clock in the Morning. And we do likewise desire, that the Lord Mayor and Court of Aldermen of the City of *London* would be present at the same Time;

and that the Common-council would appoint Fifty of their Number
to be there likewise. And hereof we desire them not to fail.

> Given at *St. James's*, the Three-and-twentieth
> Day of *December*, 1688.
>
> W.H. Prince of Orange.
>
> *By his Highness' special Command,*
> C. Huygens.

C.J., x, 5.

5. The address of the assembly, 1688.

[26 Dec. 1688]

We who have served as Members of Parliaments during the Reign
of the late King *Charles* the Second, together with the Court of
Aldermen, and Members of the Common-Council of the City of
London, assembled at your Highness' Desire, in this Extraordinary
Conjuncture, do, with an unanimous Consent, tender to your Highness
our humble and hearty Thanks, for your coming into this Kingdom,
and exposing your Person to so great Hazards, for the Preservation of
our Religion, Laws, and Liberties, and rescuing us from the Miseries of
Popery and Slavery:

And do desire your Highness, that, in pursuance of those Ends, and
for the Preservation of the Peace of the Nation, your Highness will
take upon you the Administration of public Affairs, both Civil and
Military, and the Disposal of the public Revenue.

We do also desire, that your Highness will take into your particular
care, the present condition of *Ireland*; and endeavour, by the most
speedy and effectual Means, to prevent the Dangers threatening that
Kingdom.

All which, we desire your Highness to undertake and execute, until
the Meeting of the intended Convention, the Two-and twentieth of
January next . . .

C.J., x, 6.

6. Directions for electing the convention, 1688.

Whereas the Lords Spiritual and Temporal, the Knights, Citizens and
Burgesses, heretofore Members of the Commons House of Parliament,
during the reign of *Charles* the Second, residing in and about the City
of *London*, together with the Aldermen, and divers of the Common-

Council of the said city, in this extraordinary Conjuncture at our Request, severally assembled, to advise us the best Manner how to attain the Ends of our Declaration, in calling a free Parliament, for the Preservation of the Protestant Religion, and Restoring the Rights and Liberties of the Kingdom, and Settling the same, that they may not be in Danger of being again subverted, have advised and desired us to cause our Letters to be written and directed, for the Counties, To the Coroners of the respective Counties or any One of them, and, in default of the Coroners, To the Clerks of the Peace of the respective Counties; and for the Universities, To the respective Vice-Chancellors; and for the Cities, Boroughs and Cinque-Ports, To the Chief Magistrate of each respective City, Borough and Cinque-Port; Containing Directions for the choosing, in all such Counties, Cities, Universities, Boroughs and Cinque-Ports, within Ten Days after the Receipt of the said respective Letters, such a Number of Persons to represent them, as from every such Place is or are of Right to be sent to Parliament: Of which Elections, and the Times and Places thereof, the respective Officers shall give Notice; the Notice for the intended Election, in the Counties, to be published in the Market-Towns within the respective Counties, by the Space of Five Days, at the least, before the said Election; and for the Universities, Cities, Boroughs and Cinque-Ports, in every of them respectively, by the Space of Three Days, at the least, before the said Election: The said Letters, and the Execution thereof, to be returned by such Officer and Officers who shall execute the same, to the Clerk of the Crown in the Court of Chancery, so as the Persons, so to be chosen, may meet and sit at *Westminster* the Two-and-Twentieth Day of *January* next.

We, heartily desiring the Performance of what we have in our Said Declaration expressed, in pursuance of the said Advice and Desire, have caused this our Letter to be written to you, to the Intent that you, truly and uprightly, without Favour or Affection to any Person, or indirect Practice or Proceeding, do and execute what of your Part ought to be done, according to the said Advice, for the due Execution thereof; the Elections to be made by such Persons only, as, according to the ancient Laws and Customs, of Right, ought to choose Members for Parliament: and that you cause a Return to be made, by Certificate under your Seal, of the Names of the Persons elected, annexed to this our Letter, to the said Clerk of the Crown, before the said Two-and-Twentieth Day of *January*.

Given at *St. James's*, the Nine-and-Twentieth Day of *December*, in the Year of our Lord 1688.

C.J., x, 7.

7. The succession question, 1689.

Jan. 29 [1689] The Lords entered into consideration of the same matter, wher severall motions were made to the same purpas as ther was the day before in the Hous of Commons. Some were for recalling the King upon conditions (but thos very few); others for the government to be continued in the Kings name, and the Prince to have the executive power of it by name of regent or protectour; others for haveing the King forfeit the crown and the Prince of Orange elected into it; others for haveing the said Prince and Princess crowned, as it was in the case of Philip and Mary, and to hould it by descent in right of his wife, without takeing notice of the Prince of Wales, who was to be made incapable to succeed, bycaus a papist, being christined in that Church. At last the Lords voated to agree with the Commons in the maine as to the vacancy of the crown, only differing in some words, and adjurned the debate till the next day. That voat was only carried by three.

A. Browning, *Memoirs of Sir John Reresby* (Glasgow, 1936), p. 546.

8. Conference on 'abdicated' and 'vacant', 1689.

[6 February 1689]

THE EARL OF NOTTINGHAM. Gentlemen, I intend to state the objection so: That first Reason of yours I take to be this in effect, that our word 'deserted' being applied to the government, implies our agreeing that the king hath deserted the throne, those two being in true construction the same; and then, by our own confession, the throne is vacant as to him.—To this you say, my lords have given no answer: truly, I think it is a clear answer, that the word 'deserted' may have another sense and doth not necessarily imply renouncing entirely of a right, but a ceasing of the exercise. But then, if that does not vacate the throne as to him, the other Reason [of the Commons] comes to be considered, how came you to desire the Prince of Orange to take the administration upon him, and to take care of Ireland till the Convention, and to write his Letters circularly for this meeting? And to renew your Address to the Prince, and to appoint a Day of public Thanksgiving?—In answer to that, my lords say, that though the king's deserting the government (as they agree he has done) did imply the throne to be vacant, yet they might justly do all those acts mentioned in the commons Reasons; because, if barely the exercise of the government were 'deserted', there must be a supply of that exercise in some persons taking the administration; and as none so fit, because of the Prince's relation to the crown (and his presence here) to address unto about it, so none so proper to make that Address as the lords: for in the absence of the king, they are the king and kingdom's Great Council, and might have done it by themselves without the commons; but being met in a full representative body, they joined with them.—Mr. Pollexfen indeed has said, There is no distinction in law between the kingship and the exercise of it: and, That it is the same crime, in consideration of the law, to take away that exercise, as to take away the kingship.—I shall not dispute with that learned gentleman (whom I very much honour for his knowledge in the profession of the law) what offence either of them would be now; for we are not discoursing concerning a Regency, how the government should be administered, but we are barely upon the question, whether the throne be vacant, so that we may have another king? But if we should grant a vacancy, as to the king himself, we are then told, the next in succession cannot take, because no one can be heir to one that is alive. Yet, I think, the answer given by my lords before is a very good one, That though the king be not dead naturally, yet if (as they infer) he is so civilly, the next of course ought to come in as by hereditary succession; for I know not any distinction between successors in the case of a natural death, and those in the case of a civil one.—For I would know if the next heir should be set aside in this case, and you put in another, whether that king shall be king of England to him and his heirs, and so being once upon the throne, the ancient lineal succession be altered? If that be so, then indeed it is sufficiently an elective kingdom, by taking from it the right heir.—If it be not so, then I would ask, whether such king as shall be put in, shall be king only during king James's life; that, I suppose, for many reasons is not your meaning; but, at least he must be made king during his own life; and then if there be a distinction made as to the succession between a natural and a civil death, if king James should die during the life of the new king, what would become of the hereditary monarchy? Where must the succession come in, when the next heir to king James may not be next heir to the present successor?—Therefore we must reduce all to this point, which my lords have hinted at in their Reasons, whether this will not make the kingdom elective? For if you do once make it elective, I do not say that you are always bound to go to election, but it is enough to make it so, if by that precedent there be a breach in the hereditary succession; for I will be bold to say, you cannot make a stronger tie to observe that kind of succession, than what lieth upon you to preserve it in this case.—If you are under an obligation to it, it is part of the constitution. I desire any one to tell me what stronger obligation there can be? and that, I say, is reason enough for my lords to disagree to it, it bringing in the danger of a breach upon the constitution.—Next, gentlemen, I would know of you, if the throne be vacant, whether we be obliged to fill it? If we be, we must fill it either by our old laws, or by the humour of those that are to chuse; if we fill it by our own old laws, they declare, that it is an hereditary kingdom, and we are to take the next to whom the succession would belong, and then there would be no need of standing upon a vacancy.—If we are to fill it according to the humour of the times, and of those that are to make the choice, that diverts the course of inheritance, and puts it into another line: and I cannot see by what authority we can do that, or change our ancient constitution, without committing the same fault we have laid upon the king.—These are the Objections against the Vacancy of the Throne, which occur to me; and we, gentlemen, desire a satisfaction to them before we agree to the Vacancy.—And, I think, the answering them will lead us unto that which I take to be the main point in question, whether the Vacancy of the Throne, and filling it again, will not, as my lords say, endanger the turning this hereditary monarchy of ours into an elective one?

.   .   .

MR SOMERS. My lords, your lordships, as a Reason against the words 'abdicate,' say it is not a word known in our common law. But the word 'vacant', about which we are now disputing, cannot have that objection made to it; for we find it in our Records, and even applied in a parallel case to this of ours, in 1 Hen. 4 where it is expressly made use of more than once, and there it doth import what I think it doth import in this Vote of the house of commons, now in debate; and to require any farther or other explication of it than the Record gives, will be very hard and unreasonable; for we are here to give the commons reasons for maintaining their own Vote, and nothing else.—If your lordships please to look into the Record in that case, there was first a Resignation of the crown and government made and subscribed by king Rd. 2, and this is brought into the parliament, and there they take notice, that the 'Sedes Regalis' (those are the words) 'fuit vacua'; and the Resignation being read both in Latin and English, in the great hall at Westminster, where the parliament was then assembled, it was accepted by the lords and commons.—After that, it proceeds farther; and there are Articles exhibited against Rd. 2, and upon these Articles they went on to Sentence of Deposition and Deprivation, and then follow the words in the record; 'Et confessim ut constabat ex præmissis & eorum occasione regnum Angliæ cum pertinentiis suis vacare.' Then Henry 4 riseth up out of his place as duke of Lancaster, where he sat before, and standing so high that he might be well enough seen, makes this claim to the crown: the words in the Record are, 'Dictum regnum Angliæ sicut præmittitur vacans una cum corona vendicat.'— After that, the Record goeth on, That upon this Claim the lords and commons being asked, what they thought of it? they unanimously consented, and the archbishop took him by the hand, and led him 'ad sedem regalem prædictam,' &c—Nay, after all this, it is there taken notice of, and particularly observed, that 'prius vacante sede regali,' by the lesion and deposition aforesaid, all the public officers ceased; there is care taken for Henry 4's taking the Royal Oath, and granting of new commissions.—My lords; the commons do therefore appre- hend, that with very good reason and authority they did in their Vote declare the throne to be vacant. But as to the going farther to enquire into the consequences of that, or what is to be done afterwards, is not our commission, who came here only to maintain their expressions in their Vote against your lordships amendments.

. . .

THE EARL OF CLARENDON. I would speak one word to that Record which Mr. Somers mentioned, and which the lord that spoke last hath given a plain answer unto, by making that difference (which is the great hinge of the matter in debate) between hereditary and elective kingdoms. But I have something else to say to that Record. First, It is plain in that case king Rd. 2 had absolutely resigned, renounced, or (call it what you please) 'abdicated' in writing under his own hand. What is done then? After that, the parliament being then sitting, they did not think it sufficient to go upon, because that Writing might be the effect of fear, and so, not voluntary; thereupon they proceed to a formal deposition upon Articles, and then comes in the claim of Hen. 4. After all this, was not this an election? He indeed saith, that he was the next heir, and claimed it by descent from Henry 3; yet he that was really the next heir did not appear, which was the earl of March; so that Henry 4 claimed it as his undubitable right, being the next heir that then appeared.—But, gentlemen, I pray consider what followed upon it; all the kings that were thus taken in (we say elected, but the election was not of God's approbation) scarce passed any one year in any of their reigns, without being disturbed in the possession.—Yet, I say, he himself did not care to owe the crown to the election, but claimed it as his right. And it was a plausible pretence, and kept him and his son (though not without interruption) upon the throne. But in the time of his grandson Henry 6 there was an utter overthrow of all his title and possession too: for if you look into the Parliament Roll 1. Edward 4, the proceedings against king Rd. 2, as well as the rest of the acts during the Usurpation (as that Record rightly calls it) are annulled, repealed, revoked, reversed, and all the words imaginable used and put in, to set those proceedings aside as illegal, unjust and unrighteous. And, pray what was the reason? That Act deduceth down the pedigree of the royal line, from Henry 3 to Rd. 2, who died without issue, and then Henry 4, (saith the Act) usurped; but that the Earl of March, upon the death of Rd. 2, and consequently Edward 4 from him, was undoubted king by conscience, by nature, by custom, and by law. The Record is to be seen at length, as well as that 1 Hen. 4; and being a latter act, is of more authority.—And after all this, (I pray consider it well) the right Line is restored, and the Usurpation condemned and repealed. Besides, gentlemen, I hope you will take into your consideration, what will become of the kingdom of Scotland if they should differ from us in this point, and go another way to work; then will that be a divided kingdom from ours again. You cannot but remember how much trouble it always gave our ancestors, while it continued a divided kingdom; and if we should go out of the Line, and invert the Succession in any point at all, I fear you will find a disagreement there, and then very dangerous consequences may ensue.

. . .

SIR GEORGE TREBY. . . . My lords, it is very well known, and readily agreed by us, that Edw. 4 came in, in disaffirmance of the title of the house of Lancaster—As those times went, whenever there was any turn in government, (as there were several) there were new and contrary declarations about the title to the crown made constantly in parliament; and what one parliament had settled, another undid. But then this advantage we have on our side, that as we have this precedent for us, so we have the last; for I need go no farther, than the Parliament-roll of 1 Hen. 7. 12. 16. where the Record is set right again.—The act for deposing Richard 2 is indeed by 1 Edw. 4 repealed, and saith, that Henry 4 usurped the crown, and murdered Richard 2; and thereupon it proceeds to attaint Henry 6. But then comes in Henry 7; and 1 Henry 7 there is an act made, that sets aside all the acts and attainders made against his line, and consequently repealed 1 Edw. 4 which repealed 1 Hen. 4—And I would observe one thing, by the way, concerning Henry 7. He was of the line of Lancaster, and when he came to the crown, would not endure to have his crown reckoned only matrimonial, or suffer the stile to go in the names of Henry and Elizabeth, as he must have done if he had stuck to the title of the right line of succession; no, he always stood up for his own title, though he had the heiress of the house of York in his bosom.—Therefore, my lords, his act for restoring the Record of 1 Henry 4 again, is as good an authority as it was before, and somewhat better; for it hath the last act on its side, which is unrepealed to this day. . . .

THE EARL OF NOTTINGHAM. After this long debate, pray let us endeavour to come as near as we can to an agreement: . . . Upon the whole matter, you seem to understand your own words to signify less than they do really import.—I do not find that you purpose to make the kingdom elective; and yet you talk of supplying the vacancy by the lords and commons. You do not say, that the king has left the crown for himself and his heirs; and yet your words speak of a vacancy, and nothing of the succession: but you do not tell us what you mean . . . —If the kingdom were indeed elective, we were in a capacity of electing, but 'pro hac vice,' according to the constitution, this question would be greater than what it was before; but then the great debate in it would only be, who should first have the honour of laying the very foundation of the new government.—But as this case stands upon the foot of our ancient laws, and fundamental constitution, I humbly beseech you to consider, whether at the same time that, in this way, you get an established government, you do not overturn all our legal foundations.

P.H., v, 91-107.

The Free Conference being ended, the Lords returned. . . . And, after Debate, the Question was put,

"Whether to agree with the House of Commons in the Word ["abdicated"], instead of the Word ["deserted"]; and to the Words that follow, ["and that the Throne is thereby vacant"]?"

Resolved in the Affirmative.

L.J., XIV, 118.

9. William and the Crown, 1689.

There was a great meeting at the Earl of Devonshire's, where the dispute ran very high between Lord Halifax and Lord Danby; one for the Prince, the other for the Princess: at last Lord Halifax said, he thought it would be very proper to know the Prince's own sentiments, and desired Fagel would speak, who defended himself a great while, by saying he knew nothing of his mind upon that subject, but if they would know his own, he believed the Prince would not like to be his wife's gentleman usher; upon which Lord Danby said, he hoped they all knew enough now, for his part he knew too much, and broke up the assembly, as Sir Michael Wharton who was present told me.

From Dartmouth's Notes on Burnet's History, quoted by J. Dalrymple, Memoirs of Great Britain and Ireland (1783), II, App. part I, p. 342.

10. The Bill of Rights, 1689.

An act for declaring the rights and liberties of the subject and settling the succession of the crown.

Whereas the lords spiritual and temporal, and commons, assembled at West-minster, lawfully, fully, and freely representing all the estates of the people of this realm, did upon the thirteenth day of February, in the year of our Lord one thousand six hundred eighty eight,[1] present unto their Majesties, then called and known by the names and stile of William and Mary, prince and princess of Orange, being present in their proper persons, a certain declaration in writing, made by the said lords and commons, in the words following: viz.

Whereas the late King James The Second, by the assistance of divers evil counsellors, judges, and ministers employed by him, did endeavour to sub-vert and extirpate the protestant religion, and the laws and liberties of this kingdom.

[1] 1688/9.

1. *By assuming and exercising a power of dispensing with and suspending of laws, and the execution of laws, without consent of parliament.*

2. *By committing and prosecuting divers worthy prelates, for humbly petitioning to be excused concurring to the said assumed power.*

3. *By issuing and causing to be executed a commission under the great seal for erecting a court called,* The court of commissioners for ecclesiastical causes.

4. *By levying money for and to the use of the crown, by pretence of prerogative, for other time, and in other manner, than the same was granted by parliament.*

5. *By raising and keeping a standing army within this kingdom in time of peace, without consent of parliament, and quartering soldiers contrary to law.*

6. *By causing several good subjects, being protestants, to be disarmed, at the same time when papists were both armed and employed, contrary to law.*

7. *By violating the freedom of election of members to serve in parliament.*

8. *By prosecutions in the court of King's bench, for matters and causes cognizable only in parliament; and by divers other arbitrary and illegal courses.*

9. *And whereas of late years, partial, corrupt, and unqualified persons have been returned and served on juries in trials and particularly divers jurors in trials for high treason, which were not freeholders.*

10. *And excessive bail hath been required of persons committed in criminal cases, to elude the benefit of the laws made for the liberty of the subjects.*

11. *And excessive fines have been imposed; and illegal and cruel punishments inflicted.*

12. *And several grants and promises made of fines and forfeitures, before any conviction or judgment against the persons, upon whom the same were to be levied.*

All which are utterly and directly contrary to the known laws and statutes, and freedom of this realm.

And whereas the said late King James the Second having abdicated the government, and the throne being thereby vacant, his highness the Prince of Orange (whom it hath pleased Almighty God to make the glorious instrument of delivering this kingdom from popery and arbitrary power) did (by the advice of the lords spiritual and temporal, and divers principal persons of the commons) cause letters to be written to the lords spiritual and temporal, being protestants; and other letters to the several counties, cities, universities, boroughs, and cinque-ports, for the choosing of such persons to represent them, as were of right to be sent to parliament, to meet and sit at Westminster upon the two and twentieth day of January, in this year one thousand six hundred eighty eight,[1] in order to such an establishment, as that their religion, laws, and liberties might not again be in danger of being subverted: upon which letters, elections have been accordingly made,

And thereupon the said lords spiritual and temporal, and commons, pursuant to their respective letters and elections, being now assembled in a full and free representative of this nation, taking into their most serious consideration the best means for attaining the ends aforesaid; do in the first place (as their ancestors in like case have usually done) for the vindicating and asserting their ancient rights and liberties, declare;

1. *That the pretended power of suspending of laws, or the execution of laws, by regal authority, without consent of parliament, is illegal.*

2. *That the pretended power of dispensing with laws, or the execution of laws, by regal authority, as it hath been assumed and exercised of late, is illegal.*

3. *That the commission for erecting the late court of commissioners for ecclesiastical causes, and all other commissions and courts of like nature are illegal and pernicious.*

4. *That levying money for or to the use of the crown, by pretence of prerogative, without grant of parliament, for longer time, or in other manner than the same is or shall be granted, is illegal.*

5. *That it is the right of the subjects to petition the King, and all committments and prosecutions for such petitioning are illegal.*

6. *That the raising or keeping a standing army within the kingdom in time of peace, unless it be with consent of parliament, is against law.*

7. *That the subjects which are protestants, may have arms for their defence suitable to their conditions, and as allowed by law.*

8. *That election of members of parliament ought to be free.*

9. *That the freedom of speech, and debates or proceedings in parliament, ought not to be impeached or questioned in any court or place out of parliament.*

10. *That excessive bail ought not to be required, nor excessive fines imposed; nor cruel and unusual punishments inflicted.*

[1] 1688/9.

11.   *That jurors ought to be duly impanelled and returned, and jurors which pass upon men in trials for high treason ought to be freeholders.*

12.   *That all grants and promises of fines and forfeitures of particular persons before conviction, are illegal and void.*

13.   *And that for redress of all grievances, and for the amending, strengthening and preserving of the laws, parliaments ought to be held frequently.*

And they do claim, demand, and insist upon all and singular the premisses, as their undoubted rights and liberties; and that no declarations, judgments, doings or proceedings, to the prejudice of the people in any of the said premisses, ought in any wise to be drawn hereafter into consequence or example.

To which demand of their rights they are particularly encouraged by the declaration of his highness the prince of Orange, as being the only means for obtaining a full redress and remedy therein.

Having therefore an entire confidence, That his said highness the Prince of Orange will perfect the deliverance so far advanced by him, and will still preserve them from the violation of their rights, which they have here asserted, and from all other attempts upon their religion, rights, and liberties.

II.   *The said lords spiritual and temporal, and commons, assembled at Westminster, do resolve, That William and Mary prince and princess of Orange be, and be declared, King and Queen of England, France and Ireland, and the dominions thereunto belonging, to hold the crown and royal dignity of the said kingdoms and dominions to them the said prince and princess during their lives, and the life of the survivor of them; and that the sole and full exercise of the regal power be only in, and executed by the said prince of Orange, in the names of the said prince and princess, during their joint lives; and after their deceases, the said crown and royal dignity of the said kingdoms and dominions to be to the heirs of the body of the said princess; and for default of such issue to the princess Anne of Denmark and the heirs of her body; and for default of such issue to the heirs of the body of the said prince of Orange. And the lords spiritual and temporal, and commons, do pray the said prince and princess to accept the same accordingly.*

III.   *And that the oaths hereafter mentioned be taken by all persons of whom the oaths of allegiance and supremacy might be required by law, instead of them; and that the said oaths of allegiance and supremacy may be abrogated.*

I A.B. do sincerely promise and swear, That I will be faithful, and bear true allegiance, to their Majesties King William and Queen Mary:

So help me God.

I A.B. do swear, That I do from my heart abhor, detest, and abjure as impious and heretical, that damnable doctrine and position, That princes excommunicated or deprived by the pope, or any authority of the see of Rome, may be deposed or murdered by their subjects, or any other whatsoever. And I do declare, That no foreign prince, person, prelate, state, or potentate hath, or ought to have any jurisdiction, power, superiority, pre-eminence, or authority, ecclesiastical or spiritual, within this realm:

So help me God.

IV. *Upon which their said Majesties did accept the crown and royal dignity of the kingdoms of England, France, and Ireland, and the dominions thereunto belonging, according to the resolution and desire of the said lords and commons contained in the said declaration.*

V. *And thereupon their Majesties were pleased, That the said lords spiritual and temporal, and commons, being the two houses of parliament, should continue to sit, and with their Majesties royal concurrence make effectual provision for the settlement of the religion, laws and liberties of this kingdom, so that the same for the future might not be in danger again of being subverted; to which the said lords spiritual and temporal, and commons, did agree and proceed to act accordingly.*

VI. Now in pursuance of the premisses, the said lords spiritual and temporal, and commons, in parliament assembled, for the ratifying, confirming and establishing the said declaration, and the articles, clauses, matters, and things therein contained, by the force of a law made in due form by authority of parliament, do pray that it may be declared and enacted, That all and singular the rights and liberties asserted and claimed in the said declaration, are the true, ancient, and indubitable rights and liberties of the people of this kingdom, and so shall be esteemed, allowed, adjudged, deemed, and taken to be, and that all and every the particulars aforesaid shall be firmly and strictly holden and observed, as they are expressed in the said declaration; and all officers and ministers whatsoever shall serve their Majesties and their successors according to the same in all times to come.

VII. And the said lords spiritual and temporal, and commons, seriously considering how it hath pleased Almighty God, in his marvellous providence, and merciful goodness to this nation, to provide and preserve their said Majesties royal persons most happily to reign over us upon the throne of their ancestors, for which they render unto him from the bottom of their hearts their humblest thanks and praises, do truly, firmly, assuredly, and in the sincerity of their hearts think, and do hereby recognize, acknowledge and declare, That King *James* the Second having abdicated the government, and their Majesties having accepted the crown and royal dignity as aforesaid, their said Majesties did become, were, are, and of right ought to be, by the laws of this realm, our sovereign liege and lady, King and Queen of *England, France,* and *Ireland,* and the dominions thereunto belonging, in and to whose princely persons the royal state, crown, and dignity of the said realms, with all honours, stiles, titles, regalities, prerogatives, powers, jurisdictions and authorities to the same belonging and appertaining, are most fully, rightfully, and intirely invested and incorporated, united and annexed.

VIII. And for preventing all questions and divisions in this realm, by reason of any pretended titles to the crown, and for preserving a certainty in the succession thereof, in and upon which the unity, peace, tranquillity, and safety of this nation doth, under God, wholly consist and depend, The said lords spiritual and temporal, and commons, do beseech their Majesties that it may be enacted, established and declared, That the crown and regal government of the said kingdoms and dominions, with all and singular the premisses thereunto belonging and appertaining, shall be and continue to their said Majesties, and the survivor of them, during their lives, and the life of the survivor of them; And that the intire, perfect, and full exercise of the regal power and government be only in, and executed by his Majesty, in the names of both their Majesties during their joint lives; and after their deceases the said crown and premisses shall be and remain to the heirs of the body of her Majesty; and for default of such issue, to her royal highness the princess *Anne* of *Denmark,* and the heirs of her body; and for default of such issue, to the heirs of the body of his said Majesty; And thereunto the said lords spiritual and temporal, and commons do, in the name of all the people aforesaid, most humbly and faithfully submit themselves, their heirs and posterities for ever; and do faithfully promise, That they will stand to, maintain, and defend their said Majesties, and also the limitation and succession of the crown herein specified and contained, to the utmost of their powers, with their lives and estates against all persons whatsoever, that shall attempt any thing to the contrary.

IX. *And whereas it hath been found by experience, that it is inconsistent with the safety and welfare of this protestant kingdom, to be governed by a popish prince, or by any King or Queen marrying a papist;* the said lords spiritual and temporal, and commons, do further pray that it may be enacted, That all and every person and persons that is, are or shall be reconciled to, or shall hold communion with, the see or church of *Rome,* or shall profess the popish religion, or shall marry a papist, shall be excluded, and be for ever incapable to inherit, possess, or enjoy the crown and government of this realm, and *Ireland,* and the dominions thereunto belonging, or any part of the same, or to have, use, or exercise any regal power, authority, or jurisdiction within the same; and in all and every such case or cases the people of these realms shall be, and are hereby absolved of their allegiance; and the said crown and government shall from time to time descend to, and be enjoyed by such person or persons, being protestants, as should have inherited and enjoyed the same, in case the said person or persons so reconciled, holding communion, or professing, or marrying as aforesaid, were naturally dead.

X. And that every King and Queen of this realm, who at any time hereafter shall come to and succeed in the imperial crown of this kingdom, shall on the first day of the meeting of the first parliament, next after his or her coming to the crown, sitting in his or her throne in the house of peers, in the presence of the lords and commons therein assembled, or at his or her coronation, before such person or persons who shall administer the coronation oath to him or her, at the time of his or her taking the said oath (which shall first happen) make, subscribe, and audibly repeat the declaration mentioned in the statute made in the thirtieth year of the reign of King *Charles* the Second, intituled, *An act for the more effectual preserving the King's person and government, by disabling papists from sitting in either house of parliament.* But if it shall happen, that such King or Queen, upon his or her succession to the crown of this realm, shall be under the age of twelve years, then every such King or Queen shall make, subscribe, and audibly repeat the said declaration at his or her coronation, or the first day of the meeting of the first parliament as aforesaid, which shall first happen after such King or Queen shall have attained the said age of twelve years.

XI. All which their Majesties are contented and pleased shall be declared, enacted, and established by authority of this present parliament, and shall stand, remain, and be the law of this realm for ever; and the same are by their said Majesties, by and with the advice and consent of the lords spiritual and temporal, and commons, in parliament assembled, and by the authority of the same, declared, enacted, and established accordingly.

XII. And be it further declared and enacted by the authority aforesaid, That from and after this present session of parliament, no dispensation by *non obstante* of or to any statute, or any part thereof, shall be allowed, but that the same shall be held void and of no effect, except a dispensation be allowed of in such statute, and except in such cases as shall be specially provided for by one or more bill or bills to be passed during this present session of parliament.

XIII. Provided that no charter, or grant, or pardon, granted before the three and twentieth day of *October* in the year of our Lord one thousand six hundred eighty nine shall be any ways impeached or invalidated by this act, but that the same shall be and remain of the same force and effect in law, and no other than as if this act had never been made.

1 Will. & Mary, sess. 2, c. 2: S.L., IX, 67.

11. The convention declares itself a parliament, 1689.

An act for removing and preventing all questions and disputes concerning the assembling and sitting of this present parliament.

For preventing all doubts and scruples which may in any wise arise concerning the meeting, sitting, and proceeding of this present parliament; be it declared and enacted . . .

II. That the lords spiritual and temporal, and commons, convened at *Westminster*, the two and twentieth day of *January* . . . and there sitting on the thirteenth day of *February* following, are the two houses of parliament, and so shall be, and are hereby declared, enacted, and adjudged to be, to all intents, constructions, and purposes whatsoever, notwithstanding any want of writ or writs of summons, or any other defect of form or default whatsoever, as if they had been summoned according to the usual form: and that this present act, and all other acts, to which the royal assent shall at any time be given before the next

D

prorogation after the said thirteenth of *February*, on which day their said Majesties, at the request, and by the advice of the lords and commons, did accept the crown and royal dignity of King and Queen of *England*, *France*, and *Ireland*, and the dominions and territories thereunto belonging.

III. [The old oaths of allegiance, etc, not to be taken by members, 30 Car. II, stat. 2, c. 1.]

IV. [New oaths substituted in the place of the old]

V. And it is hereby further enacted . . . That the oaths above appointed by this act, to be taken in the stead and place of the oaths of allegiance and supremacy, shall be in the words following, and no other. . . . [See Bill of Rights, p. 29.]

VIII. Provided always, and be it declared, That this present parliament may be dissolved after the usual manner, as if the same had been summoned and called by writ.

1 Will. & Mary, c. 1: S.L., IX, 1.

12. Mutiny Act, 1689.

An Act for punishing Officers or Soldiers who shall Mutiny or Desert Their Majestyes Service.

Whereas the raising or keeping a Standing Army within this Kingdome in time of Peace unlesse it be with Consent of Parlyament is against Law And whereas it is judged necessary by Their Majestyes and this present Parliament That dureing this time of Danger severall of the Forces which are now on foote should be continued and others raised for the Safety of the Kingdome for the Common Defence of the Protestant Religion and for the reduceing of Ireland

And whereas noe Man may be forejudged of Life or Limbe or subjected to any kinde of punishment by Martiall Law or in any other manner than by the Judgement of his Peeres and according to the knowne and Established Laws of this Realme Yet neverthelesse it being requisite for retaineing such Forces as are or shall be raised dureing this Exigence of Affaires in their Duty an exact Discipline be observed And that Soldiers who shall Mutiny or stirr up Sedition or shall desert Their Majestyes Service be brought to a more Exemplary and speedy Punishment then the usuall Forms of Law will allow

II. Bee it therefore Enacted . . . That from and after the Twelfth day of Aprill in the Yeare of our Lord One thousand six hundred eighty nine every Person being in Their Majestyes Service in the Army and being Mustered and in Pay as an Officer or Soldier who shall at any time before the Tenth Day of November in the Yeare of our Lord One thousand six hundred eighty nine Excite Cause or Joyne in any Mutiny or Sedition in the Army or shall desert Their Majestyes Service in the Army shall suffer Death or such other Punishment as by a Court-Martiall shall be Inflicted

III. And it is hereby further Enacted and Declared That Their Majestyes or the Generall of Their Army for the time being may by vertue of this Act have full Power and Authority to grant Commissions to any Lieftenants Generall or other Officers not under the Degree of Collonells from time to time to Call and Assemble Court Martialls for Punishing such Offences as aforesaid

IV. And it is hereby further Enacted and Declared That noe Court Martiall which shall have power to inflict any punishment by vertue of this Act for the Offences aforesaid shall consist of fewer then thirteene whereof none to be under the degree of Captaines.

V. Provided alwayes That noe Field Officer be Tryed by other than Field Officers And that such Court Martiall shall have Power and Authoritie to administer an Oath to any Witnesse in order to the Examination or Tryall of the Offences aforesaid

VI. Provided always that nothing in this Act contained shall extend or be construed to Exempt any Officer or Soldier whatsoever from the Ordinary Processe of Law

VII. Provided alwayes That this Act or any thing therein contained shall not extend or be any wayes construed to extend to or concerne any the Militia Forces of this Kingdome

VIII. Provided alsoe that this Act shall continue and be in Force untill the said Tenth day of November in the said Yeare of our Lord One thousand six hundred eighty nine and noe longer

IX. Provided alwayes and bee it enacted That in all Tryalls of Offenders by Courts Martiall to be held by vertue of this Act where the Offence may be punished by death every Officer present at such Tryall

before any Proceeding be had thereupon shall take an Oath upon the
Evangelists before the Court (and the Judge Advocate or his Deputy
shall and are hereby respectively Authorized to Administer the same)
in these words That is to say

You shall well and truely Try and Determine according to your
Evidence the Matter now before you betweene Our Soveraigne Lord
and Lady the King and Queens Majestyes and the Prisoner to be Tryed.

Soe helpe you God.

X.   And noe Sentence of Death shall be given against any Offender in
such Case by any Court Martiall unlesse nine of Thirteene Officers
present shall concurr therein And if there be a greater number of
Officers present then the Judgment shall passe by the concurrence of
the greater part of them soe Sworne and not otherwise and noe Proceedings Tryall or Sentence of Death shall be had or given against any
Offender but betweene the houres of Eight in the Morning and One
in the Afternoone.

1 Will. & Mary, c. 5: S.R., VI, 55.

13. Coronation oaths (old and new), 1685 and 1689.

An act for establishing the coronation oath.

*Whereas by the law and ancient usage of this realm, the Kings and Queens
thereof have taken a solemn oath upon the evangelists at their respective
coronations, to maintain the statutes, laws, and customs of the said realm,
and all the people and inhabitants thereof, in their spiritual and civil rights
and properties: but forasmuch as the oath itself on such occasion administred,
hath heretofore been framed in doubtful words and expressions, with relation
to ancient laws and constitutions at this time unknown: to the end thereof
that one uniform oath may be in all times to come taken by the Kings
and Queens of this realm, and to them respectively administred at
the times of their and every of their coronation; may it please your
majesties that it may be enacted:*

II.   And be it enacted . . . That the oath herein mentioned, and hereafter expressed, shall and may be administred to their most excellent
majesties King *William* and Queen *Mary*, (whom God long preserve)
at the time of their coronation in the presence of all persons that shall
be then and there present at the solemnizing thereof, by the Archbishop of *Canterbury*, or the Archbishop of *York*, or either of them, or
any other bishop of this realm, whom the King's majesty shall there-

unto appoint, and who shall be hereby thereunto respectively authorized; which oath followeth and shall be administred in this manner; that is to say,

[As prescribed by the Coronation Order of James II.]

Archbishop.

Sir, will you grant and keep and by your Oath confirm to ye people of England ye Laws and Customs to them granted by ye Kings of England, your lawfull, and Religious predecessors; And namely ye Laws, Customs, and Franchises granted to ye Clergy by ye glorious King St. Edward, your predecessor; According to ye Laws of God, ye true profession of ye Gospel establish'd in this Kingdom, and agreeing to ye prerogative of ye Kings thereof, and ye ancient Customs of ye Realm?

King.

I grant, and promise to keep them.

Archbishop.

Sir, will you keep peace, and godly Agreement entirely according to your power, to ye holy Church, ye Clergy and the people?

King.

I will keep it.

Archbishop.

Sir, will you to your power cause Law, Justice, and Discretion in

[As prescribed by the Coronation Oath Act.]

The archbishop or bishop shall say,

III. *Will you solemnly promise and swear to govern the people of this kingdom of England, and the dominions thereunto belonging, according to the statutes in parliament agreed on, and the laws and customs of the same?*

The King and Queen shall say,

I solemnly promise so to do.

Archbishop or bishop.

Will you to your power cause law and justice in mercy to be executed

37

Mercy and Truth to be executed in all your Judgements?

in all your judgements?

King.
I will.

King and Queen.
I will.

Archbishop.
Sr, will you grant to hold, and keep ye rightfull customs, wch. ye commonaltie of this your Kingdom have? And will you defend, and uphold them, to the Honour of God, so much as in you lieth?

Archbishop or bishop.
Will you to the utmost of your power maintain the laws of God, the true profession of the gospel, and the protestant reformed religion established by law? And will you preserve unto the bishops and clergy of this realm, and to the churches there committed to their charge, all such rights and privileges as by law do or shall appertain unto them, or any of them?

King.
I grant, and promise so to do.

Then shall follow ye petition, or Request of ye Bishops to ye King; to be read wth. a clear voice by one of them in ye name of ye Rest, standing by.

Bishop.
Our Lord, and King, We beseech you to pardon Us; and to grant, and preserve unto Us, and ye Churches committed to our Charge all Canonical privileges, and due Law and Justice: and yt. you will protect, and defend Us; as every good King in his Kingdom ought to be Protectour, and Defender of ye Bishops, and Churches under their Government.

The King answereth,

King.
With a willing, and devout Heart I promise and grant You my

King and Queen.
All this I promise to do.

38

Pardon; and that I will preserve, and maintein to you, and the Churches committed to your Charge all Canonical privileges and due Law and Justice. And that I will be your Protectour and Defender to my power by the assistance of God; as every good King in his Kingdom ought in Right to protect, and defend the Bishops and Churches under their Government.

Then ye King ... laying his Hand upon ye Holy Gospels, shall say,

King.

The things wch. I have here before promis'd, I will perform and keep: so help me God, and ye Contents of this Book.

After this, the King and Queen laying his and her hand upon the holy gospels, shall say,

King and Queen.

The things which I have here before promised, I will perform and keep: so help me God.

Then the King and Queen shall kiss the book.

IV.   And be it further enacted, That the said oath shall be in like manner administred to every King or Queen that shall succeed to the imperial crown of this realm, at their respective coronations, by one of the archbishops or bishops of this realm of *England*, for the time being, to be thereunto appointed by such King or Queen respectively, and in the presence of all persons that shall be attending, assisting, or otherwise present at such their respective coronations; any law, statute, or usage to the contrary notwithstanding.

1 Will. & Mary, c. 6: *S.L.* IX, 3; and L. G. Wickham Legg, *English Coronation Records* (1901), pp. 296–7.

14. Those who must take the new oaths, 1689.

An act for the abrogating of the oaths of supremacy and allegiance, and appointing other oaths.

Whereas *by a statute* [1 Eliz. c. 1.] ... *The persons therein mentioned were obliged to take an oath therein mentioned, commonly called the* Oath of

Supremacy: *and whereas by another statute* [3 Jac. I, c. 4.] . . . *another oath, commonly called the* Oath of Allegiance or Obedience, *was required to be taken by the persons therein mentioned:*

II.   [The old oaths of allegiance and supremacy abrogated.]

III.   [The new oaths and declaration by whom and how to be taken.]

IV.   [Before whom the new oaths are to be taken, and declaration to be made and subscribed.]

V.   [All persons which shall be in office shall take the oaths, &c. The Penalty for neglect.]

VI.   [Persons now in office neglecting, the office to be void.]

VII.   And be it further enacted . . . That if any archbishop or bishop, or any other person now having any ecclesiastical dignity, benefice, or promotion, shall neglect or refuse to take the oaths by this act appointed to be taken, in such manner as by this act is directed, before the first day of *August*, in the year one thousand six hundred eighty-nine, every such person and persons so neglecting or refusing, shall be . . . suspended from the execution of his or their office by the space of six months, to be accounted from the said first day of *August*: and if the said person or persons (so having neglected or refused) shall not within the said space of six months take the said oaths in such manner, court, or place, as they ought to have taken the same, before the first day of *August*; then he or they shall be *ipso facto* deprived, . . . of his and their offices, benefices, dignities, and promotions ecclesiastical.

VIII.   And be it further enacted, That if any person or persons now being master, governor, head, or fellow of any college or hall, in either of the two universities, or of any other college, or master of any hospital or school, or professor of divinity, law, physick, or other science in either of the said universities, or in the city of *London*, shall neglect or refuse to take the oaths . . . before the first day of *August*, in the year one thousand six hundred eighty-nine; every such persons . . . [will undergo similar penalties.]

IX.   And be it further enacted, That if any such other person or persons (other than the persons specially above-mentioned) shall refuse to take the said oaths . . . the person . . . tendring the said oaths . . . shall commit the said person and persons so refusing to the common gaol or house of correction, there to remain without bail or main-prize for the space of three months, unless such offender shall pay down to the said person . . . so tendring the said oaths, . . . such sum of money, not exceeding forty shillings, as the said person . . . shall require such offender to pay for his or her said refusal; which money shall be paid to the churchwardens or overseers of the poor, for the relief of the poor of the parish or place where such offender did last inhabit: And if at the end of three months after such refusal, the person or persons so refusing shall again refuse to take the said oaths . . . the said person . . . so tendring the said oaths, . . . shall commit the said person and persons so refusing to the common gaol or house of cor-rection, there to remain for the space of six months, unless every such offender shall pay . . . such sum of money, not exceeding ten pounds, nor under five pounds . . . then every person . . . refusing [a third time] shall be adjudged incapable of any office, civil or military within this kingdom, and shall likewise be and remain bound to the good behaviour, until he or they do take the said oaths. And in case such person or persons shall refuse also to make and subscribe the declaration mentioned in the statute [30 Car. II, stat. 2, c. 1.] . . . such person and persons shall suffer all pains, penalties, forfeitures, and disabilities as a popish recusant convict, and be taken and deemed a popish recusant convict, to all intents and purposes whatsoever.

X.   And be it further enacted by the authority aforesaid, That all and every commission-officer and officers, and non-commission or warrant-officer and officers, that are already imployed in their Majesties service by sea or land, shall take the said oaths, and also make, repeat, and sub-scribe the declaration mentioned in the said statute made in the thirtieth year of the reign of King *Charles* the Second, . . . and all and every such officer or officers, that shall refuse to take the said oaths, and make and subscribe the said declaration, shall be incapable of receiving, taking, holding, or executing such office or imployment.

XI.   [The oath and declaration appointed by two acts of 13 & 14 Car. II, c. 3 & 4 made void.]

XII.   And be it enacted, That the oaths that are intended and required to be taken by this act, are the oaths in these express words hereafter following [see Bill of Rights, p. 29]

XIII.   [Names of persons who take the oaths to be inrolled]

XIV and XV. [Provision for members of corporations and officers who could not take the abrogated oaths.]

XVI.   Provided always . . . That it be left to the King, to allow to such of the clergy as shall refuse the oaths prescribed by this act, as he shall think fit, not exceeding the number of twelve, an allowance out of their ecclesiastical benefices or promotions for their subsistence, not exceeding a third part, and to continue during his Majesty's pleasure, and no longer.

1 Will. & Mary, c. 8: S.L., IX, 5.

15. Toleration Act, 1689.

An Act for exempting their Majesties protestant subjects, dissenting from the church of England, from the penalties of certain laws.

Forasmuch as some ease to scrupulous consciences in the exercise of religion may be an effectual means to unite their Majesties protestant subjects in interest and affection:

II.   Be it enacted . . . That neither the statute made in the three and twentieth year of the reign of the late Queen *Elizabeth*, intituled, *An act to retain the Queen's Majesty's subjects in their due obedience*; nor the statute made in the twenty-ninth year of the said Queen, intituled, *An act for the more speedy and due execution of certain branches of the statute* . . . viz. the aforesaid act; nor that branch or clause of a statute made in the first year of the reign of the said Queen, intituled, *An act for the uniformity of common prayer and service in the church* . . . whereby all persons, having no lawful or reasonable excuse to be absent, are required to resort to their parish church or chapel, or some usual place where the common prayer shall be used, upon pain of punishment by the censures of the church, and also upon pain that every person so offending shall forfeit for every such offence twelve pence; nor the statute made in the third year of the reign of the late King *James* the First, intituled, *An act for the better discovering and repressing popish recusants*; nor that other statute made in the same year, intituled, *An act to prevent and avoid dangers which may grow by popish recusants*; nor any other law or statute of this realm made against papists or popish recusants; except the statute made in the five and twentieth year of King *Charles* the Second, intituled, *An act for preventing dangers which may happen from popish recusants*; and except also the statute made in the thirtieth year of the said King *Charles* the Second, intituled, *An act for the effectual preserving the King's person and government, by disabling papists from sitting in either house of parliament;* shall be construed to extend to any person or persons dissenting from the church of *England,* that shall take the oaths mentioned in a statute made by this present parliament (1 Will. and Mary, c. 1, p. 29) . . . and that shall make and subscribe the declaration mentioned in a statute made in the thirtieth year of the reign of King *Charles* the Second . . . which oaths and declaration the justices of peace at the general sessions of the peace . . . are hereby required to tender and administer to such persons as shall offer themselves to take, make, and subscribe the same, and thereof to keep a register: and likewise none of the persons aforesaid shall give or pay, as any fee or reward, to any officer or officers belonging to the court aforesaid, above the sum of sixpence, nor that more than once, for his or their entry of his taking the said oaths, and making and subscribing the said declaration; nor above the further sum of sixpence for any certificate of the same, to be made out and signed by the officer or officers of the said court.

III. And be it further enacted . . . That all . . . persons already convicted or prosecuted in order to conviction of recusancy . . . grounded upon the aforesaid statutes . . . that shall take the said oaths mentioned in the said statute in this present parliament made, and make and subscribe the declaration aforesaid . . . and to be thence respectively certified into the Exchequer, shall be thenceforth exempted and discharged from all the penalties, seizures, forfeitures, judgements, and executions, incurred by force of any of the aforesaid statutes, without any composition, fee, or further charge whatsoever.

IV. And be it further enacted . . . that all . . . persons that shall . . . take the said oaths, and make and subscribe the declaration aforesaid, shall not be liable to any pains, penalties, or forfeitures, mentioned in an act made in the five and thirtieth year of the reign of the late Queen *Elizabeth* (35 Eliz. c. 1.) . . . nor an act made in the two and twentieth year of the late King *Charles* the Second (22 Cha. II, c. 1.) . . . nor shall any of the said persons be prosecuted in any ecclesiastical court, for or by reason of their non-conforming to the church of *England.*

V. Provided always . . . That if any assembly of persons dissenting from the church of *England* shall be had in any place for religious worship with the doors locked, barred, or bolted, during any time of such meeting together, all and every person or persons, which shall come to and be at such meeting, shall not receive any benefit from this law, but be liable to all the pains and penalties of all the aforesaid laws recited in this act, for such their meeting, notwithstanding his taking the oaths, and making and subscribing the declaration aforesaid.

VI.   Provided always, That nothing herein contained shall . . . exempt any of the persons aforesaid from paying of tythes or other parochial duties, or any other duties to the church or minister, nor from any prosecution in any ecclesiastical court, or elsewhere for the same.

VII.   [Officers scrupling the oaths &c. allowed to act by deputy.]

VIII.   And be it further enacted . . . That no person dissenting from the church of *England* in holy orders, or pretended holy orders, or pretending to holy orders, nor any preacher or teacher of any congregation of dissenting protestants, that shall make and subscribe the declaration aforesaid, and take the said oaths . . . and shall also declare his approbation of and subscribe the articles of religion mentioned in the statute (13 Eliz. c. 12.) . . . except the thirty-fourth, thirty-fifth, and thirty-sixth, and these words of the twentieth article, *viz.* '*The church hath power to decree rites or ceremonies, and authority in controversies of faith, and yet*' shall be liable to any of the pains or penalties mentioned in an act (17 Cha. II, c. 2.) . . . nor the penalties mentioned in the aforesaid act (22 Cha. II, c. 1.) . . . for or by reason of such person's preaching at any meeting for the exercise of religion; nor to the penalty of one hundred pounds mentioned in an act (13 & 14 Cha. II, c. 4.) for officiating in any congregation for the exercise of religion permitted and allowed by this act. . .

IX.   [Taking the oaths, &c. to be registered. Meeting—door to be unlocked.]

X.   *And whereas some dissenting protestants scruple the baptizing of infants;* be it enacted . . . That every person in pretended holy orders, or pretending to holy orders, or preacher, or teacher, that shall subscribe the aforesaid articles of religion, except before excepted, and also except part of the seven and twentieth article touching infant baptism and shall take the said oaths, and make and subscribe the declaration aforesaid . . . every such person shall enjoy all the privileges, benefits, and advantages, which any other dissenting minister, as aforesaid, might have or enjoy by virtue of this act.

XI. And be it further enacted . . . That every teacher or preacher in holy orders, or pretended holy orders, that is a minister, preacher, or teacher of a congregation, that shall take the oaths herein required, and make and subscribe the declaration aforesaid, and also subscribe such of the aforesaid articles of the church of *England*, as are required by this act . . . shall be thenceforth exempted from serving upon any jury, or from being chosen or appointed to bear the office of church-warden, overseer of the poor, or any other parochial or ward office, or other office in any hundred of any shire, city, town, parish, division, or wapentake.

XII. [A J.P. may require a person going to a religious meeting to take the oaths, &c. Penalty for refusal shall be imprisonment; for second refusal the person shall be taken for a popish recusant convict.]

XIII. *And whereas there are certain other persons, dissenters from the church of* England, *who scruple the taking of any oath;* be it enacted . . . That every such person shall make and subscribe the aforesaid declaration, and the declaration of fidelity following, *viz.*

I A.B. do sincerely promise and solemnly declare before God and the world, that I will be true and faithful to King William *and Queen* Mary; *and I do solemnly profess and declare, That I do from my heart abhor, detest, and renounce as impious and heretical, that damnable doctrine and position, That princes excommunicated or deprived by the pope, or any authority of the see of* Rome, *may be deposed or murthered by their subjects, or any other whatsoever. And I do declare, that no foreign prince, person, prelate, state, or potentate hath, or ought to have, any power, jurisdiction, superiority, pre-eminence, or authority, ecclesiastical or spiritual, within this realm.*

And shall subscribe a profession of their christian belief in these words:

I A.B. profess faith in God the father, and in Jesus Christ his eternal son, the true God, and in the holy spirit, one God blessed for evermore; and do acknowledge the holy scriptures of the Old and New Testament to be given by divine inspiration.

. . . . And every such person that shall make and subscribe the two declarations and profession aforesaid . . . shall be exempted from all the . . . penalties of all . . . the aforementioned statutes made against popish recusants, or protestant nonconformists, and also from the penalties of an act (5 Eliz. c. 1.) . . . and also from the penalties of an act (13 & 14 Cha. 2, c. 1.); and enjoy all other the benefits, privileges, and advantages . . . which other dissenters shall or ought to enjoy by virtue of this act.

XIV & XV.   [Prescribe for purging after refusal of the oaths.]

XVI.   Provided always, and it is the true intent and meaning of this act, That all the laws made and provided for the frequenting of divine service on the Lord's day, commonly called *Sunday* shall be still in force, and executed against all persons that offend against the said laws, except such persons come to some congregation or assembly of religious worship, allowed or permitted by this act.

XVII.   Provided always . . . That neither this act, nor any clause, article, or thing herein contained, shall . . . extend to give any ease, benefit, or advantage to any papist or popish recusant whatsoever, or any person that shall deny in his preaching or writing the doctrine of the blessed Trinity, as it is declared in the aforesaid articles of religion.

XVIII.   [Disturbers of religious worship how punished.]

XIX.   Provided always, That no congregation or assembly for religious worship shall be permitted or allowed by this act, until the place of such meeting shall be certified to the bishop of the diocese, or to the archdeacon of that archdeaconry, or to the justices of the peace at the general or quarter sessions of the peace for that county, city, or place in which such meeting shall be held and registered in the said bishop's or archdeacon's court respectively, or recorded at the said general or quarter sessions; the register or clerk of the peace whereof is hereby required to register the same, and to give certificate thereof to such person as shall demand the same, for which there shall be no greater fee nor reward taken than the sum of sixpence.

1 Will. & Mary, c. 18: *S.L.* IX, 19.

16. Legalisation of the Acts of the convention, 1690.

An act for recognizing King William *and Queen* Mary, *and for avoiding all questions touching the acts made in the parliament assembled at* Westminster, *the thirteenth day of* February, *one thousand six hundred eighty eight.*[1]

We your Majesties' most humble and loyal subjects, the lords spiritual and temporal, and commons, in this present parliament assembled, do

1 1688/9.

beseech your most excellent Majesties that it may be published and declared in this high court of parliament, and enacted by authority of the same, That we do recognize and acknowledge, your Majesties were, are, and of right ought to be, by the laws of this realm, our sovereign liege lord and lady King and Queen of *England, France,* and *Ireland,* and the dominions thereunto belonging, in and to whose princely persons the royal state crown, and dignity of the said realms, with all honours, stiles, titles, regalities, prerogatives, powers, jurisdictions, and authorities to the same belonging and appertaining, are most fully, rightfully, and intirely invested and incorporated, united, and annexed.

II.   And for the avoiding of all disputes and questions concerning the being and authority of the late parliament assembled at *Westminster* the thirteenth day of *February* one thousand six hundred eighty eight,[1] we do most humbly beseech your Majesties that it may be enacted, and be it enacted by the King's and Queen's most excellent Majesties, by and with the advice and consent of the lords spiritual and temporal, and commons, in this present parliament assembled, and by the authority of the same, That all and singular the acts made and enacted in the said parliament were and are laws and statutes of this kingdom, and such as ought to be reputed, taken and obeyed by all the people of this kingdom.

2 Will. & Mary, c. 1: *S.L.*, IX, 75.

17. The 'Sacheverell Clause', 1690.

[10 January 1689/90.]

A Motion was made, That a Clause in the Bill, beginning Press 8, Line 3, to the End of That Press, may [be] left out of the Bill: Which Clause is as follows;

"And whereas it is necessary, for the sake of publick Justice, and securing the Government for the future, That such open Attempts upon the Constitution, and so notorious Violations of Oaths and Trusts, should not go wholly unpunished, lest hereafter ill Men might be encouraged to the like Guilt, in hopes to come off with Impunity, though they should fail, with Success: be it Enacted, by the Authority aforesaid, That every Mayor, Recorder, Alderman, Steward, Sheriff, Common Council Man, Town Clerk, Magistrate or Officer, who did

[1] 1688/9.

47

take upon him to consent to, or join in any such Surrender or Instrument, purporting such Surrender as aforesaid; or did solicit, procure, prosecute, or did pay or contribute to the Charge of prosecuting any *Scire Facias*, *Quo Warranto*, or Information in the Nature of a *Quo Warranto* by this Act declared void, shall be and is hereby Declared, Adjudged, and Enacted to be, for the Space of Seven Years, uncapable and disabled to all Intents and Purposes, to bear or execute any Office, Employment, or Place of Trust, as a Member of such respective Body Corporate, or in or for such respective City, Town, Borough, or Cinque Port, whereof or wherein he was Member, at or before the Time of the making such Surrender, or Instrument purporting such Surrender, or the suing out, or prosecuting such *Scire Facias*, *Quo Warranto*, or instrument in the nature of a *Quo Warranto*; any thing in this Act contained, or any other Law, Statute, or any Ordinance, Charter, Custom, or Thing to the contrary, in any-wise notwithstanding.

Thereupon arose a long Debate.

C.J., x, 329.

DEBATE ON THE CORPORATION BILL

MR. SACHEVERELL.   That this Bill is very necessary, no man but thinks. Surrenders of Charters are crimes notorious, but all are not equally guilty of it. . . . therefore, as a friend to the Bill, I proffer a clause, "For incapacitating, for seven years, all such as had any ways acted in the surrender of Charters of Corporations, from bearing any office in the said corporations."

. . .

MR SOLICITOR SOMERS . . . To destroy corporations, and to make parliaments at the pleasure of the crown, this is the thing, and these persons are complained of for it.   This is the worst means to arrive at the worst ends imaginable; they have broken their oaths and trust to subvert the government.   Is there any thing more just and natural than that these offenders should be laid aside?   And to put these men out of condition to play the same trick again!   All you restore were the old members of the Church of England but not that corrupt part of the Church of England who endeavoured to destroy the government. Honest men are now electors, to supply the place of those ill men.

... It is said, 'This is a bill of pains and penalties' but you are not doing that; you are only laying them aside that, you have had experience, would have betrayed the government. There is no possible inconvenience in this proviso; you will have better men and unspotted men in their stead; therefore I would not reject the clause.

MR. FOLEY. The question is, 'Whether this clause shall be rejected, or not?' It was endeavoured, the two last reigns, to pack a parliament to subvert all our constitutions. There was a design for a clause in a bill, 'That all Corporations should surrender their Charters by such a time, or else they should be void, and justices of the county should act in all towns, &c.' Had that design succeeded, there had been no need of *Quo Warrantos*. Your Books will tell you, it was not in the power of that house to make such an alteration. It was part of this king's Declaration to restore all corporations to the condition they were in before the *Quo Warrantos* and surrenders. We have ill ministers, and they are concerned that the same thing may be done again. Men have done all they can to annihilate their corporations, and we must not annihilate, but restore these men. If there be any in corporations who are sorry for what they have done, they will take this for a very merciful proviso, that they may do no more mischief to corporations and to the king; therefore retain the proviso.

. . .

MR FINCH. . . . If these men be put out of the bill, you put out the men of estates, and the ancient corporations are put into the hands of men of little or no fortune, and some call them the *mobile*. There is a clause in the bill that declares all Surrenders void; where is the danger of these men doing the same thing again? The former are in their offices and employment again. Leave this clause out, and you put in the rich men of the Corporations, and if this stands part of the bill, you put those in of no estates, and that have given no testimony of their affections to the government.

P.H., V, 508–15.

18. Triennial Act, 1694.

An act for the frequent meeting and calling of parliaments.

Whereas by the ancient laws, and statutes of this kingdom frequent parliaments ought to be held; and whereas frequent and new parliaments tend very much to the happy union and good agreement of the King and people; . . . it is hereby declared and enacted . . . That from henceforth a parliament shall be holden once in three years at the least.

II.   And be it further enacted . . . That within three years at the farthest, from and after the dissolution of this present parliament, and so from time to time for ever hereafter, within three years at the farthest, from and after the determination of every parliament, legal writs under the great seal shall be issued by directions of your Majesties your heirs and successors, for calling, assembling and holding another new parliament.

III.   And be it further enacted . . . That from henceforth no parliament whatsoever, that shall at any time hereafter be called, assembled or held, shall have any continuance longer than for three years only at the farthest, to be accounted from the day on which by the writs of summons the said parliament shall be appointed to meet.

IV.   And be it further enacted . . . That this present parliament shall cease and determine on the first day of *November*, which shall be in the year of our Lord one thousand six hundred ninety six, unless their Majesties shall think fit to dissolve it sooner.

6 & 7 Will. & Mary, c. 2: S.L. IX, 331.

19. Civil List Act, 1697.

An act for granting to his Majesty a further subsidy of tunnage and poundage, towards raising the yearly sum of seven hundred thousand pounds, for the service of his Majesty's household, and other uses therein mentioned, during his Majesty's life.

WHEREAS *your Majesty's most dutiful and loyal subjects the commons of England in parliament assembled, being deeply sensible of the great blessings which, by the goodness of Almighty God, we and all other the subjects of your Majesty's realms and dominions, in the free exercise of the true christian religion (the most valuable benefit which can be bestowed upon any nation or people) as also in our liberties and properties, do fully enjoy under your Majesty's most auspicious government; and being desirous to make a grateful acknowledgment of your Majesty's unparalleled grace and favour to us your commons, and particularly for the great and successful undertakings and achievements, whereby your Majesty hath been the happy instrument of securing the aforesaid blessings to us and our posterities;* have therefore freely and unanimously resolved to increase your Majesty's revenue during your Majesty's reign (which God long continue) and do give and grant unto your most excellent Majesty the further rates, duties, and sums of money, hereinafter mentioned; and do humbly beseech your Majesty that it may be enacted; and be it enacted . . . That over and above all subsidies and tunnage and poundage, and over and above all additional duties, impositions, and other duties whatsoever, by any other act or acts of parliament, or otherwise howsoever, already due or payable, or which ought to be paid to his Majesty, for or upon any wines, goods or merchandizes whatsoever, imported or to be imported, there shall be raised, levied, collected, paid, and satisfied unto his Majesty, one other subsidy called *Tunnage*, for and upon all wines, which from and after the last day of *January*, which shall be in the year of our Lord one thousand six hundred and ninety nine,[1] at any time or times, during his Majesty's life, shall be imported or brought into the kingdom of *England*, dominion of *Wales*, or town of *Berwick* upon *Tweed*, . . . [here follow the various rates]

IV. . . . And one further subsidy called Poundage (that is to say) of all manner of goods and merchandizes of every merchant, natural born subject, denizen, and alien, to be imported or brought into this realm, or any his Majesty's dominions to the same belonging, at any time or times after the said last day of *January*, one thousand six hundred ninety nine,[1] during his Majesty's life, by way of merchandize, of the value of every twenty shillings of the same goods and merchandizes, according to the several and particular rates and values of the same goods and merchandizes, as the same are particularly and respectively rated and valued in the aforesaid book of rates, twelve pence, and so after that rate;

. . .

XIV. *And whereas it is intended, that the yearly sum of seven hundred thousand pounds shall be supplied to his Majesty for the service of his household and family, and for other his necessary expences and occasions, out of the hereditary rates and duties of excise upon beer, ale and other liquors, which were granted to the crown in the twelfth year of the reign of King Charles the Second, and out of the rates and duties of excise upon beer, ale*

[1] 1699/1700.

and other liquors, payable for the terms of his Majesty's life, by an act of parliament made and passed in the second year of the reign of his Majesty and the late Queen of blessed memory, after all the tallies charged upon the weekly sum of six thousand pounds issuing out of the said several rates and duties of excise, pursuant to an act of parliament passed in the seventh year of his Majesty's reign in that behalf, and still remaining unsatisfied (with the interest thereof) shall be fully paid off and cleared; and out of the revenue of the general letter office or post office, or the office of the postmaster general, after all the tallies charged upon the weekly sum of six hundred pounds, issuing out of that revenue pursuant to the said act of parliament for the seventh year of his Majesty's reign, and still remaining unsatisfied, and all the interest thereof shall be fully paid and discharged; and out of the small branches of his Majesty's revenues herein mentioned and expressed, that is to say, The first fruits and tenths of the clergy; the fines for writs of covenant and writs of entry payable in the alienation office; the post fines; the revenue of the wine licences; the monies arising by sheriffs profers and compositions in the Exchequer, and by the seizures of uncustomed and prohibited goods; the revenue of the duchy of Cornwall, and any other revenue arising by the rents of lands in England or Wales, or for fines of leases of the same, or any of them; and the duty of four and a half per centum in specie, arising in Barbadoes and the Leeward islands in America; and out of the monies which from and after the commencement of this act shall arise by the further subsidies and duties hereby granted; be it therefore further enacted, and it is hereby enacted and provided by the authority aforesaid, That if the said great and small branches and revenues herein before mentioned, and out of which the said yearly sum of seven hundred thousand pounds is intended to be supplied as aforesaid, and every or any of them, shall produce in clear money more than the yearly sum of seven hundred thousand pounds, to be reckoned from the five and twentieth day of *December,* which shall be in the year of our Lord one thousand six hundred ninety nine, that then the overplus of such produce (being more than the said yearly sum of seven hundred thousand pounds) shall not be issued, disposed, made use of or applied to any use or purpose, or upon any pretext whatsoever, without the authority of parliament: and that all grants and dispositions whatsoever hereafter to be made of such over-plus, or any part thereof, from time to time, without the authority of parliament, shall be utterly void and of none effect; and the grantees, or other persons to whom such grants or dispositions, or any of them, shall be made, of such overplus, or any part thereof, shall be adjudged uncapable in law to take, hold, keep, detain or enjoy the same; any law, custom or usage to the contrary notwithstanding.

9 & 10 Will. III, c. 23: *S.L.*, x, 145.

20. Trial of Treasons Act, 1696.

An act for regulating of trials in cases of treason and misprision of treason.

Whereas nothing is more just and reasonable, than that persons prosecuted for high treason and misprision of treason, whereby the liberties, lives, honour, estates, blood, and posterity of the subjects, may be lost and destroyed, should be justly and equally tried, and that persons accused as offenders therein should not be debarred of all just and equal means for defence of their innocencies in such cases; in order thereunto, and for the better regulation of trials of persons prosecuted for high treason and misprision of such treason; be it enacted . . . That . . . all and every person or persons whatsoever, that shall be accused and indicted for high treason, whereby any corruption of blood may or shall be made . . . or for misprision of such treason, shall have a true copy of the whole indictment, but not the names of the witnesses, delivered unto them, or any of them, five days at the least before he or they shall be tried for the same, whereby to enable them, and any of them respectively, to advise with counsel thereupon, to plead and make their defence, his or their attorney or attorneys, agent or agents, or any of them, requiring the same, and paying the officer his reasonable fees for writing thereof, not exceeding five shillings for the copy of every such indictment; and that every such person so accused and indicted, arraigned or tried for any such treason, as aforesaid, or for misprision of such treason . . . shall be received and admitted to make his . . . defence, by counsel learned in the law, and to make any proof that he . . . can produce by lawful witness or witnesses, who shall then be upon oath, for his . . . just defence in that behalf; and in case any person . . . so accused or indicted shall desire counsel, the court before whom such person . . . shall be tried, or some judge of that court, shall and is hereby authorised and required immediately, upon his . . . request to assign . . . such and so many counsel, not exceeding two as the person . . . shall desire to whom such counsel shall have free access at all reasonable hours; any law or usage to the contrary notwithstanding.

II. And be it further enacted, That . . . no person . . . whatsoever shall be indicted, tried, or attainted, of high treason, whereby any corruption of blood may or shall be made . . . or of misprision of such treason, but by and upon the oaths and testimony of two lawful witnesses, either both of them to the same overt act, or one of them to one, and the other of them to another overt act of the same treason; unless the party indicted, and arraigned, or tried, shall willingly, without violence, in open court, confess the same, or shall stand mute, or refuse to plead, or in cases of high treason shall peremptorily challenge above the number of thirty five of the jury; any law, statute, or usage, to the contrary notwithstanding.

III. Provided always, That any person or persons, being indicted, as aforesaid . . . may be outlawed, and thereby attainted of or for any of the said offences of treason, or misprision of treason; and in cases of the high treasons aforesaid, where-by the law, after such outlawry, the party outlawed may come in, and be tried, he shall, upon such trial, have the benefit of this act.

IV. And be it further enacted . . . That if two or more distinct treasons or divers heads or kinds shall be alledged in one bill of indictment, one witness produced to prove one of the said treasons, and another witness produced to prove another of the said treasons, shall not be deemed or taken to be two witnesses to the same treason, within the meaning of this act.

V. And to the intent that the terror and dread of such criminal accusations may in some reasonable time be removed, be it further enacted . . . That . . . no person or persons whatsoever shall be indicted, tried or prosecuted, for any such treason as aforesaid, or for misprision of such treason, that shall be committed or done within the kingdom of *England*, dominion of *Wales*, or town of *Berwick* upon *Tweed*, . . . unless the same indictment be found by a grand jury within three years next after the treason or offence done or committed.

VI. . . . always provided and excepted, That if any person or persons whatsoever shall be guilty of designing, endeavouring, or attempting, any assassination on the body of the King, by poison or otherwise, such person or persons may be prosecuted at any time, notwithstanding the aforesaid limitation.

VII. And that all and every person . . . who shall be accused, indicted, and tried for such treason as aforesaid, or for misprision of such treason . . . shall have copies of the panel of the jurors who are to try them, duly returned by the sheriff, and delivered unto them . . . two days at the least before he or they shall be tried for the same; and that all persons so accused and indicted for any such treason as aforesaid, shall have the like process of the court where they shall be tried, to compel their witnesses to appear for them at any such trial or trials, as is usually granted to compel witnesses to appear against them.

VIII.   And be it further enacted, That no evidence shall be admitted or given of any overt act that is not expressly laid in the indictment against any person or persons whatsoever.

IX.   Provided also . . . That no indictment for any of the offences aforesaid, nor any process or return thereupon, shall be quashed on the motion of the prisoner, or his counsel, for mis-writing, mis-spelling, false or improper *Latin*, unless exception concerning the same be taken and made in the respective court where such trial shall be, by the prisoner or his counsel assigned, before any evidence given in open court upon such indictment; nor shall any such mis-writing, misspelling, false or improper *Latin*, after conviction on such indictment, be any cause to stay or arrest judgment thereupon: but nevertheless any judgment given upon such indictment, shall and may be liable to be reversed upon a writ of error, in the same manner, and no other, than as if this act had not been made.

X.   *And whereas by the good laws of this kingdom in cases of trials of commoners for their lives, a jury of twelve freeholders must all agree in one opinion before they can bring a verdict, either for acquittal or condemnation of the prisoner:*

XI.   *And whereas upon the trials of peers or peeresses, a major vote is sufficient, either to acquit or condemn;* be it further enacted . . . That upon the trial of any peer or peeress, either for treason or misprision, all the peers who have a right to sit and vote in parliament shall be duly summoned, twenty days at least before every such trial, to appear at every such trial; and that every peer, so summoned and appearing at such trial, shall vote in the trial of such peer or peeress so to be tried, every such peer first taking the oaths mentioned in an act of parliament [1 William and Mary, c. 8. See p. 39] . . . and also every such peer subscribing and audibly repeating the declaration mentioned in An act [30 Car. II, stat. 2, c. 1.] . . .

XII. Provided always, That neither this act, nor any thing therein contained, shall any ways extend to, or be construed to extend to any impeachment or other proceedings in parliament, in any kind whatsoever.

XIII. Provided always That neither this act, nor any thing therein contained, shall any ways extend to any indictment of high treason, nor to any proceedings thereupon, for counterfeiting his Majesty's coin, his great seal, or privy seal, his sign manual, or privy signet.

7 & 8 Will. III, c. 3: S.L., ix, 389.

21. Act of Settlement, 1701.

An act for the further limitation of the crown, and better securing the rights and liberties of the subject.

Whereas in the first year of the reign of your Majesty, and of our late most gracious sovereign lady Queen Mary (of blessed memory) an act of parliament was made, intituled, An act for declaring the rights and liberties of the subject, and for settling the succession of the crown, [No. 10] wherein it was (amongst other things) enacted, established, and declared, That the crown and regal government of the kingdoms of England, France, and Ireland, and the dominions thereunto belonging, should be and continue to your Majesty and the said late Queen; during the joint lives of your Majesty and the said Queen, and to the survivor: and that after the decease of your Majesty and the said Queen, the said crown and regal government should be and remain to the heirs of the body of the said late Queen; and for default of such issue, to her royal highness the Princess Anne of Denmark, and the heirs of her body: and for default of such issue, to the heirs of the body of your Majesty. And it was thereby enacted, That all and every person and persons that then were, or afterwards should be reconciled to, or should hold communion with the see or church of Rome, or should profess the popish religion, or marry a papist, should be excluded, and are by that act made for ever uncapable to inherit, possess, or enjoy the crown and government of this realm, and Ireland, and the dominions thereunto belonging, or any part of the same, or to have, use or exercise any regal power, authority, or jurisdiction within the same: and in all and every such case and cases the people of these realms shall be and are thereby absolved of their allegiance: and that the said crown and government shall from time to time descend to and be enjoyed by such person or persons, being protestants, as should have inherited and enjoyed the same, in case the said person or persons, so reconciled, holding communion, professing or marrying, as aforesaid, were naturally dead. After the making of which statute, and the settlement therein contained, your Majesty's good subjects, who were restored to the full and free possession and enjoyment of their religion, rights and liberties, by the providence of God giving success to your Majesty's just undertakings and unwearied endeavours for that purpose, had no greater temporal felicity to hope or wish for, than to see a royal progeny descending from your Majesty, to whom (under God) they owe their tranquillity, and whose ancestors have for many years been principal assertors of the reformed religion and the liberties of Europe, and from our said most gracious sovereign Lady, whose memory will always be precious to the subjects of these realms: and it having since pleased Almighty God to take away our said sovereign Lady, and also the most hopeful prince William *duke of* Gloucester *(the only surviving issue of her royal highness the princess* Anne *of* Denmark*) to the unspeakable grief and sorrow of your Majesty and your said good subjects, who under such losses being sensibly put in mind, that it standeth wholly in the pleasure of Almighty God to prolong the lives of your Majesty and of her royal Highness, and to grant to your Majesty, or to her royal Highness, such issue as may be inheritable to the crown and regal government aforesaid, by the respective limitations in the said recited act contained, do constantly implore the divine mercy for those blessings: and your Majesty's said subjects having daily experience of your royal care and concern for the present and future welfare of these kingdoms, and particularly recommending from your throne a further provision to be made for the succession of the crown in the protestant line, for the happiness of the nation, and the security of our religion; and it being absolutely necessary for the safety, peace, and quiet of this realm, to obviate all doubts and contentions in the same, by reason of any pretended title to the crown, and to maintain a certainty in the succession thereof, to which your subjects may safely have recourse for their protection, in case the limitations in the said recited act should determine:* therefore for a further provision of the succession of the crown in the protestant line . . . be it enacted . . . That the most excellent princess *Sophia*, electress and duchess dowager of *Hanover*, daughter of the most excellent princess *Elizabeth*, late Queen of *Bohemia*, daughter of our late sovereign lord King *James* the First, of happy memory, be and is hereby declared to be the next in succession, in the protestant line, to the imperial crown and dignity of the said realms of *England*, *France*, and *Ireland*, with the dominions and territories thereunto belonging, after his Majesty, and the princess *Anne*, of *Denmark*, and in default of issue of the said princess *Anne*, and of his Majesty respectively: and that from and after the deceases of his said Majesty, our now sovereign lord, and of her royal highness the princess *Anne*, of *Denmark*, and for default of issue of the said princess *Anne*, and of his Majesty respectively, the crown and regal government of the said kingdoms of *England, France*, and *Ireland*, and of the dominions thereunto belonging with the royal state and dignity of the said realms, and all honours, stiles, titles, regalities, prerogatives, powers, jurisdictions and authorities, to the same belonging and appertaining, shall be, remain, and continue to the said most excellent princess *Sophia*, and the heirs of her body, being protestants: and thereunto the said lords spiritual and temporal, and commons, shall and will, in the name of all the people of this realm, most humbly and faithfully submit themselves, their heirs and posterities; and do faithfully promise, That after the decease of his Majesty, and of her royal highness, and the failure of the heirs to their respective bodies, to stand to, maintain, and defend the said princess *Sophia*, and the heirs of her body, being protestants, according to the limitation and succession of the crown in this act specified and contained, to the utmost of their powers, with their lives and estates, against all persons whatsoever that shall attempt any thing to the contrary.

II.   Provided always . . . That all and every person and persons, who shall or may take or inherit the said crown, by virtue of the limitation of this present act, and is, are or shall be reconciled to, or shall hold communion with, the see or church of *Rome*, or shall profess the popish religion, or shall marry a papist, shall be subject to such incapacities, as in such case or cases are by the said recited act provided, enacted, and established; and that every King and Queen of this realm, who shall come to and succeed in the imperial crown of this kingdom by virtue of this act, shall have the coronation oath administered to him, her or them, at their respective coronations, according to the act of parliament made in the first year of the reign of his Majesty, and the said late Queen *Mary*, intituled, *An act for establishing the coronation oath*, [No. 13] and shall make, subscribe, and repeat the declaration in the act first above recited mentioned or referred to, in the manner and form thereby prescribed.

III.   *And whereas it is requisite and necessary that some further provision be made for securing our religion, laws and liberties, from and after the death of his Majesty and the princess* Anne *of* Denmark, *and in default of issue of the body of the said princess, and of his Majesty respectively;* be it enacted . . .

That whosoever shall hereafter come to the possession of this crown, shall join in communion with the church of England, *as by law established.*

That in case the crown and imperial dignity of this realm shall hereafter come to any person, not being a native of this kingdom of England, *this nation be not obliged to engage in any war for the defence of any dominions or territories which do not belong to the crown of* England, *without the consent of parliament.*

That no person who shall hereafter come to the possession of this crown, shall go out of the dominions of England, Scotland, *or* Ireland, *without consent of parliament.*

That from and after the time that the further limitation by this act shall take effect, all matters and things relating to the well governing of this kingdom, which are properly cognizable in the privy council by the laws and customs of this realm, shall be transacted there, and all resolutions taken thereupon shall be signed by such of the privy counsel as shall advise and consent to the same.

That after the said limitation shall take effect as aforesaid, no person born out of the kingdoms of England, Scotland, *or* Ireland, *or the dominions thereunto belonging (although he be naturalized or made a denizen, except such as are born of* English *parents) shall be capable to be of the privy council, or a member of either house of parliament, or to enjoy any office or place of trust, either civil or military, or to have any grant of lands, tenements or hereditaments from the crown, to himself or to any other or others in trust for him.*

That no person who has an office or place of profit under the King, or receives a pension from the crown, shall be capable of serving as a member of the house of commons.

That after the said limitation shall take effect as aforesaid, judges commissions be made quamdiu se bene gesserint, *and their salaries ascertained and established; but upon the address of both houses of parliament it may be lawful to remove them.*

That no pardon under the great seal of England *be pleadable to an impeachment by the commons in parliament.*

IV. *And whereas the laws of* England *are the birthright of the people thereof, and all the Kings and Queens, who shall ascend the throne of this realm, ought to administer the government of the same according to the said*

laws, and all their officers and ministers ought to serve them respectively
according to the same: the said lords spiritual and temporal, and commons,
do therefore further humbly pray, That all the laws and statutes of
this realm for securing the established religion, and the rights and
liberties of the people thereof, and all other laws and statutes of the
same now in force, may be ratified and confirmed, and the same are
by his Majesty, by and with the advice and consent of the said lords
spiritual and temporal, and commons, and by authority of the same,
ratified and confirmed accordingly.

12 & 13 Will. III, c. 2: S.L., x, 357.

22. William's opinions, 1688–90.

Dec 30 [1688] Note, a treat jealousie of being thought to bee governed.
That apprehension will give uneasiness to men in great places.

. . .

Said that the Commonwealth party was the strongest in England;
hee had then that impression given. . . .

Said that at the best, they would have a Duke of Venice; In that
perhaps hee was not so much mistaken.

Said, hee did not come over to establish a Commonwealth.

Said, hee was sure of one thing; hee would not stay in England, if
K. James came again.

. . .

Feb. 14. [1689]

Hee said with the strongest asseverations, that hee would go, if they
went about to make him Regent.—

Said, I am a young King, and a young Secretary and that hee required my help.—

Hee was desirous to bee King yet really shrunk at the burthen, at
the very first putting on of his crown.—

M^dm hee made a good deal of objection to the making Ld Shrewsbury
Secretary, when I mooved him to him.

Said hee fancyed, hee was like a King in a play—

Against taking in a greater number into his Councell.

In that hee committed a mistake.—

Double the number would have done no hurt, and would have
ingaged men of quality.

Had a wrong notion of the Privy Councell; thought the Govt was to reside there.

• • •

Mar. 28

Hee often repeated to mee, that hee was a Trimmer. Said the Commons used him like a dog.—
Their coarse usage boyled so upon his Stomack, that hee could not hinder himselfe from breaking out sometimes, against them.

• • •

? April

By the want hee hath of the Commons and by his not coming to the house of Lds where hee might see, how necessary they are to the support of his Crown; hee doth not think them of much moment.

• • •

? April

Said he had a mind to propose a warre against France upon the assistance given by that K. to K. James. Note. this was a good while before the warre was declared.
His eagernesse that way never ceased; it may bee a question whether that thought was not the greatest inducement to his undertaking,—

• • •

April 21

Said it was to be considered, whether all the Articles in the Declaration [of Rights], were to be confirmed in the bill of Succession.—
Hee had no mind to confirme them, but the conditions of his affayres overruled his inclinations in it.

May 27

Said hee heard something was doing against him by the Ch[urch] party, that hee hoped to find it out.

May 23

Note hee was then farre from leaning towards them; Would have the Oaths pressed upon the Lds. Nota—

• • •

June 2

Hee hath such a mind to France, that it would incline one to think, hee tooke England onely in his way.—

. . .

June 17

Said that a K. of England who will governe by Law as hee must do, if hee hath conscience, is the worst figure in Christendome.—

Hee hath power to destroy the Nation and not to protect it.—

. . .

July 10

Speaking about the Plt. and persuading him to let it sit hee said hee was so weary of them, hee could not bear them; there must be a recesse. I argued against it, but could not alter his opinion on it.—

Note, hee was cruelly galled with their proceedings;

. . .

July 28

Said hee now discovered plainly there was a designe for a Commonwealth.

. . . Said he saw the designe, in the managing the businesse of his revenue in the house.

That they would not have it for the Q^s. life, but hee would have it for both.—

Said that the Presbyterians now delayed it for some dayes, that they might have the honour of it themselves.

Note; about this time, there seemed to bee the first turne in the K's mind, in relation to the dissenters.—

Said hee would stay a week, and if they [parliament] did nothing in the Revenue, hee would send them away.

Said the Comptroller [Wharton] was in the designe of a Commonwealth.

Said there was a designe too, on the other side, viz: to returne to a Regency, but hee should know more of it;

Note, hee never mentioned it more, which sheweth hee was then coming over to the Ch: party.—

. . .

Aug 8

Said there was nothing to bee done, but to form a party between the 2 extremes; Nota. the Church party introduced itselfe probably upon this foot.—

. . .

Aug. 11

Said it was to bee considered whether hee might rely upon the Ch: party.—

. . .

Aug 18

Said hee must absolutely go upon the bottome of the trimmers that is the good foot. Nota.—

. . .

Aug. 21

Said hee was resolved absolutely to go upon the foundation of the middle party.—

. . .

Dec 24

Speaking of the Severall parties, hee said, hee found, hee must not yet declare himselfe, but must bee a Trimmer.—

. . .

. . . Agreed the necessity of a cabinet Councill, but said hee did not know of men, who would speak freely before one another.

. . .

Said there must be a Councell to governe in his absence, and that the Queen is not to meddle.—

. . .

Feb 5

Said hee was told, a new Plt. would immediately settle a Revenue upon him, which would give him credit.—Nota—

Said if they did not presently supply him, hee would adjourne them, to which I replyed, how could hee then go on with his journey into Ireland; To this hee gave no answer.—

Said he wished, hee could trimme a little longer, but things pressed so, hee could not.—

Said hee would make a change in the Treasury take out Ld. Delemer, and give him some money for Compensation; Note, hee talketh of money upon these occasions as if hee had it.—

'Spencer House Journals' of conversations between William and Halifax, quoted by H. C. Foxcroft, *Life and Letters of Halifax* (1898), vol. II, pp. 203–47.

23. William III and the parties, 1693.

For the KING [1693]

SIR,

... When your Majesty considers the present state of the kingdom, and the factions that are in it, you'll find that the two great points that require more especially your care, are how to manage the partyes soe as to maintain yourself against your enemies abroad, and at the same time so to preserve your authority at home, that the necessity of doing the one may not bring you to such circumstances that it will be impossible for you to keep the other; and this task is more difficult, because the Toreys, who are friends to prerogative, are so mingled with Jacobites, that they are not to be confided in during the war; and the Whigs, who are, for that reason, of necessity to be employed to support your cause against the common enemy, will at the same time endeavour all they can to make use of that opportunity to lessen your just power. And let them pretend what they will to your Majesty, the several instances they have given this session of their intentions that way, puts this matter out of all doubt to any person who has taken the least pains to observe them, and it's beyond all dispute manifest, that though they will give money to keep out King James, yet they'll never give you one vote to support your just right in any point where (what they please to call) the interest of the people is concerned.

This being the condition of your partye, which I presume your Majesty will allow to be too true, I am confident, when you look into the funds that are given for the service of this year, and consider how much they lessen and incumber your hereditary revenue; and when you know, Sir, that if the war continue, it will be impossible to save the customs (which is the only tax now left you can expect will ever be given for a longer time than from year to year) from being likewise pawned for five years at least: I presume to say, Sir, these things considered, your Majesty will be of opinion that it is more your interest, with relation to your affairs at home, to have a peace this summer, than ever it was since you sat upon the throne of England; and that if you have it not, as things have been managed, the next year's expences will so anticipate those branches of the revenue that ever have been kept hitherto for the ordinary support of the government, that it will be scarce possible that your Majesty should ever see an easy day, though it should please God hereafter to give you such a peace as yourself could wish: and the ground-work on which I build this assertion is, that it ever was and ever will be impracticable for any king of England to be the least happy, who must depend upon a parliament every year to give him a million of money for his common and necessary support;

. . .

A new parliament will not help this matter, for let who will be the givers, there will remain still the same ways of giving; . . . and in my humble opinion it seems to be unquestionably your interest, if the war continue, to continue the parliament; and if the war ends, to let that end with it. And my reasons for this opinion are:

1st, These are the same men that engaged your Majesty in the war, and are obliged by their votes to support you in it.

2dly, The experience you have that this house will do it, ought to be an unanswerable argument against parting with it, for a new one, when you do not know whether they will be for you or not.

3dly, The great reason that's given for dissolving this, being, because it's said they have an ill reputation, ought not to sway in this affair, but the contrary; since that is only a scandal raised by the enemys of the government; and the supporting your Majesty being the crime they lay to their charge, your Majesty's friends ought to esteem them for that, for which they are hated by their enemys.

4thly, Your Majesty has for this 4 years last past been giving all employments to members of the house, which though it has not signified much in any party business, yet in the grand affair of carrying on the war, they have been of mighty service, for there is but very few instances of any of them but which upon occasion appear to be hearty for your government, in relation to the foreign dispute, and many of these will be left out in a new choice, which will be no small prejudice to your Majesty, considering that most of your enemys in the house of commons are made so, because they have not places like the rest.

But what's the most dangerous consequence of a new election is, that it will throw the ballance too much on the one side or the other, for either the Whigs will, according to their expectation, get it into their hands intirely, and then I fear your Majesty will think the impositions they'll be laying upon you unreasonable; or otherwise the Torys will have the ascendant, and then it's to be doubted that they, in revenge to the Whiggs, will, for the major part, be governed by the artifices of the Jacobites, and from such a misfortune nothing less than destruction can proceed.

Whereas, as the house is now constituted, the Whigs are not strong enough to make use of the necessitys of your government as much as they are inclined to do; neither are the Tories numerous enough to resent your Majesty's favouring the Whiggs. Sir, upon the whole I shall presume to conclude as I began, that the parliament that begun with the war, should likewise end with it, and not before.

And if it please God to grant your Majesty an honourable peace, and you would then be pleased to sett up for a party of your own, and lett all people see that if they expected your favour they must depend upon you for it, and not lett any one hope for promotion for being true to a faction, but by serving of you; I presume to say that the war being ended, a new parliament called, and such measures pursued, your Majesty would quickly find, that the Jacobites would turn moderate churchmen, and loyall subjects, and the Whiggs much more obsequious courtiers, and easier servants than now they are. . . .

Your Majesty's most dutifull
and obedient subject and servant,
[Godolphin][1]

J. Dalrymple, *Memoirs of Great Britain and Ireland* (1783), vol. II, App. part II, p. 5.

[1] Date and author attributed by Dalrymple.

CHAPTER 2

THE CENTRAL GOVERNMENT

In theory, the country was governed by three separate powers, king, lords and commons, each checking and balancing the others (24); and any change in the constitution (such as parliamentary reform) was usually opposed on the grounds that it would 'upset the balance of the constitution'. In practice, means had to be found to ensure harmony between them, for the extent of their powers had never been demarcated. The Revolution Settlement had laid down certain things that the king could not do: what he could do was not defined. Thus conflict was inherent in the system, for while the executive power was in the hands of the king, the means for carrying it out had to be provided by parliament; and clashes could only be avoided, on the one hand, by the king's appointment of ministers and adoption of measures agreeable to parliament; and, on the other, by the moulding of opinion in parliament by effective oratory and by the manipulation of 'influence'. The alternatives to these were deadlock or instability; and no government which wished to stay in power and to avoid what George III once called the 'total stagnation of Public Business' could afford to neglect the problem of 'managing' the House of Commons. For this reason, first ministers like Walpole, Pelham, North, and Pitt stayed in the Commons, and those who were in the Lords, as Newcastle learned in 1754–5, had to have a man of ability to act as 'His Majesty's Minister in the House of Commons'. This was a task that not every man could perform, and few relished. Even George III could write, 'That Lord North should feel a little languid on the Approach of the Meeting of Parliament is not surprising, it is far from being a pleasant Sensation even to me.'[1]

Although 'influence' by itself was not sufficient to maintain majorities for the government, it was widely held to be 'as necessary a part of the British constitution, as any other ingredient in the composition—to be that, indeed, which gives cohesion and solidity to the whole'.[2] An uninfluenced House of Commons, it was felt, would 'engross the power to itself' (25), and upset the balance. The question was: who should wield the 'influence'? Douglas in 1761 said that the ministers of George I and George II had used it to 'put the sovereign into leading strings' by turning parliament into 'an appendage of administration' (26); Paine in 1776 could say that having locked the door against absolute monarchy they had put the crown in possession of the key (27).

[1] *Corresp. George III*, No. 3165.
[2] W. Paley, *Principles of Moral and Political Philosophy* (1786), p. 391.

The extent of the king's power at any moment depended on the resultant of a number of forces. In the first place, there was the situation in the House of Commons: the extent to which the independent members approved of the ministers and their policy; and the degree of unity among the groups in the ministry and among those in the opposition.[1] Secondly, it depended on the ability of his ministers: a powerful first minister, in control of his colleagues, skilful at 'business', the manipulation of 'influence' and debating, could force measures down the king's throat. In the third place, the personality of the monarch was important: Anne was weaker than William III; and George III in his manhood was firmer than his grandfather in his old age. And, finally, much depended on policy, on whether there was any great issue at stake, and whether his ideas on it were in line with those of the bulk of his subjects. George III, even in his later years, was able to write 'that he cannot *ever* agree to any *concessions to the Catholics* which his confidential servants may in future propose to him, and that under these circumstances, and after what has passed, his mind cannot be at ease, unless he shall receive *a positive assurance from them, which shall effectually relieve him from all future apprehension*'.[2]

The relations between king and parliament could reach (though very rarely) two possible extremes. On the one hand, the monarch could be devoted to a minister with no parliamentary following; and, on the other, parliament might force on him a minister he could not tolerate. Neither of these situations could last very long. In the case of the first, it had become an established convention that parliament could force the dismissal of ministers of whom they disapproved (28). In the case of the second, it was far from established that parliament could dictate appointments to the king. Neither could they do it for long in practice. It was one thing for the shifting groups and individuals to unite long enough to bring a minister down, but quite another for this unity to endure long enough to maintain a minister in power against the king's wishes: that development had to await the emergence of disciplined parties in the nineteenth century.

Governments were not often in those straits, however, and most ministries were well within those limits; while the really enduring ones were exactly in the middle, when the choice of king and parliament coincided, as they did on Walpole and the younger Pitt.

The Revolution Settlement had left the monarch in a very strong position, and during most of this period he was truly the head of the executive government. Certainly, the first two Hanoverians were not 'kings in toils', but took a forceful and positive role in all matters of government, great and small (29). They appointed ministers and determined policy, as Walpole's advice to Pelham shows (30). Ministers had to follow the king's wishes (31),

[1] See pp. 173–6.　　　　　[2] H.M.C., *Dropmore*, vol. IX, p. 118 (17 March 1807).

or talk him out of them; and they were able to do the latter because they had to 'face the music' in parliament. And if the king or his ministers wandered too far from what was acceptable to the House of Commons, then the ministers could be forced out, as Walpole was. The joint resignation of the Pelhams in 1746 (though a rare occurrence) illustrates the weakness of the king's position if he backed a minister without parliamentary support (32). A king had to be a man of iron to succeed in such a policy, and George II 'had not courage nor activity or sufficient knowledge of the country or perhaps of mankind to take such a line'.[1] On the other hand, parliament could rarely force a minister *into* office if the king really put his foot down (31, 33). On the death of Pelham, George II told the rest of the cabinet that 'he hoped they would not think of recommending to him any person who has flown in his face'.[2]

However, one of the opposition cries under the first two Georges was that the king should 'place himself at the head of his people' and govern with the help of the best men, irrespective of party (34, 35); and George III started out with those intentions (36, 37). The Whig magnates, on the other hand, were determined to preserve the power they had exercised in George II's old age. 'If a King of England', wrote the Duke of Devonshire at the time, 'employs those people for his ministers that the nation have a good opinion of, he will make a great figure; but if he chuses them merely thro' personal favour, it will never do, and he will be unhappy.'[3] But since George III was more stubborn than his predecessors, the great struggles of Whig legend (which were inherent in the post-Revolution system) were bound to ensue, reaching their climax in the years 1780–84. At a time of defeat in America, the independent members swung away from the king. As George put it, 'the sudden change of Sentiments of one Branch of the Legislature . . . totally incapacitated Him';[4] and North was forced out as Walpole had been (38, 39). Then came the king's prolonged refusal to 'give himself up to a set of men'; while opposed to him was the new doctrine that he should choose the ministers that parliament wanted (45).[5] The Rockinghams were able to force him to make promises on measures (40), and on men (41). These, however, were the views of the future (as was Buckingham's plan in 1802 to demand *carte blanche* from the king (42). For most men believed that it was unconstitutional to 'storm the closet' (43). The elder Pitt wrote in 1766, 'I shall never set my foot in the closet' if I 'owe my coming thither to any court cabal or ministerial connection. The

---

[1] Lord Fitzmaurice, *Life of Shelburne* (1912), vol. I, p. 37.
[2] P. C. Yorke, *Life of Hardwicke* (Cambridge, 1913), vol. II, p. 205.
[3] Ilchester, *Henry Fox, First Lord Holland* (1920), vol. II, p. 203.
[4] George's draft abdication message, March 1782, *Corresp. George III*, No. 3601.
[5] 'Which till this year was never attempted', wrote Henry Fox in 1762. (Ilchester, *Henry Fox*, vol. II, p. 202.)

King's pleasure and gracious commands alone shall be a call to me.'[1] Even Charles James Fox admitted in the 1784 debates that it was 'undoubtedly the prerogative of his Majesty to appoint his ministers', even though it might not be 'prudent, wise and politic' to continue them in office without the confidence of the House of Commons.[2] As it happened, the determination of the king and Pitt rallied the majority (44), and, as Wilberforce put it in 1812, it was determined that the House should not 'have a negative on the appointment of ministers of the Crown' (46).

Though this view continued to be held for the rest of the reign and the next, the Foxite ideals gradually became reality under the impact of various forces which were demolishing the eighteenth-century system of government. 'Economical Reform',[3] and administrative reform in the years following (47, 48), the professionalisation of the Civil Service, and Curwen's Act[4] were all weakening the 'influence' of the crown. By 1822, the Secretary of the Treasury was fearing disaster from this development. 'In this manner', he wrote, 'the just and necessary influence of the Crown is from day to day attacked; and . . . it will be quite impossible for any set of men to conduct the government of this country, unless practices of this kind shall be successfully resisted.'[5] At the same time, other factors were strengthening the power of the House of Commons: the Industrial Revolution, the development of public opinion, the spread of education, the radical movement and the growth of modern political parties. All these developments were steadily eating away at the area of the king's choice until eventually he had no choice; and, although this point was not reached in our period, the process was well under way in its last years.

It was also during this later part of the period that the opposition came to be accepted as part of the natural order of things, though as early as 1784 Mackenzie, in a work approved of by Pitt, had declared that it was a beneficial part of the constitution (49). Earlier politicians sometimes pretended that opposition was 'disloyal', though few made any bones about it in practice. Oppositions, like governments, were made up of diverse elements, some of whom, like the Tories under the first two Georges, had no expectation, or even desire, of office. The active politicians, though, were quite clear what they were after, and tactics depended upon circumstances. Sometimes, they could be 'distressful to the ministry' by taking up some popular cause (51), for, as the elder Pitt put it, one of the sources of 'consideration and weight in the House of Commons' was 'weight in the Country, sometimes arising from opposition to public measures.'[6] If the king was getting on in years, it made sense to rally round their heir to the throne, and join his

---

[1] W. S. Taylor and J. H. Pringle, *Correspondence of Chatham* (1839), vol. III, p. 12.
[2] *P.H.*, XXIV, 364. [3] See pp. 198–206. [4] See p. 206.
[5] *P.D.* (N.S.), VI, 1174. [6] P. C. Yorke, *Life of Hardwicke*, vol. II, p. 203.

'shadow cabinet', in the expectation of succeeding to office when he acceded to the throne (50). But that was a long-term policy: in the short run, it was better for ambitious men to make as much of a nuisance of themselves as possible, in the hope that the government would buy them out by taking them in. And normally they did not expect a general removal of the government and a wholesale appointment of men from the Opposition. Carteret and Pulteney, for example, were not leading a crusade against Walpole: they simply wanted places for themselves and a few friends (51). North, in February 1782, wrote to the king that 'as the House of Commons seems now to have withdrawn their confidence' from him, perhaps 'it may be feasible to divide the Opposition, and to take in only a part'.[1] Most changes of government were only adjustments, and their negotiation was a matter of considerable delicacy, since, for every enemy taken in, a friend had to be jettisoned (52, 108). And in the normal run of things, these reconstructions did not result in any great changes of policy. All oppositions had war-cries and slogans, and sometimes they even signed programmes, but office usually cooled their ardour. Only in the second half of this period do men begin to differ violently on great issues, and to practise in office what they had preached in opposition, but by that time the eighteenth-century constitution is beginning to dissolve.

Governments were called 'cabinets' throughout this period, even though Charles James Fox said in 1806: 'There is nothing in our constitution that recognises any such institution as a Cabinet council.'[2] The modern cabinet is the direct descendant of the 'inner' or 'efficient' cabinet of the eighteenth century, which crystallised out of the 'cabinet council' of the seventeenth century, which in its turn had grown out of the Privy Council. In each case the parent body became too big for efficiency and secrecy, particularly in time of war. 'A cabinet council of 12 or 13 men,' wrote Sunderland in 1693, 'of which no one takes himself to be particularly concerned in the general conduct of affairs, where there is neither secrecy, despatch or credit, is a monstrous thing.'[3] Naturally, these developments received no publicity, and the House of Commons was constantly suspicious of methods of government whereby responsibility for advice could not be pinned down to a known minister (28, 53).[4] On the other hand, the monarchs throughout this period felt themselves free to consult anybody they wished (54); a practice which led to attacks in parliament on 'secret advisers', 'ministers behind the curtain', 'double cabinets' and so on (32, 55, 56).

In William III's reign the 'cabinet council' was sufficiently established to have a recognised membership of the holders of certain offices (57); but there was also an inner cabinet to deal with secret affairs (58). Under Anne

---

[1] *Corresp. of George III*, No. 3535.
[3] Quoted by J. P. Kenyon, *Earl of Sunderland* (1957), p. 263.
[2] *P.D.*, VI, 308.
[4] See p. 59.

there were regular weekly meetings of both, and she sat with the 'Cabinet council', which seems to have acted as a kind of second chamber to the 'efficient cabinet' or 'lords of the committee' (59).[1] George I continued this system till 1717,[2] after which the monarch ceased to sit with the cabinet except rarely. In the middle of the eighteenth century the 'cabinet council' (of about fourteen members) used to give formal sanction to the decisions of the 'efficient cabinet' (of about five members) (60, 61). In George III's time, Lord Mansfield was 'much averse to frequent Councils'. He felt that 'they only make quarrels in Ministry that they should be only kept for sanction to the efficient Ministers on great occasions'.[3] And this is what happened. For the 'cabinet council' had become too big for active government, and during the remainder of the period it met, in the presence of the king, as the Hanging Cabinet, and as the Grand Cabinet to hear the king's speech at the beginning of each parliamentary session. The king, of course, consulted members of it (54); but the feeling against irresponsible advisers was strong enough by 1801 for Addington to tell Loughborough, the ex-Chancellor, not to appear at cabinet meetings (62).

Much of the daily work of government was carried out by individual ministers conferring with the king in his Closet and never came before the cabinet at all. When the king referred a question to the cabinet, the result of their deliberations would be delivered to the king (now that he no longer sat with them) in the form of a minute, or perhaps of a despatch (65). At some stage during the reign of George III the cabinet began to consider matters without waiting for the king's orders, a practice which the king said in April 1782 was 'quite new' (64), but which was firmly established in the period described by Lord Holland (66). This document also brings out how vague and constantly changing was cabinet procedure, varying according to the personalities of the monarchs and the ministers, and according to the extent to which the cabinet was the king's choice or not.

The feeling of cabinet unity grew only haltingly, and varied from ministry to ministry with the characteristics of the political groups which composed them and with the personality of the first minister; and, although collective responsibility was recognised earlier (66, 67), a full corporate sense had to await the growth of political parties. Cabinets were especially liable to division if the chief minister was not the king's choice. The Pelhams had that trouble after the fall of Walpole (30). Philip Yorke wrote: 'Nothing afforded so melancholy a prospect at this time [1744], as the want of union

[1] J. H. Plumb, 'The Organisation of the Cabinet in the Reign of Queen Anne', *T.R.H.S.*, 5th series, vol. VII (1957), p. 137.

[2] J. H. Plumb, *The First Four Georges* (1956), pp. 56–7.

[3] R. R. Sedgwick, *Letters from George III to Lord Bute* (1939), p. 212 (1 April 1763).

in the Cabinet,—the two leaders there the D. of Newcastle and Ld Carteret were not upon good terms enough to dine together.'[1] A similar situation was common in the early part of George III's reign (63): and only disappeared as the factors mentioned earlier brought about the gradual withdrawal of the king from active politics.

This slow and irregular process, the elimination of the crown, and the establishment of the cabinet as the central organ of government, was naturally accompanied by the growth of the office of Prime Minister. There have always been first ministers in our history, and the problem of when to begin calling them 'prime ministers' depends on our definition of that term. Under William III, who ruled the country himself, we can hardly use it. Anne, lacking the ability, needed a chief minister; but, though the term 'prime minister' was sometimes used about Godolphin and Oxford (68, 69), they had insufficient personal ascendancy over parliament, their colleagues or the queen to merit it. In any case, they sat in the House of Lords (as did Sunderland), and it was Walpole who made the important innovation by remaining in the Commons. He was strong because he drew support from the two chief sources of power: he was the king's choice, and he had a majority in the House of Commons. And since he had to defend the measures of the former in the latter, he had to dominate all aspects of government, and his post of First Lord of the Treasury became (as Hardwicke described it in 1755) 'an employment of great business, very extensive, which always went beyond the bare management of the revenue' (73). George II may have objected to this extension of the Treasury's power, but later in 1827 Wellington was convinced that it would be 'embarrassing, if not impossible, for the First Minister to hold any other office'.[2] This control of patronage gave Walpole a firmer hold over parliament and over his colleagues than had previously been enjoyed by a first minister (70); and he was accused of a 'most heinous offence against our constitution' by becoming prime minister (71), a charge which he denied (72), though neither side in the argument was using the term exactly in our sense. After his fall there was a period of confusion till Pelham forced himself on a reluctant king into roughly the same position. After 1754 the logic of the situation was not accepted (for Newcastle sat in the Lords, and the Pelhams had no talent in the Commons capable of dealing with Fox and Pitt) and there was no clear case of a prime minister till the younger Pitt; though it was becoming recognised that such an officer was a necessity to unify the government (74, 75, 76), though not, at this stage, to dominate the king (77).

[1] Quoted by J. B. Owen, *The Rise of the Pelhams* (1957), p. 206.
[2] Wellington (ed.), *Despatches, Correspondence and Memoranda of the Duke of Wellington* (1871), vol. IV, p. 25.

24. Blackstone on the constitution, 1765.

It is highly necessary for preserving the balance of the constitution, that the executive power be a branch, though not the whole of the legislative. The total union of them, we have seen, would be productive of tyranny; the total disjunction of them, for the present, would in the end produce the same effects, by causing that union against which it seems to provide. The legislative would soon become tyrannical, by making continual encroachments, and gradually assuming to itself the rights of the executive power.

. . . To hinder therefore any such encroachments, the king is himself a part of the parliament: and, as this is the reason of his being so, very properly therefore the share of legislation, which the constitution has placed in the crown, consists in the power of *rejecting* rather than *resolving*; this being sufficient to answer the end proposed. For we may apply to the royal negative, in this instance, what Cicero observes of the negative of the Roman tribunes, that the crown has not any power of *doing* wrong, but merely of *preventing* wrong being done. The crown cannot begin of itself any alterations in the present established law; but it may approve or disapprove of the alterations suggested and consented to by the two houses. The legislative therefore cannot abridge the executive power of any rights which it now has by law, without it's own consent; since the law must perpetually stand as it now does, and unless all the powers will agree to alter it. And herein indeed consists the true excellence of the English government, that all the parts of it form a mutual check upon each other. In the legislature, the people are a check upon the nobility, and the nobility a check upon the people; by the mutual privilege of rejecting what the other has resolved: while the king is a check upon both, which preserves the executive power from encroachments. And this very executive power is again checked and kept within due bounds by the two houses, through the privilege they have of inquiring into, impeaching and punishing the conduct (not indeed of the king, which would destroy his constitutional independence; but, which is more beneficial to the public,) of his evil and pernicious counsellors. Thus every branch of our civil polity supports and is supported, regulates and is regulated, by the rest: for the two houses naturally drawing in two directions of opposite interest, and the prerogative in another still different from them both, they mutually keep each other from exceeding their proper limits; while the whole is prevented from separation, and artificially connected together by the mixed nature of the crown, which is a part of the legislative, and the sole executive magistrate. Like three distinct powers in mechanics, they jointly impel the machine of government in a direction different from what either, acting by itself, would have done; but at the same time in a direction partaking of each, and formed out of all; a direction which constitutes the true line of the liberty and happiness of the community.

W. Blackstone, *Commentaries on the Laws of England* (15th ed., 1809), vol. I, p. 153.

25. Hume on the necessity of influence, 1741.

The share of power allotted by our constitution to the House of Commons is so great, that it absolutely commands all the other parts of the government. The king's legislative power is plainly no proper check to it. For though the King has a negative in framing laws, yet this, in fact, is esteemed of so little moment, that whatever is voted by the two houses is always sure to pass into a law, and the royal assent is little better than a form. The principal weight of the crown lies in the executive power. But besides that the executive power in every government is altogether subordinate to the legislative; besides this, I say, the exercise of this power requires an immense expense, and the Commons have assumed to themselves the sole right of granting money. How easy, therefore, would it be for that house to wrest from the crown all these powers, one after another; by making every grant conditional, and choosing their time so well, that their refusal of supply should only distress the government, without giving foreign powers any advantage over us? Did the House of Commons depend in the same manner on the King, and had none of the members any property but from his gift, would not he command all their resolutions, and be from that moment absolute? As to the House of Lords, they are a very powerful support to the crown, so long as they are, in their turn, supported by it; but both experience and reason show, that they have no force or authority sufficient to maintain themselves alone without such support.

How, therefore, shall we resolve this paradox? And by what means is this member of our constitution confined within the proper limits; since, from our very constitution, it must necessarily have as much power as it demands, and can only be confined by itself? How is this consistent with our experience of human nature? I answer, that the interest of the body is here restrained by that of the individuals, and that the House of Commons stretches not its power, because such an usurpation would be contrary to the interest of the majority of its members. The crown has so many offices at its disposal, that, when assisted by the honest and disinterested part of the house, it will always command the resolutions of the whole, so far, at least, as to preserve the ancient constitution from danger. We may, therefore, give to this influence what name we please, we may call it by the invidious appellations of *corruption* and *dependence*; but some degree and some kind of it are inseparable from the very nature of the constitution, and necessary to the preservation of our mixed government.

D. Hume, Essays Moral, Political, and Literary (1862), p. 25.

26. The evils of influence in ministers' hands, 1761.

Such is the happy distribution of supreme power in this country, that the sovereign finds it his interest to pursue no measures but such as are agreeable to the representatives of the people; and the necessity of obtaining parliamentary concurrence has increased since the revolution; from which period, by separating the civil list from the other charges of government, annual sessions must be held, and annual supplies granted. Ministers, therefore, who wanted to force themselves into employments in court, saw that they should gain their point, if they could convince the sovereign that they had the power over parliament. But how could any particular set of men acquire such a power? It was impossible that the whole body of the people, in this great country, should concur in enslaving their sovereign and themselves, to any junto of their fellow-subjects; and it was obvious that a parliament *chosen freely* and composed of gentlemen of real property, whose inclination it would be to *vote freely*, were not likely to act the despicable part of tools to a narrow party cabal of ambitious courtiers.

In this situation, therefore, there was no alternative; the scheme of putting the sovereign into the leading-strings of party must be abandoned, or else such methods put in practice, as might check the freedom of election, and procure such a parliament as might support a particular set of ministers. The real disaffection that existed at the accession of George the First, furnished those who then got possession of the closet, with a specious pretence to employ secretly the court influence upon certain important occasions; and having once prevailed upon the king to look upon such *secret* influence, as necessary for the security of his family, they knew it would answer a more immediate purpose to themselves, by giving them the means of perpetuating their own power; a point, in their opinion, not too dearly purchased, by a most enormous expence of public money, and by establishing venality and corruption into a system, as necessary engines of government.

To consider the English constitution in theory, it's stability would be supposed to arise from parliament. But parliaments, when once they become appendages of administration, must open the widest door to slavery. In this case, they become a mere *state engine* in the hands of the minister, to *stamp* a value on the basest metal, and to give every bad measure the sanction of national consent. And no chains are so heavy as those which we put on ourselves; for we shall bear from our representatives, what prerogative, openly exerted, never will venture to put in practice. . . .

J. Douglas, Seasonable Hints from an Honest Man (1761) p. 24.

27. The evils of influence in the king's hands, 1776.

That the crown is the overbearing part in the English constitution needs not be mentioned, and that it derives its whole consequence merely from being the giver of places and pensions is self-evident, where fore, though we have been wise enough to shut and lock a door against absolute Monarchy, we at the same time have been foolish enough to put the Crown in possession of the key.

T. Paine, Common Sense (1776), p. 11.

28. House of Commons requests dismissal of ministers, 1701.

[16 April 1701]

MOST GRACIOUS SOVEREIGN,

We, Your Majesty's most dutiful and Loyal Subjects, the Commons in Parliament assembled, do humbly crave Leave to represent to Your Majesty the great Satisfaction we have, from our late Inquiry concerning the Treaty of Partition, made in the Year One thousand Six hundred Ninety-eight, on which the Treaty of One thousand Six hundred Ninety-nine was founded, to see Your Majesty's great Care of your People, and this Nation, in not entering into that Negotiation without the Advice of Your *English* counsellors, and finding, That

John Lord *Somers*, on whose Judgement Your Majesty did chiefly rely in that so important Affair, did, in Concert with *Edward* Earl of *Orford*, and *Charles* Lord *Hallifax*, advise Your Majesty to enter into that Treaty, of so dangerous a Consequence to the Trade and Welfare of this Nation; and who, to avoid the Censure which might justly be apprehended to fall on those who advised the same, endeavoured to insinuate, That Your Majesty, without the Advice of Your Council, entered into that Treaty; and under Your sacred Name to seek Protection for what themselves had so advised: Of which Treatment of Your Majesty, we cannot but have a just Resentment: And, that they may be no longer able to deceive Your Majesty, and abuse Your People, we do humbly beseech Your Majesty, That you will be pleased to remove *John* Lord *Somers*, *Edward* Earl of *Orford*, and *Charles* Lord *Hallifax*, from Your Council and Presence for ever; and also *William* Earl of *Portland*, who transacted these Treaties, so unjust in their own Nature, and so fatal in their Consequences to this Nation, and the Peace of *Europe*: And we humbly crave Leave, upon this Occasion, to repeat our Assurances to Your Majesty, That we will always stand by, and support, Your Majesty, to the utmost of our Power, against all Your Enemies, both at home and abroad.

C.J., XIII, 497.

29. George II and electioneering, 1754.

[Newcastle's notes for his audience with the King.]

Newcastle House, March 21st 1754.

Evesham Election.

The Agreement was that everything above 1500 £ should be paid by the King—That Sum is now spent—he has received nothing—No one can say what the expence will be—Mr. West judges, that it will amount to 1500 £—Ald^n Porter was recommended to Mr West, upon whose Interest he stands at Evesham.—

Evesham

Ald^n Porter
S^{ir} J. Rushout
Mr Rudge

Lord Coventry offers, that Sir J. Rushout, & Mr Rudge should pay Ald^n Porter's expences if he would desist, & by that means the expence of 1500 will be saved To receive the King's pleasure upon it—Mr Ald^n Porter desires not to give it up.

Minutes about Evesham

(8 April 1754)

Alderman Porter	*Evesham*
represents, that he has complied with his Promise, & has now spent 1700 £, and that, if the election should now be given up, tho' his expences were repaid, he apprehends, it would be a Prejudice to Him, in his Character and Rank in the City—Mr West strongly declares against the composition—Mr West proposes, that Mr. Ald^n Porter should now have 1000 £. & have in all events 500, in case it is necessary	To lay this Affair again before the King & receive H.M$^{ty's}$ Orders upon it—and to acquaint Lord Coventry with the State of it—That I could do nothing in it, but left it entirely to Ald^n Porter— & Mr West—

Add. MSS. 32995, ff. 114, 203.

30. Walpole's advice on managing George II, 1743.

LORD ORFORD TO H. PELHAM.

Houghton, Oct. 20th, 1743.

DEAR SIR,

I never think of the present situation of public affairs, but I am full of wonder and concern; amazed at the conduct of the first agent [Carteret], and deeply affected with the difficulties that surround you on all sides. I cannot conceive, what measures this bold adventurer forms to himself, to secure success in the king's business. To stick at nothing to gain the king, to indulge him in all his unhappy foibles, and not to see his way through a labyrinth of expectations, which he must have raised, deserves no better title than infatuation; wherein, if he miscarries, his labour is all lost, and his credit must sink, with the disappointments he shall meet. What then must be his reasonings? He suffers not the king to doubt, but promises him success in all his undertakings. Upon what representations must these hopes be grounded? Why, that Mr. Pelham, in his station, must answer for the same majority in the House of Commons, that carried through the business last year. . . . How then, must you combat him, in this order of battle? It may be impossible for you, if you are never so willing, to run all the lengths of foreign flattery, that he will lead you into; and your friends, if they are not satisfied with the administration, may be very difficult to be brought into what is expected. But then, on the other hand, it will be utterly impossible for him, to shew the king any method of bringing the Tories into that system, that must be the foundation of all his interest. The distinction, of Hanover and England, is too much relished by them, to imagine, that any consideration will bring them into the support of Hanoverian measures. They see how much private discontents and disaffection, have been improved by this unhappy turn; and the party will not part with the advantage, that they are sensible they have gained, by labouring this point; and the more it hurts and wounds the king, the more it will be pushed and insisted upon.

On the other hand, the Whigs may be sorry for what they will endeavour to soften and palliate; and every thinking man, that wishes the support of this establishment, will enter into the cause of the king; and now that he, and indeed he alone, is personally attacked, the Jacobite opposition from the Tories, will provoke the Whigs, and engage them to go farther than they would naturally be inclined to do. In this light, and it is a most true one, the king must, with tenderness and management, be shewn, what he may with reason depend upon, and what, he will be deceived and lost, if he places any confidence and reliance in. The king saw last year, what part the Whigs acted; and, I should hope, he may be convinced, that the Whig party will stand by him, as they have done, through his whole reign, if his majesty does not surrender himself into hands, that mean and wish nothing but his destruction, and want to be armed with his authority and power, only to nail up his cannon, and turn it against himself. Upon this ground, you will be able to contend with Carteret. He gains the king, by giving in to all his foreign views; and you shew the king, that what is reasonable and practicable, can only be obtained by the Whigs, and can never be hoped for by any assistance from the Tories. He promises, and you must perform. . . .

. . . This leads me to the most tender and delicate part of the whole; I mean your behaviour, and your manner of treating this subject with him. It is a great misfortune, that you have not time; for time and address have often carried things, that met at first onset, with great reluctance; and you must expect to meet the king instructed, and greatly prepared in favour of the points which Carteret has in view to drive. Address and management are the weapons you must fight and defend with: plain truths will not be relished at first, in opposition to prejudices, conceived and infused in favour of his own partialities; and you must dress up all you offer, with the appearance of no other view or tendency, but to promote his service in his own way, to the utmost of your power. And the more you can make any thing appear to be his own, and agreeable to his declarations and orders, given to you before he went, the better you will be heard: as, the power to treat with such persons, as should be necessary to carry on his service in your hands; the encouragement and hopes to be given to the Whigs, by you, as arising from himself. Hint, at first, the danger he will run, in deviating from his own rule; shew him the unavoidable necessity there will be, of dissolving this parliament, if he departs from the body of the Whigs; and let him see the consequences of going to a new election, in the height of the war, which will certainly end in a rank Tory parliament, that will at once put a stop to all the measures that are now in practice, and for ever defeat all his views and desires, which are made the pretences to him, of hazarding the change.

W. Coxe, *Pelham Administration* (1829), vol. I, p. 103.

31. George II and ministerial appointments, 1750.

NEWCASTLE TO PELHAM

Hanover Sept. 2nd–13th, 1750

... and then, or in talking of the duke of Bedford's removal, he [George II] said, 'but, my lord, you and I cannot do it alone; we must have the council with us:' and named no particular person to consult; but, to be sure, the whole meant yourself. He said once, very significantly (I think upon my lord Sandwich's subject), 'they are caballing; I know, or you may be sure, that they are caballing at this very time.' Though he spoke this, by way, rather of apprehension than resentment, I am, from this, as well as from the king's whole conduct in this affair, fully convinced myself, that the Duke of Cumberland's parties with the duke of Bedford, and public and open support and predilection for my lord Sandwich, and the duke of Bedford, is one, if not the chief cause of the king's present intention of removing the duke of Bedford from the office of Secretary of State; and though the king has never let drop one word like it to me, if you will give him the least handle to talk upon it, I am persuaded he will own it to you, and talk fully upon it to you. This is only my own suspicion, from my knowledge of the king, without having any other grounds for it. The king asked me, whom I had thought on, for Secretary of State; or, who should be the man? (when I state things in two ways, it is because I cannot positively say, which the king said; you see by this, my care not to mislead you), I replied, 'I think your Majesty has choice enough.'

He then said, of himself, 'I have been thinking of Holdernesse.' I said, he had named the man that I should have named to his Majesty, if I had taken the liberty to name any body. He then said much, and, indeed, I think with great justice, in favour of Holdernesse; how well he behaved in Holland; and I told him, for I had not then your letter, that you was very well satisfied with lord Holdernesse's behaviour in Holland, and had owned, it was better than you had expected. And then, says the king, 'Albemarle shall come to England; and Walde-grave go embassador to France; and then he will be qualified to be Secretary of State.' And his Majesty hinted to me, that if I had let him send Waldegrave to Aix la Chapelle, he might have been Secretary of State now. I objected to lord Albemarle's leaving Paris, whilst it was necessary to have an embassador there, and chiefly on account of the great expense of a new embassador. 'Oh!' says the king, 'that is but a trifle; £.1,500 or £.2,000.' I told him, you had told me, £.7,000; but he seemed determined that Albemarle should come home; and I think that is another scheme of the lady, . . . and that I know, and am, therefore, for keeping him where he is. . . .

I wonder you reason upon it as you do. As to Halifax, I love him and esteem him, and think he has very efficient talents; but he is the last man in the kingdom, except Sandwich, that I should think of for the Secretary of State. In the first place, the whole council, all of us put together, could not make the king do it. In the next place, he is so conceited of his parts, that he would not be there one month, without thinking he knew as much, or more of the business, than any one man; and I am sure it would be impracticable to go on with him. He hates the duke of Bedford and Sandwich, I know; and I know also, neither of the others do, but they are both honest men, and I own I do not desire they should hate the duke of Bedford. All I desire is, that they should not list under him, or cabal with him. Besides, if this change is ever made, as it solely arises from the king, so it shall, for me, end with him. That is, as the king cannot reproach me with having said one word to him, since I have been here, relating to the removal of the duke of Bedford (as I told him very plainly the other day) and as, therefore, (if it is done) it arises singly from his Majesty himself; so the successor shall be his own choice, that I may have no reproach, from him at least, about it.

W. Coxe, Pelham Administration (1829), vol. II, p. 385.

32. Joint resignation of the Pelhams, 1746.

SIR JAMES GREY (ENVOY IN VENICE) TO SIR THOMAS ROBINSON

Venice, March 26th, N.S. 1746

DEAR SIR,

...I am very happy to be able, in some measure, to satisfy your curiosity about what has passed lately at home; and will venture to transcribe part of a letter, which seems to give a true and natural account of the whole transaction.

'I gave you a hint, last week, of an insurrection in the closet, and of lord Bath's having prevented Pitt's being secretary at war. The ministry gave up that; but finding a change had been made, in a scheme of foreign politics, which they had laid before the king, and for which he had thanked them; and perceiving some symptoms of an invitation to dismiss them, at the end of the session; they came to a sudden resolution not to do lord Granville's business, by carrying the supplies, and then to be turned out; so on Monday morning, to the astonishment of every body, the two secretaries of state threw up the seals; next day, Mr Pelham, with the Treasury; duke of Bedford, with the Admiralty; lord Gower, and lord Pembroke, gave up too; the dukes of Devonshire, Grafton, and Richmond, the lord Chancellor Mr Winnington, and almost all the great officers, and offices, declaring they would do the same. Lord Granville had immediately both seals, one for himself, and the other to give to whom he pleased. Lord Bath was named first commissioner of the Treasury, lord Carlisle privy seal, and lord Winchelsea reinstated in the Admiralty.

'Thus far all went swimmingly. They had only forgot one little point; which was, to secure a majority in both Houses. In the Commons, they unluckily found, they had nobody to take the lead, better than Sir John Rushout, Sir John Barnard having refused to be chancellor of the Exchequer; so did lord Chief Justice Wills to be chancellor; and the wildness of the scheme soon prevented many from giving into it. Hop, the Dutch minister, did not a little help to increase the confusion, by declaring, that he had immediately dispatched a courier to Holland, and did not doubt but the States would send to accept France's own terms. I should tell you, that lord Bath's being of the enterprize, helped hugely to poison the success of it. In short, his lordship, whose politics were never characterized by steadiness, had not courage enough to take the Treasury.

'On the Wednesday after the Monday, on which the changes happened, he went to the king, and told him he had tried the House of Commons, and *found it would not do*. Bounce went all the projects into shivers, like the vessels in the Alchymist, when they are on the brink of the Philosopher's Stone. The king, who had given into these alterations, was fatigued and perplexed; shut himself up in his closet; and refused to admit any more of the people, who were pouring in upon him, with white staffs, gold keys, commissions, &c. At last he sent for Mr Winnington, and told him he was the honestest man about him, and should have the honour of the reconciliation; and sent him to Mr Pelham, to desire they would all return to their employments. Lord Granville is as jolly as ever; laughs and drinks; owns it was mad, and that he would do it again tomorrow.'

In another letter, I am told lord Cholmondeley was to be the other secretary, the duke of Bolton lord lieutenant of Ireland, and the duke of Portland master of the horse. Upon lord Granville's resignation, Sir William Stanhope said, that his only surprise was, how he had kept it so long; and another joker observed, that it was not safe to walk the streets at night, for fear of being pressed for a cabinet counsellor.

W. Coxe, *Pelham Administration* (1829), vol. I, p. 290.

33. Royal veto on promotion for Pitt, 1754.

MR. PITT TO THE LORD CHANCELLOR

Bath, April 4th, 1754.

MY LORD,

. . . It is very kind and generous in your Lordship to suggest a ray of distant general hope to a man you see despairing, and to turn his view forward from the present scene to a future. But, my Lord, give me leave to say that after having set out, ten years ago, under such general suggestions of future hope, and bearing long a load of obloquy for supporting the King's measures, without ever obtaining in recompence the smallest remission of that [royal] displeasure, I vainly laboured to soften, I am come finally to feel all ardour for public business extinguished, as well as to find myself deprived of all consideration, by which alone I could have been of any use. For indeed, my Lord, I am persuaded I can be of no material use under such circumstances; nor have I the heart or the presumption to attempt an active, much less a leading part, in Parliament. The weight of the irremovable Royal displeasure is too heavy for any man to move under, who is firmly resolved never to move to the disturbance of Government; it must crush any such man; it has sunk and exanimated me; I succumb under it, and wish for nothing but a decent and innocent retreat wherein, by being placed out of the stream of Cabinet Council promotion, I may no longer seem to stick fast aground and have the mortification to see myself, and offer to others the ridiculous amusement of seeing, every boat pass by me that navigates the same river. To speak without a figure; I will presume so far upon your Lordship's great goodness to me as to declare my earnest wish. It is that, (since I cannot be admitted into a subordinate share in government under His Majesty's principal ministers, upon equal terms with those of no more than equal pretensions), a retreat not void of some advantages, nor derogatory to the rank of the office I hold,[1] might (as soon as practicable) be opened to me. In this view I take the liberty of recommending myself to your Lordship's friendship, as I have done to the Duke of Newcastle. Out of his Grace's immediate province patent offices of this kind arise, and to your joint protection and to that only, I wish to owe the future quiet and satisfaction of my life.

P. C. Yorke, Life of Hardwicke (Cambridge, 1913), vol. II, p. 214.

34. The Patriot King, 1752.

To espouse no party, but to govern like the common father of his people, is so essential to the character of a PATRIOTIC KING, that he who does otherwise forfeits the title. It is the peculiar privilege and glory of this character, that princes who maintain it, and they alone, are so far from the necessity, that they are not exposed to the temptation,

---

[1] Pitt had been Paymaster of the Forces since 1746.

of *governing by a party*: which must always end in the government of a *faction*: the faction of the *prince*, if he has ability; the faction of his *ministers*, if he has not; and, either one way or other, in the oppression of the people. For *faction* is to *party* what the *superlative* is to the *positive*: *party* is a political evil, and *faction* is the *worst* of all *parties*. The true image of a free people, governed by a PATRIOTIC KING, is that of a patriarchal family, where the head and all the members are united by one common interest, and animated by one common spirit: and where, if any are perverse enough to have another, they will soon be borne down by the superiority of those who have the same; and, far from making a *division*, they will but confirm the *union* of the little state. That to approach as near as possible to those ideas of perfect government, and social happiness under it, is desirable in every state, no man will be absurd enough to deny. The sole question is, therefore, how near to them is it possible to attain? For, if this attempt be not absolutely impracticable, all the views of a PATRIOTIC KING will be directed to make it succeed. Instead of abetting the divisions of his people, he will endeavour to unite them, and to be himself the centre of their union: instead of putting himself at the head of *one party* in order to govern *his people*, he will put himself at the head of *his people* in order to govern, or more properly to subdue, *all parties*. Now, to arrive at this desirable union, and to maintain it, will be found more difficult in some cases than in others, but absolutely impossible in none, to a wise and good prince.

Bolingbroke, Idea of a Patriot King (1752), p. 162.

35. Advice to George III on his accession, 1761.

A King who would hope for a reign of consequence, and ease, must begin with such a steadiness of conduct, as may convince every one who approaches him, that he knows it is the duty of his ministers to depend on him, and has too much spirit to depend on his ministers. If he shews his inclination to continue particular persons, in high office, he must at the same time, shew his resolution to break all factious *connections* and *confederacies*.

A new King surrounded by a set of grasping courtiers, each aiming at the management of him, like a virgin beset by her lovers, must, upon occasion, be able to check their importunity, and steadily say, No. The judicious use of this short, but expressive monosyllable, will save a world of trouble, and be the only means of preserving his future honor and dignity. But if once it be discovered, that he durst not say this on one occasion, his independence will, on every occasion, be attacked, till, at last, by repeated compliances, he sees himself doomed, through his whole reign, to suffer violence from every one who shall have insolence enough to make the attempt.

In a word, if a monarch do not begin his sovereignty by such a conduct, as will let the candidates for power see, that he will not permit them to force it from him, he will at last see himself the servant of his own servants; the fountain of all honors, without being able to bestow any; with a right to dispose of every office however great, without being allowed to name any one of the lowest; and if ever he should endeavor to extricate himself out of this unhappy state, he will then learn, by dear-bought experience, that it is much easier to preserve independence, than to throw off subjection; and that one moment of steadiness, at the beginning of his reign, would have saved him years of trouble and distress, in the progress of it. . . .

To hear some folks talk of the necessity the crown is under to submit to the direction and management of confederated ministers, one would imagine, that the times of the *old barons* were revived, when by their feudal superiorities, military vassals, and numerous retainers, they could, at any time, if they united together, measure swords with their sovereign: but thank God, those times have been long at an end, and the great men of this country have no means of making themselves considerable, and of procuring dependants, but such as the crown furnishes them with, by instructing them with the direction of that influence which is its own, which may be resumed at pleasure, and which whenever it is resumed, must leave the greatest leader of a ministerial confederacy, as insignificant as he was before thought formidable. If there have been instances in modern times, that seem to contradict my assertion, this hath not arisen from real power in the subject, but from weak timidity and ill judged compliance in the crown. . . .

. . . Our kings have sometimes given such unlimited indulgence to their ministers, that those put into employments, scarcely ever looked beyond the ministers to own an obligation. The natural consequence of this was, that ministers employed the influence of the crown to make it submit to themselves; and having once acquired a number of dependants, purchased by doleing out the king's bounty, they had the insolence to urge the number of their dependants, as a reason why the king should bow to their ministerial omnipotence.—A prince who can be intimidated by the cabals of those who derive all their importance and influence from the unlimited disposal they have had of his favours, scarcely deserves pity, because he has the means of liberty, but wants spirit to assert it. Let him once shew that he is determined to be looked upon as master, and he will soon feel he will be respected as such: and if any over-grown minister should think this an encroachment on his office, and begin to show his inclination to distress government, which he can no longer manage without controul, he will soon find that his supposed friends were only the friends of his power, and will continue firm to him no longer than while he has possession of the means of gratifying them. In the age we live in there are but few individuals, I am sure there are but few retainers of a court, so little attentive to their own interest, as to forget that the crown is permanent, and administrations temporary; that a king is such all the days of his life, and that ministers exist only by his pleasure. To suppose, therefore, that a discarded leader of a party, should find his myrmidons willing to continue faithful to his standard, when it is set up in opposition to that of the king, is to suppose them capable of a conduct to which their leader himself must know they are entire strangers. . . .

Indeed, in one case, and in one case only, can the sovereign of this country, ever fear the resentment of a disgusted minister, or of a discarded party; and that is, when a plausible pretence for opposition can be taken up, and the bulk of the nation induced to interest itself in it, and to believe that it was formed by the leaders of it, not on account of their disappointment in the struggle for power, but on account of their honest disapprobation of the public plan of government.—But I think I may venture to give it as my opinion, that, were it possible to conceive there should be, at present, an intention in any combination of men to oppose government, they could not find such a pretence for opposition, as they could lay hold of with any appearance of decency, or hopes of success.

J. Douglas, *Seasonable Hints from an Honest Man* (1761), p. 7.

36. George III's programme, 1763.

EARL OF BUTE TO DUKE OF BEDFORD

London, April 2, 1763

. . . Three things the King is determined to abide by, and to make the basis of his future administration as they have been of his present.

1st. Never upon any account to suffer those ministers of the late reign who have attempted to fetter and enslave him ever to come into his service while he lives to hold the sceptre.

2dly. To collect every other force, and above all, that of your Grace and Mr Fox to his councils and support.

3rdly. To show all proper countenance to the country gentlemen acting on Whig principles, and on those principles only supporting his government.

J. Russell, Correspondence of the Duke of Bedford (1846), vol. III, p. 224.

37. George III and government without party, 1766.

THE KING TO THE EARL OF CHATHAM

St. James's, m. past eleven, p.m.
[December 2, 1766]

LORD CHATHAM,

On my return from the ball-room, I found your letter containing the Duke of Bedford's extravagant proposal. Indeed I expected, from his choosing to deliver his answer in person that he meant to attempt obtaining an office or two in addition to those offered; but could not imagine that even the rapaciousness of his friends could presume to think of more than that.

I know the uprightness of my cause, and that my principal ministers mean nothing but to aid in making my people happy; therefore I cannot exceed the bounds you acquainted Lord Gower were the utmost that would be granted. This hour demands a due firmness; it is that has already dismayed all the hopes of those just retired, and will I am confident, show the Bedfords of what little consequence they also are. A contrary conduct would at once overturn the very end proposed at the formation of the present administration; for to rout out the present method of parties banding together, can only be obtained by a withstanding their unjust demands, as well as the engaging able men, be their private connections where they will. I shall be ready to receive you tomorrow at two o'clock at the Queen's house.

GEORGE R.

W. S. Taylor and J. H. Pringle, *Correspondence of William Pitt, Earl of Chatham* (1838–40), vol. III, p. 137.

38. The fall of North, 1782.

LORD NORTH TO THE KING

[18 March 1782]

SIRE.—Mr Grosvenor today in the House of Commons desired me to appoint him an hour tomorrow morning, as he had a matter of importance to communicate to me, and I have since learned from good authority, that it is his intention to represent to me, in his own name, and in those of some other Country Gentlemen "*That, being now convinced that the present Administration cannot continue any longer, they are of opinion that vain and ineffectual struggles tend only to public mischief and confusion, and that they shall think it their duty henceforward to desist from opposing what appears to be clearly the sense of the House of Commons.*" If these gentlemen persist in this resolution, Your Majesty will perceive that we shall infallibly be in a Minority even on Wednesday next, when the House will be moved, in direct terms, to resolve "*That it is their opinion that the management of public affairs ought not to be continued in the hands of the present Ministers.*"

When I had the honour of an audience of Your Majesty this morning, I humbly endeavoured to state to Your Majesty my reasons for thinking that the fate of the present Ministry is absolutely and irrecoverably decided; The votes of the Minorities on Friday sevennight, and on Friday last contained, I believe, the genuine sense of the House of Commons, and I really think, of the Nation at large; Not that I suppose the minds of men in general exasperated against the individuals who compose the Administration, but they are tired of the Administration collectively taken, and wish at all events to see it alter'd. The torrent is too strong to be resisted; Your Majesty is well apprized that, in this country, the Prince on the Throne, cannot, with prudence, oppose the deliberate resolution of the House of Commons: Your Royal Predecessors (particularly King William the Third and his late Majesty) were obliged to yield to it much against their wish in more instances than one: they consented to changes in their Ministry which they disapproved because they found it necessary to sacrifice their private wishes, and even their opinions to the preservation of public order, and the prevention of these terrible mischiefs, which are the natural consequence of the clashing of two branches of the Sovereign Power in the State. The concessions they made were never deemed dishonourable, but were considered as marks of their wisdom, and of their parental affection for their people. Your Majesty has graciously and steadily supported the servants you approve, as long as they could be supported: Your Majesty has firmly and resolutely maintained what appeared to You essential to the welfare and dignity of this Country, as long as this Country itself thought proper to maintain it. The Parliament have altered their sentiments, and as their sentiments, whether just or erroneous, must ultimately prevail, Your Majesty having persevered, as long as possible, in what You thought right, can lose no honour if you yield at length, as some of the most renowned and most glorious of your Predecessors have done, to the opinion and wishes of the House of Commons. . . .

NORTH.

Monday night

Corresp. George III, No. 3566.

39. George III accepts a reverse, 1782.

THE KING TO LORD NORTH

Queen's House, March 27th, 1782.

LORD NORTH—At last the fatal day is come which the misfortunes of the times and the sudden change of sentiments of the House of Commons have drove me to, of changing the Ministry, and a more general removal of other persons than, I believe, ever was known before: I have to the last fought for Individuals, but the number I have saved except My Bed-chamber is incredibly few. You would hardly believe that even the D. of Montagu was strongly run at, but I declared I would sooner let confusion follow than part with the late Governor of my Sons, and so unexceptional a Man; at last I succeeded, so that He and Lord Ashburnham remain. The effusion of my sorrows has made me say more than I had intended, but I ever did and ever shall look on You as a friend as well as faithful servant. Pray acquaint the Cabinet that they must this day attend at St. James's to resign; I shall hope to be there if possible by one, and will receive them before the Levee, as I think it would be awkward to have the new People presented at the Levee prior to the resignations. G.R.

Where is Robinson's Warrant?

Corresp. George III, No. 3593.

40. George III coerced on measures, 1782.

Queen's House, April 12th, 1782.

m. 10 pt. 9 A.M.

. . . When necessity made me yield to the advice of Ld. Shelburne in permitting him to offer the Treasury to the Marquis of Rockingham, four propositions were insisted upon by that Quarter:—

1°. No veto to the Independence of America.

2°. Contractor's Bill.

3°. Disqualification of Revenue Officers from voting at Elections of Members of Parliament.

4°. The Reduction of several offices as proposed in Mr. Burke's Establishment Bill, and rigid Oeconomy in the Administration of the Civil List.

The answers I gave were, I hope, cautious and not unsatisfactory as to the three first, and therefore need not be repeated here; as to the last I declared a willingness to introduce the most rigid oeconomy, but that I trusted it could not be meant under that word either to affect the Dignity of the Crown by reducing such Offices as had any Peculiar Attendance on the Person of the King, or to diminish its comforts by disabling it from those acts of Benevolence which alone make the Station bearable, but that I suppose it could be now settled by interior regulations, and was the object for the Attention of the Cabinet, as far as related [to] the interests of the Crown, as I thought Public Oeconomy the object of Parliament. Thus things stood till last week, when I found the language of the Marquis of Rockingham changed, and that his ideas began to run entirely on bringing the Civil List before Parliament, and within these two days he has avowed that he means to introduce the whole of Mr Burke's Bill, and it was with the utmost difficulty I could prevent his taking such a step in the House of Commons without previously laying the matter before the Ministers, saying it was one of his four propositions, and therefore did not require any consultation. He means today to lay a Message before the Cabinet, which though I tried to avoid it, he obliged me to read yesterday, but on which I did not utter a syllable.

Corresp. George III, No. 3648.

41. George III coerced on men, 1783.

MEMORANDUM BY THE KING

... Being thus baffled in every endeavour,[1] on Wednesday March 12th [1783] I sent for Lord North and told him provided an Administration could be formed on a broad basis, and that I could on the whole approve of the Plan of Arrangements, that then I would not object to the Duke of Portland being at the head of the Treasury, and therefore authorized him to go to that Duke with a Message to that purpose, and desiring when they had formed a joint plan that Lord North might bring it to me; this he hoped to effect in two days. ...

... [On] Friday March 21st ... as soon as I returned from St. James's I saw the Duke of Portland, who said—his object in wishing to see Me was to acquaint that the cause of difference between his friends and Lord North no longer existed, they have withdrawn their objection to Lord Stormont; that the Duke of Portland could now therefore shew me the names of the proposed Cabinet Ministers; I declined seeing it, referring to the letter of March 18th which I had written to Lord North and which had been communicated to Him, by which I had declared that I must see and examine the whole Plan of Arrangements before I could give any opinion on particular parts of it. He to my astonishment said this was want of confidence in him for that the Cabinet once laid before Me, he expected that on his coming to the head of the Treasury, I should rely on his making no propositions but such as he thought necessary for my affairs and consequently that I should acquiesce in them. This unexpected idea, I fortunately did not treat with the warmth it deserved, but on finding that [the] Duke would not see the singularity of the proposition and that on discussing it he began to grow warm, said I must have time to consider of a proposition I thought so novel.

Therefore the next morning I sent for Lord North and did not disguise from him the indecency of the proposal; but pretended to immagine it was not meant, and insisted on his going to the Duke of Portland, and on their joint plan of Arrangement being sent to Me in the course of the Evening.

... After the drawing Room the Duke of Portland asked an Audience, when he said he came in consequence of the intimation through Lord North, that he had drawn up no Plan, but was ready

---

[1] To form an administration other than the Fox–North coalition.

to shew Me the list of Efficient Cabinet Ministers: I answered I was sorry to return to what past on Friday; the only alteration in his language was to press much for my looking at that list, which I desired to decline from an intention which I avowed again of not entering into parts of the Plan till he had enabled Me to examine the whole; but he pressed so much for my looking at his Paper that I so far complied, and then returned it to Him. He then complained of my not saying I approved of the Names; this I told him I had before declined doing, and repeated my words. He upon that said he could not think of forming any Plan, and that he thought I might trust the Seven Persons mentioned and could not propose anything but what it would be right for me to Acquiesce in. This I replied was asking more than any Man above forty could engage to do, and insisted he should in the evening send either his Plan or a refusal of doing it.

MEMORANDUM BY THE KING

[April 1783]

The total stagnation of Public Business by no Administration in reality subsisting at a time when the Definitive Treaties ought to be prosecuted; the Navy and the Army reduced to a state of Peace and Taxes laid for defraying the Expenses of the State and for settling the unpaid Debt obliged Me no longer to defer submitting to the erection of an Administration whose conduct as individuals does not promise to deserve collectively my confidence

I therefore on Tuesday evening, April 1st 1783, sent for Ld. North and enquired if the Seven Persons named by the D. of Portland and him were ready to accept the Employments proposed, on his answering in the affirmative I authorized him to acquaint them they might accept them the next day, after which the D. of Portland and He should plan the arrangements of Employments. . . .

Corresp. George III, Nos. 4268, 4271.

42. Buckingham's views on the formation of cabinets, 1802.

MARQUIS OF BUCKINGHAM TO LORD GRENVILLE

1802, November 1. Stowe.—You will easily believe that my mind and every moment of my time has been most fully occupied by the very interesting communications which Tom has made to me from you, and upon which I am only prepared to offer you the very crude and undigested reflections that have occurred to me, in the discussion with him of what I understood now to be the proposition floating in your mind, namely of assisting Mr. Pitt to form a Cabinet composed of Mr Addington and Lord Hawkesbury, Mr Dundas, Lord Spencer, Mr Windham and yourself, with the addition of the Lord Chancellor, and of the Duke of Portland or some other person of that description from amongst the present ministers, or with some other not very material change. It seems difficult to ascertain correctly from the long details of your conversation with Mr. Pitt, how far you stand *engaged* to him, supposing Lord Spencer and Mr Windham willing to accede to such an arrangement; and under that uncertainty I feel some little awkwardness in giving you the first blush of my opinions; and should have paused upon it if Tom had not urged me to state them to you immediately. You must therefore take them undigested and unarranged, but they will at least occupy your thoughts so far as to enable you to satisfy my mind upon them when we meet, which, for the reasons given in Tom's letter which he has read to me, and which I enclose to you, I trust will be. I clearly understand the proposition to be, not that of forming an administration in the usual way, that is with *carte blanche* from the king, and with materials or rather persons acting in unison of opinions together; but to be an arrangement of infinite difficulty, having for its object the placing Mr Pitt at the head of government, notwithstanding his public and private *embarrassments* of every sort, and consequently with an imperious call for great sacrifice of whatever stands in the way of that object. The first sacrifice is that which I know you make, but for which no one will give you a moment's belief, namely, your own personal wishes for personal ease out of office. The next sacrifice is that of your own feelings when called upon to sit in a Cabinet with Mr Addington and Lord Hawkesbury, to whose ignorance, imbecility, and deception on the public, as well as their criminal annihilation of the internal and external political strength of the country, you have imputed and must still more strongly continue to impute the present tremendous crisis.

H.M.C., *Dropmore*, VII, 117.

43. The king's power of forming governments, 1782.

[10 July, 1782]

EARL OF SHELBURNE: . . . It was true indeed, that his principles differed in some respects from those of some of his then colleagues; but when they pleaded consistency, it was but fair that he should stand upon his consistency as firmly as they did upon theirs; and it would have been very singular indeed, if he should have given up to them all those constitutional ideas, which for seventeen years he had imbibed from his master in politics, the late Earl of Chatham; that noble earl had always declared, that this country ought not to be governed by any party or faction; that if it was to be so governed, the constitution must necessarily expire; with these principles he had always acted; they were not newly taken up for ambitious purposes; their lordships might recollect a particular expression that he had used some time ago, when speaking of party, he declared that he never would consent that the "King of England should be a King of the Mahrattas," among whom it was a custom for a certain number of great lords to elect a peshaw, who was the creature of an aristocracy, and was vested with the plenitude of power, while the King was, in fact, nothing more than a royal pageant or puppet.

These being his principles, it was natural for him to stand up for the prerogative of the crown, and insist upon the King's right to appoint his own servants. If the power which others wished to assume, of vesting in the cabinet the right of appointing to all places, and filling up all vacancies, should once be established, the King must then resemble the king of the Mahrattas, who had nothing of the sovereignty but the name: in that case the monarchical part of the constitution would be absorbed by the aristocracy, and the famed constitution of England would be no more.

P.H., XXIII, 191.

44. Appointment of ministers: Pitt's views, 1784.

MR PITT: [20 Feb. 1784]

Prerogative, Sir, has been justly called a part of the rights of the people, and sure I am it is a part of their rights, which the people were never more disposed to defend, of which they were never more jealous than at this hour. Grant only this, that this House has a negative in the appointment of ministers, and you transplant the executive power into this House. Sir, I shall call upon gentlemen to speak out: let them not come to resolution after resolution, without stating the grounds on which they act; for there is nothing more dangerous among mixed powers, than that one branch of the legislature should attack another by means of hints and auxiliary arguments, urged only in debate, without daring to avow the direct grounds on which they go; and without stating in plain terms on the face of their resolution, what are their motives, and what are their principles which lead them to come to such resolutions. Above all, Sir, let this House beware of suffering any individual to involve his own cause, and to interweave his own interests in the resolutions of the House of Commons. The dignity of the House is for ever appealed to: let us beware that it is not the dignity of any set of men; let us beware that personal prejudices have no share in deciding these great constitutional questions. The right hon. gentleman [Fox] is possessed of those enchanting arts whereby he can give grace to deformity; he holds before your eyes a beautiful and delusive image: he pushes it forward to your observation; but as sure as you embrace it, the pleasing vision will vanish, and this fair phantom of liberty will be succeeded by anarchy, confusion, and ruin to the constitution. For in truth, Sir, if the constitutional independence of the crown is thus reduced to the very verge of annihilation, where is the boasted equipoise of the constitution? Where is that balance among the three branches of the legislature which our ancestors have measured out to each with so much precision? Where is the independence—nay, where is even the safety of any one prerogative of the crown, or even of the crown itself, if its prerogative of naming ministers is to be usurped by this House, or if, (which is precisely the same thing) its nomination of them, is to be negatived by us without stating any one ground of distrust in the men, and without suffering ourselves to have any experience of their measures? Dreadful, therefore, as the conflict is, my conscience, my duty, my fixed regard for the constitution of our ancestors, maintain me still in this arduous situation. It is not any proud contempt, or defiance of the constitutional resolutions of this House; it is no personal point of honour; much less is it any lust for power that makes me still cling to office; the situation of the times requires of me, and I will add, the country calls aloud to me, that I should defend this castle; and I am determined, therefore, I will yet defend it.

P.H., XXIV, 663.

45. Appointment of ministers: Fox's views, 1784.

Mr Fox: [1 March 1784]

Since the unfortunate reigns of the Stuarts, prerogative had never been so much the topic of discussion as it had become of late in parliament. His ideas of whatever the constitution had vested in the crown were no secret: he ever had and ever would avow them. No prerogative of the crown was, in his opinion, distinct or unconnected with the whole of that free and liberal system in which our government chiefly consisted. The people were the great source of all power, and their welfare the sole object for which it was to be exerted; but who in this case were to be the judges? The House of Commons undoubtedly were competent to protect the rights of the people, to pronounce on whatever they deemed an encroachment on their privileges; and the moment they could not prevent everything which struck them as such, they were not equal to the design of such an institution. This he called a due seasoning or modification of that enormous power devolved by the constitution on the executive government of the country. The House of Commons consequently were possessed of the power of putting a negative on the choice of ministers; they were stationed as sentinels by the people, to watch over whatever could more or less remotely or nearly affect their interest, so that whenever they discovered in those nominated by his Majesty to the several great offices of state, want of ability, want of weight to render their situations respectable, or want of such principles as were necessary to give effect to the wishes of the House; in any or all of such cases they were entitled to advise his Majesty against employing such persons as his faithful Commons could not trust.

P.H., xxiv, 690.

46. Appointment of ministers: views of 1812.

[21 May 1812]

MR STUART WORTLEY . . . then moved, "That an humble Address be presented to his royal highness the Prince Regent, humbly praying, that he will be pleased to take such measures as will enable him, under the present circumstances of the country, to form a strong and efficient Administration . . ."

MR EYRE opposed it, as unconstitutional to interfere with the prerogative of the crown in the formation of an administration. There was no instance upon record of this House having so interfered. They had interfered, when an administration had been formed, and found inefficient; but they had never come forward with their previous advice. It was their duty to watch over and controul the crown;

but there was no doctrine in the constitution better understood than that they had no right to interfere with the crown in the nomination of its servants . . .

Mr Wilberforce [said] he was old enough to recollect, that 30 years ago the question, whether the House should have a previous negative on the appointment of the ministers of the crown, had been decided. It had then been determined, that it should not; and then it was only when either or both of the Houses of Parliament had had experience of some of the measures of ministers, that, if they could not confide in the administration, it became their duty to address the throne and express their judgment. The amendment of the honourable baronet (Sir F. Burdett) near him was objectionable on the same ground. It was unconstitutional. The hon. baronet seemed to think that previous pledges ought to be required of ministers. This was not the part they had to act; they were not to call to the bar of the House the person chosen, or whom they imagined would be chosen by the Prince, and interrogate them as to the opinions which they held, and the advice they intended to give. The crown had first to do its part;—the House would then judge of the measures of the administration, and proceed accordingly. These were the old-fashioned principles of the constitution . . .

The Hon. J. W. Ward . . . did not see that it was unconstitutional,— he was sure it was not without precedent for that House to advise the sovereign on the formation of an administration. He admitted that this interference was not to be resorted to frequently, or on slight occasions.

P.D., xxiii, 252.

47. Administrative reform (commission of enquiry), 1785.

An act for appointing commissioners to enquire into the fees, gratuities, perquisites, and emoluments, which are, or have been lately received in the several publick offices therein mentioned; to examine into any abuses which may exist in the same; and to report such observations as shall occur to them, for the better conducting and managing the business transacted in the said offices.

Whereas *it is highly expedient for the publick service, that an inquiry should be made respecting the expences in the different offices and depart-*

ments of his Majesty's government hereinafter mentioned, and the fees, gratuities, perquisites, and emoluments, received and taken therein, with a view to such regulations as shall be judged expedient and proper for the correction of abuses which may have arisen, and to effect such savings as may be made in each . . . be it therefore enacted . . . That the lords commissioners of his Majesty's treasury, for the office of the treasury, for the office of paymaster general of his Majesty's forces, the offices of customs and excise in *England* and *Scotland* respectively, the offices of taxes, stamps, and salt duties, the offices of the postmaster general, surveyor general, and auditors of the land revenue, surveyor general of the woods and forests, and also for the offices for hackney coaches, and for hawkers and pedlars, respectively; that the commissioners for executing the office of lord high admiral of *Great Britain*, for the admiralty, for the treasurer of the navy, for the offices of the navy and victualling, and for sick and hurt seamen, respectively; and the principal secretaries of state for their several offices, the master general of the ordnance for the office of ordnance, his Majesty's secretary at war for his office, shall with all convenient speed, lay the returns of the fees, gratuities, perquisites, and emoluments, usually taken, demanded, or received by any clerk or officer within any of the before-mentioned offices or departments respectively, or copies thereof, together with copies of the annual establishments, and also of the incident bills for defraying the contingent expences of the said offices or departments, as they respectively stood in the year one thousand seven hundred and eighty-two, or in such preceding and subsequent years as they shall judge most convenient, before sir *John Dick* baronet, and *William Molleson* esquire, comptrollers of the army accounts, together with *Francis Baring* esquire, who are hereby constituted commissioners for making the enquiries intended by this act: and that the said commissioners or any two of them, shall and they are hereby required to take into their consideration all the said returns, establishments, and incident bills, and shall proceed thereupon according to such instructions and directions as they shall from time to time receive from the King's most excellent majesty in council; and the said commissioners shall, from time to time report and certify their proceedings, in writing under the hands and seals of them, or any two of them, to the King in council, upon each office or department, specifying what officers and clerks belong to or are employed in the same, and what is the duty, services, and attendance required of them, together with the fees, gratuities, perquisites, and emoluments, which the said officers and clerks, or their substitutes or under clerks, may or ought lawfully to have and take for in respect of their several offices and places; adding, at the same time, such observations as shall occur to them and such plans, either for correction and improvement, or for abolishing or regulating any of the said fees, gratuities, perquisites, and emoluments, or for carrying into execution the general purposes of this act, as may appear to them proper to be adopted for the time to come; and in particular, the said commissioners shall, in all cases in which they shall be of opinion that any fees ought to continue to be taken in any of the said offices or departments, consider and report whether it will be practicable to appoint a person to receive and distribute the same, under the directions of the several boards or principal officers, in such manner, and in such proportions as shall be hereafter settled.

25 Geo. III, c. 19: S.L., XXXV, 44.

48. Administrative reform (public audit), 1785.

An act for better examining and auditing the publick accounts of this kingdom.

WHEREAS *the present method of accounting for the receipts, issues, and expenditures of the publick money, before the auditors of the imprest, is become insufficient to answer the good purposes intended thereby; for remedy whereof, it is important that a more effectual method shall be provided in future for examining the publick accounts of the kingdom, and for preventing, so far as possible, all delays, frauds and abuses, in delivering in and passing same: and whereas it is expedient, for the effecting thereof, that the right vested in the right honourable lord* Sondes, *and the right honourable* John Stuart *commonly called* Lord Viscount Mountstuart, *now lord* Cardiff, *which they derive from the patents granted to them respectively, as auditors of the imprest, should cease and determine, on due compensation being made to them for their interest in the same; and that all fees, gratuities, and perquisites, in the office of the auditors of the imprest, should be forthwith abolished; and that every officer and clerk in the said office or department should be paid by the publick a certain fixed annual salary, in lieu of all such fees, gratuities, and perquisites:* be it therefore enacted ... That, from and after the fifth day of *July,* one thousand seven hundred and eighty-five, the patents granted by his late and present Majesty, under the great seal of *Great Britain*, to the said lord *Sondes*, and the said lord *Mountstuart*, as auditors of the imprest, shall be vacated; and all powers, authorities, rights, privileges, and advantages, thereby granted and given, shall cease and determine from the fifth day of *July*, one thousand seven hundred and eighty-five; from and after which time, no fee, gratuity, perquisite, or emolument, shall be received or taken by any person or persons whomsoever, employed in the making up, passing, or auditing any publick accounts under the authority of this act.

IV. And, in order effectually to provide such examination of all publick accounts in future as may be necessary for the security of the publick interest, be it further enacted, That it shall and may be lawful for his Majesty, his heirs and successors, to nominate and appoint five commissioners, by letters patent under the great seal of *Great Britain*, two of whom shall be the comptrollers of the army accounts, now and hereafter for the time being; and to grant fixed salaries to each of the said commissioners, to be paid out of the aggregate fund, not exceeding in the whole the sum of four thousand pounds clear of all deductions annually, who shall be stiled, *The commissioners for auditing the publick accounts*, and shall hold their offices *quam diu se bene gesserint*, (except the said comptrollers of the army accounts, who shall continue to be commissioners for auditing the publick accounts so long only as they shall be comptrollers of army accounts;) and shall, before they shall enter upon the execution of the powers vested in them by this act, take an oath before the chancellor of the exchequer, which he is hereby authorised and required to administer, the tenor whereof shall be as followeth; (that is to say:)

I A. B. *do swear, That, according to the best of my skill and knowledge, I will faithfully, impartially, and truly execute the several powers and trusts vested in me by an act* for better examining and auditing the publick accounts of this kingdom. So help me God.

V. And be it further enacted, That the lord high treasurer, or the commissioners of the treasury, or any three of them, shall be, and he or they are hereby authorised to appoint such officers and clerks, and other persons, as shall appear to them to be necessary, from time to time, for making up and preparing for declaration the several publick accounts of the kingdom, with such fixed salaries to each as they shall judge proper; and to allow such reasonable sums, as to them shall seem fit, from time to time, for stationary, coals, candles, and other incidental charges to be incurred in the office for auditing the public accounts, to be paid out of the aggregate fund, not exceeding in the whole the annual sum of six thousand pounds clear of all deductions, which shall be to the several officers, clerks, and other persons, in lieu of all fees, gratuities, and perquisites whatsoever.

25 Geo. III, c. 52: S.L., xxxv, 225.

49. The value of the opposition, 1784.

It is material to consider whence arises this general safe-guard, which the public possesses, against the malversation of ministers, against the intentional abuse, or the ignorant misapplication, of the powers with which they are intrusted. The popular nature of our government furnishes a check, of which the operation is constant, because it is excited by natural and increasing causes. The opportunity which parliament affords to the young, the bustling, and the ambitious, of canvassing public measures, is one of those salutary counterpoises which our constitution affords against the weight of the Executive Power. The Opposition in Britain is a sort of public body, which, in the practice at least of our government, is perfectly known and established. The provision of this ex-official body, when it acts in a manner salutary to the state, is to watch with jealousy over the conduct of administration; to correct the abuses, and to resist the corruptions of its power; to restrain whatever may be excessive, to moderate what may be inconsiderate, and to supply what may be defective in its measures.

Mackenzie, *History of the Proceedings of the Parliament of* 1784, quoted by G. Rose: *Observations respecting the Public Expenditure and the Influence of the Crown* (1810), p. 77.

50. The Prince of Wales's 'shadow cabinet', 1749.

[18 July 1749]

This day I arived at Kew about eleven o'clock. The Prince received me most kindly, and told me he desired me to come into his service upon any terms, and by any title I pleased: that he meant to put the principal direction of his affairs into my hands: and what he could not do for me in his present situation, must be made up to me in futurity. All this in a manner, so noble and frank, and with expressions so full of affection and regard, that I ought not to remember them, but as a debt, and to perpetuate my gratitude. This passed before dinner.

After dinner, he took me into a private room, and of himself began to say, that he thought I might as well be called Treasurer of the Chambers, as any other name: that the Earl of Scarborough, his Treasurer, might take it ill, if I stood upon the establishment with higher appointments than he did: that his Royal Highness's destination was, that I should have 2000 £. per annum. That he thought it best to put me upon the establishment at the highest salary, only, and that he would pay me the rest himself. I humbly desired, that I might stand upon the establishment without any salary, and that I would take what he now designed for me, when he should be King, but nothing before. He said, that it became me, to make him that offer, but it did not become him to accept it, consistent with his reputation, and therefore, it must be in present. He then immediately added, that we must settle what was to happen in reversion, and said, that he thought a Peerage with the management of the House of Lords, and the seals of Secretary of State, for the Southern Province, would be a proper station for me, if I approved of it. Perceiving me to be under much confusion at this unexpected offer, and at a loss how to express myself; he stopped me, and then said, I now promise you on the word and honour of a Prince that, as soon as I come to the Crown, I will give you a Peerage and the Seals of the Southern Province. Upon my endeavouring to thank him, he repeated the same words, and added (putting back his chair) and I give you leave to kiss my hand upon it, now, by way of acceptance, which I did accordingly.

He then continued to say, that he would provide for my friends, whom he knew I valued more than myself: that he promised Mr. Furness, the Treasury: Sir Francis Dashwood, the Treasury of the Navy, or Cofferrer: Mr. Henley, Solicitor General, and gave me leave to tell them so, adding, that he would confirm it to them himself. . . .

George Bubb Dodington, *Diary* (1784), p. 4.

51. Opposition tactics: Chesterfield's advice, 1741.

THE EARL OF CHESTERFIELD TO GEORGE DODINGTON

Spa. September 8th. 1741.

Having at last found a safe way of sending you this letter, I shall, without the least reserve, give you my thoughts upon the contents of your's of 30th of May O.S.

By the best judgement I can form of the list of this present parliament, and I have examined it very carefully, we appear to be so strong, that I think we can but just be called the minority; and I am very sure that such a minority, well united and well conducted, might soon be a majority. But,

Hoc opus hic labor est.

It will neither be united nor well conducted. Those who should lead it will make it their business to break and divide it; and they will succeed. I mean Carteret and Pulteney. Their behaviour these few years has, in my mind, plainly shewn their views and their negotiations with the court: but, surely, their conduct at the end of last session puts that matter out of all dispute. They feared even the success of that minority, and took care to render it as insignificant as possible. Will they then not be much more apprehensive of the success of this; and will not both their merit and their reward be much the greater for defeating it? If you'll tell me that they ought rather to avail themselves of these numbers, and, at the head of them, force their way where they are so impatient to go, I will agree with you, that in prudence they ought; but the fact is, they reason quite differently, desire to get in, with a few by negotiation, and not by victory with numbers, who they fear might presume upon their strength, and grow troublesome to their generals.

On the other hand, sir Robert must be alarmed at our numbers, and must resolve to reduce them before they are brought into the field. He knows by experience, where and how to apply for that purpose; with this difference only, that the numbers will have raised the price, which he must come up to. And this is all the fruit I expect from this strong minority. You will possibly ask me, whether all this is in the power of Carteret and Pulteney? I answer, yes; in the power of Pulteney alone. He has a personal influence over many, and an interested influence over more. The silly, half-witted zealous Whigs consider him as the only support of Whigism; and look upon us as running headlong into Bolingbroke and the Tories. The interested Whigs, as Sandys, Rushout, and Gibbon, with many others, are as impatient to come into court as he can be; and, persuaded that he has opened that door a little, will hold fast by him to squeeze in with him, and think they can justify their conduct to the publick, by following their old leader, under the colours (tho' false ones) of whigism.

What then, is nothing to be done? Are we to give it up tamely, when the prospect seems so fair? No; I am for acting, let our numbers be what they will. I am for discriminating, and making people speak out; tho' our numbers should, as I am convinced they will, lessen considerably by it. Let what will happen, we cannot be in a worse situation than we have been in for these last three or four years. Nay, I am for acting at the very beginning of the sessions, and bringing our numbers the first week; and points for that purpose, I am sure, are not wanting. Some occur to me now, many more will, I dare say, occur to others; and many will, by that time, present themselves.

For example, the court generally proposes some servile and shameless tool of their's to be chairman of the committee of privileges and elections. Why should not we, therefore, pick out some Whig of a fair character, and with personal connections, to set up in opposition? I think we should be pretty strong upon this point. But as for opposition to their speaker, if it be Onslow, we shall be but weak; he having, by a certain decency of behaviour, made himself many personal friends in the minority. The affair of Carthagena will of course be mentioned; and there, in my opinion, a question, and a trying one too, of censure, lies very fair, that the delaying of that expedition so late last year was the principal cause of our disappointment. An address to the king, desiring him to make no peace with Spain, unless our undoubted right of navigation in the West Indies, without molestation or search, be clearly, and in express words, stipulated; and till we have acquired some valuable possession there, as a pledge of the performance of such stipulation: such a question would be a popular one, and distressful enough to the ministry.

I entirely agree with you, that we ought to have meetings to concert measures some time before the meeting of the parliament; but that I likewise know will not happen, I have been these seven years endeavouring to bring it about, and have not been able. Fox-hunting, gardening, planting, or indifference, having always kept our people in the country, till the very day before the meeting of the parliament. Besides, would it be easy to settle who should be at those meetings? If Pulteney and his people were to be chose, it would be only informing them beforehand, what they should either oppose or defeat; and if they were not there, their own exclusion would in some degree justify, or at least colour, their conduct.

W. Coxe, *Memoirs of the Life and Administration of Sir Robert Walpole, Earl of Orford* (1798), vol. III, p. 579.

52. Government tactics: Walpole's advice, 1743.

LORD ORFORD TO THE DUKE OF NEWCASTLE

[October 1743]

My Dear Lord,

I had the favour of y^{rs} by the bearer of this, & altho' my last letter to Mr Pelham makes it allmost unnecessary to add any thing upon the subject of domesticks, I make no scruple to say a word or two in further explanation of my poor thoughts. Cobham insists upon two conditions, a total discarding of Ld Bath & his friends, & upon an admission of 3 or 4 Tories, as 'tis called, wth his Party. The first seems to carry no difficulty, for if you do not remove them, 'tis plain by their conduct, they will obstruct or betray you, as soon & as often as they can, or dare, & it cannot be otherwise, for you have gott what they wanted,[1] & the only price of their satisfaction is to recover what they have publickly been disappointed in, & by whom? answer that question, & and I think you no longer doubt. As to bringing in Tories, I can only say necessity has no Law, lett them remember, that *three* or *four* is the number demanded; I am afraid, that will soon be forgott, but if they must be had, all prudent means must be used to make those easy that will naturally be uneasy, & I should hope if they see the necessity, they will be convinced. If then Ld Privy Seal's [Gower] & Ld Cobham's Party, are to be purchased, for so I understand this System, the former question is over, for how can you bring in two new Setts of men, wthout removing some that are in, & can they be, but those we are talking of? The opinion you mention of some of y^r best friends viz. *To suffer those that are at present in to remain in, or be transfer'd to Employments of no Trust Power or Confidence, & to take in the opposing Whigs, even with a mixture of three or four Tories,* seems to me utterly impossible. Have you wherewithal?

[1] Henry Pelham received the Treasury on the death of Wilmington, not Bath.

But what part will Ld Carterett act? His professions to you do not correspond wth his Conduct. His total silence upon most material things denote [sic] no confidence or cordial freindship. But by ye next messenger He will write more fully; I don't believe it. There can be no doubt but they depend upon Him, for wthout that, they have no ground at all to stand upon, but you must carry Him along with you if you can; and I shall imagine Stair's behaviour to Carterett, may drive C. to be reasonable wth you. Stair's memorial is unpardonable, & as He will be communicative about it, it will be in every Bodies mouth, to fit the blame where their inclinations lead them. In truth the King only is attack'd but publickly Carterett must be ye Butt, And these Representations of Stair's, will be the foundation of renewing and aggravating the odious distinction of England & Hanover, here Carterett must be wth you, for you must defend the King, & consequently espouse his cause. But perhaps 'tis not impossible but Carterett may have suggested to Bath to take this Plea to recomend himself & his friends to the King's protection. This thought I am sure should be a lesson to Cobham, for He & his wild youth must cease to make *Hanover* their darling Topick of familiarity, if they hope to enable you to serve them at Court.

Add. MSS. 32701, ff. 148-9.

53. Commons attack on the cabinet council, 1692.

[23 Nov. 1692]

M_R F_{OLEY} [after criticising the government's mismanagement of the war]

. . . I move you to come to this Resolution, 'That the great affairs of the Government, for the time past, have been unsuccessfully managed; and that the king be moved, for the future, to employ men of known integrity and fidelity.'

S_{IR} W_M. S_{TRICKLAND}. I cannot tell where it is we are wounded. I would not have the management in such hands for the future; but this cannot be while we have a Cabinet-Council.

M_R W_{ALLER}. 'Cabinet-Council' is not a word to be found in our Law-books. We knew it not before; we took it for a nick-name. Nothing can fall out more unhappily than to have a distinction made of the 'Cabinet' and 'Privy Council.' It has had this effect in the country, and must have, that, in the country, the justices of the peace, and deputy-lieutenants, will be afraid to act: they will say, 'they cannot go on;' and why? Because several of them have been misrepresented, and are not willing to act; they know not who will stand by them; and are loth to make discoveries, unless seconded. If some of the Privy Council must be trusted, and some not, to who must any gentleman apply? Must he ask, 'Who is a Cabinet Counsellor?' This creates mistrust in the people. I am sure, these distinctions of some being more trusted than others, have given great dissatisfaction. This is what I have met with this summer; and therefore I second the motion.

Sir Rd. Temple. All governments reduce their Council to a few: Holland does; and the French king to three.

Mr. Waller. We have reduced our Secretaries from two to one. The question proposed was, 'That the king be advised, that all matters of state be advised on in the Privy-Council, and that the management of them by a Cabal is dangerous.'

... Mr Goodwin Wharton. ... The method of this cabinet is not the method nor the practice of England. As for private councils, all kings have their favourites; and I wish the king had such a secretary as Mazarine, to secure the interest of the nation, and not himself. The method is this; things are concerted in the Cabinet, and then brought to the Council; such a thing resolved in the cabinet, and brought and put upon them, for their assent, without showing any of the reasons. That has not been the method of England. I am credibly informed, that it has been complained of in council, and not much backed there. If this method be, you will never know who gives advice. If you think it convenient, I shall be of your mind; but I think that this method is not for the service of the nation.

Mr Foley. I would have every counsellor set his hand to his assent, or dissent, to be distinguished.

P.H., v, 731.

54. 'Confidential cabinet', 1771.

THE KING TO LORD NORTH

Lord North—Nothing can be more handsome than the Duke of Grafton's manner of accepting the Privy Seal, which convinces Me that He would have been hurt if it had not been offered to him; I must bear testimony that He ever thought the confidential Cabinet too numerous and that on Lord Bristol's getting the Privy Seal he therefore desired it might be stipulated that he should not be of those

Meetings; and as He thinks the same in his own case I cannot see any reason for Summoning him on Ministerial Questions except when they regard some affair to be debated in the House of Lords; on other occasions if his advice is asked he will undoubtedly give it privately. You will give Lord Suffolk notice to bring the Privy Seal.

> *Queen's House*
> June 11th 1771$^{m}_{43}$ pt. 7 p.m.

Corresp. George III, No. 964.

55. North on advice and responsibility, 1784.

[12 January 1784]

LORD NORTH said . . . Secret influence . . . was now openly avowed. A peer of parliament had given secret advice, and gloried in it. He would not say that a peer, or a privy counsellor, had not a right to advise the crown; but he would contend, that the moment he gave such advice, he ought to take the seals and become a minister, that advice and responsibility might go hand in hand,

P.H., XXIV, 290.

56. Spencer Perceval on ministerial responsibility, 1813.

SPENCER PERCEVAL TO SIR WILLIAM MANNERS[1]

[18 March 1813]

It has been therefore and still is out of my power to tell you at what time you may expect it [a peerage]. As this is the case it is necessary that I should at present trouble you with any inquiries into the particulars of this written promise, which at least is so far out of the ordinary course of matters of this description as to put me under the necessity of making such enquiries before I can satisfy myself that it is consistent with my duty to advise H.R.H. to grant this peerage, for you must be aware that, by the Constitution of the country, H.R.H. cannot, either as Regent or King, exercise any of the prerogatives of the Crown but under the advice of some responsible Minister and consequently that such Minister has a duty which requires him to know the circumstances which are connected with any promise which he may be desirous to carry into execution.

A. Aspinall (ed.), *Letters of King George IV, 1812–1830* (Cambridge, 1938), vol. I, p. 245, n. I.

[1] See No. 85.

57. Cabinet Council membership under William III, 1701.

LORD SUNDERLAND'S ADVICE TO LORD SOMERS

... None to be of the Cabinet Council, but who have, in some sort, a right to enter there by their employment.

Archbishop, Lord Keeper, Lord President, Lord Privy Seal, Lord Steward, Lord Chamberlain, First Commissioner of the Treasury, Two Secretaries of State; the Lieutenant of Ireland must be there, when he is in England. If the King would have more, it ought to be the First Commissioner of the Admiralty, and the Master of the Ordnance. If these two are excluded, no one can take it ill, if he be not admitted. They may be summoned, when any thing relating to their charge is debated. It would be much for the King's service, if he brought his affairs to be debated at that Council.

Hardwicke, *State Papers* (1778), vol. II, p. 461.

58. Inner and Outer Cabinets under William III, 1694.

(1) THE DUKE OF SHREWSBURY TO THE KING

Whitehall, May 11–21, 1694.—Sir; you were pleased not only to allow, but to command me, to apply to yourself, in any thing I thought most proper to be communicated to you alone. It has happened, that within these two days, I have been engaged in a negotiation, of which I think it absolutely necessary to give your majesty an account, just as it fell out.

By her majesty's directions, I suppose, Mr Secretary Trenchard, upon Wednesday last, writ letters to my lord keeper, lord Portland, privy seal, lord Sydney, and myself, to meet at his office to consult about the two services that are now expected from the fleet, viz. that of the Mediterranean and the attempt upon Brest. This being at Mr Secretary's office, where many people come in upon business, could not be a secret, but the Marquis of Normanby hearing of it, came to me yesterday morning, and so positively assured me, that your majesty had, in express terms, promised him to be called to all councils, when any, in what place soever, should be summoned, that he could not believe but this proceeding of the queen, in leaving him out in any consultations, must proceed from a mistake, and therefore desired me to go to her majesty, and to acquaint her, how he understood himself to be left here, entrusted with your majesty's business of the most secret concerns. I waited upon the queen accordingly, and she was pleased to permit me to tell my lord again, that your majesty's instructions to her were, that there should be no cabinet council; but lords should be summoned, sometimes one, and sometimes another, as they should be judged most proper for the business they were to advise about; only some whose employments belong to the crown, made it necessary they should not be excluded. . . .

(2) THE KING TO THE DUKE OF SHREWSBURY

May 22—June 1, 1694.—Since the departure of the last courier, I received, at Loo, your letter of the 11th, and here this morning those of the 15th and 18th. It is true, that I did promise my lord Normanby, that when there was a cabinet council, he should assist at it; but surely this does not engage either the queen or myself, to summon him to all the meetings, which we may order, on particular occasions, to be attended solely by the great officers of the crown, namely, the lord keeper, the lord president, the lord privy seal, and the two secretaries of state. I do not know the reason why lord Sydney [Master of the Ordnance] was summoned to attend, unless it was on account of some business relative to the artillery, which, however, might have been communicated to him. I do not see that any objection can be made to this arrangement, whenever the queen summons the aforesaid officers of the crown, to consult on some secret and important affair. Assuredly that number is fully sufficient, and the meeting cannot be considered as a cabinet council, since they are distinguished, by their offices, from the other counsellors of state, and therefore no one can find fault if they are more trusted and employed than others.

I agree entirely with you, that if lord Normanby is admitted, all those who have ever attended any cabinet council, should likewise have a seat. Doubtless the queen communicates to him the business, that is to be discussed, and places confidence in him, with which he ought to be contented; but if he forces us to have a regular cabinet council, merely that he may attend, and when we do not deem it advantageous for the welfare of our service, it is assuming too much.

W. Coxe (ed.), *Correspondence of the Duke of Shrewsbury* (1821), p. 33.

59. Cabinets under Anne: Lord Dartmouth's notes, 1710.

(1) THE 'LORDS OF THE COMMITTEE'

Cockpitt   Ld Stew[ard][1]: Ld Pres[ident][2]: D[uke of]
Oct 13th/1710   Queens[bury][3]: Ld Dart[mouth]:[4]

Sr John Leak[5] & Sr Geor: Bings[6] were called in and desiered to give their opinions upon Mr Slangerlands letter to the D. of Marlborough[7] about the expedition upon the Coast and then were desiered to give their opinions in writting which they desiered to withdraw upon and consult with one another about and then gave it in in writteing.

Mr Craggs of the Ordinance gave in a Paper, and says all the ordinance stores are ready on board, and only wait for a convey to carry them to the downs which he understands from the Admiralty is ready.

Mr Coleby of the transports says all the transports are ready for the troops in the Isle of Wight.

Mr Coleby of the victualling office says there are 2,000 bags of Bisquit ready to be embarked upon Sunday next and that 2,000 more will be ready he thincks at furthest in ten days, and that there are provissions on board the transports at portsmouth for 6,000 men for 4 months at large allowance and for 6 at short

Ordered that I should give my Ld Marlborough an account of what they all say & send him word the Queen has been at so great an expence and so great a number of men has been diverted from any other servis in expectation of this expedition that she would have it goe on if Practicable.

Ordered that the memorial from the Admiralty about sending ships to the Mediteranian to releive Sr John Norris shall be laid before the Queen at Hampton Court on Monday next

I acquainted the Lds that the victuals and transports were ready for the recruits for Spain, Ordered that I should writte to the Admiralty for a convey for them to Corke & thence to Barcellona And to writte to the transports to goe for Corke immediatly & that an order should be sent to the Lds Justices of Ireland for their embarkation

Ordered that the Petition from the Leghorne Merchants shall be considered at a fuller Board.

[1] Duke of Buckingham.   [2] Earl of Rochester.   [3] Secretary for Scotland.
[4] Secretary of State (South).   [5] First Lord of the Admiralty.
[6] A Lord of the Admiralty.   [7] Commander-in-Chief.

(2) THE 'CABINET COUNCIL'

Hampton Court   Q[ueen]
Oct 16/1710   Ld Pres: Ld Cham[berlain]¹: D. Queens:
                 Mr Har[ley]²: Ld Dart:

---

ordered to writte to the Duke of Marlborough and lett him know no answer can be given to his letter of the 20th N.S. till he has sent an answer to mine of the 13th O.S. but that if he thincks fitt to goe on with the design all things are ready here and the 2 ships he mentions in his last will be so to if he sends directions for them

agreed that the Queen will take the 2,000 Horse for Spain upon the Terms propossed, but that I should writte to Ld Townshend³ to press the States as much as possible to agree to there Part, and in the mean while till we have an answer what they will doe not lett count Gallas⁴ know the Queen will take the troops otherwise than in conjunction with the States. and that I should writte to Mr Fryberg⁵ to press the States in this matter.

Ordered that I shall writte to Ld Townshend to press verry ernestly with the States to send as many ships as they can into the Mediterranian there being an account come to the Queen of a verry great Force fitting out at Toulon and that Mr Fryberg be desiered to acquaint the States with the Hazard her fleet runs upon their haveing withdrawn their squadron and that therefore they will send as many as they can as fast as they can without staying for there Marchant ships.

that the Lords of the Admiralty shall send to Sr Charles Hedges for his oppinion what directions are proper to be given in relation to the 2 Genoesse ships that are carried to Port Mahon

to send to the Ordinance upon my Ld Shannons demand of Tents for the men in the Isle of wight and also the demand for the men at Corke sent me from the Secretary of warr

---

¹ Duke of Shrewsbury.
² Chancellor of the Exchequer.
³ British plenipotentiary at the Hague.
⁴ Austrian envoy.
⁵ Dutch envoy.

(3) THE 'LORDS OF THE COMMITTEE'

Cockpitt   Ld Pres: Ld Cham: D. Queens: Ld Dart.
Oct 17/1710

Sr J Leak & Sr G. Byngs attended. & were called in. Ordered that the 2 shipps which attend at Helvettsluce for my Ld Rivers shall have orders from the Admiralty to follow my Ld Marlboroughs directions & that if the expedition requiers it before my Ld Rivers arrives he should make use of them if not there shall be two others ordered for that servis which I am to acquaint my Ld Marlborough with, the ships are the Pool and Experiment.

Count Gallas was desierd to come in, And he desired in the name of his master that the 2,000 Horse may be received & transported upon the same foot that several other reinforcements have been sent to Spain

Ordered that I should inquier what orders have been sent by my Ld Sunderland[1] to Sr J. Norris for obeying the King of Spain's orders in relation to Count Gallas's request that he may have orders to assist in the reduction of Siscily & the Coast of Tuscany and that it shall be considered another day.

Ordered that a copy of the Admiralty letter to me in relation to the fleet in the Mediteranian upon the Dutch squadrons being come away shall be sent to Ld Townshend. the Portugall Envoy was desired to come in, and Prosposes that there should be an assurance given to the King of Portugall that in case the King of Spain demands the assistance of the Portugesse troops in Spain the Queen will Protect Portugall, He was desierd to give in his propossal in writting.

Ordered to writte on Fryday next to Mr Chetwynds of Teurin and Genoa to acquaint them with the agreement for the 2000 Horse and that they should make preparations accordingly for transporting them into Spain.

To writte to Ld Shannon that I will Lay his letter before the Queen

To send Mr Roop's letter to the Admiralty

To send the Post Masters letter about the Paquet Boat for Lisbon to the Treasury, and to lett the Post Masters know that there is verry

---

[1] The previous Secretary of State (South).

great notice taken of all Peoples letters being opened which is supposed to be a fault in their own officers and that they should take cair to prevent such complaints for the future.

that Mr Harcourts Petition be reffered to the Treasury.

Dartmouth MSS., Oct. 13, 16 and 17, 1710. (I am grateful to Dr. J. H. Plumb for bringing these documents to my notice; and I wish to acknowledge the kindness of Lord Dartmouth and the Librarian of the William Salt Library, Stafford, who have granted permission to print them.)

60. Privy Council, Cabinet Council, and Inner Cabinet under George II, 1739.

DUKE OF ARGYLE [1 Mar 1739]

I remember, my lords, a very good saying of a noble lord, who once sat in this House, it was the late lord Peterborough: when he was asked by a friend, one day, his opinion of a certain measure; says my lord, in some surprise, 'This is the first time I ever heard of it.' 'Impossible,' says the other, 'why you are a privy counsellor.' 'So I am,' replies his lordship, 'and there is a cabinet counsellor coming up to us just now; if you ask the same question of him, he will perhaps hold his peace, and then you will think he is in the secret, but if he opens once his mouth about it, you will find he knows as little of it as I do.' My lords, it is not being in privy council, or in cabinet council, one must be in the minister's council to know the true motives of our late proceedings.

P.H., x, 1136.

61. Inner and Outer Cabinet minutes under George II, 1755.

(1) INNER CABINET

Newcastle House April 17th 1755

Present

Lord Chancellor	Earl of Holdernesse [Secretary of State]
Lord President	Lord Anson [First Lord of the Admiralty]
Duke of Newcastle [First Lord of the Treasury]	Sir Thomas Robinson [Secretary of State]

An extract of a letter from M. de Rouillé[1] to the Duc de Mirepoix,[2] dated the 13th Inst, and delivered by Him, this Day, to Sir Thomas

[1] French Minister of State.   [2] French Ambassador.

Robinson, was read to their Lordships, who were humbly of Opinion, that the said Extract should be laid, on Monday next, before the Lords of the Cabinet Council, by whom the Counter Project, and the last Answer, given to M. de Mirepoix, had been approved:—And that orders should be sent to the Lords of the Admiralty to add Three more Ships of the Line, and Frigate of Fifty Guns, to the Seven Ships of the Line, already under the Command of Vice Admiral Boscawen; and to direct Him to proceed immediately, therewith, to North America.

Their Lordships were, also, humbly of Opinion, that, as the Sending such a considerable Force to North America, will greatly weaken the remaining Fleet; It is now become absolutely necessary, that Twelve Hundred Land Forces should immediately be put on board the said remaining Fleet, till a sufficient Number of Marines can be raised, for the purpose.

(2) OUTER CABINET

Whitehall, April 22nd 1755

Present

Lord Chancellor   Duke of Dorset [Master of the
                                              Horse]
Lord President   Marquess of Hartington [Ld. Lieut.
                                              of Ireland]
Lord Privy Seal   Earl of Holdernesse [Secretary of
                                              State]
Lord Steward   Earl of Rochford [Groom of the
                                      Stole, and First Lord of the
                                              Bedchamber]
Lord Chamberlain   Lord Anson [First Lord of the
                                              Admiralty]
Duke of Argyle [Keeper of the   Mr Fox [Secretary at War]
    Great Seal]
Duke of Newcastle [First Lord   Sir Thom.ˢ Robinson [Secretary of
    of the Treasury]   State]

The Extract of M. de Rouillé's Letter of the 13th Inst, communicated to Sir Thomas Robinson by M. de Mirepoix, having been taken into Consideration, Their Lordships were humbly of Opinion, that an Answer, to the Purport of the inclosed Paper, should be delivered to the French Ambassador

Their Lordships were, likewise, of Opinion, that Directions should be sent to Vice Admiral Boscawen to proceed without loss of Time, to North America, with the Eleven Ships of the Line, and one Frigate, under His Command, pursuant to his former Instructions:—And that Twelve Hundred Land Forces should be immediately put on board the remaining Fleet, till a sufficient Number of Marines can be raised to replace them. Add. MSS., 32996, ff. 77 and 89.

62. Cabinet membership, 1801.

ADDINGTON TO LOUGHBOROUGH

Downing Street, April 25th, 1801.

MY DEAR LORD,

A misconception appears to have taken place, in consequence of which I am led to trouble your Lordship from various considerations, and particularly from a sense of duty to the King. I have reason to believe that his Majesty considered your Lordship's attendance at the Cabinet as having naturally ceased upon the resignation of the Seals,[1] and supposed it to be so understood by your Lordship. Much as I should feel personally gratified in having the benefit of your Lordship's counsel and assistance, I will fairly acknowledge to you, that I did not offer to his Majesty any suggestion to the contrary; and, indeed, I must have felt myself precluded from doing so by having previously in more instances than one expressed and acted upon the opinion, that the members of the Cabinet should not exceed that of the persons whose responsible situations in office require their being members of it. Under these circumstances, I feel that I have perhaps given way to a mistaken delicacy, in not having sooner made the communication to your Lordship; but I am persuaded you will see that I should be wanting in duty to the King, and in what is due to yourself, if I delayed it beyond the time when a minute of Cabinet with the names of the persons present must be prepared in order to be submitted to his Majesty.

I hope your Lordship will give me full credit for the motives by which I can alone be actuated upon this occasion, as well as for the sincere sentiments of esteem and regard with which I am, my dear Lord,

Your Lordship's most obedient and faithful servant,

HENRY ADDINGTON.

Lord J. Campbell, Lives of the Chancellors (1850), vol. VI, p. 314.

[1] He had been Chancellor.

63. A divided cabinet, 1779.

Lord North has the honour of informing his Majesty, that he has great reason to beleive that the object of Lord Shelbourne's motion in the House tomorrow, & of Lord Upper Ossory's in the House of Commons on Monday next is to blame in the strongest terms the delays which have prevail'd respecting Ireland, & to direct the whole blame at Lord North. That the movers expect to be supported by Lord Gower & his friends, & do not despair of the assistance of the Chancellor [Thurlow]. This expectation, wild as it appears, is not absolutely impossible, Lord Chancellor & Lord Stormont [Secretary of State] both on Saturday last & yesterday, have given in the Cabinet the strongest marks of their dislike to Lord North. As they are two of the ablest, if not, the two ablest servants which his Majesty has, their dislike to and disapprobation of Lord North will render it almost impracticable for his Majesty's affairs to be carried on by the present Ministry. His Majesty had better part with Lord North a thousand times than lose the assistance of the other two. The Chancellor not only strongly reprobates the conduct of Lord North in the meetings of the Cabinet, but in his communication with several persons frequently repeats that it is necessary that Lord North should be removed. Lord North hardly thinks that he will in a public Debate say anything tomorrow which may amount to an open breach, but his sentiments are so well known that the opposition have conceived great hopes of the part he will act tomorrow. It is said that these two motions are to be followed by an impeachment of Lord North, from whence Lord North expects no mischief personally to himself & which he wishes to meet, if possible, out of office, & trust to his innocence alone & the protection of the Law. What, however, concerns him only is a matter not worth a moment of his Majesty's consideration, but it deserves well the matured deliberation, whether in the midst of these growing difficulties it is not become indispensable necessary for his Majesty to turn in his thoughts some new arrangement. Lord North himself is so broken in memory, in spirits, & in bodily strength that he cannot hope to be able to serve well much longer, however ready he may [be] to sacrifice all his wishes, and all his feelings to his Majesty's commands. After the declarations of Lord Rockingham's friends & of Mr Fox on the first day of the Session, Lord North conjectures that Lord Shelburne

& his little party may be easily induced to make up an administration with Lord Chancellor, Lord Stormont, Lord Gower & His friends, especially while the effect of the Majorities at the opening of the Session remains, but that moment will pass, & these persons be plunged into a determined opposition against a divided Cabinet, who will not, in that case, be able to do right in any one of the great questions which are before us. To this misfortune must be added that Lord North disapproved by his brethren in Cabinet will not be fairly supported in the House as the long conversation he has had with the Attorney General gives him every reason to doubt whether he will not leave him soon on some very material question. Lord North thought it his duty to mention all these circumstances to the King that his Majesty may be able to determine what is best for himself & for the public. Lord North will be fairly driven away in the course of the Session, & a party coming in victoriously will carry their expectations very high indeed. . . .

Downing Street. Nov. 30. 1779.

Corresp. George III, No. 2855.

64. The king and cabinet procedure, 1782.

LORD SHELBURNE TO THE KING

29 April, 1782.

. . . I must take that, or some opportunity of stating what I conceive the natural course of business to be, first for the Department to submit any business to Your Majesty, and to be consider'd afterwards by the Cabinet under Your Majesty's Reference.

KING TO LORD SHELBURNE

Queen's House, April 29th, 1782
m. past A.M. [sic]

. . . Certainly it is quite new for business to be laid before the Cabinet and consequently advice offered by the Ministers to the Crown unasked; the Minister of the Department used always to ask the permission of the King to lay such a point before the Cabinet, as he cldnt chuse to venture to take the direction of Crown upon without such sanction; then the Advice came with propriety.

Corresp. George III, Nos. 3699, 3700.

65. Cabinet procedure, 1796.

LORD GRENVILLE TO GEORGE III

1796, January 30, Downing Street.—Lord Grenville has the honour to submit to your Majesty the draft of a dispatch to Sir Morton Eden, which was this day read and approved at the meeting of your Majesty's confidential servants, as a measure which the circumstances and situation of public affairs appear to render necessary and expedient. Considering the great importance of the subject, Lord Grenville does not presume to take this step without previously submitting it to your Majesty's consideration, but he would not discharge his duty to your Majesty if he did not take the liberty to add that, as far as he is capable of forming a judgement upon the subject, such a declaration or communication as is there mentioned, especially if it can be made jointly in your Majesty's name and that of the Emperor, could not but produce the most advantageous effects both at home and abroad . . .

. . . Lord Grenville is by no means insensible that to these considerations others of great weight may be opposed, as is natural with respect to a subject so extensive in its nature and so important in its consequences. In humbly submitting to your Majesty those arguments and that opinion which prevail in his judgement, he discharges the duty which he owes to your Majesty, and he trusts to the experience which he has often had of your Majesty's goodness for a favourable interpretation of them. If your Majesty should on the whole be pleased to authorise him to send the dispatch in its present form, it will, he presumes, be necessary to make communications of a similar import (as far as the difference of circumstances may permit) to your Majesty's other allies, and Lord Grenville will in that case lose no time in executing the business in that shape.

GEORGE III TO LORD GRENVILLE

1796, January 31, Windsor.—I have this morning received Lord Grenville's note accompanying the draft of a dispatch to Sir Morton Eden, read and approved yesterday at a meeting of the Cabinet, which [in] the circumstances and situation of public affairs appeared to them to be necessary and expedient. I do not in the least mean to make any obstinate resistance to the measure proposed, though I own I cannot feel the utility of it; my mind is not of a nature to be guided by the object of obtaining a little applause, or staving off some abuse; rectitude of conduct is my sole aim. I trust the rulers in France will reject any proposition from hence short of a total giving up of every advantage we may have gained, and therefore that the measure proposed will meet with a refusal.

H.M.C., *Dropmore*, III, 169.

66. Cabinet procedure, 1806.

[written in 1837]

When I came into office, [1806] I was curious to understand the course of proceeding or interior constitution of our Government. It is vague in the extreme, and often irregular and inconvenient. The Cabinet, which is legally only a Committee of the Privy Council appointed by the King on each distinct occasion, has gradually assumed the character and in some measure the reality of a permanent council, through which advice on all matters of great importance is conveyed to the Crown. But though the necessity of a well-concerted or party Government in a limited monarchy and popular constitution, has generally established the wholesome doctrine, that each and every member of the Cabinet is in some degree responsible for the measures adopted by the Government while he is a member of it, yet there are no precise laws nor rules, nor even any well-established or understood usages which mark what measures in each department are or are not to be communicated to the Cabinet. Measures of foreign policy seem indeed more emphatically designated by the history of the origin of this committee in Charles the Second's time, by usage and by reason as the objects of their deliberation. Yet there is nothing but private agreement or party feeling generally, or the directions of the King accidentally, which obliges even a Secretary for Foreign Affairs to consult his colleagues on any of the duties of his office before he takes the King's pleasure upon them. In all Administrations I believe, and in ours I am sure, his dispatches, his measures, and even his appointments were more generally submitted to the judgment of the Cabinet than those in any other department. When a Cabinet is held at a publick office, it is generally at the Foreign Office. The acts of that office, however, are not invariably nor necessarily laid before the Cabinet; and the Secretary of State at his own discretion advises and completes many without any such consultation. In the other branches of administration, such as the Treasury, the Home Secretaryship, the

Chancery, the Admiralty, the discretion is yet larger as to the matters in their respective departments on which the Ministers take the King's pleasure directly or previously consult their colleagues before they advise him. Nomination to places is, for obvious reasons, seldom submitted to the consideration of the Cabinet. Yet by usage, arising out of the necessity of placing a large portion of that species of power in one department, the patronage does *not* always in practice or substance belong to those officers who are the legal channels, and consequently in a strict constitutional sense, the sole legal and ostensible advisers, of the appointment. Thus, for instance, the First Lord of the Treasury actually and constantly takes the King's pleasure on the appointment to many dignities and places, to the warrant, patent, or instrument for which he neither affixes signature nor seal, but which are conferred by the Great Seal, the Privy Seal, and the Signet. Such an undefined distribution of authority, and the want of a distinct line between the jurisdiction of the Cabinet and the individual Ministers who compose it, as well as between the jurisdiction of their respective offices, is sometimes convenient to the publick service; inasmuch as the person whose abilities qualify him for the largest share of power, may from other circumstances be incapacitated from holding the office which would technically render him responsible for the exercise of it. On the other hand, the looseness of the obligation of referring the measures of each department to the Cabinet, and the undefined limits of the authority of many of the high offices, afford great scope for intrigue and cabal with the Crown. A favourite might by these means contrive insensibly to separate his interests from those of his colleagues, and at the secret suggestion of a King thwart the measures and defeat the views of a council which, though not technically, is virtually responsible to the publick for the whole conduct of affairs. These remarks are speculations resulting from reflection, not the fruit of experience.

Lord Holland, *Memoirs of the Whig Party* (1852), vol. II, p. 84.

67. Collective responsibility, 1806.

Debate on Lord Chief Justice Ellenborough's seat in the Cabinet 3 Mar 1806.

CASTLEREAGH . . . Being unable to sustain his argument either on the ground of precedent or analogy, the right hon. gent. (Mr Fox) endeavours at once to get rid of the motion, by assuming that there is no such body known to the law or constitution, as a Cabinet council; that responsibility cannot attach to the individuals composing such a body, and that the constitution knows no responsibility except in those executive officers of the crown, who in their respective departments carry the king's orders into execution. . . . Is not the Cabinet, in the modern practice of the constitution, as well known to parliament as if the existence of such a council had been an object of express legislative provision? have not the members of the Cabinet been always considered by the country, and have they not always considered themselves, whatever may have been their offices, or even if they sat there without office, both as individually and collectively responsible for the measures of government? It may frequently be more difficult to establish the fact of participation in the guilt of any criminal measure against the minister who has only advised, than it would be to prove it against the minister who has executed a measure, no other evidence being required in the latter case, than the order or instrument by which the criminal act has been either directed or performed. But the greater or less degree of difficulty which may attend the proofs of the fact, in particular instances, cannot affect the general question of responsibility. When the commons impeached lord Somers, lord Halifax, and lord Orford, on account of the Partition Treaty, neither the lord Treasurer, lord Halifax nor lord Orford, who presided at the Admiralty, could in the right hon. gent.'s sense of responsibility be deemed responsible; yet the house of commons never hesitated to consider them as equally answerable for that measure with their colleagues in the government. The right hon. gent. has admitted that any privy counsellor is liable to answer for the advice which he may give to the crown; but he cannot by such admission exempt those privy counsellors who are avowedly selected, habitually to advise his majesty on the current affairs of his government, from that general responsibility which results of course from their being charged with the duty of giving that advice constantly and systematically, which other privy counsellors are in the habit of giving only occasionally, if at all. Independently, however, of the application of the right hon. gent's argument to the present question, it is of no small importance that the country at large, and that Europe should be informed, whether the Cabinet council generally, with the noble lord (Grenville) at its head, is to be considered as responsible for all the measures of government, or whether those alone who carry into execution the respective acts are answerable? It is right that it should be distinctly understood, whether the only security we have for the administration of foreign affairs on wise and sound principles is the right hon. gent. himself; whether the military system of the country is exclusively committed to the separate responsibility of the secretary of state for the war department, and whether the first lord of the treasury's responsibility is in the present administration, to be really viewed upon all the questions not immediately relating to his own immediate department, in no other light than in that of an ordinary privy counsellor?

P.D., VI, 326.

68. 'Primere' Minister, 1711.

[April, 1711]

... the Duke of Newcastle sent for me to his house, and told me ... that nothing in the present posture of affairs could establish the security of the Protestant religion, and the tranquillity of England, but Mr Harley's taking the white staff, and thereby becoming the "Primere" Minister.

H.M.C., *Portland*, V, 655 (Memoirs of the Harley family).

69. Chief Minister, 1714.

On the State of Party at the Accession of George I by Mr Wortley

... Mr Walpole is already looked upon as the chief minister, made so by Lord Townshend; and when he is in the Treasury, it will be thought that the King has declared him so. The Duke of Albemarle, Lord Shaftesbury, Lord Clifford, afterwards Treasurer, were all Commissioners at a time. In King William's [reign] Lord Godolphin was third Commissioner of the Treasury after having been Secretary of State. Lord Montagu was one of the seven Regents in King William's absence. Great men have generally been of the Treasury; and when a Commissioner of the Treasury has equal favour with any of the other ministers, he will be first minister.

Can it be for the honour of the Government to have a man marked for corruption declared first minister? Can he bear the envy of having such a post? especially when he has the places of two Paymasters, and a place for his uncle, though a Tory.

If he is to be in it (*the treasury*), is it reasonable he should make all the rest?

The Commissioners of the Treasury has [*sic*] commonly been all men of great figure, and independent of one another, chose by the King's favour.

If the list of the Commissioners of the Treasury in King William's time be looked over, it is plain he chose men not likely to be of the same opinion; in King Charles's time it was plainly so too.

My Lord Oxford was the first commissioner that chose all his brethren, and it is plain what was the ill consequence of giving him so uncontrolled a power.

If there be one or two in the commission who are not of Mr Walpole's choosing, they cannot hinder any of his projects, so that they can do no harm; and can do no good but to inform the King of his affairs. This is what Mr Walpole will endeavour to prevent all he can.

Lord Wharncliffe (ed.), *Letters and Works of Lady Mary Wortley Montagu* (1837), vol. I, p. 127.

70. Walpole and the cabinet, 1735.

Whatever step Sir Robert Walpole took in England with regard to all these negotiations, though concerted solely, and concluded absolutely, in reality by the Queen and him in her closet, wore the face of being always as much the act of the whole Cabinet Council as theirs, not a letter coming from Hanover relating to these things that was not communicated to the Cabinet Council, nor any piece of advice sent thither but what was signed by them. So that Sir Robert Walpole, with a dexterity equal to his power, whilst in fact he did everything alone, was responsible for nothing but in common, whilst those ciphers of the Cabinet signed everything he dictated, and, without the least share of honour or power, bound themselves equally with him in case this political merchant should be bankrupt.

John, Lord Hervey, *Memoirs of Reign of George II* (1931), ed. R. Sedgwick, vol. II, p. 469.

71. Walpole accused of being Prime Minister, 1741.

Mr Sandys

. . . I know, Sir, it will be objected, that as every material step in the late conduct of our public affairs, either at home or abroad, has been authorized or approved of by parliament, what I have said must be looked on as a general charge against his majesty's counsels and our parliaments, rather than a personal charge against any one minister;

but this, upon a due consideration, becomes the most heavy, and the most evident charge against the minister I aim at. According to our constitution, we can have no sole and prime minister: we ought always to have several prime ministers or officers of state: every such officer has his own proper department; and no officer ought to meddle in the affairs belonging to the department of another. But it is publicly known, that this minister, having obtained a sole influence over all our public counsels, has not only assumed the sole direction of all public affairs, but has got every officer of state removed that would not follow his direction, even in the affairs belonging to his own proper department. By this means he hath monopolized all the favours of the crown, and engrossed the sole disposal of all places, pensions, titles, and ribbons, as well as of all preferments, civil, military or ecclesiastical.

This, Sir, is of itself a most heinous offence against our constitution: but he has greatly aggravated the heinousness of his crime; for, having thus monopolized all the favours of the crown, he has made a blind submission to his direction at elections and in parliament, the only ground to hope for any honours or preferments, and the only tenure by which any gentleman could preserve what he had. This is so notoriously known, that it can stand in need of no proof. Have not many deserving gentlemen been disappointed in the preferment they had a just title to, upon the bare suspicion of not being blindly devoted to his personal interest? Have not some persons of the highest rank and most illustrious characters been displaced, for no other reason than because they disdained to sacrifice their honour and conscience to his direction in parliament? As no crime, no neglect, no misbehaviour could ever be objected to them, as no other reason could ever be assigned for depriving the crown of their service, this only could be the reason. Nay, has not this minister himself not only confessed it, but boasted of it? Has he not said, and in this House too, that he would be a pitiful fellow of a minister who did not displace any officer that opposed his measures in Parliament?

Can any gentleman who heard this declaration desire a proof of the minister's misconduct, or of his crimes? Was not this openly avowing one of the most heinous crimes that can be committed by a minister in this Kingdom? Was it not avowing that he had made use of the favours of the crown for obtaining a corrupt majority in both Houses of Parliament, and keeping that majority in a slavish dependence upon himself alone? Do not we all know, that even the King himself is not, by our constitution, to take notice of any man's behaviour in parliament, far less to make that behaviour a means by which he is to obtain, or a tenure by which he is to hold, the favour of the crown?

And shall we allow a minister not only to do, but openly to avow, what he ought to be hanged for, should he advise his sovereign to do so? It is by means of this crime, Sir, that the minister I am speaking of has obtained the authority or approbation of parliament in every step of his conduct, and therefore that authority or approbation is so far from being an alleviation, that it is a most heavy aggravation of every wrong step which he has thus got authorised or approved of by parliament. For this reason, in considering any particular step of his conduct, its being authorised or approved by parliament can have no weight in his favour, whatever it may have against him. If the step was in itself weak or wicked, or if it now appears from its consequences to have been so, its having been approved of, or authorised by parliament, must be supposed to have proceeded either from his having misled the parliament by false glosses and asseverations, or from his having over-awed a majority by means of that crime which he has since openly avowed.

P.H., XI, 1232.

72. Walpole denies being Prime Minister, 1741.

SIR ROBERT WALPOLE

... Have gentlemen produced one instance of this exorbitant power, of the influence which I extend to all parts of the nation, of the tyranny with which I oppress those I oppose, and the liberality with which I reward those who support me? But having first invested me with a kind of mock dignity, and styled me a prime minister, they impute to me an unpardonable abuse of that chimerical authority which they only have created and conferred. If they are really persuaded that the army is annually established by me, that I have the sole disposal of posts and honours, that I employ this power in the destruction of liberty, and the diminution of commerce, let me awaken them from their delusion. Let me expose to their view the real condition of the public weal; let me show them that the crown has made no encroachments, that all supplies have been granted by parliament, that all questions have been debated with the same freedom as before the fatal period in which my counsels are said to have gained the ascendancy;

an ascendancy from which they deduce the loss of trade, the approach of slavery, the proponderance of prerogative, and the extension of influence. But I am far from believing that they feel those apprehensions which they so earnestly labour to communicate to others, and I have too high an opinion of their sagacity not to conclude that, even in their own judgement, they are complaining of grievances that they do not suffer, and promoting rather their private interests than that of the public.

What is this unbounded sole power which is imputed to me? How has it discovered itself, or how has it been proved?

What have been the effects of the corruption, ambition and avarice, with which I am so abundantly charged?

Have I ever been suspected of being corrupted? A strange phenomenon, a corrupter himself not corrupt! Is ambition imputed to me? Why then do I still continue a commoner? I, who refused a white staff and a peerage. I had, indeed, like to have forgotten the little ornament about my shoulders, which gentlemen have so repeatedly mentioned in terms of sarcastic obloquy. But surely, though this may be regarded with envy or indignation in another place, it cannot be supposed to raise any resentment in this House, where many may be pleased to see those honours which their ancestors have worn, restored again to the Commons.

Have I given any symptoms of an avaricious disposition? Have I obtained any grants from the crown since I have been placed at the head of the treasury? Has my conduct been different from that which others in the same station would have followed? Have I acted wrong in giving the place of auditor to my son, and in providing for my own family? I trust that their advancement will not be imputed to me as a crime, unless it shall be proved that I placed them in offices of trust and responsibility for which they were unfit.

But while I unequivocally deny that I am sole and prime minister, and that to my influence and direction all the measures of government must be attributed, yet I will not shrink from the responsibility which attaches to the post I have the honour to hold; and should during the long period in which I have sat upon this bench, any one step taken by government be proved to be either disgraceful or disadvantageous to the nation, I am ready to hold myself accountable.

To conclude, Sir, though I shall always be proud of the honour of any trust or confidence from his majesty, yet I shall always be ready to remove from his counsels and presence, when he thinks fit; and therefore I should think myself very little concerned in the event of the present question, if it were not for the encroachment that will thereby be made upon the prerogatives of the crown. But I must think, that an address to his majesty to remove one of his servants, without so much as alleging any particular crime against him, is one of the greatest encroachments that was ever made upon the prerogatives of the crown; and therefore, for the sake of my master, without any regard for my own, I hope all those that have a due regard for our constitution, and for the rights and prerogatives of the crown, without which our constitution cannot be preserved, will be against this motion.

P.H., XI, 1295, note.

73. George II and the First Lord of the Treasury, 1755.

LORD CHANCELLOR [HARDWICKE] TO THE DUKE OF NEWCASTLE

Powis House, Jan. 3rd, 1755. At night.

... After we had looked at each other rather more than a minute, the King made the usual sign when he dismisses one. I said not one syllable more about Joe,[1] but instantly said I thought it my duty to mention to His Majesty that, though I had not seen your Grace, I had received a letter from you last night, by which I found you were under the greatest concern that His Majesty should interpret the opinion you gave him for suspending the disposition of the Groom of the Stole for the present, as proceeding from any other motive than the real one, a desire that it might be further considered by His Majesty. The King grew warm, and said, "The Duke of Newcastle meddles in things he has nothing to do with. He would dispose of my Bedchamber, which is a personal service about myself, and I wont suffer anybody to meddle in. I know what he wanted; he wanted to recommend my Lord Lincoln or his brother-in-law." Here I interposed, and assured His Majesty that I did, in my conscience, believe your Grace did not intend to have proposed any particular person, much less my Lord Lincoln or the Duke of Leeds, and that you had never given me the least hint of it. ... His Majesty then talked of his Father's having been in the right in resolving to have no Groom of the Stole, and of Sunderland's having forced him to make him etc.; that the Treasury was the Duke of Newcastle's department, and that was business enough etc.; that

---

[1] Colonel Joseph Yorke, his son.

your Grace had begun at the wrong end, and proposed Lords of the Bedchamber to him before there was any vacancy there. To this I said that the head of his Treasury was indeed an employment of great business, very extensive, which always went beyond the bare management of the revenue; that it extended through both Houses of Parliament, the members of which were naturally to look thither; that there must be some principal person to receive applications, to hear the wants and the wishes and the requests of mankind, with the reasons of them, in order to lay them before His Majesty for his determination; that it was impossible for the King to be troubled with all this himself. This he in part admitted, but there were some things nobody should meddle in etc. I said it was only a method of laying things before him, and the absolute final decision was in *him*; that it had been always the usage in this Country, and I supposed was so in others; that without it no administration could be enabled to serve him, that ministers bore all the blame and resentment of disappointed persons, and they could never carry on his affairs without having some weight in the disposition of favours. The King said, he had seen too much of that in this Country already, and it was time to change it in some degree. . . .

P. C. Yorke, *Life of Hardwicke* (Cambridge, 1913), vol. II, p. 224.

74. George III and the Prime Minister, 1764.

MR GRENVILLE'S DIARY

Friday, 23rd [March, 1764]. When Mr Grenville went to the King, His Majesty talked to him with more than ordinary goodness, said he was sensible of the weight and authority that he had given to his government, that it was always his opinion that it would be so, but that now, all the world confessed it as well as himself; that it was necessary to lodge the power of the government in one man alone, and that Mr Grenville was the person in whom he wished to see it; that when Lord Egremont was alive, it was necessary from particular circumstances to make that power more equal in the three Ministers; that he meant it should be in him; that to him he gave, and would give his confidence; that it would be necessary for Mr Grenville to keep certain managements with the two Secretaries of State and the Duke of Bedford, but that must be at his own discretion, for that it was his desire and purpose that all recommendations and appointments should come through Mr Grenville.

W. J. Smith (ed.), *Grenville Papers* (1852–3), vol. II, p. 499.

75. Prime Minister: North's view, 1778.

LORD NORTH TO THE KING

[10 Nov. 1778]

There are two points, which Lord North has the honour of submitting to his Majesty's consideration, & which he conceives very important for the government of his country.

The first is, That the Public business can never go on as it ought, while the Principal & most efficient offices are in the hands of persons who are either indifferent to, or actually dislike their situation.

The second is, That in critical times, it is necessary that there should be one directing Minister, who should plan the whole of the operations of government, & controul all the other departments of administration so far as to make them co-operate zealously & actively with his designs even tho contrary to their own.

Lord North conceives these two rules to be wise & true, & therefore, thinks it his duty to submit the expediency of his Majesty's removing him as soon as he can, because he is certainly not capable of being such a minister as he has described, & he can never like a situation which he has most perfectly disliked even in much better and easier times.

Corresp. George III, No. 2446.

76. Prime Minister: Pitt's view, 1803.

LORD MELVILLE TO MR ADDINGTON

Walmer Castle, March 22, 1803.

. . . Besides this consideration, he [Pitt] stated, not less pointedly and decidedly, his sentiments with regard to the absolute necessity there is in the conduct of the affairs of this country, that there should be an avowed and real Minister, possessing the chief weight in the council, and the principal place in the confidence of the King. In that respect there can be no rivality or division of power. That power must rest in the person generally called the First Minister, and that Minister ought, he thinks, to be the person at the head of the finances. He knows, to his own comfortable experience, that notwithstanding the abstract truth of that general proposition, it is noways incompatible with the most cordial concert and mutual exchange of advice and intercourse amongst the different branches of executive departments; but still if it should come unfortunately to such a radical difference of opinion that no spirit of conciliation or concession can reconcile, the sentiments of the Minister must be allowed and understood to prevail, leaving the other members of the administration to act as they may conceive themselves conscientiously called upon to act under such circumstances. During the last administration such a collision of opinion I believe scarcely ever happened, or, at least, was not such as the parties felt themselves obliged to push to extremities; but still it is possible, and the only remedy applicable to it is in the principle which I have explained.

Earl Stanhope, *Life of William Pitt* (1867), vol. IV, p. 24.

77. George III demands guarantees on policy, 1807.

GEORGE III TO LORD GRENVILLE

1807, March 17. Windsor Castle.—The King has lost no time in dictating the answer to the minute of Cabinet. Lord Grenville will receive it enclosed, and his Majesty desires he will communicate it to his colleagues, trusting at the same time that Lord Grenville will see the propriety, with a view to the prevention of all future mistakes, that when they shall have duly considered the latter part of his Majesty's answer, their determination should be stated on paper.

Enclosed.

1807, March 17. Windsor Castle.—The King having fully considered what is submitted in the minute of Cabinet which he received yesterday morning, desires Lord Grenville will communicate to those of his confidential servants who were present, his sentiments and observations upon the contents of that minute, as hereafter expressed. His Majesty has learned with satisfaction that they have determined not to press forward any further the discussion of the Bill depending in Parliament,[1] and he is sensible of the deference shown to his sentiments and his feelings. But he regrets that, while they have felt bound as his Ministers to adopt this line of conduct, they should as individuals consider it necessary to state to Parliament opinions which are known to be so decidedly contrary to his principles, at a moment too, when it is the declared object of his Government not to encourage any dispositions on the part of the Roman Catholics of Ireland to prefer a petition to Parliament.

[1] To grant commissions in the forces to Roman Catholics.

From the latter part of the minute the King must conclude that, although the Bill now depending is dropped, they have been unable to make up their minds not to press upon him in future, measures *connected with a question* which has already proved so distressing to him; nor can his Majesty conceal from them, that *this intimation* on their part, *unless withdrawn*, will leave the matter in a state most embarrassing and unsatisfactory to him, and, in his opinion not less so to them. The King therefore considers it due to himself, and consistent with the fair and upright conduct which it has and ever will be his object to observe towards everyone, to declare at once, most unequivocally, that upon this subject his sentiments never can change, that he cannot *ever* agree to any *concessions to the Catholics* which his confidential servants may in future propose to him, and that under these circumstances, and after what has passed, his mind cannot be at ease, unless he shall receive *a positive assurance from them, which shall effectually relieve him from all future apprehension.*

LORD GRENVILLE TO GEORGE III

1807, March 18. Downing Street.—Lord Grenville has the honour most humbly to lay before your Majesty the minute of a meeting of such of your Majesty's servants as are therein named, which was held tonight at Earl Spencer's House.

Enclosure

CABINET MINUTE

1807, March 18. At the Earl Spencer's.

Present:

The Lord Privy Seal	Lord Henry Petty.
Earl Spencer.	Lord Grenville.
Earl of Moira.	Mr Secretary Windham.
Viscount Howick.	Mr Grenville.

Your Majesty's servants have considered with the most respectful and dutiful attention the answer which your Majesty has done them the honour to return to their minute of the 15th instant. They beg leave most humbly to represent to your Majesty that, at the time when your Majesty was graciously pleased to call them to your councils, no assurance was required from them inconsistent with those duties which are inseparable from that station. Had any such assurance been demanded, they must have expressed, with all humility and duty, the absolute impossibility of their thus fettering the free exercise of their judgment. Those who are entrusted by your Majesty with the administration of your extensive empire, are bound by every obligation to submit to your Majesty without reserve the best advice which they can frame to meet the various exigences and dangers of the times. The situation of Ireland appears to your Majesty's servants to constitute the most formidable part of the present difficulties of the empire. This subject must, as they conceive, require a continued and vigilant attention and a repeated consideration of every fresh circumstance which may call for the interposition of your Majesty's Government or of Parliament. In forbearing to urge any further while employed in your Majesty's service, a measure which would in their judgment have tended to compose the present uneasiness in Ireland, and have been productive of material benefit to the empire, they humbly submit to your Majesty that they have gone to the utmost possible limits of their public duty; but that it would be deeply criminal in them, with the general opinions which they entertain on the subject, to bind themselves to withhold from your Majesty under all the various circumstances which may arise, those councils which may eventually appear to them indispensably necessary for the peace and tranquillity of Ireland, and for defeating the enterprizes of the enemy against the very existence of your Majesty's empire.

Your Majesty's servants must ever deeply regret that any difficulty should arise on their part, in giving the most prompt obedience to any demand which your Majesty considers as indispensable to the ease of your Majesty's mind. But it is not possible for them consistently with any sense of those obligations which must always attach on the sworn councillors of your Majesty, to withdraw a statement which was not made without the most anxious consideration of every circumstance which could be suggested by their earnest desire for your Majesty's ease, comfort, and happiness; or to give assurances which would impose upon them a restraint incompatible with the faithful discharge of the most important duty which they owe your Majesty.

H.M.C., Dropmore, IX, 118.

CHAPTER 3

PARLIAMENT

I. LORDS AND COMMONS

Though the House of Commons was the stronger of the two Houses of Parliament, owing to its representative nature and to its exclusive power of initiating financial measures, the upper House was still possessed of enormous resources of power. Its assent was necessary to all legislation; and when the ministers and the Lords were in harmony (as they usually were) it formed a very useful 'longstop' to measures which the government could not kill, or did not wish openly to kill, in the Commons (78). But its influence was far more extensive. Most cabinet ministers sat in the Lords, and, in any case, individual lords had the right to offer the Crown advice even if they were not in the government. Through their property they controlled large numbers of constituencies and therefore of members of the House of Commons (79). The leaders of the army, the navy, the civil departments, the Church and local government sat in the Lords, and thus their influence was felt in all aspects of government throughout the length and breadth of the kingdom.

The relations between the two Houses partook of that harmony which the eighteenth-century system of government managed to achieve most of the time. The Lords tended to support the king; the king and his ministers had disciplinary powers over them through the bishops,[1] the Scottish representative peers (80) and the creation of new peers; and the Lords had their constitutional, and extra-constitutional control over the Commons. However, Blackstone's 'three distinct powers in mechanics' sometimes failed to 'jointly impel the machinery of government'[2] and one result could be quarrels between the two Houses, as in Queen Anne's reign,[3] when the eighteenth-century system was not fully established, and later, when it was beginning to disintegrate.

78. House of Lords as 'longstop', 1772.

LORD NORTH TO THE KING

[3 April, 1772]

Lord North was prevented from paying his duty to his Majesty yesterday at St James's by business which required his early attendance

---

[1] See Chapter 5, pp. 326–7.   [2] See No. 24, p. 75.
[3] For example, over the case of *Ashby* v. *White*: see pp. 221–2.

at the House of Commons and detained him till near five o'clock. He had the honour of his Majesty's commands yesterday Evening, and had soon after a meeting of the Principal Members of Parliament concerning the Dissenters petition. The Gentlemen continued till eleven o'clock in Downing Street, discussing the proper course to be held today. Lord North is sorry to inform his Majesty, that upon the best information that he has received there is not merely a possibility or a probability but a certainty that he will be beat if he opposes this measure in the House of Commons: The Opposition are all united in favour of it, and one half of the friends of Government will either stay away, or vote with the Opposition. The greater number of the gentlemen, who were with Ld North last night strongly dissuaded him from attempting to throw it out in the House of Commons: Those whose elections principally depend upon Presbyterians, must vote for this petition; Those, who have a few dissenting constituents would avoid voting at all, as they are sure that their Dissenting friends would resent it, and that their Church of England would not thank them: Upon the whole, they look'd upon it as one of those bills, which ought to be thrown out by the House of Peers and not by the Commons, and conceiving that they had given evident proofs of their attachment to the Church in two instances during the present Sessions, think it hard to be press'd a third time in a case, where their conduct may endanger their own seat, but where the Lords may act with perfect freedom, and without the least apprehension.

Lord North will not fail to attend his Majesty at St James's this morning, when he will explain the matter more at large.

Downing Street *Friday morn:*

Corresp. George III, No. 1049.

79. Electoral influence of the Lords, 1719.

A restraint upon the Number of the Lords will necessarily restrain the Influence of that Body in the Election of Members to serve in the Lower House. It is very well known, that few Members of the House of Commons are advanc'd to Peerage, who have not one or more Corporations under their Direction: Nay, that very often, this is one Reason for their Promotion. If, therefore, this perpetually increasing Body of Lords continues on the foot it is now, in Proportion as their Number is augmented, their Influence in Elections will grow more general, till at length, as the Upper House are the Creature of the

Crown, the Lower House may be in a great Measure the Creature of the Lords: And it is worth while to consider, whether in Process of Time, unless seasonably prevented, the House of Commons may not be filled with Stewards and Bayliffs of our Peers.

The Old Whig (1719), Number 1, para. 21.

80. Bishops and Scottish peers, 1780.

[10 Mar. 1780]

THE EARL OF EFFINGHAM . . .

The influence of the crown could hardly be denied; hopes and fears were created in the breasts of men according to their different tempers and dispositions. The influence of preferment, in expectation, or the anxiousness of retaining what we already held, was a pervading principle. The right reverend bench, for instance, were not affected by any fear of losing the very respectable rank and emoluments they held in the state; but still, in some minds, translations to higher dignities and greater emoluments might be not entirely overlooked. A certain part of the peerage, whose seats in that House stood upon a different footing from those who enjoyed that right by inheritance, he meant the peerage of Scotland; those two descriptions threw a great weight into the scale of the crown.

P.H., XXI, 229.

II. ELECTIONS

THE PATRONS

The choosing of representatives was quite separate from the choosing of ministers. The hustings was a different world from the lobby; its contests were fought at different times, on different issues, by different methods. General elections, which, after the Septennial Act (**116**), took place at fairly regular intervals every seven years till 1784, did not coincide with changes of government; and the electorate chose Members of Parliament, not governments or programmes, and they based their choice on local and personal, and seldom on national, issues. Left to itself, the system would have produced a House of Commons of independent members; and government would have been impossible had not ministers and magnates imposed some sort of pattern by 'influencing' the elections. This was the oil for the 'machinery of government', which, in the absence of the secret ballot and in the presence of eighteenth-century standards of public morality, lubricated the whole system, as Brown puts it, 'from the lowest *Cobler* in a *Borough*, to the *King's* *first Minister*' (**81**). By its operation ministers ensured the election of a number of members sufficient to facilitate (though not to eliminate) the task of binding the House of Commons to their will, thus making government possible (**82**). Such a member toed the line because of one, or a combination of several, of the following circumstances. He might have, or expect to have, a place, or a pension, or a government contract for himself or for a friend or relation (**83**). He might sit for a government borough; or for a private borough of a member or a supporter of the government (**84**). Or he might have been given financial support by the government to fight a seat for himself (**92**). The government had private seats available because their owners expected places or high honours in return (**85**), which they felt they deserved as a reward for their 'slavery' (**86**), or as 'interest on the capital sunk' (**87**). A candidate with no 'interest' in a seat had to find a patron, or buy himself a seat at great expense (**88**); and purchase was the only resource for a candidate who wished to retain his political independence, unless he was lucky enough to find a patron who would allow him to vote as he wished (**89**), or unless he was a statesman of the rank of a Fox or a Pitt.

The organisation of this vast and delicate web of 'influence', the ramifications of which are described by Douglas (**83**), was the task principally of the First Lord of the Treasury and his Secretary, whose work went on continuously, and was not confined to those septennial periods of excitement known as 'making a parliament'. And a statesman would not for long have the chance (as Carteret put it) 'to make kings and emperors, and to maintain the balance of Europe',[1] unless he also had his eyes on the freeholders of the smallest villages in England (**90, 91, 92, 100, 105**); for in the opposition there were plenty of patrons waiting to do his work for him (**93**).

81. 'Influence' in general: a critic's view, 1758.

The Restraints laid on the royal Prerogative at the Revolution, and the Accession of Liberty thus gained by the People, produced two Effects with Respect to Parliaments. One was that, instead of being *occasionally*, they were thence-forward *annually* assembled: The other was, that whereas, on any trifling Offence given, they had been usually *intimidated* or *dissolved*, they now found themselves possessed of new *Dignity* and *Power*; their consent being necessary for raising the *annual Supplies*.

No body of Men, except in the simplest and most virtuous Times, ever found themselves possessed of Power, but many of them would attempt to turn it to their private Advantage. Thus the Parliaments

---

[1] H. Walpole, *Memoires of the Last Ten Years of the Reign of George the Second* (1822), vol. I, p. 147.

finding themselves *of Weight*, and finding at the same Time that the Disposal of all *Lucrative Employments* was vested in the *Crown*, soon bethought themselves that, in Exchange for *their* Concurrence in granting Supplies, and forwarding the *Measures* of *Government*, it was but equitable that the Crown should *concur* in vesting Them, or their *Dependants*, with the *Lucrative Employs* of State.

If this was done, the Wheels of Government ran smooth and quiet: But if any large Body of Claimants was dissatisfied, the political Uproar began; and public Measures were obstructed or over-turned.

William the *Third* found this to be the national Turn; and set him-self, like a Politician, to oppose it: He therefore silenced all he could, by Places or Pensions: And hence the origin of MAKING of PARLIA-MENTS.

. . . this new Principle of Self-Interest began to work deeper every Day in its Effects. As a Seat in Parliament was now found to be of considerable selfish Importance, the Contention for *Gain*, which had begun in *Town*, spread itself by Degrees into the *Country*. *Shires* and *Boroughs*, which in former Times had *Paid* their Representatives for their Attendance in Parliament, were now the great Objects of *Re-quest*, and *political Struggle*.

And as the Representatives had already found their Influence, and made their Demands on the *Crown*; so now, the *Constituents* found *their* Influence, and made *their* Demands on the *Representatives*.

Thus the great Chain of political Self-Interest was at length formed; and extended from the *lowest Cobler* in a *Borough*, to the *King's first Minister*.

. . . Besides this, the lucrative *Employs* of our *Country* not being near so numerous as the Claimants are, in every Degree of political *Power* and *Expectation*; the Spirit of selfish Faction arose of Course in its Strength, from unsatisfied Demands, and disappointed Avarice.

It hath been much debated, whether the Ministers or the People have contributed more to the Establishment of this System of Self-Interest and Faction. On Enquiry it would probably appear, that at different Periods the Pendulum hath swung at large on both sides. It came down, in former Times, from the Minister to the Represent-ative, from the Representative to the managing Alderman, from the Alderman to the Cobler. In later Times, the Impulse seems to have been chiefly in the contrary Direction: From the Cobler to the managing

Alderman; from him, to the Member; from the Member, to the *great Man* who ruled the Borough; and thence to the Minister.

Rev. John Brown, *Estimate of the Manners and Principles of the Times* (7th ed., 1758), vol. I, p. 107.

82. The government interest, 1734.

GEORGE DODINGTON TO THE DUKE OF DORSET

Jan 15 [1734] The whole bent and view not only of the Court but of the nation is at present employed about the ensuing elections. That there will be a Whigg Parliament there is no doubt, and I think, considering the reall weight that the families, fortunes, and interest of those in the King's service naturally give us, separate from the vast influence of the power and very great revenue of the Crown (if either should be made use of), I say I think there is no room to doubt but that it will be a Court Parliament. If I should be mistaken in this opinion of our natural strength, and it should be thought advisable to employ the revenue and power of the Crown to procure, by means of the returning officers, a majority to be returned, and that majority should afterwards (as no doubt they will) fortify and increase themselves by the decision of the elections in the Committee, yet then it will still be a Court Parliament, and the Opposition will have nothing either to boast of or to hope. But if this should be the case, their influence upon the people might be apprehended, because it might be productive of ill consequences if the people should be perswaded to believe that the majority of the Parliament were two degrees removed from being their representatives—one by the partiality of the returns; the other by that of the decisions of the Committee.

H.M.C., *Stopford-Sackville*, I, 151.

83. Resources of government 'influence', 1761.

I am sensible, that there are many well-meaning persons who seem to think, that without *corruption*, there might be danger apprehended from *Democratical* encroachments on prerogative.—But they who are really struck with the above objection, certainly forget that tho' the wings of *prerogative* have been clipt, the *influence* of the crown is greater than ever it was in any period of our history. For when we consider, in how many boroughs the government has the voters at its command; when we consider the vast body of persons employed in the collection of the revenue in every part of the kingdom; the inconceivable number of placemen, and candidates for places in the *customs*, in the *excise*, in the *post office*, in the *ordnance*, in the *salt office*, in the *stamps*, in the *navy* and *victualing* offices, and in a variety of other departments; when we consider again the extensive influence of the *money corporations*, *subscription jobbers*, and *contractors*; the endless dependence created by the obligations conferred on the bulk of the gentlemen's families throughout the kingdom, who have relations preferred, or waiting to be preferred, in our *navy*, and numerous *standing army*; when, I say, we consider how wide, how binding a dependence on the crown is created by the above enumerated particulars, no lover of monarchy need fear any bad consequences from shutting up the Exchequer at elections; especially, when to the endless means the crown has of influencing the votes of the *electors*, we add the vast number of employments, which the fashion of the times makes the *elected* desirous of, and for the obtaining which, they must depend upon the crown.

But, I believe, I have expressed myself improperly, when I spoke of the influence of the crown; for to say the truth, we may have observed from experience, that in proportion as the crown had the power of *obliging*, ministers, by being permitted to assume the universal direction of all those who had been *obliged*, have too frequently been enabled to make use of the dependents on the crown, to bring it into subjection to themselves; and at the same time, while they became formidable to the prince, they have had it in their power to make attempts on the liberties of the people. For when the crown influence lies dispersed in its several distinct channels; when every placeman, or public officer, is left at full freedom to vote for the candidate he likes best; numerous as these gentlemen are throughout the kingdom, they never can be supposed united in any scheme to hurt public liberty. But when they are to pass in muster before a first minister, when they are taught to look upon him as their commander in chief, and know that disobedience to his orders will be construed *mutiny*, and punished as such; when instructions are dispatched by the parliamentary undertaker, to every servant of the crown to support and oppose particular candidates; when every placeman, from the *excise-man* and *tide-waiter* up to the *commissioner* and *courtier*, has a ministerial list delivered to him; when the influence of the crown, I say, is thus moulded with one connected mass, and trusted to the direction of a single minister, What object can be strong enough to resist its force? And how fatally will it operate in destroying the independence of parliament, even though the *flood-gate* of *corruption* should be stopt?

If the interposition of a lord of parliament, in any particular election, be carefully provided against (as we know it is by the standing orders of the house of commons) as inconsistent with the constitution, how much more daring an attack is it upon the very essence of parliament, to see a minister presume to *undertake*, not for one or two members only, in places where he has a natural interest, but for hundreds of representatives, in boroughs scarcely known to him by name? What notion can any one have of the freedom of elections, if the writs for a new parliament issued by the crown, are accompanied by private instructions from a minister, like so many *congé d'élires*, which must implicitly be obeyed?

John Douglas, *Seasonable Hints from an Honest Man* (1761), p. 37.

84. A patron seeks a candidate, 1775.

1775, September 6.—Hinchingbrook. The Earl of Sandwich to John Robinson. My younger son's case is quite desperate. When a vacancy happens at Huntingdon, I could wish to have a candidate ready to start immediately. I should not like a merchant or a meer moneyed man, for reasons which I have allready told you, and yet a sum of money will be necessary, tho' upon such terms as no one would refuse. The terms in short that I must have are 2,000 £. to be lent to me for five years on my bond, and to pay the expenses of the election, which in all probability would not amount to 300 £.

I think there are many people in the world who would gladly accept these conditions; while I am now writing one occurs to me, namely, Lord Carmarthen; but I now write only for your opinion, and to desire as a friend that you would suggest to me one or more persons who you think would come up to my description, and who would be agreeable to Lord North; I cannot as yet authorize you to make the proposal to any one for reasons I am going to mention to you, and I write merely that I may not be unprepared, and have more than one string to my bow.

Mr Banks who is now with Captain Phipps in Yorkshire, has sounded him about coming into Parliament through my means. I think he is not unlikely to accept my proposals, and I have now written to tell him the conditions on which alone I can take him by the hand, namely, the *thinking and acting as I do in all American points and supporting the present administration in their whole system*. I know his connection with opposition is entirely at an end, and that he wants much to come into Parliament; therefore my opinion is that he will accept my offer, and if he does I think he will be a very good acquisition to us in the House of Commons. A week longer will bring this affair to a decision between Phipps and me, and by that time I shall have heard fully from you in answer to this letter.

W. T. Laprade (ed.), Parliamentary Papers of John Robinson (1922), p. 26.

85. A patron claims his reward: a peerage, 1813.

SIR WILLIAM MANNERS TO COLONEL MCMAHON [PRINCE REGENT'S PRIVATE SECRETARY]

Oxford Street, West end,
April 16 [1813].

Allow me to ask you two questions. Since I last had the honour of writing to you, a great change in politics has taken place.

Parties being nothing to me, my Parliamentary interest will always follow the politics of Carlton House. Have you any friends of the same sentiments desirous of securing seats for the next Parliament without trouble, opposition, or even attendance? If you have, & will refer them to me, or name them, I will enter into arrangements with them to their satisfaction, either for Ilchester, where I have reduced the votes to fifty two, all of whom are tenants at will, or for Grantham, where I own by inheritance & purchase the chief part of the parish, & have the Duke of Rutland at my command. Therefore any opposition there is now out of the question.

My second question is, whether you can form an idea at what time the promise of the peerage will be realised to me.

[P.S.] I will return your letter, if you desire it.

A. Aspinall (ed.), Letters of King George IV (Cambridge, 1938), No. 271.

86. A patron's problems, 1788.

THE MARQUIS OF BUCKINGHAM TO W. W. GRENVILLE

1788, June 7. Phoenix Lodge [Dublin] . . . You will easily see that I point at your re-election for the county.[1] If you cannot vacate before

---

[1] Pitt had offered Grenville a post.

the prorogation, I necessarily have the option of the 54 days canvass for you, or the abandonment of the county; for I must look upon the idea of General Grenville's election as wholly visionary, the man being absolutely unknown, and most absolutely unfit for any such attempt. To the 54 days canvass I have given my answer [against], and to the question of the abandonment I am ready to sacrifice that or any other object to my favourite wish of forwarding your political situation. I do not pretend to be insensible to the proposal of giving up the fruits of 15 years' personal slavery and of 14,000 £. which I have paid at different times for that seat; but I know that I would, with my eyes open, have engaged in that slavery and in that expense, twice told, to have contributed to your success in life; and I feel, therefore, that on this head we cannot have a shadow of difference. If therefore you ask me whether you shall hazard any of the great considerations which ought to guide you in this question for the sake of such a miserable object as the county of Buckingham, either as a personal feather to you, or as a trust estate for my family, I do not pause a moment in the answer. You well remember that when you undertook it, we calculated your political steps much slower than your industry, abilities, and character now hold out to you; but we both saw the incumbrance which a county representation threw upon the shoulders of a political man; and perhaps it might be a question well worth consideration to decide whether it is not almost incompatable, in its various unpleasant bearings, with your new situation. . . .

H.M.C., *Dropmore*, I, 333.

87. A patron's interest on his capital, 1810.

EDWARD HARBORD TO LORD SUFFIELD

My Dear Brother,   Oct. 7th [1810]

As to my being justifiable in thus abandoning the interests of my family after all the money that has been spent in bringing me into Parliament for Yarmouth, I have only to answer that money so spent has, I think, been well spent. Your Lord Lieutenancy and Petre's Receiver Generalship have been the consequence. In point of pecuniary advantage to the family, the Receiver Generalship pays more than the interest of the capital sunk, and I am sure you will not rate your desire of being Lord Lieutenant of the County so low, as to say the attainment of that object was worth nothing. I think I have shown that all the money that has been spent upon bringing me into Parliament for Yarmouth has been spent well; now there is no longer a family to draw upon for Yarmouth expenses, nor am I bound in duty to take any trouble which I do not like. As to withdrawing from Parliament, time will prove whether I shall do so, but I do not choose to entail upon myself any further trouble respecting Yarmouth; and if I should take my seat for any other place, I shall do so upon terms which will not render me amenable to any one for my political conduct.

. . . I am etc. E. HARBORD

R. M. Bacon (ed.), *A Memoir of the Life of Edward, Third Baron Suffield* (Norwich, 1818), p. 45.

88. A candidate seeks a patron, 1714.

LADY MARY WORTLEY MONTAGU TO HER HUSBAND, MR WORTLEY MONTAGU

(1)

. ... I hope you are convinced I was not mistaken in my judgment of Lord Pelham; he is very silly but very good natured. I don't see how it can be improper for you to get it represented to him that he is obliged in honour to get you chose at Aldburgh, and may more easily get Mr Jessop chose at another place. I can't believe but you may manage it in such a manner, Mr Jessop himself would not be against it, nor would he have so much reason to take it ill, if he should not be chose, as you have after so much money fruitlessly spent. I dare say you may order it so that it may be so, if you talk to Lord Townshend about it, etc. I mention this, because I cannot think you can stand at York or anywhere else, without a great expense. . . . After all, I look upon Aldburgh to be the surest thing. Lord Pelham is easily persuaded to anything, and I am sure he may be told by Lord Townshend that he has used you ill; and I know he'll be desirous to do all things in his power to make it up. In my opinion, if you resolve upon an extraordinary expense to be in Parliament, you should resolve to have it turn to some account. . . .

(2)

You seem not to have received my letters, or not to have understood them: you had been chose undoubtedly at York, if you had declared in time; but there is not any gentleman or tradesman disengaged at this time; they are treating every night. Lord Carlisle and the Thompsons have given their interest to Mr Jenkins. I agree with you of the necessity of your standing this Parliament, which, perhaps, may be more considerable than any that are to follow it; but, as you proceed, 'tis my opinion, you will spend your money and not be chose. I believe there is hardly a borough unengaged. I expect every letter should tell me you are sure of some place; and, as far as I can perceive you are sure of none. As it has been managed, perhaps it will be the best way to deposit a certain sum in some friend's hands, and buy some little Cornish borough: it would, undoubtedly, look better to be chose for a considerable town; but I take it to be now too late. If you have any thoughts of Newark, it will be absolutely necessary for you to enquire after Lord Lexington's interest; and your best way to apply yourself to Lord Holdernesse, who is both a Whig and an honest man. He is now in town, and you may enquire of him if Brigadier Sutton stands there; and if not, try to engage him for you. Lord Lexington is so ill at the Bath, that it is a doubt if he will live 'till the elections; and if he dies, one of his heiresses, and the whole interest of his estate, will probably fall on Lord Holdernesse.

'Tis a surprize to me, that you cannot make sure of some borough, when a number of your friends bring in so many Parliament-men without trouble or expense. 'Tis too late to mention it now, but you might have applied to Lady Winchester, as Sir Joseph Jekyl did last year, and by her interest the Duke of Bolton brought him in, for nothing; I am sure she would be more zealous to serve me, than Lady Jekyl.

Lord Wharncliffe (ed.), *Letters and Works of Lady Mary Wortley Montagu* (1861), vol. I, p. 211.

89. A member achieves independence, 1812.

[November, 1812] Before the Bristol election, the Duke of Norfolk offered, in case I should be unsuccessful at that place, to bring me into Parliament without any other expense than just that of a dinner to the electors, which was always usual. He said that he would either have me returned at the general election, or, if I thought that my being already elected would operate at all to my prejudice at Bristol, he would reserve a seat for me till the contest there should be over. He told me that it was to be fully understood that I was to vote, when in Parliament, just as I should think proper; and that, if I accepted his offer, he should consider it as an obligation conferred on him. This very kind and liberal offer I accepted; and Mr. Henry Howard, the Duke's relation, who was elected to represent Gloucester, was also returned for Arundel, with an intention that he should elect to sit for Gloucester, and leave Arundel open for me.

I had formerly, determined never to come into Parliament but by a popular election, or upon the purchase by myself of a seat from the proprietor of some borough, and I refused an offer which the late Marquis of Lansdowne made me, to come in for Calne, a great many years ago; and more recently (in 1805) declined accepting a seat which the Prince of Wales had procured for me. The alteration, however, which has taken place in the Law, and the change in my own situation, have made that quite unobjectionable to which there appeared to me formerly to be the strongest objection. Since Curwen's Bill[1] has declared illegal the purchase of seats in the manner which was formerly practised, there is no choice for a person like myself, but to come into Parliament on such an offer as is now made to me, or to decline Parliament altogether, and I cannot think it is my duty to decline it. The objection to coming into Parliament upon the nomination of some nobleman or other great landed proprietor, is, that you come in shackled with his political opinions and subservient to his will; but, after the part that I have already acted in Parliament, no doubt can be entertained that the Duke of Norfolk is quite sincere in telling me that I shall be quite independent of him.

. . . 21st, [December, 1812] Mon. I was elected without opposition. An opposition, however, was threatened up to the moment of the election taking place. None that would have been made could have been effectual. The right of election is in the inhabitants paying scot and lot; and of 310, the whole number of electors, 195 were decided supporters of any candidate the Duke of Norfolk might recommend. After the election, about fifty of the principal inhabitants and electors dined with the Duke at the Castle.

Memoirs of the Life of Sir Samuel Romilly (1840), vol. III, pp. 72, 74.

90. 'Making a parliament': Newcastle, 1733.

R. BURNETT[2] TO DUKE OF NEWCASTLE

Burwaish sept 20th, 1733

MAY IT PLEASE YOUR GRACE

Your Grace will I sopose have herd from Broomham what Company wass there from Hasting & Rye, & yesterday, I mett Mr Pelham

---

[1] No. 127.   [2] Newcastle's election agent in Sussex.

& Mr Butler hear, where, there Rod out to meet them about a mile out of town Mr Jurden¹ Dr Burrell Mr Collins Mr Luxford, & between thirty & forty of ye freeholders of Burwaish, who are most of them Duble votes, for Mr [Henry] Pelham & Mr Butler. the Gentlemen Dined with Mr Hussey & ye freeholders att ye Bear, aughter Dinnor Mr Pelham & ye Gentlemen Came & stayd till Five of the Clock aughter which Mr Pelham & ye Company went to Wadhurst, & Left Mr Atkins & my selfe to take Care of ye Company heare, who wass all very well taken Care of, in the evning the soldiers that are Quarterd hear wass gott Drunk & Insulted ye Chancelor & some of ye Gentlemen, but we soon Gott the better of them & spent the evning very Quiatly I am now Going to meet Mr Pelham att Mayfeild in his way to haland. And am

Your Graces most Dutyfull
And obedient servant
R. BURNETT.

Add. MSS. 32688, f. 357.

91. 'Making a parliament': Newcastle, 1753.

MARLBOROUGH TO NEWCASTLE

Blenheim Sep: 3, 1753

MY DEAR LORD

As your Grace well knows the necessity of troubling one's friends during a county election, I hope you will lett that be my excuse for the present request, which is a pardon for a poor woman in Oxford gaol under sentence of transportation for stealing a shift and an old cloack, it is I am assured her first offence the judge will I believe make a favorable report; I am desired to beg this favour by these, I can't at present well refuse, several freeholders in Oxfordshire I am with the greatest truth

Your Graces
Most faithfull &
Obedient humble servant
MARLBOROUGH.

The woman's name is
Ann Grant

Add. MSS. 32732, f. 601.

¹ Vicar of Burwash, Prebendary and Chancellor of Chichester.

92. 'Making a parliament': George III, 1782.

LORD NORTH TO THE KING

[18th April, 1782]

Lord North has the honour of sending to His Majesty the State of the Election Account, three Quarterly Accounts, together with the lists of Pensions and payments by Sir Grey Cooper and Mr Robinson, upon which He takes the liberty to make some observations.

The Election Account contains not only the expenses of the General Election, but of the preceding and subsequent years.

Although the whole expense is £103,765 : 15 : 9 yet as the contributions from several individuals amounted to £31,010 : 17 : 0, the expense that falls upon His Majesty is only £72,754 : 18 : 9, a sum larger, but not very considerably larger than has been paid on other occasions of a similar nature. The causes were, the strength of the Opposition to Government, which comprehending many powerful and rich families, and being very eager and zealous in their cause, were enabled to stir up and maintain many, and those formidable, contests in several of the Counties and Boroughs of England and Scotland: add to this, that the difficulties of the Times obliged several of the friends of Government to apply for assistance from Administration, who could have helped themselves better if the times had been more favourable for obtaining pecuniary assistance or credit from private persons.

The sums which were paid to the Government candidates were to enable them to defray the necessary, legal and concomitant expenses which arose from the different canvasses, Polls and Trials before the Committees, and were not given as bribes. No part of these expenses are, in that sense of the word, *corruption*.

Perhaps, it may be answered, that the sums paid to the Gentlemen who have the command of Boroughs, for their interest, are to be considered as *Bribes*. But those bargains are not usually called by that name, and the money disbursed in that manner does not exceed what has been disbursed on all former occasions.

Some of the expense should likewise be added.

Westminster   Election cost above £8,000; the expense of both candidates fell on the Crown.

Bristol   There were *two* elections, both contested, which brought on an expense of £6,000.

Tamworth   Lord Townshend's distresses obliged him to sell his seat there for £4,000. Mr. Courtney, the member, returned this favour to Government by supporting them always with great abilities and zeal.

Surry   £4,000 was paid to Lord Onslow to enable him to maintain the Contest for that County.

Gloucestershire Upon Mr Chester's Death, there was a debt remaining in the County in consequence of the great contest, which was very embarrassing to the friends of Government at the last vacancy. £2,000 was paid in part of that Debt; the expense of the Government party there at the two Elections had been immense.

Coventry   In the course of the year and a half, there were three contested Elections, and the two Trials before Committees. At the end of all these expenses Lord Sheffield and Mr Yeo applied for £2,000.

Hampshire   £2,000 was issued to support the D. of Chandos and Sir Richd. Worsley in 1779.

The expenses of Windsor, and in Scotland, were new but appeared unavoidable. They amount to about £5,000 in all.

Lord North did not apply for Secret Service Warrants to defray these expenses, as he knew that the remainder would, by degrees, be defrayed by the £1,000 a month out of the Privy Purse, and as these expenses would be very small during the rest of the Parliament.

Corresp. George III, No. 3668.

93. The Prince of Wales buys Old Sarum, 1749.

MEMORANDUM, UNSIGNED, UNDATED, AND SOMEWHAT MUTILATED, IN DR. AYSCOUGH'S HANDWRITING

[1749, May or June. London.]—Mr. [Thomas] Pitt according to Mr. Godfrey's calculation, will owe his Royal Highness at Midsummer 1749, 120£. 0. 0.

His Royal Highness is willing (in order to accommodate Mr. Pitt's affairs) to remit to him the above sum, and to add to it as much as shall make up the sum of 3000£, and to put Mr. Pitt in the receipt of his allowance and salary of 1500£ a year, on the following condit[ions]. That his Royal Highness shall have the nomination of [each] and every Member of Parliament that shall be e[lected] at the borough of Old

Sarum for the term of —— years, without any further expence to [his] Royal Highness, except the sum of forty pounds to p[ay] usual fees, at each election. Mr. Pitt shall deposite the deeds and l[eases] of the estates, to which the right of voting belongs, [in] such hands as his Royal Highness shall approve of; and further to secure to his Royal Highness the right of [nomi]nating and electing at the borough of Old Sarum [for] the term of years aforesaid, against the chance [of] Mr. Pitt's dying before that term be expired, Mr. [Pitt] shall immediately make his will and constitute . . . Dr. Ayscough his sole executor; who shall be [authorized] to act in respect of all elections in the same m[anner] as Mr. [Pitt.]

H.M.C., Dropmore. I, 134.

III. ELECTIONS: THE CONSTITUENCIES

The Boroughs

The main area of activity for the organisers of 'influence' was in the boroughs. It is difficult to speak generally about them, for they varied widely in size and type of franchise, and historians have usually divided them into five main groups:

1. *Potwalloper Boroughs*, where the vote was with those who kept their own house and 'dressed their own meat'. The technique of managing these depended on the size of the electorate. In a small borough like Tregony (**94**), a candidate could buy votes with money, hogs or tin; or buy the mayor, who would discount votes on the other side. Taunton, a medium-sized borough, illustrates further methods of dealing with poor voters, and shows also how it was necessary to prevent one 'interest' (the dissenting manufacturers) from opposing another 'interest' (the Mayor and Corporation) (**95**).

2. *Scot-and-Lot Boroughs*,[1] where those who paid the local rates had the vote. The problems were similar to those in the potwalloper boroughs, and the documents illustrate electioneering in Abingdon at the beginning and at the end of this period (**96, 97**). The earlier one brings out other inducements that a candidate might offer other than money: a place in the excise for individuals, and favours from the Admiralty and the Army for the town as a whole.

3. *Freemen Boroughs*, where freemen, by apprenticeship, birth or purchase, had the vote. Here again size was very important. The corporation of a small borough would carefully restrict the creation of freemen in order to keep the numbers within manageable proportions. The opposite tactics were sometimes employed by the corporations of large boroughs, where the

---

[1] See also No. **89**, p. 148.

electorate might be swamped by the creation of large numbers of non-resident freemen for purely electoral purposes (98). At the same time, candidates had to employ the appropriate 'nursing' techniques (99). In some freemen boroughs, freeholders also had the vote, as at Nottingham where the electorate consisted of some 2,000 freemen and forty-shilling freeholders. No patron could be certain of a body of voters of these dimensions, and thus Nottingham was an 'open borough'. The documents (100) illustrate some of the various expedients resorted to by the leaders of the Whig and Tory 'interests' there in preparation for the election of 1754: what Namier calls 'a system of organised bullying which worked from the top downwards'.[1]

4. *Corporation Boroughs*, where the mayor and corporation chose the members. The documents show the Earl of Bristol nursing Bury St Edmunds over a period of years (101).

5. *Burgage Boroughs*, where the vote was with the owner, in some cases, or the tenant, in others, of certain lands held by an ancient tenure called 'burgage tenure'. These, especially the former, were the most likely to become 'pocket boroughs', for a patron simply had to buy up a majority of the tenements to secure absolute control, free from the necessity of 'keeping sweet' a number of human beings. The documents illustrate the beginning of this process at Boroughbridge (102) and the finished product at Appleby (103). Great Bedwyn is an example of the second, more complicated sort, where properties were let to voters for a few days just before an election (104).

THE COUNTIES

In the counties the franchise was uniform: it went to all those who held freehold to the annual value of forty shillings, the word 'freehold' being broad enough to include leasehold for life, annuities, mortgages and so on, and life-offices in Church and State. The two seats in each county were usually in the hands of the great landed families, aristocratic or otherwise. The vulgar arts of bribery found in the boroughs were inappropriate among the gentlemen who dominated the affairs of the countryside. 'Influence', of course, there was, but it was the social and economic influence of landed magnates over their relations, their servants, their tenants, their shopkeepers; of patrons of livings over their incumbents; of Lord Lieutenants over the J.P.s; of aristocrats and gentry over their social inferiors (105). Everything was done to avoid a contest, which, owing to the size of the electorate, could be ruinously expensive, even by eighteenth-century standards; and in order 'to preserve the peace of the county' a compromise was usually

---

[1] Namier, *Structure of Politics* (1957), p. 93; where there is an account of the borough of Nottingham.

arrived at between the leading 'interests': between two rival families, or between Whigs and Tories, or between the peers and the gentry. Sometimes these 'compositions' involved the boroughs in the county as well (106).

94. Potwalloper borough: Tregony (*c.* 100 votes), 1696.

HOUSE OF COMMONS PROCEEDINGS, 5 MARCH 1696

Upon the several Petitions of Sir *Jos. Tredenham*, and *Seymour Tredenham* Esquire, complaining of an undue Election of *Francis Roberts* Esquire, and *James Mountague* Esquire:

The Committee have examined the Merits of That Election.
That, upon the Poll, the numbers were thus;

For Mr *Roberts*	93
For Mr *Mountague*	99
For Sir *Jos. Tredenham*	88
For *Mr Tredenham*	60

That it was agreed, That all such Inhabitants of the said Borough as did provide for themselves, whether they lived under the same Roof or not, had a Right to vote.

But the Petitioners insisted, That the Mayor ought not to have voted; and that the capital Burgesses, if they were not House-Keepers, had no Right to vote: Which was denied by the Counsel for the Sitting Members.

That the Sitting Members had given Exceptions to Nine of them that polled for the Petitioners; which the Petitioners insisted they could justify; and also would justify 17 others, that would have voted for them, and were refused by the Mayor to be polled.

That the Petitioners also insisted, That many ill Practices had been used by the Sitting Members or their Agents, with relation to the Said Election.

And, for the Petitioners, were first called,

Henry Greby: Who said, That the Town had been a long time dissatisfied with the Election of Strangers: That about 140 went to Sir *Joseph Tredenham's* House, and desired him to stand for the Said Borough; and that the Mayor had promised to do what he could for him: But Mr *Harvey*, Mr *Boscawen's* Steward, said, His Master expected both Votes; at which the Town being dissatisfied, they desired Mr *Seymour Tredenham* to stand:

That it was given out, That such as were Mr *Boscawen's* Friends, if they would give a single Vote, they should have 6d a Day; and if a double Vote, 12d a Day: And that the Mayor said, Sir *Joseph* would lose it, unless he did as they did: And that one *Melchisedeck Kinsman*, who voted for Mr *Roberts* and Mr *Mountague* had before promised Sir *Joseph*; and, being asked, Why he went off? he said, He got Two Hogs by it; one of which Hogs, he believes, was worth 30s.:

That *Woolridge* said, He had 1000 £ Weight of Tin, which he was to distribute: And that, a little before the Election, the Mayor said, He could have 100 £ for Ten Voices.

To prove the 9, that had polled, and was now objected to, had a Right, they called,

Henry Greby, Ja. Triscawen: Who said, That *Tho. May* was a House-Keeper, and had lived in Town above Four Years:

But, on the other Side, it was testified, He was a poor Man, and had lived that Time under Presentments:

. . . That *Henry Triscawen* was a House-Keeper, and solicited for the Sitting Members; and said, He might have 6 £.:

On the other Side, it was testified, That, all the Time of the Election, he lay in a Hog-stye:

That *John Morse* had an Estate in *Tregony* of 14 or 16 £ a Year, and was a House-Keeper . . .

That *Wm. Barnicote* was a House-Keeper:

On the other Side, it was testified, That he worked in a Chamber, and had no Chimney:

That *Peter Gummer* kept a Shop:

On the other Side, it was testified, That he lodged with his Brother, and had neither Pot, nor Bed.

. . .

C.J., XI, 491.

95. Potwalloper borough: Taunton (*c.* 500 votes), 1781.

JOHN HALLIDAY TO JOHN ROBINSON
(SECRETARY OF THE TREASURY)

1781, December 17.—Parliament Street. Monday morning. Mr. Halliday presents his respectful compliments to Mr. Robinson and begs to offer, for his opinion, the inclosed proposal, which at present strikes him (from the perfect knowledge he has of the various characters that interest themselves in the elections of Taunton) as most likely if managed with address to prevent any contest of consequence if an election for that place should shortly become necessary.

1781. December 17.—Enclosure. It may be proposed by one of the members of T[aunton] to some of the principal manufacturers there; to induce them to decline engaging in an opposition to the corporation, if an election should be occasioned by the death of the other member, that, to preserve the peace of the town, and thereby not only prevent the injury and interruption that will necessary [necessarily] happen from a contested election to the newly established silk manufacture, but to encourage the further progress of that manufacture and the more extensive employment of the poor in the town. He would propose to give in premiums in the manner as shall be recommended by a majority of the master workmen in that branch already introduced, and also to promote the engaging in other branches of the silk manufacture the sum of — and to be applied towards preserving the woollen manufacture now on its decline in the town in premiums in manner and in proportion as shall be recommended by a majority of the principal persons engaged in that manufacture.

[The writer suggests in the margin of the paper five hundred pounds as necessary for the silk manufacturers and three hundred pounds for the woollen manufacturers.]

If the above proposal should be approved of, the whole remaining expence will be (as 'tis apprehended that after the vacancy happens, it will not be proper to open any houses of entertainment): To 250 poor persons who have now a right to vote at an election, 29s. each, 525 £. To a publick dinner after the election and a piece of plate to the mayor, about 105 £. making a total of 1,430 £.

N.B. It has been usual to give to the poor voters after the election is over 1 guinea each and a piece of plate to the Mayor of about 15 £ value.

It must be observed that all the principal manufacturers of T[aunton] are Dissenters and much at enmity with the corporation, who will not admit any person of that description to become a magistrate of the town. An opposition to any candidate that the corporation approve is therefore mostly to be apprehended from them. It is proposed to prevent any effectual opposition by endeavouring to stop it at the fountain head in the manner here recommended, which 'tis believed will have that effect.

W. T. Laprade (ed.), *Parliamentary Papers of John Robinson* (1922), p. 38.

96. Scot-and-Lot borough: Abingdon (*c.* 250 votes), 1699.

HOUSE OF COMMONS PROCEEDINGS, 3 MARCH 1699

Upon the Petition of *William Huckes* Esquire, complaining of an undue Election and Return of *Simon Harcourt* Esquire to serve for the Borough of Abbingdon:

That the Election for the said Borough was upon the 21st. of July: That, upon the Poll, there was,

For Mr *Harcourt*   – – 252

For Mr *Huckes* – – – 264

... The Counsel for the Sitting Member acknowledged, That as the Poll was taken, the Numbers were as above; but said, They should take off a great many of the Petitioner's Votes; viz. 16, as receiving constant Alms; and 65 others, as Inmates, or Lodgers, Boarders, or living in the same Houses with others that had voted; and some others that were induced to vote for the Petitioner by Promises of Reward.

That the Sitting Member's Counsel insisted on several Irregularities on the Part of the Petitioner: And called several Witnesses;

Mr *Rawlins* said, That the 21th *June*, being *Sunday*, he was at the *King's Head* in the *Old Change*, and a Porter came from *Mr Huckes* the Petitioner, to desire him to come to him: That, accordingly, he went to the Petitioner; who told him, That Mr *Sellwood* had promised him his Interest, and he desired his, the said Mr *Rawlins*', Voice; but he told him, He could not be for him: That the Petitioner told him, If he was a Parliament man, he should be a Commissioner of Excise; and That would be worth 1,500 £ a Year to him; which he reckoned thus; viz. The Salary 800 £ a Year, Perquisites 200 £; and he told the said Mr *Rawlins*, that what he, the Petitioner, could do, would be 500 £ a Year more to him: That the said Mr *Rawlins* told the Petitioner, He thought Mr *Sellwood* would not believe him: He told him, Yes; for he had promised to remit 300 £ that he owed him, whether he, the said Petitioner, had the place or not: That he advised the Petitioner to stand at Wallingford; but he said, No, he must turn out Mr *Harcourt*, or he should not have the Place ...

... *Charles Mortimer* said, That Mr *Watkyns* sollicited Votes for the Petitioner; and reported, That the Petitioner was promised a Place in the Excise Office; and told the said *Mortimer*, He should have a Place there himself, if he would be for the Petitioner.

Richard Eley, Jos. *Stockwell*, Mr *John Bush*: Who testified, That, at the News-house in *Abingdon*, a pretty while before the Election, a Letter was produced, and read; and subscribed *Charles Medlecott*; by which it was desired, to the Effect following; viz. That an Interest might be made for the Petitioner against Mr *Harcourt*, because he was a disaffected Person; and, if he got into the house, he would go nigh to be Speaker; and if Mr *Harcourt* was put by, it would be a great Service to them; for That the Lords of the Admiralty would protect their Watermen or Bargemen from being pressed; and that they should have some of the Lord of *Oxford's* Regiment, if they desired the same; and, if they desired they should have no Soldiers quartered upon the Town:

C.J., xii, 542.

97. Scot-and-Lot borough: Abingdon (*c.* 250 votes), 1796.

30th [May, 1796] Selwood, Town Clerk of Abingdon, and Bowles, of the Corporation, called me out of the Court of the King's Bench. The electors of Abingdon are 240 scot and lot; about 70 of them take money. About half of the 240 go with the corporation. The Dissenters, headed by the Tomkiss's and Fletchers, are the next best interest. Child, the brewer, and his friends, have also considerable weight. If all three sets can agree, they carry the place in defiance of all opposition. The corporation sent to sound me. I answered as to my present secure situation, but would think of it, and endeavour to know what Child thought of me; but the whole subject to my further consideration. The election (unopposed) would cost within 300£., and annual subscriptions afterwards about 100£ a year. Politics free.

Lord Colchester (ed.), *Diary and Correspondence of Charles Abbot, Lord Colchester* (1861), vol. I, p. 55.

98. Freemen borough: Colchester (over 1000 votes), 1711.

HOUSE OF COMMONS PROCEEDINGS, 27 JANUARY 1711

Mr *Freeman* also reported from the Committee of Privileges and Elections, the Matter, as it appeared to them, touching the Election for the Borough of *Colchester*, in the County of *Essex*, and the Resolutions of the Committee thereupon . . .

That the Poll was thus:

693 for the sitting Member:
685 for the Petitioner.

That the Right of Election was agreed to be in the Mayor, Aldermen, Common Council, and Burgesses.

That the Question was, whether the Mayor, of his own Authority, without consent of the Common Council, can make Foreigners free.

Against such Authority, in the Mayor, several Entries in the Town Books were produced; *viz.*

In 1654 an Order, that no Foreigner should be made free, without Consent of the Majority of the Common Council.

And several Instances were produced of Persons, admitted by the Mayor and Common Council in the Years 1656, 57, 58, 85, and 93.

In 1694 a Disfranchisement, in the Town Book, of Alderman *Mott*, for Misdemeanors.

And *William Boyle*, and *Sam. Hayward*, said, one of those Misdemeanors was, for making a Person free in the Year of his Mayoralty (which was the precedent Year) without Consent of the Common Council.

In *July*, 1697, an Order of the Town Book, that no Foreigner should be admitted, without Consent of the Majority of the free Burgesses assembled in the Common Hall.

John Potter, Esquire, said, that *John Raynham*, when he was Mayor in 1705/6, Two Days before the Election to Parliament, without Consent of the Common Council made 100 Foreigners free, and swore them in the Night-time, in Alehouses and Taverns, without the Town Clerk, who ought to swear them publickly in the Town Hall.

That the Counsel for the sitting Member called *Oliver Birkin*, *Thos. Grigson*, and *Tho. Glascock*; who said, that all the Mayors since 1697, but One or Two, have of themselves admitted Foreigners; and that there are some Instances of Admittances of the same Nature before that Time, but they are very few.

And that the Committee came to this Resolution:

Resolved, That it is the Opinion of the Committee, That the Mayor of the Borough of *Colchester*, in the County of *Essex*, cannot make Foreigners free of the said Borough, without the consent of the Majority of the Aldermen, and Common Council.

And upon this the sitting Member's Counsel admitted, the Petitioner had a Majority.

C.J., XVI, 470.

99. Freemen borough: Carlisle (450 votes), 1712.

HOUSE OF COMMONS PROCEEDINGS, 23 FEBRUARY 1712

Mr *Freeman*, according to Order, reported from the Committee of Privileges and Elections, the Matter, as it appeared to them, touching the Election for the City of *Carlisle*, and the Resolution of the Committee thereupon . . .

That the Right of Election was agreed to be in the Mayor, Aldermen, Bailiffs, and Freemen, resident or not resident;

That it was also agreed, That the Sons of Freemen, born after their Fathers Freedom, and Persons serving Seven Years within the City, have a Right to be made free;

That the Poll was thus;

> 277 for the Sitting Member;
> 167 for the Petitioner.

. . . *Joseph Nixon* said. That, upon the 20th of *September* 1710, the Petitioner came to the Shoemakers Company, and desired to be admitted a Brother of it: That he was accordingly admitted, and then gave that Company Two Silver Candlesticks, and a Salver; and ordered them 10s. apiece to drink at several Houses in the Town; which they had accordingly:

That at the same Time he requested their Votes in the next Election; and told them, He should, after a while, have occasion for 700 Pair of Shoes for his Regiment, which the Shoemakers in That Town should make for him.

C.J., xvii, 106.

100. Open borough: Nottingham (over 2000 votes), 1753.

(1)

JOHN CLAY [NEWCASTLE'S AGENT AT NOTTINGHAM] TO NEWCASTLE

[13 Aug 1753]

This morning's Post brought me the Honour of Your Letter and I shall with the greatest pleasure endeavour to execute Your Grace's Commands for the Service of My Lord Howe at the next Election, But I think it my Duty to acquaint Your Grace that too great a number of the Common Burgesses of this Town are most unhappily prejudiced against Lord Howe on account of his Lordship haveing subscribed towards carrying on the Law Suit now depending between the Corporation and the Burgesses in favour of the Corporation, And this very thing has been for a long time and still is so inveterately resented and exaggerated to My Lord Howe's disadvantage that I am fully convinced Nothing but the united Interest of Your Grace and My Lord Middleton[1] can reconcile it.

I . . . am now inform'd there is a Project on foot to joyn Mr. Plumptre with Sir Charles Sedley in opposition to Lord Howe and it is generally believ'd Lord Middleton will favour it, This Scheme is now so publickly mentioned that I really believe it is actually intended, And in Failure of it they say Two Gentlemen shall be putt up in the Opposite Interest which will be much worse still, ffor in such Case I greatly fear this Burrough would be lost. Will it not therefore be proper that Your Grace should settle Things with My Lord Middleton before I begin to make Your Grace's Pleasure known to any body? I am well satisfied my appearing in it at present will prove fatal.

Add. MSS. 32732, f. 456.

(2)

JOHN CLAY TO NEWCASTLE

[24 Oct. 1753]

In begining of last week My Lord Howe began to walk the streets of this Town and to ask Votes and yesterday morning the whole was finished, His Lordship was attended by the Mayor & Aldermen and by Mr Sherwin, Mr Hartopp and other the Chief Gentlemen of our Town and by myself every day And I have the Pleasure to tell Your Grace that Lord Howe has the promiss of a considerable Majority of Votes, I never saw the Whig Interest more united. This Day the Opposite Candidates caused an Advertisemt to be printed & dispersed amongst the Burgesses (one of which I thought proper to inclose herein) by which it now very plainly appears what we are to expect And for my part I cannot construe it any otherwise than as a manifest and Open Violation of the Compromise between Yo[r] Grace and Lord Middleton as Sir Willoughby Aston who is Ld Middleton's Friend has joyn'd with Mr Plumptre, And we are inform'd with great certainty that Ld Middleton & divers other Gentlemen in this Neighbourhood

---

[1] Head of the Tory 'interest'.

have already subscribed Great Sums of money to carry on this Design, And therefore it is plain that the next Election here will be a thorough Triall between the Whig & Tory Interest, ffor Mr Plumptre cannot be chose by the Whigs tho' he may perhaps in some measure divide that Interest wch will be some prejudice to us, And if we should loose it will prove a very fatal thing hereafter. I would willingly hope Your Grace will even yet prevent Mr Plumptre's Standing, Otherwise I can't say what may be the Consequence ffor without doubt there are five hundred Burgesses at least who may and will be bought. Mr Plumptre is now in Kent but is expected here in a fortnight, This Place is already in great Confusion and will be much more so if not made easy by Yo^r Grace's kind Interposition. I can't send Yo^r Grace an exact Account of the Votes promised and desired (the Books being not yet fully cast up and settled) but hope to do it by Saturdays or Monday's Post. . . .

Add. MSS. 32733, ff. 122–3.

(3)

JOHN CLAY TO NEWCASTLE

[31 Oct 1753]

. . . I forgott in my former Letters to acquaint Your Grace that Mr Smith our Banker & his two Sons had most heartily engaged themselves in Ld Howe's Interest and That both the Sons walk'd the Town with us and exerted themselves greatly in perswading the Burgesses which added great Weight to our Endeavours And were so remarkably zealous and warm upon all Occasions that none could doubt of their being sincere, Which will make the following Relation very surprizing. My Lord Middleton hearing of the Extraordinary zeal of the Smith's ffamily (and having constantly a very great sum of money lying dead (as to himself) in their hands which they employ to their own profit) sent his Steward on ffryday last to them threatening that unless they immediately chang'd their behaviour and acted in a quite different manner he would take his money out of their hands & perswade all his ffriends to do the like, This Message had such Effect upon the mean Spirits of the Smith's Family (whose Idol is money) that one of the sons went next day to Ld Middleton in the name of his ffather, His brother & himself gave up Lord Howe and his Interest (as much as in them lay) and promised to do as Ld Middleton should direct them.

was not fully satisfied of the truth of this Monstrous Revolt untill Monday last when I sent to Ld Howe to desire him to come hither and yesterday he came and alighted at my House where after my relating to him the Affair and consulting upon it he took a Resolution to continue to proceed in his Interest in manner as if this thing had not happen'd and to show his Open Contempt of the Smith's Family, In wch I think His LdShip judged very rightly, I doubt not but Your Grace very well remembers how this Family behaved at the last Election, I fear this will be of considerable Detriment to my Lord Howes Election tho' I am this Moment told that the Eldest Son (George Smith who married a relation of Ld Howes) denies that his Brother had any Consent of his to go to Lord Middleton & say what he did And declares he will still be with us tho' his ffather & Brother are gone from us. I doubt Your Grace will think me troublesome in writing so often but I cannot think I ought to keep anything materiall from Your Grace's Knowledge.

If Your Grace cannot perswade Mr Plumtre You may prevent him by makeing him Sherriff of the County next Year but it must be a secret untill the very time it is done . . .

Add. MSS. 32733, ff. 174–5.

(4)

JOHN CLAY TO NEWCASTLE

[10 Nov 1753]

I write these at request of Lord Howe to acquaint Yo^r Grace that there are some Burgesses of this Town residing at Newark who cannot be prevail'd upon at present to promise their Votes for His Lordship but by the Assistance of Yo^r Grace's Steward Mr Spraggin of Newark it is thought they may be gain'd, My Lord Howe therefore begs You will be pleas'd to send directions to Mr Spraggin to use his Endeavours on this Occasion, And a List of their Names shall be sent him. Sir Willoughby Aston & Mr Francis Plumptre (as representative of his Brother) made their Publick Entry here on Monday last on horseback and ever since have walk'd the Town & ask'd Votes joyntly but have not gott thro' half the Town as yet, They are accompanied thro' the Streets by Ld Middleton's two Sons, Sir Cha. Sedley, Sir Tho. Parkyns Mr Chaworth & severall other country Gentlemen & by severall Tradesmen of this Town, They make great Boastings of their Success but I would yet willingly hope Ld Howe will succeed. Mr Smith's Eldest Son continues yet with us, but we are great Sufferers by the late behaviour of his ffather & Younger brother. . . .

Add. MSS. 32733, ff. 234-5.

(5)

JOHN CLAY TO ROBERT SPRAGGING [NEWCASTLE'S STEWARD]

[14 Nov 1753]

The Underwritten is a List of some Person's Names who are Burgesses of this Town and reside in Newarke, They have been applied to on behalf of My Lord Howe for their Votes at the next Election for this Town but as yet have not been prevailed upon to promise, His Grace the Duke of Newcastle is greatly attached to the Interest of Lord Howe and You will very soon have His Grace's Directions to use Your best Endeavours to gain the Votes of these Persons for Lord Howe, And you will please to perswade as many of them as You can to give their Votes for Lord Howe Only. And be so good as to favour me with a Line of Your Success herein, I am Sir

Yo^r most humble Servt
JOHN CLAY

Mr Marshall of Newark has spoke to them and can inform You of them.

Wm Derry a Joyner	Saml. Moor a Staymaker
Benja. Piggot a Glazier	Danl. Harvey Innholder
Tho. Groves a Tanner	John Herring a Joyner
John Keep a Breeches Maker	Tho. Robinson a Joyner
John Traman a Grocer	Wm. Briggs Huntsman.

Add. MSS. 32733, f. 288.

(6)

JOHN CLAY TO NEWCASTLE

[2 Dec 1753]

. . . Our Election Affairs have since my last continued without any material Alteration till yesterday when the Mayor happening to sumon a Hall to do some Corporation Business A great number of the comon people (our Adversaries) who pretended to have a Right to be made

164

Burgesses assembled at the Hall and required to be sworn, The Mayor told them in a very civil manner he had not called the Hall with that intent to make Burgesses of any side and desir'd them to depart, But they stayd at the Hall Door till the Mayor broke up the Meeting And then they mobbd & insulted him quite thro' the Streets of the Town to his own house at Noon Day. This Usage justly provok'd him to issue his Warr^t for apprehending two of the Ringleaders and to send One to the Gaol & the other to the House of Correction where they yet remain. The Mobb towards the Evning gave out they would pull down the Gaol and Great Numbers of them went about in the Streets all night but the Mayor ordering all his Constables & many others to their Assistance to walk the Streets all night no harm was done, But this day Disputes have run very high amongst us And some of our ffriends have desired the Mayor to petition Y^r Grace to send us some Soldiers but I am clearly of opinion it would be wrong to do that at present. . . .

Add. MSS. 32733, f. 397.

(7)

JOHN CLAY TO NEWCASTLE

[31 Dec 1753]

. . . Your Grace's first Order to me being to promote Lord Howe's Interest together with such other Gentleman as Ld. Middleton should nominate I comunicated it to all Your Friends and Tenants and Ld. M. heard of it & was well pleas'd, But as Things have been quite altered since that time I presume Your Grace will now think proper to direct that Yo^r Tenants and Myself shall vote for Ld Howe Only as it is the most Effectual Way to serve him, And yet I must acquaint Your Grace that Ld. M. (as is publickly given out) pretends he has sett up Sir W. Aston and that Mr Plumptre is sett up by the Comon Burgesses and tho' a Junction is brought it is what his Ld Ship cannot help, but I take this to be an Artifice to mollify Y^r Grace's Orders in suffering Y^r Ten^{ts} & me to vote for Sir W. A. as well as for Lord Howe.

There are three or four of Your Grace's Tenants who will not promise to vote for Lord Howe, must I not give them warning to quitt their Tenemnts? I think it should be so, but as I know it will occasion a great Clamour amongst us I dare not do it without Your Grace's Order. In this I desire to know Yo^r Grace's Pleasure as soon as maybe.

A great Alteration begins now to appear in their behaviour of the

poorer sort of Burgesses towards both Parties—Money and the best
Bidders is become the By-Word amongst them and I plainly foresee
an immense sum will be spent, I must desire Your Grace's Directions
with regard to the Expences I have born & shall be at which are more
or less every day for I cannot walk the Streets or even keep within my
house but my pockett is pick'd (as I call it) I very seldom give above
sixpence or a Shilling at a time but that with my other Expences in
publick Houses has already amounted to near Eight pounds and perhaps may rise to Twenty pounds or more before the Election if Your
Grace does not restrain me. . . .

Add. MSS. 32733, f. 619.

101. Corporation borough: Bury St. Edmunds (37 votes), 1718–25.

(1)

TO YE WORSHIPFUL MR CARY, ALDERMAN OF BURY ST. EDMUNDS

SIR Dec. 2, 1718.

You being chief magistrate of a town I have ever felt a most innate
affection for, makes me address myself to you as the properest person
to contrive ye best disposal of a small Charity I intend towards the
relief of those poor families who are afflicted with ye small pox. My
steward Oliver has direction from me by the same hand which conveys
this to you to pay one hundred pounds to such person or persons as you
& your brethren of ye Corporation (to every member whereof I desire
you would make my service always acceptable) shall think fitt to
appoint; and when yee are mett to deliberate on ye most impartial
method of distribution, which I'm sure by these means will be observd,
I hope you will do me the favour to make them accept of six bottles of
wine, which will be likewise orderd for such a meeting (whenever
you'l appoint it) by, Sir, your etc.

S.H.A.H., Letter-Books of John Hervey (Wells, 1894), vol. II, p. 68.

(2)

LORD BRISTOL TO LADY BRISTOL

Ickworth, Sept. 2, 1721.

MY EVER-NEW DELIGHT

. . . Yesterday I gave the Corporation a dinner of twenty nine dishes
(warm), at which there were above fourty of our friends present, who

all agreed there were [sic] never was seen a more noble entertainment at any time or place, and indeed I thought so too; and such I beleive you will think it ought to have been, after I have told you it cost above five and twenty pounds, besides my own beef and mutton, veale and venison. Had it, or could it have been better, they woud have deservd it all, since they rememberd you with such particular respect and esteem that I shall ever love them more for that than for all the trust and confidence they have putt in me and my family, by sending them so many years for their representatives to Parliament, especially Alderman Chamberlain, who when I drank a health to all our wives, woud pledg only to your own, saying that not only their but no other mens wives health was worthy to be mingled with the virtuous, beautiful Countess of Bristol's.

S.H.A.H., Letter-Books of John Hervey (Wells, 1894), vol. II, p. 177.

(3)

London, March 6, 1724/5.

Mr Alderman

You having a double title to be troubled on the present occasion, both as Cheif Magistrate of Bury and as one of my first-rate friends in the Corporation, makes me address this to you, to let you know there is a very near prospect of Mr. Sergeant Reynolds's being declared a judge, and that you would be so kind as to convene all our fast friends together at your own house or any other place you or they shall think more proper to drink a glass of wine together, and then & there to acquaint them that I intend to sett up my son, the Lord Hervey, to supply the Sergeant's vacancy as your representative in Parliament; and that as soon as the warrant is signd for his being a judge you and they may depend on seeing both my son & me at Bury to sollicite his election, which is as firmly depended on by us & all other friends to the present Government as you may reckon upon being reimbursd whatever charges you may be at in doing what is desird of you & them by your most obligd friend to serve you & them, Bristol.

My son sends his most humble service to all our friends.

S.H.A.H., Letter-Books of John Hervey (Wells, 1894), vol. II, p. 379.

167

102. Burgage borough: Boroughbridge (*c.* 70 votes), 1711.

W. WENMAN [NEWCASTLE'S AGENT] TO CHARLES WILKINSON [NEWCASTLE'S AGENT IN ALDBURGH, YORKS]

Welbeck, July 8th, 1711.

MR WILKINSON,

SIR,

As to the subject of your letter, my Lord [John Holles, Duke of Newcastle] says he shall be very willing to support your Brother's,[1] and your interest in Boroughbridge, so far as just reason requires. But my Lord says, what your Brother sees now, his Grace discovered from the intimates of Sir Bryan [Stapylton][1] many years ago. That if Sir Bryan did not sell his estate to my Lord, he did intend at what price soever to overthrow the Wilkinson interest in Boroughbridge. And my Lord says the fundamental mismanagement was when Sir Bryan offered my Lord his estate at 22 years purchase that your father and brother did not fright Sir Bryan into the conclusion of the bargain, as they might have done. And now the buying little single burgages at such extravagant rates has given the townsmen a handle to enhance their prices beyond measure. For it is certain that a great many Boroughs in England may be bought for half the rate that is now at your Borough. And land about London and all other parts of England is fallen at least 4 or 5 years purchase upon the great difference of advantage between money and land. Sir Bryan's party is now so uppish that it cannot be imagined he will sell my Lord his Estate at any price as will make amends for paying so dear for other purchases—so that the only method my Lord can think of for preventing your, and your Brother's interest sinking entirely, and the utmost assistance you can in all reason expect from his Grace is to this effect. That my Lord will be willing to give 26 years purchase for Henlock's. And any other Burgages you can buy according to such rents as you will undertake to take them at. And his Grace will not buy upon any other condition. And though it can hardly be supposed at this time a-day they are to be bought at that price, therefore, your Brother may take it under his consideration whether to lay down 4 or 5 years purchase on the remainder of the price you can agree for, until so many are bought as will secure an undoubted majority for two. And when that is done there may be methods found for making your brother no loser.

[1] Principal burgage-holders.

And to show the utmost goodwill he can to your Brother my Lord says if your brother has not money enough to go through with this matter his grace will accomodate him and be very easy with the interest, being good security. . . .

I am etc.,

W. WENMAN.

T. Lawson-Tancred, *Records of a Yorkshire Manor* (1937), p. 231.

103. Burgage borough: Appleby (*c.* 100 votes), 1802.

PHILIP FRANCIS TO HARRIET FRACE

Appleby Castle,
Wednesday morning, 7 July, 1802

MY OWN DEAR HARRIET,

The Fact is that yesterday morning, between 11 & 12 I was unanimously elected by one Elector, to represent this Ancient Borough in Parliament, and I believe I am the very first Member returned in the whole Kingdom. There was no other Candidate, no Opposition, no Poll demanded, Scrutiny, or petition. So I had nothing to do but to thank the said Elector for the Unanimous Voice by which I was chosen. Then we had a great Dinner at the Castle, and a famous Ball in the evening for that part of the Community which my lady calls the Raggamuffins. On Friday Morning I shall quit this Triumphant Scene with flying Colours, and a noble Determination not to see it again in less than seven years.

B. Francis and E. Keary (ed.), *The Francis Letters* (1901), vol. II, p. 493.

104. Burgage borough: Great Bedwyn (100 votes), 1729.

HOUSE OF COMMONS PROCEEDINGS, 26 MARCH 1729

Mr *Earle* (according to Order) reported from the Committee of Privileges and Elections, the Matter, as it appeared to them, touching the Election for the Borough of *Great Bedwyn*, in the County of *Wilts*, and the Resolutions of the Committee thereupon . . .

That the Counsel for the Petitioner insisted, that this Borough is a Borough by Prescription; and that the Right of Election is in the

Freeholders, and Inhabitants of ancient Messuages within the Borough; and called

Thomas Rosier, *Thomas Street*, and *Robert Byrd*; who spoke for Fifty, Forty, and Thirty Years past; and said, that Freeholders and Lease-holders of ancient Burgage Houses, not receiving Alms, always voted; and that new Houses, built on old Foundations, did so likewise: And said, that the Commoners have also voted, that did not receive Alms; and that they had heard, there was a Charter, but that it was delivered up: And said, that the Freeholders, though they did not live within the Borough, have also voted, and that Certificate Men were not allowed. And *Robert Byrd* said, there was no such qualification required as Forty Days Possession; and that it was a general Rule, to let Houses for Four or Five Days at the Time of an Election; and that the same was done at Lord *Bruce*'s and Mr *Pollexfen*'s Election in 1708; and that they never knew any body refused, for want of Forty Days Possession; and that the taking of Houses against Elections is so usual, that they take no Notice of it. . . .

C.J., XXI, 294.

105. County: Sussex, 1740.

NEWCASTLE TO MR PELHAM, JUNIOR

Claremont July 21st. 1740.

DEAR SIR,

I am very much obliged to you for your Letter, which I received by Chapman, and the account you sent me of the Meeting at the Star on Friday last. You will see by the indecent & impertinent Advertisement in the London Evening Post of Thursday last, that We are to expect a very warm Contest, & Mr Champion's appearance looks, as if Sir Tho: Dyke was to be the Man; Tho' I rather think it will end in the two old ones. —— I doubt not, but that, if our Friends will do their Parts, we shall beat Them by a much larger Majority, than we did the last time. I am very willing to do every thing in my power; But the necessary —— attendance upon the Business of the Office, at this very busy & critical Conjuncture, will not allow me to give so much Time to our Election Affairs, as I am afraid They will require, and I should otherwise be very glad to give; so that We must depend upon you, and the rest of our Friends; For my poor Brother cannot be expected to do much in the Condition He is at present in.

The first Thing to be done is, to get a good Meeting of considerable

Friends at Horsham; and I have been under great Difficulty, what to determine about it. I have at last taken of the Poll, all the Baronets, Esquires, and most of those, that are called Gentlemen, and all the Clergy, that voted for us the last Time. They amount in the whole to about 230. I shall send the Lists for the three Western Rapes, to Arch Deacon Ball, Major Battine, Mr Jewkes, & Jack Butler; and hope They will take Care to speak to the Gentlemen in their Lists to be at the Assizes at Horsham on Monday the 4th of August. But I have given Them a great Caution not to let one suspect, that the Summons comes from me: But that our Friends are desired to meet at Horsham to consider of proper Persons to stand Candidates for the County at the ensuing Election.

I enclose to you those for the three Eastern Rapes, and beg you will immediately consult with Burnet,[1] to send the proper Notice to the Persons mentioned in the Three Lists. But you & Burnet will take particular Care, That the summons may not seem to come from me; But that there is to be a Meeting at the Assizes at Horsham, where these Gentlemen are desired to be. If the Dean of Chichester is not in our Parts, I should think, Mr Clark would be the properest Clergyman to be consulted, for the Clergy of Pevensey Rape; Mr Bland, for the Clergy of Lewes Rape; and Mr Chancellor Jordan, and Mr Ashburnham, for the Clergy of Hasting Rape. You will take Sir William Gage and Mr Hay, into your concert if they like it. . . .

The great Point is, to get the principal Gentlemen, to come to Horsham. You say nothing of Jack Spence; I wish He would send his son Luke to Horsham. If Burnet could get Mr Walter Roberts of Warbleton, Mr Peckham of Salehurst, Mr Fowle, Mr Tho: Fuller of Gatehouse, Mr Michael Baker, of Mayfield, and Mr John Newnham (for Will. Newnham, I daresay, will come) It would have a very good Effect; and I beg you would take Care, if possible, to get Masters of Brighthelmston, Sir Willm. Gage is the Man to work with Him. My Brother was of the Opinion, That we should have as large a Meeting of Considerable People, as we could get; but not to descend too low; and except the Clergy (and I don't see, how we could distinguish amongst Them) I think there are not twenty People, That could have been left out; and I don't reckon we shall, upon the whole, have above an Hundred; and That is not too many.

I have one Difficulty, which I don't know how to get over, and

---

[1] See No. 90.

That is, where They shall go at Horsham: We are all to be at Col. Ingram's:—and yet a Meeting at a private House is not so clever, for a publick Declaration. I should think, the best would be, either to meet at some publick House in Horsham, for half an Hour before, and there make the Declaration, and then go afterwards to Col. Ingram's, to drink Success; or else to meet at Col. Ingram's on Monday night, and then determine to meet at a Publick House the next Day, to make the Declaration: But that we may determine at the Time. Get but our Friends to Horsham, and we shall do well enough with Them there. If there is any Gentlemen, that is unwilling to come, and that a letter from me would bring Him, upon the first notice from you, I will write to any Body, that you shall direct. . . .

I am,

&tc. HOLLES NEWCASTLE.

To Mr Pelham, Junior

Add. MSS. 32694, f. 211.

106. A compromise: Bedfordshire, 1753.

P. YORKE TO LORD HARDWICKE

5 August 1753

. . . We had at the Meeting [at Bedford] all the principal Gentlemen of both Parties; of the Whigs, besides myself, were Sr Rowland, & Mr Alston, (who appeared very cool & grave,) Mr Farrer, Mr Orlebar, Mr Ongley &c.—of the Torys, Ld St John, who declared their concurrence, in this short sentence, after some silence in that side,—My Lord, (addressing himself to the Duke, who had called upon them to declare,) I beleive none of this side, have any objection.—besides his Lordship were Sr H. Monoux, Sir B Chernocke, Sr C. Chester, &c— The Gentlemen all dined together, the H. Sheriff Mr Herne, (who is possessed of the Napier Estate,) was put at the head of the Table, & the Duke was very civil & gracious to every body . . .

The Duke of Bedford & the Corporation have settled their affairs for the next Election. The Duke brings in Mr Ongley, & the Corporation Mr Herne. His Grace is also to chuse Alderman Dickenson (who is reckoned a moderate Tory) for one of his Boroughs. Mr Crawley of Luton has been the chief mediator in this business between his Grace & the Torys.

Sr. R. Alston is very desirous that his Son should come in again for the County. If the Young Man is in any tolerable State of Sanity,

I do not see, that any other choice can be made in order to keep up the Whig Interest here, & I know the Duke of Bedford is very willing to consent, & does not think of any body else.

Add. MSS. 35351, f. 249.

IV. PARTIES

Though the election of M.P.s might seem to have depended on factors unconnected with the interests of the nation, nevertheless the House of Commons was not filled with unprincipled time-servers. The owner of a corrupt little burgage borough, once he reached Westminster, could be in a position of greater independence than any M.P. today. The law reformer Romilly considered the purchase of a borough 'as almost the only mode by which Parliament was accessible with honour to one who had no family connexion, or local interest which could procure his return'.[1] In fact, the political managers at the centre (the Court and its allies and the leaders of the opposition) controlled or influenced less than half the total membership of the House of Commons.[2] The remainder were independent of the political leaders, a feature which renders the eighteenth-century political system peculiarly remote to us who are accustomed to the two-party system. George III's mother said to Dodington: 'The *party*, this; and the *party*, that: but I could never understand what the party was; I have endeavoured to learn, and I could never find, that the party was anything else, but the Duke of Devonshire, and his son, and old Horace Walpole.'[3] This may be exaggeration, but in those days there were no parties in our sense, that is to say, national organisations supporting certain policies, controlling the bulk of the M.P.s and obeying the orders of leaders at the top. Politicians called themselves (or their opponents) 'Whigs' or 'Tories', but less than half were organised into 'parties', and those that were belonged to one of a number of small groups, bound to leaders by ties of relationship, friendship, 'interest', or similarity of general attitude, rather than of support for a specific programme. Not that they were unprincipled, but rather that they conceived political office not as receiving a mandate to put into force a certain platform, but rather as receiving power to deal with political problems as they came along: a not inappropriate approach at a time when the bulk of these problems concerned foreign affairs.

That is one broad division, then, that can be discerned in the eighteenth-century House of Commons: between the active politicians on the one hand, and the independent members on the other (**38, 107**).[4] The former provided

---

[1] S. Romilly, *Memoirs of the Life of Sir Samuel Romilly* (1840), vol. II, p. 121.
[2] L. Namier, *Structure of Politics* (1957), p. 150.
[3] H. P. Wyndham (ed.), *Diary of George Bubb Dodington* (1784), p. 328.
[4] See also No. **132**, p. 220.

the leaders of the governments and the oppositions, and competed amongst themselves for the support of the latter. When one or more of these active groups formed a ministry, they required the support of the 'Queen's Servants', the 'King's Friends' or what has been called 'the Court and Treasury Party' (108). As Harley once put it, 'I take it for granted that no party in the House can carry it for themselves without the Queen's servants join with them; That the foundation is, persons or parties are to come in to the Queen, and not the Queen to them.'[1] This was a group of 100 to 200 'placemen' of various kinds: civil servants, court and household officers, government contractors and members sitting for government boroughs— what Liverpool called 'that strength which belongs to Government as such, and which may be considered as transferable from one Administration to another'.[2] Various 'Place Acts' attempted to whittle down the size of this group, but nothing really effective was achieved till the administrative reforms at the end of the century. In fact, the Place Act of 1742 (120) expressly omitted senior civil servants from its operation. These were the secretaries and under-secretaries mentioned in section III of the Act, who formed the efficient core of the Court and Treasury Party. Like so many other characters in constitutional history, they were at some stage in the metamorphosis from personal servant to state official. Some regarded themselves as working for the king rather than for the ministers who came and went (109), and were thus semi-permanent, and independent of party manoeuvre: a necessary position if continuity and efficiency were to be maintained in their offices. On the other hand, ministers needed servants they could trust, appointed by themselves, not by their predecessors, perhaps their enemies; and so some civil servants did come and go with governments (110). These latter were certainly not politically neutral; but neither were the former, so long as their master the king was in politics. The two types are difficult to distinguish during most of the period till the reforms at the end, when the former, like their master, began to be excluded from politics. They were the ancestors of the permanent-secretaries of later times; just as the latter developed into the modern parliamentary-secretaries.

The ministers needed the placemen, then, and to complete their majority they required (and usually received) the votes of those independent members who usually conceived it their duty to support the king's government. The remaining active groups lead the opposition, supported by the remainder of the independent members, and (in some periods) by the Prince of Wales and *his* little group of placemen (111).

---

[1] H.M.C., *Bath*, I, 74.

[2] C. D. Yonge, *Life of Liverpool* (1868), vol. I, p. 219. C. J. Fox called them: 'That band of janissaries who surround the person of the prince and are ready to strangle the minister at the nod of the moment.'—Quoted by S. Maccoby, *English Radicalism, 1762–1785* (1955), p. 403.

Thus our more or less permanent division is cut across by the more ephemeral division into government and opposition, or 'Court' and 'Country'. Add to this a third division, between Whigs and Tories, cutting across the first two, and the obscure nature of the history of party in this period becomes understandable. For the names, and the emotions associated with them, survived for generations after the issues which had called them into being were dead; and they generated more heat in local affairs than they did at the centre. The Revolution destroyed the theoretical foundations of Toryism and divided the party into at least three groups[1]; and Whigs were now to be found supporting the prerogative of the king they had placed on the throne. A correspondent of Harley thus describes the situation at the very beginning of our period: '... Parliament ... seems so divided at present with Tories, Whigs, Court Whigs, and Tory Whigs, which are the names at present given us.'[2] After 1714 the Tories were proscribed, and the active politicians of 'Court' and 'Country' were Whigs; and it was widely recognised that these party distinctions were 'vain names' (112). The Tories were permanently in opposition (136 strong, for example, in 1742[3]) and the policies they adopted bear no relation to those on which the party was founded. Except for the little group of Jacobites, there was no strict Tory position to take (113). There was a 'Country' position to take, and the Tories were joined in this by those independent members of the opposition who called themselves 'Whigs', and both were exploited by the active politicians of the opposition who also called themselves 'Whigs'. Typical 'Country' policies can be seen in Document No. 111. In this, the Prince of Wales promises to 'abolish for the future all Distinction of Party'—a principle reiterated by Bolingbroke (112), and inherited by George III, thus becoming a 'Court' principle later in the century (114, 37). In opposition to George III, the Rockingham Whigs developed a theory in active support of party (115), realising that 'without the organisation which the party system alone could give, the unreformed House of Commons lay at the mercy of the occupant of the throne'.[4] To complicate the situation, these same Whigs inherited most of the remainder of the 'Country' policies mentioned in No. 111. And a minority of these Whigs, the Foxites, linking up with the popular movements outside Parliament in connection with the Wilkes affairs, the American Revolution and the French Revolution, added a further doctrine: Parliamentary Reform.[5] This group cornered the name 'Whig' for itself and in time fastened the name 'Tory' on all those who rallied round the king in defence of the constitution. This development

---

[1] See No. 7.
[2] H.M.C., *Portland*, III, 446.
[3] J. B. Owen, *Rise of the Pelhams* (1957), p. 66.
[4] D. A. Winstanley, *Lord Chatham and the Whig Opposition* (Cambridge, 1910), p. 32.
[5] See Part VI of this chapter, p. 208.

occurred at a time when the eighteenth-century system was disintegrating: when the king was withdrawing from active politics, when the size of the 'Court and Treasury Party' was tapering off, when the independent members were gradually being drawn into one group or another, when the number of groups was being reduced to two, and when the world outside parliament was making itself felt—in other words, when the two-party system as we know it was being born.

107. The independent members, 1781.

HOUSE OF COMMONS PROCEEDINGS, 8 MAY 1781

LORD FEILDING ... Let them draw the comparison between the present state of court influence, and what it was under sir Robert Walpole, and he would ask the gentlemen over the way, in what period of that minister's reign, so few placemen were in parliament? When would they find four only of the twelve grooms of the bed-chamber in that House? But not to mention the Nullum Tempus Act, the Act for securing independence of the judges, or that great barrier to parliamentary freedom, Mr. Grenville's Bill, (all since that minister's time) there was still a stronger circumstance arisen. Where were those regularly trained parties, for which that period was so remarkable? He would ask an hon. gentleman, over against him, could he, could the ablest political muster-master so exactly calculate the strength on each side as to be able previously to determine which way many, he might almost say any, great popular question would be carried? No; he could not, that was effectually prevented by a new, a third party, having sprung up in that House, unknown to former periods. He meant the country gentlemen; the balance of power in that House was taken out of the hands of the minister, and placed in those of the country gentlemen; in the hands of men, for whom they had seen learned universities and great populous counties contending ... men neither to be frowned into servility nor huzzard into faction; by the support of these men, and not, as had been falsely asserted, by the low arts of corruption, did the present minister [North] stand. Should the noble lord in the blue ribbon, by any strange fatality, become that weak, that wicked minister, he had been unjustly called; should he become, as he had been represented, careless of the public good, attentive only to his private interest, a misleader of his sovereign, a corrupter of the parliament, an oppressor of the people, his supporters would immediately fail him; but while, on the contrary, he saw him generally supported by the most respectable characters in the House, it was to him as convincing a proof that he deserved their support and the confidence of the people at large, as it was of the worth, the generosity, or the integrity, of a private character, whom he saw countenanced and supported by the worthy, the generous, and the just.

P.H., XXII, 149.

108. State of the parties, 1706.

LORD GODOLPHIN TO ROBERT HARLEY

[1705–6, March 22] Good Friday night—I think as you do in your letter t' other day that the Tories are more numerous in this Parliament than the Whigs, and the Queen's servants much the least part of the three. My computation runs thus: of the 450 that chose the Speaker Tories 190, Whigs 160, Queen's servants 100, of the last about 15 perhaps joined with Tories in that vote of the Speaker, by which they mounted to 205, and so afterwards more or less, in almost every vote. Except in the Place Bill, that is the *clause*, the 160 voted always with the body of the Queen's servants. Now the question in my opinion is, whether it be more likely or more easy to keep the 160 which with the Queen's true servants will always be a majority, or to get [sic] from the 190. I think their behaviour in this Session has shown as much inveteracy and as little sense as was possible, however I should be always of opinion to receive such of them as would come off, but I see very little reason to depend upon that or upon them afterwards, and further it ought to be considered that for every one we are like to get from the 190 we shall lose 2 or 3 from the 160, and is it not more reasonable and more easy to preserve those who have served and helped us than to seek those who have basely and ungratefully done all that was in their poor power to ruin us: and when they find themselves disappointed, they would willingly make a little fair weather again, in hopes only as I think of a better opportunity next winter, if we have ill success, and if we have good, of making a merit. As for the Clergy, they always say themselves it is easy for the Queen to get them into her interests. I think so too, if they be once thoroughly satisfied which is the right way to preferment. As for the idle stories they make not the least impression upon me, I mind only what men do, and not what others say they do, so that as far as my friendship is of any value, you need not apprehend that 'tis in the power of another to take it from you.

N   177

As to the *narrow measures* of any in the House of Lords, be they who they will, I may presume to say such measures are wrong; I take it our business is, to get as many as we can from the 190, without doing anything to lose one of the 160.

H.M.C., *Portland*, IV, 291.

109. A non-party civil servant, 1788.

WILLIAM KNOX[1] TO LORD WALSINGHAM

[25 May 1788]

... Your Lordship has probably heard of a middle party that has sprung up from the inattention and partiality of Mr Pitt in disposing of offices. He avows an inattention to men, and reliance upon measures. I apprehend the principle, and would have walked barefoot from Pembrokeshire to have given it support, but how has he adhered to this principle? [He criticizes various ministers] ... He has it in his power to fill offices in a manner that will give satisfaction to the public, and restore the expiring confidence of Parliament; but if he continues to play at Tom with the great officers of Government, he will sink in character, and be driven from Ministry. Such is the language I hear. I shall greatly regret his fall, for though he has used me ill, I admire his talents and pray for his continuance, But I owe a superior duty to the king and the country, and as he will not avail himself of my experience and judgement, I must carry them where they may be rendered usefull. I want not the paltry salary of office, but I expect civility and attention. The party I have already mentioned have applied to me for inform-ation. They disavow factious opposition, and profess attachment to the king's authority. In these points we perfectly agree; the king's servant is my minister, be he who he may. I have, therefore, con-sented to direct them, and give them creditable business to transact. I will do no mischief, but I will stimulate the Minister to do good ...

H.M.C., *Various*, VI, 201.

110. A party 'civil servant', 1758.

JAMES WEST TO NEWCASTLE

[17 Jan 1758]

I humbly presume to send Your Grace, the Estimate of the Supply for the Year 1758, in the manner Your Grace was pleased to order this

[1] Under-Secretary of State for the Colonies, 1770-1782.

morning; and as It is impossible for me to obey Your Graces other command,[1] the only instance which to the best of my recollection I have ever failed in, I most humbly beg your Graces permission to retire from the business of the Treasury, and this My Lord I find myself obliged to do, as much out of duty to Your Grace, as Justice to myself. When I was first appointed Secretary to the Chancellor of the Exchequer It was at Mr Pelham's desire, without my seeking, & upon his absolute promise that I should be Secretary of the Treasury as soon as he could provide for Mr Jeffries; after some years waiting, He told me He was so pressed by Mr Jeffries friends; that he could not remove him without some provision, & therefore desired me to take the place, as Mr Scope[2] was very old, & to allow Mr Jeffries 1000 £ p. ann., till he could provide for him wch should not exceed a year; at the same time insisting I should keep the office of Secretary to the Chancellor of the Exchequer, as some sort of recompense for the Allowance I was to make, till he could manage other wayes for him: The many repeated marks of friendship & confidence with which he honoured me, will remain deeply impressed & claim my most gratefull remembrances and acknowledgements: On Mr Scropes death (April 1752) He did me the honour to write to me then in the Countrey to congratulate me on succeeding him & being eased of my Burdensome payment. He then made Mr Jeffries his Secretary, as Chancellor of the Exchequer, with a payment from Mr Hardinge [joint Secretary of the Treasury] of 200 £ p. ann., in lieu of 1000 £ which I paid him.

From April 1752 to Nov. 1756 when your Grace quitted the Treasury, and I found myself bound by Inclination as well as duty, not to serve, under any administration without your Grace; I enjoyed the whole of the profits of one of the Secretaries of the Treasury, and I hope It is not arrogant to say, that in my poor opinion Whoever brings himself into parliament & honestly discharges the duty of the office, amply deserves the Lawfull fees of it—what I have done since to deserve their being curtailed, I am ignorant of ... Your Grace asks Is Mr Jeffries to starve? God forbid! ... May I humbly ask, am I to work for him? but indeed It is not for him but for a person I love & esteem, one who would have continued to have paid Mr Jeffries had I not quitted the Treasury with Your Grace when he chose

[1] To have John Jeffreys quartered upon him; see Namier, *Structure of Politics* (1957), pp. 402-6, for an account of him.

[2] John Scrope, Secretary of the Treasury, 1724-52.

to stay with those whom before & since he has been more closely connected with; but My Lord I went out with Your Grace & therefore I am to be punished, a Triumphant Sneer is to appear, & a Malignant Whisper to be spread thro' the House of Commons & elsewhere, that however honoured with Your Grace's Countenance, I shall be mulcted for my attachment; to which, however falsely, will not fail to be added; that he that helps to quarter upon others, is himself quartered upon.

Add. MSS. 32877, ff. 168–9.

III. Treaty of alliance between the Prince of Wales and the Tories, 1747.

Carlton House June 4 1747 ten o'Clock at Night

Present

His Royal Highness the Prince of Wales
Lord Talbot, Lord Baltimore, Dr Lee, Sr Fra^s Dashwood.

His Royal Highness was pleased to read the following Paper.

His Royal Highness has authorised Lord Talbot & Sir Fra.^s Dashwood to give the most positive Assurances to the Gentlemen in the Opposition, of his upright Intentions: that He is strongly convinced of the Distress and Calamities, that have befell, and every day are more likely to befall his Country; & therefore invites all Well-wishers to this Country & its Constitution to coalise & unite with him in the following Principles only.

1. His R.H. promises & will declare it solemnly & openly, that it is his Intentions totally to abolish for the future all Distinction of Party, & as far as it lies in his power, (and when it does lie in his power), to take away all Proscriptions from any Set of men whatever, who are Friends to the Constitution: And therefore will promote for the present, & when in his power will grant a Bill, to impower all Gentlemen to act as Justices of the Peace paying Land Tax for £300 *per ann:* in any County where they intend to serve.

2. His R.H. promiseth in like manner to support a Bill, and forthwith to grant it (whenever he shall have the Misfortune to lose His Majesty) to raise & establish a numerous Militia throughout the Kingdom.

3. His R.H. promises in like manner to support & promote, and likewise grant (when it is in his power) a Bill to exclude all Military Officers

in the Land Service under the Degree of Colonels of Regiments, & in the Sea Service under the degree of Rear-Admirals, from sitting in the House of Commons.

4. His R.H. promises, that he will (when in his power) immediately grant Inquiries into the great Number of Abuses in Offices, & does not doubt of the Assistance of all honest Men to enable him to reform & correct the same for the future.

5. His R.H. promises & will openly declare, that he will make no Agreement, or join in support of any Administration whatsoever, without previously obtaining the above-mentioned Points, on behalf of the People, & for the sake of good Governmt, upon these Conditions, & these Conditions only; & his R.H. thinks he has a Right not to doubt of a most cordial Support from all those good Men, who mean well to their Country, & this Constitution; & that they will become his & his Family's Friends, & unite with him to promote the good Government of this Country, & follow him on those Principles both in Court, & out of Court. And if he should live to form an Administration, it shall be composed, without Distinction, of Men of Dignity, Knowledge, & Probity.

6. His R.H. further promises to accept of no more, if offered him, than £800,000 for his Civil List *per annum* by Way of Rent-Charge.

. . .

Reasons for the Tories coaliting with the Prince: by Mr Powney.

1. Because he expresses a good Opinion of you, & desires your Assistance.

2. Because the present Ministry & all its Connections hate you, & will proscribe you, as long as they are in power.

3. Because, if you do not join him, you drive him into the hands, which he abhors, into those very hands, which always will oppose you.

4. Because, if you have a Share in his Councils, there can be no present danger of Reproach from such Measures & Motions, as shall be agreed upon; & you shall approve of, to be agitated in Parliament.

5. Because he offers such terms in future for securing the Liberty of the Subject, & for setting bounds to the Prerogative, as never were proposed by any one related to the Crown.

6. Because it is necessary for him to have Assurances, whereby to form a future Administration; & if you decline taking part in that, you

can be nothing but in Opposition in conjunction with the worst Set of Men in the present Ministry.

7. Because there is no other sensible Plan by which this Country can be served, the landed Interest supported, and the Parliamentary Interest of Individuals be secured.

Add. MSS. 35870, ff. 129–31.

112. Bolingbroke appeals for non-party government, 1727.

Every Body knows that, for near a *Century* past, this Kingdom hath been almost continually agitated with Contentions; occasion'd by mutual Jealousies and Uneasinesses between the *Prince* and the *People*, for *Liberty* on one Side, and the *Prerogative* on the other; in which also *Religion* has been not a little concern'd. These Disputes, which have divided the Nation into two great Factions, and brought about several wonderful Revolutions in our Government, seem, at present, to be in a great Measure terminated by the firm Establishment of the *Protestant Succession*, against all Attempts to defeat it; and by the general Affection of the People to his Majesty's Person, Family and Government.

Notwithstanding This, the Names of *Distinction* are still kept up, when our Differences are so generally reconcil'd; and we preserve the same Bitterness, Hatred and Animosity against one another, whilst we are in the *same Interest*, and pursue the *same End*, as when we professed *contrary Views*, and took *Measures* diametrically *opposite*.

If you ask a *Whig* for his opinion of a *Tory*, he'll tell you, in general, that he is a *Jacobite* or a *Papist*: a Friend to *arbitrary Government*, and against the *Liberties* of the People both in *Church* and *State*.

Take the Character of a *Whig*, in like Manner, from a *Tory*, and you will hear him describ'd to be a Man of *Republican Principles*; a *Presbyterian*; and a sworn Enemy to the Church of *England*, and the *Regal Prerogative*; nay, it will be well for him, if he is not set forth as a downright *Atheist*, or *Libertine*, and an Enemy to *all Government* whatsoever.

But will either a *Whig* or a *Tory*, if you put the same Questions separately to them, acknowledge these *Characters* to be just; or adopt such *Principles* as their own? No; there is not, I believe, one in an hundred of either Party, who would not deny them in the most solemn Manner; and exclaim very loudly against such uncharitable Treatment; the just Inference from which is, that as every Man must be supposed to wish for his own Happiness, and consequently for the

Welfare of his Country; so no Man of common Sense, who hath the last Knowledge of the Constitution of this Nation, can possibly espouse *such Principles*; and therefore it is very unjust to charge any Person with maintaining Tenets, which he solemnly denies; and which, being inconsistent with his own Interest, he cannot reasonably be supposed to maintain. . . .

What therefore is to be wish'd, in our present Circumstances, is that all Persons, however distinguish'd by party Appellations, who are truly in the Interest of the *present Government*, and desire the Continuance of it, would consolidate themselves into a Body, and unite in Measures against the *common Enemies* of their Country, whether *foreign* or *domestick*; that they would forget all their former unreasonable Animosities; and whilst they are equally exerting their Endeavours to accomplish the *same End, viz.* the Happiness of their Country, that they would not quarrel with one another about any Differences in Judgement concerning the *Means*.

Let the *true Sons of the Church*, and especially the *Clergy*, lay aside all unnecessary Fear or Apprehensions of its *Danger*; and content themselves with those Rights, Immunities and Powers, with which the Law hath invested them, without endeavouring to stretch them any farther. Let the *Protestant Dissenter* acquiesce under that *Toleration* and those *Privileges*, with which the Legislature hath thought fit to indulge him. Let the *Whig* enjoy his *Liberty* and *Property* in its fullest Latitude, without reproaching the *Tory* as an Enemy to both; and let the *Tory*, in his Turn, drop all his Bitterness and Malevolence against the *Whig*, as disaffected to *Monarchy* and *Religion*; or rather let the very Names of *Whig* and *Tory* be for ever buried in Oblivion; and let there be, for the future, no other Distinction known amongst us, but of "*Those*, (as our late *glorious Deliverer* express'd it) who are for the *Protestant Religion* and the *present Establishment*; and of Those, who mean a *Popish Prince* and a *French Government*." . . .

Bolingbroke, The Craftsman, No. 40, 24 April 1727.

113. Hervey on the state of the parties, 1727.

Whig and Tory had been the denominations by which men opposite in their political views had distinguished themselves for many years and through many reigns. Those who were called Whigs had been in power from the first accession of the Hanover family to the Crown; but the original principles on which both these parties were said to act altered so insensibly in the persons who bore the names, by the long prosperity of the one, and the adversity of the other, and those who called themselves Whigs arbitrarily gave the title of Tory to every one who opposed the measures of the administrations or whom they had a mind to make disagreeable at Court; whilst the Tories (with more justice) reproached the Whigs with acting on those principles and pushing those very points which, to ingratiate themselves with the people and to assume a popular character, they had at first set themselves up to explode and oppose.

The two chief characteristics of the Tories originally were the espousing of the prerogative and the dignity of the Church; both which they pretended were now become, if not by profession, at least by practice, much more the care of the Whigs. Nor were the Whigs quite innocent of this imputation; long service and favour had gradually taught them a much greater complaisance to the Crown than they had formerly paid to it, and the power of the crown being an engine at present in their own hands, they were not very reluctant to keep up an authority they exercised, and support the prerogative which was their own present though precarious possession. The assistance, likewise, which the Whigs in power had received from the bench of bishops in Parliamentary affairs, had made them show their gratitude there too, by supporting both them and the inferior clergy in all ecclesiastical concerns (except the suffering the Convocation to sit), with as much vigour and firmness as the most zealous of those who are called the Church Party could have done. The increase of the army and civil list, the repeated suspension of the Habeas Corpus Act, and frequent votes of credit in the late reign, were further instances that were often and not unreasonably given by the Tories of the Whigs deviating in their conduct from their original profession and principles.

Both Whigs and Tories were subdivided into two parties; the Tories into Jacobites and what were called Hanover Tories; the Whigs into patriots and courtiers, which was in plain English "Whigs in place" and "Whigs out of place." The Jacobite party was fallen so low, from the indolence of some, the defection of others, and the despair of all, that in reality it consisted only of a few veterans (and those very few) who were really Jacobites by principle, and some others who, educated in that calling, made it a point of honour not to quit the name, though their attachment to the person of the Pretender was not only weakened but, properly speaking, entirely dissolved, their consciences quiet about his title, and their reverence to his character, their compassion for his misfortunes, and their hope of his success, quite worn out.

That which kept this party still alive and gave it that little weight it yet retained in the Kingdom was that all those who were by private views piqued at the administration without being disaffected to the government joined the Jacobites in Parliament and pushed the same points, though on different motives; these only designing to distress the ministers, and those catching at anything that might shake the establishment of the Hanover family, and tend to the subversion of the whole. By these means men oftentimes seemed united in their public conduct who differed as much in their private wishes and views from one another as they did from those they opposed; and whilst they acted in concert together, both thought they were playing only their own game, and each looked upon the other as a dupe. . . .

It will not be difficult, from what has been said of the state of the party at this juncture in England, to perceive that the chief struggle now lay not between the Jacobites and Hanoverians, or Tories and Whigs, but between Whigs and Whigs, who, conquerors in the common cause, were now split into civil contest among themselves, and had no considerable opponents but one another.

R. Sedgwick (ed.), John, Lord Hervey, *Memoirs of the Reign of George II* (1931), vol. I, p. 3.

114. Douglas regards party distinctions as merely nominal, 1761.

When the private interest of a few individuals is affected, we frequently see that they have art enough to get their cause to be looked upon as the cause of a whole party. I should be sorry if this happened to be the case at present; and yet, we have been told, that, because a few *tories* have got places, attempts have been made to induce the *whigs* to consider this as an attack on their whole body: but if the *whigs* can be so far deluded as to believe this, it will give us a remarkable proof, that *party is the madness of the many, for the gain of the few*. For does any candid and intelligent man seriously believe, that at this time of day, there subsists any party distinction amongst us, that is not merely nominal? Are not the *tories* friends of the *royal family*? Have they not long ago laid aside their aversion to the dissenters? Do they not think the toleration and establishment, both necessary parts of the constitution? And can a *whig* distinguish these from his own principles? Must not, therefore, every honest man see and confess, that the cry against widening the bottom of government, is propagated by some, who, finding their own views of ambition or gain affected by this measure, endeavour to render it odious amongst the body of the party, who otherwise would have seen no reason to be alarmed, even in point of private interest? For all that the *tories* possibly can hope for, or expect, is that a few marks of confidence may be given them at present, as a proof, that the *proscription* is at an end, and as an earnest, that in the future disposal of court favors, when there are vacancies by deaths and not by removals, they will stand an equal chance of being taken notice of, with the rest of his majesty's good subjects. And here I may ask, has so much as a single *whig* been displaced, to make room for a *tory* successor? Have not the few places conferred on the formerly excluded party, been such as his majesty has created, in his own bed-chamber, by increasing the numbers of his servants? Why therefore should there be complaints, where there is so little foundation? Indeed, the thing speaks for itself. The ground of the uneasiness is not that any *whig* has been displaced, but that a nation of *whigs* as we may now justly be called, must cease for the future to be governed by the narrow maxims of faction.

John Douglas, Seasonable Hints from an Honest Man (1761), p. 32.

115. Burke's defence of party, 1770.

Party is a body of men united, for promoting by their joint endeavours the national interest, upon some particular principle in which they are all agreed. For my part, I find it impossible to conceive, that any one believes in his own politicks, or thinks them to be of any weight, who refuses to adopt the means of having them reduced into practice. It is the business of the speculative philosopher to mark the proper ends of government. It is the business of the politician, who is the philosopher in action, to find out proper means towards those ends, and to employ them with effect. Therefore every honourable connexion will avow it is their first purpose, to pursue every just method to put the men who hold their opinions into such a condition as may enable them to carry their common plans into execution, with all the power and authority of the state. As this power is attached to certain situations, it is their duty to contend for these situations. Without a proscription of others, they are bound to give to their own party the preference in all things; and by no means, for private considerations, to accept any offers of power in which the whole body is not included;

nor to suffer themselves to be led, or to be controuled, or to be over-balanced, in office or in council, by those who contradict the very fundamental principles on which their party is formed, and even those upon which every fair connexion must stand. Such a generous con-tention for power, on such manly and honourable maxims, will easily be distinguished from the mean and interested struggle for place and emolument. The very stile of such persons will serve to discriminate them from those numberless imposters, who have deluded the ignorant with professions incompatible with human practice, and have after-wards incensed them by practices below the level of vulgar rectitude. . . .

In order to throw an odium on political connexion . . . [non-party] politicians suppose it a necessary incident to it, that you are blindly to follow the opinions of your party, when in direct opposition to your own clear ideas; a degree of servitude that no worthy man could bear the thought of submitting to; and such as, I believe, no connexions (except some court factions) ever could be so senselessly tyrannical as to impose. Men thinking freely, will, in particular instances, think differently. But still, as the greater part of the measures which arise in the course of public business are related to, or dependent on, some great *leading general principles in government*, a man must be peculiarly unfortunate in the choice of his political company if he does not agree with them at least nine times in ten. If he does not concur in these general principles upon which the party is founded, and which neces-sarily draw on a concurrence in their application, he ought from the beginning to have chosen some other, more conformable to his opin-ions. When the question is in its nature doubtful, or not very material, the modesty which becomes an individual, and (in spite of our court moralists) that partiality which becomes a well-chosen friendship, will frequently bring on an acquiescence in the general sentiment. Thus the disagreement will naturally be rare; it will be only enough to indulge freedom, without violating concord, or disturbing arrangement. And this is all that ever was required for a character of the greatest uniform-ity and steadiness in connexion. How men can proceed without any connexion at all, is to me utterly imcomprehensible. Of what sort of materials must that man be made, how must he be tempered and put together, who can sit whole years in parliament, with five hundred and fifty of his fellow citizens, amidst the storm of such tempestuous passions, in the sharp conflict of so many wits, and tempers, and characters, in the agitation of such mighty questions, in the discussion of such vast and ponderous interests, without seeing any one sort of men, whose character, conduct, or disposition, would lead him to associate himself with them, to aid and be aided, in any one system of public utility?

E. Burke, 'Thoughts on the Cause of the Present Discontents', Works(1792), vol. I, p. 498.

V. DURATION, FREQUENCY AND MEMBERSHIP

The clause in the Bill of Rights (10) laying down that 'Parliaments ought to be held frequently' was given specific form in the Triennial Act of 1694 (18), though the dependence of the crown on the House of Commons, ensured by post-Revolutionary finance, required annual sessions without the necessity of legislating for them. The duration of parliament was changed once more in this period by the Septennial Act of 1716 (116), though it became part of the stock-in-trade of oppositions to demand a return to the Triennial Act (itself a 'Country' measure originally). Oppositions also paid frequent attention to parliamentary membership. A large number of measures were passed during the period all attempting (though without great success) to reduce the influence of the Court on the House of Commons by preventing certain types of government servants from sitting there, or from influencing elections. The drastic exclusion envisaged by the 'Place Clause' in the Act of Settlement (21) was moderated by the Succession to the Crown Acts of 1705 and 1707, which brought in the compromise of re-election for ministers (117). Without it the development of the constitution would have been distorted, for that beneficial mutual influence of crown and parliament which eventually produced the cabinet responsible to parliament would have been prevented. Those who were completely excluded by the various Acts of the first half of the period were different categories of revenue officers and minor civil servants (118, 119, 120). Similar in intent were the Acts imposing property qualifications for M.P.s (121); and the Acts which attempted to take disputes over the franchise and over election returns out of the hands of party-politics, that is to say, the Last Determinations Act (122) and the Grenville Committees Act (123). In the second half of the period, another burst of 'Country' activity produced the enactment by the Rockinghams of their programme of Economical Reform in 1782: the Disfranchisement of the Revenue Officers (124), the exclusion of government contractors from the House of Commons (125) and the Civil Establishment Act (126). Numerous and thorough though all these measures may seem, they had a small effect on the 'influence' of the Court compared with Curwen's Act (127, 128) and with the administrative reforms carried out under Pitt and his successors after 1784 by the government departments themselves in the interests of efficiency and economy (47, 48).

116. The Septennial Act, 1716.

An act for enlarging the time of continuance of parliaments, appointed by an act made in the sixth year of the reign of King William *and Queen* Mary, *intituled,* An act for the frequent meeting and calling of parliaments.

WHEREAS *in and by an act of parliament made in the sixth year of the reign of their late Majesties King* William *and Queen* Mary *(of ever blessed memory) intituled* An act for the frequent meeting and calling of parliaments: *it was, among other things enacted, That from thenceforth no parliament whatsoever, that should at any time then after be called, assembled or held, should have any continuance longer than for three years only at the farthest, to be accounted from the day on which by the writ of summons the said parliament should be appointed to meet: and whereas it has been found by experience, that the said clause hath proved very grievous and burthensome, by occasioning much greater and more continued expences in order to elections of members to serve in parliament, and more violent and lasting heats and animosities among the subjects of this realm, than were ever known before the said clause was enacted; and the said provision, if it should continue, may probably at this juncture, when a restless and popish faction are designing and endeavouring to renew the rebellion within this kingdom, and an invasion from abroad, be destructive to the peace and security of the government;* be it enacted ... That this present parliament, and all parliaments that shall at any time hereafter be called, assembled or held, shall and may respectively have continuance for seven years, and no longer, to be accounted from the day on which by the writ of summons this present parliament hath been, or any future parliament shall be appointed to meet, unless this present, or any such parliament hereafter to be summoned, shall be sooner dissolved by his Majesty, his heirs or successors.

1 Geo. I, stat. 2, c. 38: S.L., XIII, 282.

117. Re-election for office-holders, 1707.

XXV. And be it further enacted That no person, who shall have in his own name, or in the name of any person or persons in trust for him, or for his benefit, any new office or place of profit whatsoever under the Crown, which at any time since the five and twentieth day of *October*, in the year of our Lord one thousand seven hundred and five have been created or erected, or hereafter shall be created or erected, nor any person who shall be commissioner or sub-commissioner of prizes, secretary or receiver of the prizes, nor any comptroller of the accounts of the army, nor any commissioner of transports, nor any commissioner for any wine licences, nor any governor or deputy governor of any of the plantations, nor any commissioners of the navy employed in any of the out-ports, nor any person having any pension from the crown during pleasure, shall be capable of being elected, or of sitting or voting as a member of the house of commons in any parliament which shall be hereafter summoned and holden.

XXVI. Provided always, That if any person being chosen a member of the house of commons, shall accept of any office of profit from the crown, during such time as he shall continue a member, his election shall be, and is hereby declared to be void and a new writ shall issue for a new election, as if such person so accepting was naturally dead. Provided nevertheless, That such person shall be capable of being again elected, as if his place had not become void as aforesaid.

XXVIII. Provided also, That nothing herein contained shall extend, or be construed to extend to any member of the house of commons, being an officer in her Majesty's navy or army, who shall receive any new or other commission in the navy or army respectively.

6 Anne, c. 7: S.L., XI, 316.

118. A Place Clause: Excise-men, 1700.

An act for granting an aid to his Majesty, by sale of the forfeited and other estates and interests in Ireland, *for the several purposes therein mentioned.* 2s. in the pound.

CL. And be it enacted by the authority aforesaid, That no member of the house of commons in this present or any future parliament . . . shall . . . be capable of being a commissioner or farmer of the duty of excise upon beer, ale and other liquors, or of being a commissioner for determining appeals concerning the said duty, or controlling or auditing the account of the said duty, or of holding or enjoying in his own name, or in the name of any other person in trust for him or for his use and benefit, or of executing by himself or his deputy, any office, place or employment, touching or concerning the farming, collecting or managing the said duty of excise.

11 & 12 Will. III, c. 2: S.L., X. 306.

119. A Place Clause: Customs-men, 1700.

An act for granting an aid to his Majesty for defraying the expence of his navy, guards, and garrisons for one year, and for other necessary occasions. 2s. in the pound.

LXXXIX. And be it enacted . . . That no member of the house of commons, from and after the dissolution of this present parliament, shall be capable of being a commissioner or farmer of the customs, or of holding or enjoying in his own name, or in the name of any other person in trust for him, or for his use or benefit, or of executing by himself or his deputy, any office, place or employment, touching or concerning the farming, collecting or managing the customs.

XCI. And be it further enacted . . . That . . . no commissioner, collector, comptroller, searcher, or other officer or person whatsoever, concerned or imployed in the charging, collecting, levying, or managing the customs, or any branch or part thereof, shall by word, message, or writing, or in any other manner whatsoever, endeavour to persuade any elector to give, or dissuade any elector from giving his vote for the choice of any person to be a knight of the shire, citizen, burgess, or baron, of any county, city, borough, or cinque port to serve in parliament; and every officer, or other person offending therein, shall forfeit the sum of one hundred pounds; one moiety thereof to the informer, the other moiety to the poor of the parish where such offence shall be committed . . .

12 & 13 Will. III, c. 10: S.L., x, 371.

120. A Place Act: minor civil servants, 1742.

An act to exclude certain officers from being members of the house of commons. For further limiting or reducing the number of officers capable of sitting in the house of commons, be it enacted . . . That from and after the dissolution, or other determination of this present parliament, no person who shall be commissioner of the revenue in *Ireland,* or commissioner of the navy or victualling offices, nor any deputies or clerks in any of the said offices, or in any of the several offices following; that is to say, The office of lord high treasurer, or the commissioners of the treasury, or of the auditor of the receipt of his Majesty's exchequer, or of the tellers of the exchequer, or of the chancellor of the exchequer, or of the lord high admiral, or of the commissioners of the admiralty, or of the paymasters of the army, or of the navy, or of his Majesty's principal secretaries of state, or of the commissioners of the salt, or of the commissioners of the stamps, or of the commissioners of appeals, or of the commissioners of wine licences, or of the commissioners of hackney coaches, or of the commissioners of hawkers and pedlars, nor any persons having any office, civil or military, within the island of *Minorca*, or in *Gibraltar*, other than officers having commissions in any regiment there only, shall be capable of being elected, or of sitting or voting as a member of the house of commons, in any parliament which shall be hereafter summoned and holden.

II. And be it further enacted by the authority aforesaid, That if any person hereby disabled . . . shall nevertheless be returned as a member . . . such election and return are hereby enacted and declared to be void to all intents and purposes whatsoever; and if any person disabled, and declared incapable by this act to be elected, shall, after the dissolution, or other determination of this present parliament, presume to sit or vote as a member of the house of commons in any parliament, to be hereafter summoned, such person so sitting or voting, shall forfeit the sum of twenty pounds for every day in which he shall sit or vote in the said house of commons, to such person or persons who shall sue for the same in any of his Majesty's courts at *Westminster*; . . . and shall from thenceforth be incapable of taking, holding, or enjoying any office of honour or profit under his Majesty, his heirs or successors.

III. Provided always, and it is hereby enacted and declared by the authority aforesaid, That nothing in this act shall extend or be construed to extend, or relate to, or exclude the treasurer or comptroller of the navy, the secretaries of the treasury, the secretary to the chancellor of the exchequer, or secretaries of the admiralty, the under secretary to any of his Majesty's principal secretaries of state, or the deputy paymaster of the army, or to exclude any person having or holding any office or employment for life, or for so long as he shall behave himself well in his office; any thing herein contained to the contrary notwithstanding.

15 Geo. II, c. 22: *S.L.*, xviii, 36.

121. Property qualifications for M.P.s, 1710.

An Act for securing the freedom of parliaments, by the further qualifying the members to sit in the house of commons.

For the better preserving the constitution and freedom of parliament, be it enacted . . . That from and after the determination of this present parliament, no person shall be capable to sit or vote as a member of the house of commons, for any county, city, borough, or cinque port, within that part of *Great Britain* called *England*, the dominion of *Wales*, and town of *Berwick* upon *Tweed*, who shall not have an estate, freehold or copyhold, for his own life, or for some greater estate, either in law or equity, to and for his own use and benefit, of or in lands, tenements, or hereditaments, over and above what will satisfy and clear all incumbrances that may affect the same, lying or being within that part of *Great Britain* called *England*, the dominion of *Wales*, and town of *Berwick* upon *Tweed*, of the respective annual value hereafter limited, *videlicet*, The annual value of six hundred pounds, above reprizes, for every Knight of a shire; and the annual value of three hundred pounds, above reprizes, for every citizen, burgess, or baron of the cinque ports; and that if any person, who shall be elected or returned to serve in any parliament, as a knight of a shire, or as a citizen, burgess, or baron of the cinque ports, shall not, at the time of such election and return be seized of, or entitled of such an estate, in lands, tenements or hereditaments, as for such knight, or for such citizen, burgess or baron respectively, is herein before required or limited, such election and return shall be void.

II. Provided always, That nothing in this act contained, shall extend to make the eldest son, or heir apparent of any peer, or lord of parliament, or of any person qualified by this act to serve as knight of a shire, uncapable of being elected and returned, and sitting and voting as a member of the house of commons, in any parliament.

III. Provided always, That nothing in this act contained shall extend, or be construed to extend to either of the universities in that part of *Great Britain* called *England*, but that they and each of them may elect and return members to represent them in parliament, as heretofore they have done; any thing herein contained to the contrary notwithstanding.

9 Anne, c. 5: S.L., xii, 89.

122. Last Determinations Act, 1729.

An act for the more effectual preventing bribery and corruption in the elections of members to serve in parliament

Whereas *it is found by experience, that the laws already in being have not been sufficient to prevent corrupt and illegal practices in the election of members to serve in parliament;* for remedy therefore of so great an evil, and to the end that all elections of members to parliament may hereafter be freely and indifferently made, without charge or expence, be it enacted . . . That from and after the twenty fourth day of *June* in the year of our Lord one thousand seven hundred and twenty nine, upon every election of any member or members to serve for the commons in parliament, every freeholder, citizen, freeman, burgess or person having or claiming to have a right to vote or be polled at such election, shall, before he is admitted to poll at the same election, take the following oath (or, being one of the people called *Quakers*, shall make the solemn affirmation appointed for *Quakers*) in case the same shall be demanded by either of the candidates, or any two of the electors; that is to say,

I, A. B. do swear (or one of the people called *Quakers, I, A. B. do solemnly affirm*) *I have not received, or had by my self, or any person whatsoever in trust for me, or for my use and benefit directly or indirectly, any sum or sums of money, office, place or employment gift or reward, or any promise or security for any money, office, employment or gift, in order to give my vote at this election and that I have not before been polled at this election* . . .

III. And be it further enacted . . . That every sheriff, mayor, bailiff, headborough or other person, being the returning officer of any member to serve in parliament, shall, immediately after the reading the writ or precept for the election of such member, take and subscribe the following oath, *videlicet,*

I, A. B. do solemnly swear, That I have not directly nor indirectly, received any sum or sums of money, office, place or employment, gratuity or reward, or any bond, bill or note, or any promise or gratuity whatsoever, either by myself, or any other person to my use, or benefit or advantage, for making any return at the present election of members to serve in parliament; and that I will return such person or persons as shall, to the best of my judgment, appear to me to have the majority of legal votes.

Which oath any justice or justices of the peace of the said county, city, corporation or borough where such election shall be made, or in his or their absence, any three of the electors are thereby required and authorized to administer; and such oath so taken, shall be entered among the records of the sessions of such county, city, corporation and borough as aforesaid.

IV. And be it enacted . . . That such votes shall be deemed to be legal, which have been so declared by the last determination in the house of commons; which last determination concerning any county, shire, city, borough, cinque port or place shall be final to all intents and purposes whatsoever, any usage to the contrary notwithstanding.

V. And be it further enacted . . . That if any returning officer, elector or person taking the oath or affirmation herein before mentioned, shall be guilty of wilful and corrupt perjury, or of false affirming, and be thereof convicted by due course of law, he shall incur and suffer the pains and penalties, which by law are enacted or inflicted in cases of wilful and corrupt perjury.

VI. And be it enacted . . . That no person convicted of wilful and corrupt perjury, or subornation of perjury, shall, after such conviction, be capable of voting in any election of any member or members to serve in parliament.

VII. [Persons taking money or reward for their vote, &c. forfeit 500 £, and disabled to vote, &c.]

VIII. [Offenders in 12 months after the election discovering others, indemnified.]

IX. [The act to be read by the sheriff, &c. after reading the writ, and at the quarter-sessions after Easter.]

X. [Wilful offence forfeits 50 £.]

XI. [Prosecution to commence within two years.]

2 Geo. II, c. 24: S.L., XVI, 66.

123. Grenville Committees Act, 1770.

An Act to regulate the trials of controverted elections, or returns of members to serve in parliament.

Whereas *the present mode of decision upon petitions, complaining of undue elections or return of members to serve in parliament, frequently obstructs publick business; occasions much expence, trouble, and delay to the parties; is defective, for want of those sanctions and solemnities which are established by law in other trials; and is attended with many other inconveniences: for remedy thereof,* be it enacted . . . That after the end of the present session of parliament, whenever a petition, complaining of an undue election or return of a member or members to serve in parliament, shall be presented to the house of commons, a day and hour shall by the said house be appointed for taking the same into consideration; and notice thereof in writing shall be forthwith given, by the Speaker, to the petitioners and the sitting members, or their respective agents, accompanied with an order to them to attend the house, at the time appointed, by themselves, their counsel, or agents.

IV. And be it further enacted, That at the time appointed for taking such petition into consideration, and previous to the reading the order of the day for that purpose, the serjeant at arms shall be directed to go with the mace to the places adjacent, and require the immediate attendance of the members on the business of the house; and after his return the house shall be counted, and if there be less than one hundred members present, the order for taking such petition into consideration shall be immediately adjourned to a particular hour on the following day (*Sunday* and *Christmas* day always excepted;) and the house shall then adjourn to the said day; and the proceedings of all committees, subsequent to such notice from the said serjeant, shall be void: and, on the said following day, the house shall proceed in the same manner; and so, from day to day, till there be an attendance of one hundred members at the reading the order of the day, to take such petition into consideration.

V. And be it further enacted, That if after summoning the members, and counting the house as aforesaid, one hundred members shall be found to be present; the petitioners by themselves, their counsel, or agents, and the counsel or agents of the sitting members, shall be ordered to attend at the bar; and then the door of the house shall be locked, and no member shall be suffered to enter into or depart from the house, until the petitioners, their counsel, or agents, and the counsel or agents for the sitting members, shall be directed to withdraw as herein after is mentioned: and when the door shall be locked as aforesaid, the order of the day shall be read, and the names of all the members of the house, written or printed on distinct pieces of parchment or paper, being all as near as may be of equal size, and rolled up in the same manner, shall be put in equal number into six boxes or glasses, to be placed on the table for that purpose, and shall be shaken together; and then the clerk or clerk assistant attending the house shall publickly draw out of the said six boxes or glasses alternately the said pieces of parchment or paper, and deliver the same to the speaker, to be by him read to the house; and so shall continue to do, until forty-nine names of the members then present be drawn.

VI. Provided always, That if the name of any member who shall have given his vote at the election so complained of as aforesaid, or who shall be a petitioner complaining of an undue election or return, or against whose return a petition shall be then depending, or whose return shall not have been brought in fourteen days, shall be drawn; his name shall be set aside, with the names of those who are absent from the house.

XI. And be it further enacted, That . . . the petitioners or their agents, shall then name one, and the sitting members, or their agents, another, from among the members then present, whose names shall not have been drawn, to be added to those who shall have been so chosen by lot.

XIII. And be it further enacted, That as soon as the said forty nine members shall have been so chosen by lot, and the two members to be added thereunto shall have been so nominated as aforesaid, the door of the house shall be opened, and the house may proceed upon any other business; and lists of the forty nine members so chosen by lot shall then be given to the petitioners, their counsel or agents, and the counsel or agents for the sitting members, who shall immediately withdraw, together with the clerk appointed to attend the said select committee; and the said petitioners and sitting members, their counsel or agents, beginning on the part of the petitioners, shall alternately strike off one of the said forty nine members, until the said number shall be reduced to thirteen; and the said clerk, within one hour at farthest from the time of the parties withdrawing from the house shall deliver in to the house the names of the thirteen members then remaining; and the said thirteen members, together with the two members nominated aforesaid, shall be sworn at the table, well and truly to try the matter of the petition referred to them, and a true judgement to give according to the evidence; and shall be a select committee to try and determine the merits of the return or election appointed by the house to be that day taken into consideration; and the house shall order the said select committee to meet at a certain time to be fixed by the house, which time shall be within twenty-four hours of the appointment of the said select committee, unless a *Sunday* or *Christmas* day shall intervene; and the place of their meeting and sitting shall be some convenient room or place adjacent to the house of commons or court of requests, properly prepared for that purpose.

XVIII. And be it further enacted, That the said select committee shall have power to send for persons, papers and records; and shall examine all witnesses who come before them upon oath; and shall try the merits of the return, or election, or both; and shall determine, by a majority of voices of the said select committee, whether the petitioners or the sitting members, or either of them, be duly returned or elected, or whether the election be void; which determination shall be final between the parties to all intents and purposes: and the house, on being informed thereof by the chairman of the said select committee, shall order the same to be entered in their journals, and give the necessary directions for confirming or altering the return, or for the issuing a new writ for a new election, or for carrying the said determination into execution, as the case may require.

XXX. And be it further enacted, That this act shall continue in force seven years,[1] and till the end of the session of parliament next after the expiration of the said seven years, and no longer.

10 Geo. III, c. 16: *S.L.*, xxviii, 287.

124. Disfranchisement of the revenue officers: Crewe's Act, 1782.

An act for better securing the freedom of elections of members to serve in parliament, by disabling certain officers, employed in the collection or management of his Majesty's revenues, from giving their votes at such elections.

For the better securing the freedom of members to serve in parliament, be it enacted . . . That, . . . no commissioner, collector, supervisor, gauger, or other officer or person whatsoever, concerned or employed in the charging, collecting, levying, or managing the duties of excise, or any branch or part thereof; nor any commissioner, collector, comptroller, searcher, or other officer or person whatsoever, concerned or employed in the charging, collecting, levying, or managing the customs, or any branch or part thereof; nor any commissioner, officer or other person concerned or employed in collecting, receiving, or managing, any of the duties on stamped vellum, parchment, and paper, nor any person appointed by the commissioners for distributing of stamps; nor any commissioner, officer, or other person employed in

[1] Made perpetual by 14 Geo. III, c. 15 (1774).

collecting, levying, or managing, any of the duties on salt; nor any surveyor, collector, comptroller, inspector, officer, or other person employed in collecting, managing, or receiving, the duties on windows or houses; nor any postmaster, postmasters general, or his or their deputy or deputies, or any person employed by or under him or them in receiving, collecting, or managing the revenue of the post-office, or any part thereof, nor any captain, master, or mate, of any ship, packet, or other vessel, employed by or under the postmaster or postmasters general in conveying the mail to and from foreign ports, shall be capable of giving his vote for the election of any knight of the shire, commissioner, citizen, burgess, or baron, to serve in parliament for any county, stewartry, city, borough, or cinque port, or for chusing any delegate in whom the right of electing members to serve in parliament, for that part of *Great Britain* called *Scotland*, is vested: and if any person hereby made incapable of voting as aforesaid, shall nevertheless presume to give his vote, during the time he shall hold, or within twelve calendar months after he shall cease to hold, or execute any of the offices aforesaid, contrary to the true intent and meaning of this act, such votes so given shall be held null and void to all intents and purposes whatsoever, and every person so offending shall forfeit the sum of one hundred pounds, one moiety thereof to the informer, and the other moiety thereof to be immediately paid into the hands of the treasurer of the county, riding, or division, within which such offence shall have been committed, in that part of *Great Britain* called *England*; and into the hands of the clerk of the justices of the peace of the counties or stewartries, in that part of *Great Britain* called *Scotland*, to be applied and disposed of to such purposes as the justices at the next general quarter session of the peace to be held for such county, stewartry, riding, or division, shall think fit; . . . and the person convicted on any such suit shall thereby become disabled and incapable of ever bearing or executing any office or place of trust whatsoever under his Majesty, his heirs and successors.

II. [Not to extend to commissioners of the land tax, or persons acting under them]

III. [nor to offices held by letters patent for any estate of inheritance;]

IV. [nor to persons who shall resign their offices before Aug. 1, 1782.]

V. [Limitations of actions.]

22 Geo. III, c. 41: *S.L.*, XXXIV, 48.

125. A Place Act: government contractors, 1782.

An act for restraining any person concerned in any contract, commission, or agreement, made for the publick service, from being elected, or sitting and voting as a member of the house of commons.

For further securing the freedom and independence of parliament, be it enacted . . . That, from and after the end of this present session of parliament, any person who shall, directly or indirectly, himself, or by any person whatsoever in trust for him, or for his use or benefit, or on his account, undertake, execute, hold, or enjoy, in the whole or in part, any contract, agreement, or commission, made or entered into with, under, or from the commissioners of his Majesty's treasury, or of the navy or victualling office, or with the master general or board of ordnance, or with any one or more of such commissioners, or with any other person or persons whatsoever, for or on account of publick service; or shall knowingly and willingly furnish or provide, in pursuance of any such agreement, contract, or commission, which he or they shall have made or entered into as aforesaid, any money to be remitted abroad, or any wares or merchandize to be used or employed in the service of the publick, shall be incapable of being elected, or of sitting or voting as a member of the house of commons, during the time that he shall execute, hold, or enjoy, any such contract, agreement, or commission, or any part or share thereof, or any benefit or emolument arising from the same. . . .

III. Provided always, and be it enacted, That nothing herein contained shall extend, or be construed to extend, to any contract, agreement, or commission, made, entered into, or accepted, by any incorporated trading company in its corporate capacity, nor to any company now existing or established and consisting of more than ten persons, where such contract, agreement, or commission, shall be made, entered into, or accepted, for the general benefit of such incorporation or company. . . .   22 Geo. III, c. 45: *S.L.*, xxxiv, 56.

126. Civil Establishment Act, 1782.

An act for enabling his Majesty to discharge the debt contracted upon his civil list revenues; and for preventing the same from being in arrear for the future, by regulating the mode of payments out of the said revenues, and by suppressing or regulating certain offices therein mentioned, which are now paid out of the revenues of the civil list.

WHEREAS *his Majesty, from his paternal regard to the welfare of his faithful people, from his desire to discharge the debt on his civil list, without any new burthen to the publick, for preventing the growth of a like debt for the future, as well as for introducing a better order and œconomy in the civil list establishments, and for the better security of the liberty and independency of parliament, has been pleased to order, that the office commonly called or known by the name of* Third Secretary of State, *or* Secretary of State for the Colonies; *the office or establishment commonly known by the name and description of* The Board of Trade and Plantations; *the offices of lords of police in* Scotland; *the principal officers of the board of works; the principal officers of the great wardrobe; the principal officers of the jewel office; the treasurer of the chamber; the cofferer of the household; the officers of the six clerks of the board of green cloth; the office of paymaster of the pensions; the office of master of the harriers and fox hounds; and also the office of master of the stag hounds, should be suppressed:* wherefore, for carrying his Majesty's said gracious order into execution . . . be it enacted . . . That . . . the office commonly called or known by the name of *Third Secretary of State*, or Secretary of State for the Colonies [etc] . . . and all and every of the offices aforesaid, together with certain of the offices dependent on or connected with the same, of which a list shall be entered in the exchequer . . . are hereby utterly suppressed, abolished, and taken away . . .

IV. And whereas a new and oeconomical plan is intended to be adopted and take place, pursuant to his Majesty's gracious intentions, be it therefore enacted, That the commissioners of the treasury . . . are hereby authorized and required to direct such person or persons as they shall think most fit and capable to prepare, make up, and lay before them, for their approbation, methods accomodated to the several reforms and alterations in this act made, and to appoint or continue in office such officers as they shall judge most fit and proper for carrying such plans into execution, under the direction of the lord steward, lord chamberlain, master of the horse, and any other principal officer, to whom the said officers shall severally be subordinate; and the said lord steward, lord chamberlain, master of the horse, and such other principal officer, shall regularly, within the space of fifteen days after each and every quarter day, make out, or cause to be made out, an estimate of all the several articles of expence of his Majesty's civil government, within their distinct departments; which shall, after being inspected, and approved by the said lord steward, lord chamberlain, master of the horse, and such other principal officer, be presented to the said commissioners of the treasury; and which estimate of expence shall not be exceeded (except as is herein-after excepted and specially provided for) above five thousand pounds, in any of those departments in any one year, without sufficient reasons, to be produced to the said commissioners of the treasury, for increasing the same; and upon the expiration of the quarter, the said commissioners of the treasury shall direct so much of the monies of the civil list revenues to be issued at the receipt of the exchequer to the said lord steward, [etc] . . . or to any person or persons appointed for that purpose by the said lord steward, [etc] . . . with the consent and approbation of the commissioners of the treasury, as shall be sufficient to satisfy and pay the whole of the expence incurred in such quarter, which shall be by him distributed to and among the several persons who shall be intitled to receive the same.

V. [The court of virge, with all its lawful jurisdiction and powers, preserved.]

VI. [His Majesty's buildings to be under the direction of a surveyor or comptroller, to be appointed by his Majesty.]

VII. [The Royal gardens to be under the direction of a surveyor or comptroller, to be appointed by his Majesty.]

VIII [Directions relative to the execution of new buildings or repairs.]

IX. [Commissioners of the treasury, before payment for any such works, may order the same to be surveyed.]

X. [Where expences shall be under 1,000 £. vouchers to be produced to the lord chamberlain.]

XI [Clerks, &c. in the royal palaces, to be paid monthly.]

XII. [No new works in his Majesty's parks, &c. above a limited sum, to be undertaken without an order from his Majesty.]

XIII. [Furniture, plate, &c. to be under the management of the lord chamberlain.]

XIV. [Work formerly under the direction of the great wardrobe, how to be executed.]

XV. [The business heretofore done by the board of trade, to be executed by a committee of the privy council.]

XVII. *And, for the better regulation of the granting of pensions, and the prevention of abuse or excess therein,* be it enacted, That, . . . no pension exceeding the sum of three hundred pounds a year, shall be granted to or for the use of any one person; and that the whole amount of the pensions granted in any one year, shall not exceed six hundred pounds; a list of which, together with the names of the persons to whom the same are granted, shall be laid before parliament in twenty days after the beginning of each session, until the whole pension list shall be reduced to ninety thousand pounds; which sum it shall not be lawful to exceed by more than five thousand pounds in the whole of all the grants: nor shall any pension, to be granted after the said reduction, to or for the use of any one person, exceed the sum of one thousand two hundred pounds yearly, except to his Majesty's royal family, or on an address of either house of parliament.

XVIII. [Not to extend to persons who have served the crown in foreign courts.]

XIX. *And whereas much confusion and expence did arise from having pensions paid at various places, and by various persons; and a custom hath prevailed of granting pensions on a private list during his Majesty's pleasure, upon a supposition that in some cases it may not be expedient for the publick good to divulge the names of the persons in the said list, or that to divulge it may be disagreeable to the persons receiving such payments to have it known that their distresses are so relieved, or for saving the expence of fees and taxes on small pensions; by means of which said usage, secret and dangerous corruption may hereafter be practised: and whereas it is no disparagement for any persons to be relieved by the royal bounty in their distress, or for their desert, but, on the contrary, it is honorable, on just cause, to be thought worthy of reward:* be it therefore enacted . . . That no pension whatsoever, on the civil establishment, shall hereafter be paid but at the exchequer, and in the same manner as those pensions which are now paid and entered at the exchequer, under the head, title, and description of *Pensions,* and with the name of the person to whom, or in trust for whom, the said pension is granted;

XXI. Provided also, That it shall and may be lawful for the high treasurer, or first commissioner of the treasury for the time being, to return into the exchequer any pension or annuity, without the name of the person to whom the same is payable, on taking an oath before the barons of the exchequer, or one baron of the exchequer, or before the cursitor baron, in form following:

I A. B. do swear, That, according to the best of my knowledge, belief and information, the pension or pensions or annuity or annuities, returned without a name by me into the exchequer, is or are not, directly or indirectly, for the benefit, use, or behalf of any member of the house of commons, or, so far as I am concerned, applicable, directly or indirectly to the purpose of supporting or procuring an interest in any place returning members to parliament.

So help me GOD.

XXIV. *And, for preventing as much as may be all abuses in the disposal of monies issued under the head of secret service money, or money for special service;* be it enacted . . . That it shall not be lawful to issue or imprest from the exchequer, or order to be paid by a treasury warrant, or under sign manual, or otherwise, to any secretary or secretaries of the treasury, or to any other person or persons whatsoever, from the civil list revenues, for the purpose of secret service within this kingdom, any sum or sums of money which in the whole shall exceed the sum of ten thousand pounds in one year.

XXX. *And, for the better prevention of all practice by which such grants as of bounty may be made a colour under which pensions may be substantially granted, contrary to the true intent and meaning of this act,* it is hereby enacted, That any sum or sums of money so given as of royal bounty, to any person more than once in three years, the same is and shall be reputed a pension or pensions to all intents and purposes whatsoever.

XXXI. *And whereas the establishment of an invariable order in the payment of salaries and other charges on the civil list, will enable those who have the charge thereof the better to provide for the several services to which the said civil list revenues ought to be applied, and will be the means to prevent the incurring of debt for the future, and the following order seems just and equitable for that purpose; that is to say, first, the pensions and allowances of the royal family; secondly, the payment of the salaries of the lord high chancellor of Great Britain, lord keeper or lords commissioners of the great seal, the speaker of the house of commons, and judges of the courts of King's bench and common pleas, and barons of the exchequer, the chief justice of* Chester, *and the justices of the courts of great session in the principality of* Wales; *thirdly, the salaries of the ministers to foreign courts, being resident at the said courts; fourthly, the approved bills of all tradesmen, artificers, and labourers, for any articles supplied or works done, for his Majesty's service; fifthly, The menial servants in his Majesty's household; sixthly, The pension list, beginning with the smallest pensions; seventhly, The salaries of all other places payable out of the civil list revenues, beginning with the lowest; eighthly, The salaries and pensions of the high treasurer or commissioners of the treasury, and chancellor of the exchequer; be it* further enacted . . . That the commissioners of the treasury shall . . . draw out a plan of the establishments and payments of the said civil list revenues in classes, according to the order herein mentioned, arranging by estimate the expence of each class, . . .

XXXV. And be it enacted, That the commissioners of the treasury shall cause a regular book or books to be kept, for the charges of each of the classes and articles aforesaid, distinctly and apart; and it is hereby directed, that the result of payment in the said several books contained shall, in an orderly manner, and according to the usual method in which fair accounts are kept, be entered in a separate book at the end of each year, and the same being opposed to the receipt of the civil list cash, a balance shall be struck upon the whole.

XXXVI. *And whereas, upon abolishing the several offices suppressed by this act, sundry persons, who may have held their offices by patent for life, or may have legally, or according to the course of office, purchased the same for a valuable consideration, and may suffer hardship by the suppression thereof: and whereas others, though not within the same description, who have diligently and faithfully executed their several subordinate offices for his Majesty's service, and by such suppression will be reduced to distressful or indigent circumstances;* be it enacted by the authority aforesaid, That the commissioners of the treasury may, and they are hereby impowered, to allow to every person severally who holds his office by patent for life, or who has purchased his place in the manner before mentioned, an annuity equal to the legal emoluments of his said office; and also to allow to other persons in the subordinate offices aforesaid, upon examination into the circumstances and behaviour of the said persons, such annuities severally as the commissioners of the treasury shall think equitable and just, for the support and maintenance of such person or persons, until he or they shall be provided for in his Majesty's service, according to his or their abilities and merit.

22 Geo. III, c. 82: S.L., XXXIV, 143.

127. Corrupt practices at elections: Curwen's Act, 1809.

An Act for the better securing the Independence and Purity of Parliament, by preventing the procuring or obtaining of Seats in Parliament by corrupt Practices.

Whereas it is expedient to make further Provision for preventing corrupt Practices in the procuring of Elections and Returns of Members to sit in the House of Commons; And Whereas the giving, or procuring to be given, or promising to give or to procure to be given any Sum of Money, Gift, or Reward, or any Office, Place, Employment, or Gratuity, in order to procure the Return of any Member to serve in Parliament, if not given to or for the Use of some Person having a Right or claiming to have a Right to act as Returning Officer, or to vote at such Election, is not Bribery within the Meaning of an Act passed in the Second Year of King *George* the Second, intituled, *An Act for the more effectual preventing Bribery and Corruption in the Election of Members to serve in Parliament*, but such Gifts or Promises are contrary to the ancient Usage, Right, and Freedom of Elections, and contrary to the Laws and Constitution of this Realm; Be it declared and enacted . . . That if any Person or Persons shall, from and after the passing of this Act, either by himself, herself, or themselves, or by any other Person or Persons for or on his, her, or their behalf, give or cause to be given, directly, or indirectly, or promise or agree to give any Sum of Money, Gift, or Reward, to any Person or Persons, upon any Engagement, Contract, or Agreement, that such Person or Persons to whom, to whose Use, or on whose Behalf such Gift or Promise shall be made, shall, by himself, herself, or themselves, or by any other Person or Persons whatsoever at his, her, or their Solicitation, Request, or Command, procure or endeavour to procure the Return of any Person to serve in Parliament for any County, Stewartry, City, Town, Borough, Cinque Port, or Place, every Person so having given or promised to give, if not returned himself to Parliament for such County [etc] . . ., shall for every such Gift or Promise forfeit the sum of One thousand Pounds . . .; and every person so returned . . . shall be . . . disabled and incapacitated to serve in that Parliament for such County [etc] . . .; and any Person or Persons who shall receive or accept of, by himself, herself, or themselves, or by any other Person or Persons in trust for . . . him, her, or them, any such Sum of Money, Gift, or Reward, or any such Promise upon any such Engagement, Contract, or Agreement, shall forfeit to His Majesty the Value . . . of such Sum of Money . . ., over and above the Sum of Five hundred Pounds, which said Sum . . . he . . . shall forfeit to any Person who shall sue for the same . . .

II Provided always, and be it further enacted, That nothing in this Act contained shall extend, or be construed to extend, to any Money paid or agreed to be paid to or by any Person, for any legal Expence *bonâ fide* incurred at or concerning any Election.

III And be it further enacted, That if any Person or Persons shall, from and after the passing of this Act, by himself, herself, or themselves, or by any Person or Persons for or on his, her, or their Behalf, give or procure to be given, or promise to give or procure to be given, any Office, Place, or Employment, to any Person or Persons whatsoever, upon any express Contract or Agreement that such Person or Persons, to whom or to whose Use or on whose Behalf such Gift or Promise shall be made, shall by himself, herself, or themselves, or by any other Person or Persons at his, her, or their Solicitation, Request or Command, procure or endeavour to procure the Return of any Person to serve in Parliament for any County, [etc] . . ., such Person so returned, and so having given or procured to be given, or so having promised to give or procure to be given, or knowing of and consenting to such Gift or Promise upon any such express Contract or Agreement, shall be and is hereby declared and enacted to be disabled and incapacitated to serve in that Parliament for such County [etc] . . .; and any Person who shall receive or accept of, by himself, herself, or themselves, or by any other Person or Persons in trust for or to the Use of or on the Behalf of such Person, any such Office, Place, or Employment, upon such express Contract or Agreement, shall forfeit such Office [etc] . . ., and shall forfeit the Sum of Five hundred Pounds . . .; and any Person holding any Office under his Majesty, who shall give such Office . . . upon any such express Contract or Agreement, that the Person to whom or for whose Use such Office . . . shall be given, shall so procure or endeavour to procure the Return of any Person to serve in Parliament, shall forfeit the Sum of One thousand Pounds . . .

49 Geo. III, c. 118: *S.L.*, XLIX, 454.

128. Effect of Curwen's Act, 1812.

LIVERPOOL TO STOWELL

Fife House, September 25th, 1812

... You will, perhaps, be surprised when I tell you that the Treasury have only one seat free of expense, for which our friend Vansittart will be elected. I have two more which personal friends have put at my disposal and this is the sum total of my powers free of expenses.

Mr Curwen's bill has put an end to all money transactions between Government and the supposed proprietors of boroughs. Our friends, therefore, who look for the assistance of Government must be ready to start for open boroughs, where the general influence of Government, combined with a reasonable expense on their own part, may afford them a chance of success.

C. D. Yonge, *Life of Liverpool* (1868), vol. I, p. 444.

VI. PARLIAMENTARY REFORM

Effective or not, Place Acts, Economical Reform and administrative reform no longer satisfied a growing body of people who demanded a more radical reform of parliament, and who were no longer content to leave the opposition to the Court in the hands of the great landed families. The struggles between George III, bent on a full use of the powers of the crown, and those Whigs who were determined to regard the political victories of their predecessors over George II as constitutional precedents, did not take place in a vacuum. For at the same time violent indignation amongst the gentlemen and freeholders in the counties and the middle class and workers in the towns, stimulated by the economic dislocation caused by rapid industrialisation and the American and French Revolutionary Wars, led to attacks not merely on the power of the crown, but also on the composition of parliament; and, under the stimulus of the American Revolution, the Irish troubles, and the French Revolution, the whole eighteenth-century system was subjected to searching criticism, not merely of its practical working but even of its theoretical foundations. Principles, derived partly from seventeenth-century tradition and partly from the 'Philosophes', had returned to politics.

These principles found their way on to the Statute Book in the nineteenth century owing to the vigour with which they were supported not so much by parliament as by the electorate and the world beyond that. In the seventeenth and eighteenth centuries there was nothing unusual in Country leaders stirring up feeling outside parliament to lend weight to their attacks on the Court. They relied particularly on the freemen of the Cities of London and Westminster and the freeholders of the County of Middlesex;

and to the Closet and the House they added a third political institution: the streets of the Metropolis. However, in the changing political and economic environment of the later part of the period, the politicians found that they had constructed a Frankenstein's monster beyond their power to control. The menace first appeared in the late 1760's when the persecution of John Wilkes by a House of Commons subservient to the Court seemed to demonstrate that political freedom was not safe in the hands of the unreformed parliament. It rose up again in the late 1770's, during the economic distress and national humiliation produced by the American War, and helped to produce in 1780 what seems to have been an almost revolutionary situation. The movement used traditional techniques on a scale which made it a new force in politics: the press (**129**), county meetings, resolutions, petitions to the House, remonstrances to the king,[1] instructions to M.P.s, even forming in 1780 a central association to co-ordinate the efforts of the nation and perhaps take action itself should parliament remain unresponsive (**130**). It worked in alliance with the political magnates of the opposition in voicing the traditional 'Country' demands for the abolition of corruption, Place Acts, Economical Reform; but also (and this is where the alliance ended) campaigned in favour of parliamentary reform. Wilkes introduced the first measure for this in the Commons in 1776 (**131**); the younger Pitt, heir to some of the 'Country' tradition, made more than one attempt (**132**); the idea was taken up by the Foxites, the chief inheritors of opposition doctrines; but the most effective campaigners were the radicals called into action by the association movement of 1780 and left in charge of it when the Gordon Riots frightened most of the remainder of the opposition back into support of the 'established order of things'.[2] The French Revolution renewed the stimulus, but delayed its success by further scaring those classes who were opposed to any change. The techniques of 1780 were exploited to the full during the wars and again in the post-war period, especially in times of industrial and agrarian unrest, till by 1830 many politicians were convinced that the pressure had become irresistible. Thus, as Cobbett wrote at the time, it is as 'clear as daylight that the reform arose out of the will and resolution of the people'[3].

129. Junius to the Duke of Grafton, 1769.

TO HIS GRACE THE DUKE OF GRAFTON

MY LORD, 8 *July*, 1769.

If nature had given you an understanding qualified to keep pace with the wishes and principles of your heart, she would have made you, perhaps, the most formidable minister that ever was employed, under

---

[1] See also No. **198**.   [2] William IV's phrase.

[3] W. Cobbett, *Political Register*, 2 June 1832.

a limited monarch, to accomplish the ruin of a free people. When neither the feelings of shame, the reproaches of conscience, nor the dread of punishment, form any bar to the designs of a minister, the people would have too much reason to lament their condition, if they did not find some resource in the weakness of his understanding. We owe it to the bounty of Providence, that the completest depravity of the heart is sometimes strangely united with a confusion of mind, which counteracts the most favourite principles, and makes the same man treacherous without art, and a hypocrite without deceiving. The measures, for instance, in which your Grace's activity has been chiefly exerted, as they were adopted without skill, should have been conducted with more than common dexterity. But truly, my Lord, the execution has been as gross as the design. By one decisive step, you have defeated all the arts of writing. You have fairly confounded the intrigues of opposition, and silenced the clamours of faction. A dark, ambiguous system might require and furnish the materials of ingenious illustration; and, in doubtful measures, the virulent exaggeration of party must be employed, to rouse and engage the passions of the people. You have now brought the merits of your administration to an issue, on which every Englishman, of the narrowest capacity, may determine for himself. It is not an alarm to the passions, but a calm appeal to the judgment of the people, upon their own most essential interests. A more experienced minister would not have hazarded a direct invasion of the first principles of the constitution, before he had made some progress in subduing the spirit of the people. With such a cause as yours, my Lord, it is not sufficient that you have the court at your devotion, unless you can find means to corrupt or intimidate the jury. The collective body of the people form that jury, and from *their* decision there is but one appeal. . . .

Since the accession of our most gracious Sovereign to the throne, we have seen a system of government, which may well be called a reign of experiments. Parties of all denominations have been employed and dismissed. The advice of the ablest men in this country has been repeatedly called for and rejected; and when the Royal displeasure has been signified to a minister, the marks of it have usually been proportioned to his abilities and integrity. The spirit of the FAVOUR-ITE had some apparent influence upon every administration; and every set of ministers preserved an appearance of duration as long as they submitted to that influence. But there were certain services to be performed for the Favourite's security, or to gratify his resentments, which your predecessors in office had the wisdom or the virtue not to undertake. The moment this refractory spirit was discovered, their disgrace was determined. Lord Chatham, Mr Grenville, and Lord Rockingham have successively had the honour to be dismissed for preferring their duty, as servants of the public, to those compliances which were expected from their station. A submissive administration was at last gradually collected from the deserters of all parties, interests, and connexions: and nothing remained but to find a leader for these gallant well-disciplined troops. Stand forth, my Lord, for thou art the man. Lord Bute found no resource of dependance or security in the proud, imposing superiority of Lord Chatham's abilities, the shrewd inflexible judgment of Mr. Grenville, nor in the mild but determined integrity of Lord Rockingham. His views and situation required a creature void of all these properties; and he was forced to go through every division, resolution, composition, and refinement of political chemistry, before he happily arrived at the *caput mortuum* of vitriol in your Grace. Flat and insipid in your retired state, but brought into action, you become vitriol again. Such are the extremes of alternate indolence or fury, which have governed your whole administration. Your circumstances with regard to the people soon becoming desperate, like other honest servants, you determined to involve the best of masters in the same difficulties with yourself. We owe it to your Grace's well-directed labours, that your Sovereign has been persuaded to doubt of the affections of his subjects, and the people to suspect the virtues of their Sovereign, at a time when both were unquestionable. You have degraded the royal dignity into a base, dishonourable competition with Mr. Wilkes, nor had you abilities to carry even this last contemptible triumph over a private man, without the grossest violation of the fundamental laws of the constitution and rights of the people. But these are rights, my Lord, which you can no more annihilate, than you can the soil to which they are annexed. The question no longer turns upon points of national honour and security abroad, or on the degrees of expedience and propriety of measure at home. It was not inconsistent that you should abandon the cause of liberty in another country,[1] which you had persecuted in your own; and in the common arts of domestic corruption, we miss no part of Sir Robert Walpole's system except his abilities.

[1] Corsica.

In this humble imitative line, you might long have proceeded, safe and contemptible. You might, probably, never have risen to the dignity of being hated, and even have been despised with moderation. But it seems you meant to be distinguished, and, to a mind like yours, there was no other road to fame but by the destruction of a noble fabric, which you thought had been too long the admiration of mankind. The use you have made of the military force introduced an alarming change in the mode of executing the laws. The arbitrary appointment of Mr. Luttrell invades the foundation of the laws themselves, as it manifestly transfers the right of legislation from those whom the people have chosen, to those whom they have rejected. With a succession of such appointments, we may soon see a House of Commons collected, in the choice of which the other towns and counties of England will have as little share as the devoted county of Middlesex.

Yet, I trust, your Grace will find that the people of this country are neither to be intimidated by violent measures, nor deceived by refinements. When they see Mr. Luttrell seated in the House of Commons by mere dint of power, and in direct opposition to the choice of a whole county, they will not listen to those subtleties, by which every arbitrary exertion of authority is explained into the law and privilege of parliament. It requires no persuasion of argument, but simply the evidence of the senses, to convince them, that to transfer the right of election from the collective to the representative body of the people, contradicts all those ideas of a House of Commons, which they have received from their forefathers, and which they have already, though vainly perhaps, delivered to their children. The principles, on which this violent measure has been defended, have added scorn to injury, and forced us to feel that we are not only oppressed, but insulted.

With what force, my Lord, with what protection are you prepared to meet the united detestation of the people of England? The city of London has given a generous example to the kingdom, in what manner a king of this country ought to be addressed; and I fancy, my Lord, it is not yet in your courage to stand between your Sovereign and the addresses of his subjects. The injuries you have done this country are such as demand not only redress, but vengeance. In vain shall you look for protection to that venal vote, which you have already paid for. . . .   JUNIUS.

Junius, Letters (Woodfall's ed. 1812), vol. I, p. 163.

130. The Association Movement, 1780.

At a Meeting of Deputies from the Counties of York, Surrey, Middlesex, Sussex, Gloucester, Hertford, Kent, Huntingdon, Dorset, Bucks, Chester, Devon, and Essex; from the Cities of London and Westminster, and Gloucester, and the Towns of Newcastle and Nottingham, holden at the St. Alban's Tavern, and afterwards by several adjournments at the Great-Room in King-Street, St. James's, on Saturday the 11th, Tuesday the 14th, Wednesday the 15th, Friday the 17th, Saturday the 18th, and Monday the 20th days of March, 1780:

The Rev. Christopher Wyvill, one of the Deputies from the county of York, in the Chair.

. . .

Read and approved the following

MEMORIAL,

Containing reasons for a Plan of Association, proposed by the Deputies from the several Counties, Cities, and Towns, who have petitioned Parliament for a redress of grievances.

. . . What is our situation at present? By the operation of a despotic system, which has continued with very little intermission, near nineteen years, and is now almost compleated by a dangerous Administration, the very vitals of the Constitution have received a mortal wound, not this or that partiality of the reigning mind has been gratified, but the whole capacity of popular freedom has been struck at. We are arrived at the crisis which the wisest of political writers have uniformly marked for the downfall of Britain, when the Legislative Body shall become as corrupt as the executive and dependent upon it.

Let any man look back to the laws which have passed only in the ten last Sessions of Parliament, forming, as it were step by step, a code of Prerogative, which has already brought within its vortex the primary part of Civil, Religious, Commercial, and Military Administration, within the Kingdom or its dependencies, not excepting from its vast controul all the branches of the Royal Family, and but too probably the succession of the Crown: Let him look back to these, and then doubt if the Executive Power has not found its way to the corruption of the Legislative. Let him behold a venal majority in the House of Commons, Session after Session, moving obsequious to the nod of the Minister, and giving the Legislative sanction to propositions, not only big with the fate of their country, but often militating against the first principles of the Constitution, and the declared voice of their Constituents; while every effort of reason and argument, urged by an independent few, has only been answered by numbers, dumb to every other reply: and then let him judge how enormous that corruption must be. But let him bring his observation to the immense patronage of the Crown, diffused over this Legislative Body in the bestowel of offices, and where offices are too few, or not lucrative enough to satiate the corruption of individuals, in ruinous contracts, in profuse pensions, some known, and others studiously concealed: Let these be considered, and the terms above-mentioned, in which the crisis of British Freedom is marked, are indisputably fulfilled, the Legislative Body is as corrupt as the Executive and dependent upon it. . . .

Wherefore we do most anxiously recommend it to all classes of citizens, and especially to those who have votes for the returning of any Members to Parliament, as they value their liberties, the preservation of their remaining properties, and the rescuing of their posterity from unconstitutional dominion, to unite themselves in a firm purpose of obtaining from their Representatives those salutary reforms, (the outlines of which are hereafter submitted) by the establishment whereof, the door must be effectually shut on corruption, and jointly and severally to persevere, regardless of every consideration to the contrary, until they shall have obtained the same . . .

Resolved,

1st, That a diligent examination be made into all the branches of the receipt, expenditure, and mode of keeping and passing accounts of public money, in order to obtain the Plan of Reform requested by the Petitions of the People.

Resolved,

2nd, That there be sent to the House of Commons, in addition to the present Representatives of Counties, a number of Members not less than one hundred; to be chosen in a due proportion by the several counties of the kingdom of Great Britain.

Resolved,

3rd, That the Members of the House of Commons be annually elected to serve in Parliament.

Resolved,

4th, That it be most earnestly recommended to the Freeholders of the different counties, and to the Electors of the cities and boroughs, throughout the kingdom, to support, at the ensuing general election, such Candidates to represent them in Parliament as shall, previous to the election, by signing the Association or otherwise, have satisfied them, that they will support the above important regulations in Parliament, or so much thereof as shall not be obtained in the present Parliament.

. . .

(Signed)
By order of this Meeting of Deputies,
C. WYVILL, Chairman.

C. Wyvill, *Political Papers* (York, 1794), vol. I, p. 426.

131. Speech of John Wilkes in favour of parliamentary reform, 1776.

HOUSE OF COMMONS PROCEEDINGS, 21 MARCH 1776

MR WILKES rose and said:

... This House is at this hour composed of the same representation it was at his [Charles II] demise, notwithstanding the many and important changes which have since happened. It becomes us therefore to enquire, whether the sense of parliament can be now, on solid grounds, from the present representation, said to be the sense of the nation, as in the time of our forefathers. I am satisfied Sir, the sentiments of the people cannot be justly known at this time from the resolutions of a parliament, composed as the present is, even though no undue influence was practised after the return of the members to the House, even supposing for a moment the influence of all the baneful arts of corruption to be suspended, which, for a moment, I believe, they have not been, under the present profligate administration. Let us examine, Sir, with exactness and candour, if the representation is fair and perfect; let us consider of what the efficient parts of this House are composed, and what proportion they bear, on the large scale, to the body of the people of England, who are supposed to be represented.

The Southern part of this island, to which I now confine my ideas, consists of about five millions of people, according to the most received calculation. I will state by what numbers the majority of this House is elected, and I propose the largest number present of any recorded in our Journals, which was in the famous year 1741. In that year the three largest divisions appear on our Journals. The first is that of the 21st of January, when the numbers were 253 to 250; the second on the 28th of the same month, 236 to 235; the third on the 9th of March, 244 to 243. In these divisions the members for Scotland are included; but I will state my calculations only for England, because it gives the argument more force. The division therefore, I adopt, is that of January 21. The number of members present on that day were 503. Let me, however, suppose the number of 254 to be the majority of members, who will ever be able to attend in their places. I state it high, from the accidents of sickness, service in foreign parts, travelling and necessary avocations. From the majority of electors only in the boroughs, which return members to this House, it has been demonstrated, that this number of 254 is elected by no more than 5,723 persons, generally the inhabitants of Cornish, and other very insignificant boroughs, perhaps by not the most respectable part of the community. Is our sovereign, then, to learn the sense of his whole people from these few persons? Are these men to give laws to this vast empire, and to tax this wealthy nation? I do not mention all the tedious calculations, because gentlemen may find them at length in the works of the incomparable Dr Price, in Postlethwaite, and in Burgh's Political Disquisitions. Figures afford the clearest demonstration, incapable of cavil and sophistry. . . .

. . . I am aware, Sir, that the power, *de jure*, of the legislature to disfranchise a number of boroughs, upon the general grounds of improving the constitution, has been doubted; and gentlemen will ask, whether a power is lodged in the representative to destroy his immediate constituent? Such a question is best answered by another How originated the right, and upon what ground was it first granted? Old Sarum and Gatton, for instance, were populous towns, and therefore the right of representation was first given them. They are now desolate, and of consequence ought not to retain a privilege, which they acquired only by their extent and populousness. We ought in every thing, as far as we can to make the theory and practice of the constitution coincide. The supreme legislative body of a state must surely have this power inherent in itself. It was *de facto* lately exercised to its full extent by parliament in the case of Shoreham with universal approbation, for near a hundred corrupt voters were disfranchised, and about twice that number of freeholders admitted from the county of Sussex. . . .

. . . The disfranchising of the mean, venal, and dependent boroughs would be laying the axe to the root of corruption and treasury influence, as well as aristocratical tyranny. We ought equally to guard against those, who sell themselves, or whose lords sell them. Burgage tenures, and private property in a share of the legislature, are monstrous absurdities in a free state, as well as an insult on common sense. I wish, Sir, an English parliament to speak the free, unbiassed sense of the body of the English people, and of every man among us, of each individual, who may justly be supposed to be comprehended in a fair majority. The meanest mechanic, the poorest peasant and day labourer, has important rights respecting his personal liberty, that of his wife and children, his property, however inconsiderable, his wages, his earnings, the very price and value of each day's hard labour, which are in many trades and manufactures regulated by the power of parliament. Every law relative to marriage, to the protection of a wife, sister, or daughter, against violence and brutal lust, to every contract or agreement with a rapacious or unjust master, is of importance to the manufacturer, the cottager, the servant, as well as to the rich subjects of the state. Some share therefore in the power of making those laws, which deeply interest them, and to which they are expected to pay obedience, should be reserved even to this inferior, but most useful, set of men in the community. We ought always to remember this important truth, acknowledged by every free state, that all government is instituted for the good of the mass of the people to be governed; that they are the original fountain of power, and even of the revenue, and in all events the last resource. . . .

. . . Without a true representation of the Commons our constitution is essentially defective, our parliament is a delusive name, a mere phantom, and all other remedies to recover the pristine purity of the form of government established by our ancestors would be ineffectual, even the shortening the periods of parliaments, and a place and pension Bill, both which I highly approve, and think absolutely necessary. I therefore flatter myself, Sir, that I shall have the concurrence of the House with the motion, which I have now the honour of making, "That leave be given to bring in a Bill for a just and equal Representation of the People of England in Parliament."

P.H., XVIII, 1287.

132. Speech and resolutions of Pitt in favour of parliamentary reform, 1783.

HOUSE OF COMMONS PROCEEDINGS, 7 MAY 1783

MR WILLIAM PITT: An Englishman, who should compare the flourishing state of his country some twenty years ago with the state of humiliation in which he now beholds her, must be convinced, that the ruin which he now deplores, having been brought on by slow degrees, and almost imperceptibly, proceeded from something radically wrong in the constitution. Of the existence of a radical error no one seemed to doubt; nay, almost all were so clearly satisfied of it, that various remedies had been devised by those who wished most heartily to remove it. The House itself had discovered, that a secret influence of the crown was sapping the very foundation of liberty by corruption: the influence of the crown had been felt within those walls, and had often been found strong enough to stifle the sense of duty, and to overrule the propositions made to satisfy the wishes and desires of the people; the House of Commons (in former parliaments) had been base enough to feed the influence that enslaved its members: and thus was at one time the parent and the offspring of corruption.

... Among the various expedients that had been devised to bar the entrance of such influence into that House, he had heard principally of three. One was, to extend the right of voting for members to serve in parliament, which was now so confined, to all the inhabitants of the Kingdom indiscriminately, so that every man, without the distinction of freeholder, or freeman of a corporation, should have the franchise of a vote for a person to represent him in parliament:— and this mode, he understood, was thought by those who patronized it to be the only one that was consistent with true liberty in a free constitution, where every one ought to be governed by those laws only to which all have actually given their consent, either in person, or by their representative. For himself, he utterly rejected and condemned this mode, which was impossible for him to adopt without libelling those renowned forefathers who had framed the constitution in the fulness of their wisdom, and fashioned it for the government of freemen, not of slaves. If this doctrine should obtain, nearly one half of the people must in fact be slaves; for it was absolutely impossible that this idea of giving to every man a right of voting, however finely it might appear in theory, could ever be reduced to practice. But, though it were even practicable, still one half of the nation would be slaves; for all those who vote for the unsuccessful candidates cannot in the strictness of this doctrine, be said to be represented in parliament; and therefore they are governed by laws to which they give not their assent, either in person or by representatives. . . .

For his part, his idea of representation was this, that the members once chosen, and returned to parliament, were, in effect, the representatives of the people at large, as well as those who did not vote at all, or who, having voted, gave their votes against them, as of those by whose suffrages they were actually seated in the House. This being therefore his principle he could not consent to an innovation founded on doctrines subversive of liberty, which in reality went so far as to say, that this House of Commons was not, and that no House of Commons ever had been, a true and constitutional representation of the people; for no House of Commons had yet been elected by all the men in the Kingdom. The country had long prospered, and had even attained the summit of glory, though this doctrine had never been embraced; and he hoped that no one would ever attempt to introduce it into the laws of England, or treat it in any other light than as a mere speculative proposition, that may be good in theory, but which it would be absurd and chimerical to endeavour to reduce to practice.

The second expedient he had heard of, was to abolish the franchise which several boroughs now enjoy, of returning members to serve in parliament. These places were known by the favourite—popular appellation of rotten boroughs. He confessed that there was something very plausible in this idea; but still he was not ready to adopt it; he held those boroughs in the light of the deformities, which in some degree disfigured the fabric of the constitution, but which he feared could not be removed without endangering the whole pile . . . It must be admitted, from a variety of circumstances, which it was unnecessary for him at present to explain, that though the members returned by boroughs might be for the present the brightest patterns of patriotism and liberty, still there was no doubt but that borough members, considered in the abstract, were more liable to the operation of that influence, which every good man wished to see destroyed in that House, than those members who were returned by the counties; and therefore, though he was afraid to cut up the roots of this influence by disfranchising the boroughs, because he was afraid of doing more harm than good by using a remedy that might be thought worse than the disease, still he thought it was his duty to counteract, if possible, that influence, the instruments of which he was afraid to remove. The boroughs ought to be considered not only as places of franchise, but also as places where the franchise was in some measure connected with property by burgage tenure; and therefore, as he was unwilling to dissolve the boroughs, he would endeavour to defeat the effect of undue influence in them, by introducing and establishing a counter-balance, that should keep it down and prevent it from ruining the country.

This brought him naturally to the third expedient, that he had often heard mentioned; which was to add a certain number of members of the House, who should be returned by the counties and the metropolis. It was unnecessary for him to say, that the county members, in general, were almost necessarily taken from that class and description of gentlemen the least liable to the seduction of corrupt influence, the most deeply interested in the liberty and prosperity of the country, and, consequently, the most likely to pursue such measures, as appeared to them the most salutary to their country: in the hands of such men, the liberties of their constituents would be safe, because the interests of such representatives, and the represented, must necessarily be the same. This expedient appeared to him the most fit to be adopted, because it was the least objectionable; it had the merit of promising an effectual counterbalance to the weight of the boroughs, without being an innovation in the form of the constitution. He would not then say what number of members ought to be added to the counties; . . . he, however, would say, that, in his opinion, the number ought not to be under one hundred. . . . He was not, however, without an expedient, by degrees, to reduce the number of members, even after the addition, down to nearly the present number: his expedient was this: that whenever it should be proved before the tribunal, which happily was now established by law, to try the merits of contested elections, that the majority of any borough had been bribed and corrupted, the borough should then lose the privilege of sending members of parliament; the corrupt majority should be disfranchised, and the honest minority be permitted to vote at elections for knights of the shire.

. . . He then read his three Resolutions, which in substance, were as follow: 1. "That it was the opinion of the House, that the most effectual and practicable measures ought to be taken for the better prevention both of bribery and expense in the election of members to serve in parliament. 2. That, for the future, when the majority of voters for any borough should be convicted of gross and notorious corruption, before a select committee of that House, appointed to try the merits of any election, such borough should be disfranchised, and the minority of voters, not so convicted, should be entitled to vote for the county in which such borough should be situated. 3. That an addition of knights of the shire, and of representatives of the metropolis, should be added to the state of the representation."

P.H., XXIII, 829.

VII. PRIVILEGE

The privileges of the House of Commons were called in question several times during this period, and led to acrimonious disputes between the two Houses, between the House of Commons and the courts, and between the Court and the opposition (for party differences were usually involved). The difficulties were created partly by the fact that the traditional defence of its privileges against the crown led the Commons to exaggerate the extent of its privileges against the people; and partly by the uncertain state of the law upon the whole subject. These points are illustrated by the following cases.

Ashby v. *White* and *Paty's Case*

During the general election of 1700, a Whig voter at Aylesbury, Matthew Ashby, was prevented from giving his vote by the Mayor, William White, and three constables. Ashby recovered five pounds damages and costs at the assizes; but White successfully took the case to the Queen's Bench, where three out of the four judges decided that no action could lie since election disputes were a matter for the House of Commons and not for the courts. The dissentient judge was Lord Chief Justice Holt, whose important opinion (133) was upheld by the House of Lords, where Ashby took the case by writ of error (134). This led to a dispute between the two Houses. The Commons feared that Holt's view would give the Upper House the ultimate control over the composition of the Lower, and so they resolved that they had the sole right of deciding all matters relating to elections (135); a view which the Lords denied, publishing their reasons (136). In view of the Lords' decision, other electors, John Paty and four more, brought similar actions against the constables of Aylesbury. The House of Commons, in accordance with its previous resolutions (136), committed them to Newgate for breach of privilege; and when they applied for a writ of *Habeas Corpus* the Queen's

Bench refused it by a majority of three to one, Holt again being the dissentient (**137**). An attempt to bring the matter before the House of Lords led to a fierce contest between the Houses, which was only ended by the prorogation of Parliament. Thus the issues were still left in some doubt, but subsequent judgements have confirmed the distinction which is at the bottom of the opinion held by Holt and the Lords in the case of *Ashby* v. *White*: that is, that, though the Houses of Parliament are the sole judges of the exercise of their established privileges, the problem of the existence or not of a disputed privilege is a question of law to be decided by the courts, and not by resolutions of one of the Houses. On the other hand, Holt's view in *Paty's case* has not received such confirmation, for such judgements as de Grey's in *Brass Crosby's case* (**147**) illustrate the courts' view that the Houses have the power to commit for breaches of their privileges.

Wilkes' Case

Parliament and the courts came into conflict over another matter of privilege in the case of John Wilkes, who was committed to the Tower by the Secretary of State for the publication of No. 45 of the *North Briton*. Chief Justice Pratt discharged him on a writ of *Habeas Corpus* on the grounds that as an M.P. he was exempted from arrest for all offences except treason, felony and breach of the peace (**138**). The House of Commons subsequently passed the following resolutions: that No. 45 *North Briton* was a libel (**139** (1)); that the privilege of parliament does not extend to libel (**139** (2)); that John Wilkes was the author and that he should be expelled from the House (**139** (3)). The House of Lords concurred, though seventeen dissentient peers recorded their reasons for not doing so (**140**). Thus parliament raised again one of the issues of the *Ashby* v. *White case*: for in the case of *Wilkes* they were diminishing their privileges (i.e. altering the law of the land) by resolution in opposition to the decision of the Court of Common Pleas. Later, when parliamentary privilege was reduced in the circumstances of civil actions against members and their servants, the change was more correctly made, by Act of Parliament (**141**).

The Middlesex Elections

In these proceedings, according to some lawyers at the time, the House of Commons was similarly attempting to change the law by resolution, this time in order to extend its privileges till they became dangerous to the rights of the individual. John Wilkes, having been elected member for the County of Middlesex in 1768, was expelled from the House on 3 February 1769 (**142** (1)). He was re-elected, re-expelled, and declared incapable of being elected to serve in that parliament (**142** (2)). On his third re-election, the House declared his opponent, Luttrell, to have been elected (**142** (3)); and

Wilkes had no redress. The crux of the matter was whether the House had power to incapacitate Wilkes from being elected. If it had, then the votes cast for him in the third election were wasted, and Luttrell had had the majority. However, the precedents they relied on were shown to be unsound; and the arguments on the other side, outlined in the Lords' Protest of 2 February 1770 (143), indicate a view of the law of privilege more in keeping with Holt's judgement in *Ashby* v. *White*, and with the later thoughts of the House of Commons, when, after five failures, Wilkes succeeded, in 1782, in having these resolutions expunged from the records of the House (144).

Parliamentary Reporting

During this period, the Houses gradually ceased to exercise one of their undoubted privileges: that of prohibiting the publication of reports of their proceedings. This was a privilege of long standing, and the House of Commons, for example, regularly forbade the presence of strangers in the House, and numerous resolutions were passed making it quite clear that reporting their proceedings was a breach of privilege. In 1738 further clarification was provided by a resolution that this was the case during a recess as well as when the House was sitting (145). However, there was a considerable expansion of newspaper publishing in the second half of this period, and during the popular outbursts of the late sixties[1] members objected to seeing garbled versions of their speeches in the press. Accordingly, in February 1771, the publishers of two newspapers were summoned to attend at the bar of the House. On the advice of Alderman Wilkes, who saw here a good opportunity to strike a blow for the 'patriot' cause, they refused to appear. In March, the House ordered the printers of four other newspapers to appear. When one of them, Miller, refused, the Sergeant-at-Arms sent a Messenger to arrest him who was apprehended by a City constable on a charge of assault. The case came before the Lord Mayor (Brass Crosby) and two aldermen (Wilkes and Oliver), who discharged Miller, and would have committed the Messenger, had not the Sergeant-at-Arms appeared to bail him out. Shortly afterwards, Crosby and Oliver, who were Members of Parliament, were committed to the Tower for breach of privilege (146); and the Court of Common Pleas refused a writ of *Habeas Corpus* (147). Wilkes, however, scored a propagandist victory by concentrating everyone's attention not on parliamentary reporting but on another aspect of the case: the fact that the House of Commons was interfering with the privileges of the City of London. The consequence was that the House feared a repetition of these incidents and brought no more cases against journalists. Not that parliamentary reporting was unfettered after 1771: for

---

[1] See pp. 208–212.

journalists were not always admitted into the gallery, and until 1783 they could only take notes surreptitiously. However, although neither House was prepared to alter its standing orders on the subject, the presence of strangers was more and more winked at, until in the early nineteenth century it was regarded as normal, as Speaker Abbot's diary shows (**148**).

133. *Ashby* v. *White:* Holt's judgement, 1702.

HOLT chief justice. The single question in this case is, Whether, if a free burgess of a corporation, who has an undoubted right to give his vote in the election of a burgess to serve in parliament, be refused and hindered to give it by the officer, if an action on the case will lie against such an officer.

I am of the opinion that judgement ought to be given in this case for the plaintiff. My brothers differ from me in opinion, and they all differ from one another in the reasons of their opinion; but notwithstanding their opinion, I think the plaintiff ought to recover, and that this action is well maintainable, and ought to lie. . . .

But to proceed, I will do these two things: First, I will maintain that the plaintiff has a right and privilege to give his vote: Secondly, in consequence thereof, that if he be hindered in the enjoyment or exercise of that right, the law gives him an action against the disturber, and that this is the proper action given by the law.

I did not at first think it would be any difficulty, to prove that the plaintiff has a right to vote, nor necessary to maintain it, but from what my brothers have said in their arguments I find it will be necessary to prove it. [He quotes a number of arguments and cases] . . . But from hence it appears that every man, that is to give his vote on the election of members to serve in parliament, has a several and particular right in his private capacity, as a citizen or burgess. And surely it cannot be said, that this is so inconsiderable a right, as to apply that maxim to it, *de minimis non curat lex*. A right that a man has to give his vote at the election of a person to represent him in parliament, there to concur to the making of laws, which are to bind his liberty and property, is a most transcendant thing, and of an high nature, and the law takes notice of it in divers statutes. . . .

. . . The right of voting at the election of burgesses is a thing of the highest importance, and so great a privilege, that it is a great injury to deprive the plaintiff of it. These reasons have satisfied me as to the first point.

2. If the plaintiff has a right, he must of necessity have a means to vindicate and maintain it, and a remedy if he is injured in the exercise or enjoyment of it; and indeed it is a vain thing to imagine a right without a remedy; for want of right and want of remedy are reciprocal. . . . And I am of opinion, that this action on the case is a proper action. My brother POWELL indeed thinks, that an action upon the case is not maintainable, because here is no hurt or damage to the plaintiff; but surely every injury imports a damage, though it does not cost the party one farthing, and it is impossible to prove the contrary; for a damage is not merely pecuniary, but an injury imports a damage, when a man is thereby hindred of his right. . . .

But in the principal case my brother says, we cannot judge of this matter, because it is a parliamentary thing. O! by all means be very tender of that. Besides it is intricate, and there may be contrariety of opinions. But this matter can never come in question in parliament; for it is agreed that the persons for whom the plaintiff voted were elected; so that the action is brought for being deprived of his vote: and if it were carried for the other candidates against whom he voted, his damage would be less. To allow this action will make publick officers more careful to observe the constitution of cities and boroughs, and not to be so partial as they commonly are in all elections, which is indeed a great and growing mischief, and tends to the prejudice of the peace of the nation. But they say, that this is a matter out of our jurisdiction, and we ought not to inlarge it. I agree we ought not to incroach or inlarge our jurisdiction; by so doing we usurp both on the right of the queen and the people: but sure we may determine on a charter granted by the King, or on a matter of custom or prescription, when it comes before us without incroaching on the parliament. And if it be a matter within our jurisdiction, we are bound by our oath to judge of it. This is a matter of property determinable before us. Was ever such a petition heard of in parliament, as that a man was hindred of giving his vote, and praying them to give him remedy? The parliament undoubtedly would say, take your remedy at law. It is not like the case of determining the right of election between the candidates.

My brother POWELL says, that the plaintiff's right of voting ought first to have been determined in parliament, . . . If the house of commons do determine this matter, it is not that they have an original right, but as incident to elections. But we do not deny them their rights of examining elections, but we must not be frighted when a matter of property comes before us, by saying it belongs to the parliament; we must exert the queen's jurisdiction. My opinion is founded on the law of *England*. . . . Therefore my opinion is, that the plaintiff ought to have judgment.

Lord Raymond, Reports of Cases (4th ed., 1790), vol. II, p. 950.

134. *Ashby* v. *White:* House of Lords' reversal of Queen's Bench decision, 1704.

After hearing Counsel, at the Bar, to argue the Errors assigned upon the Writ of Error brought into this House, from Her Majesty's Court of Queen's Bench, the Sixth Day of *December* One thousand Seven Hundred and Three, wherein Judgement is entered, for *William White, Richard Talboys, William Bell,* and *Richard Heydon,* against *Matthew Ashby:*

After due Consideration of what was offered thereupon, it is this Day ORDERED and Adjudged, by the Lords Spiritual and Temporal in Parliament assembled, That the said Judgement given in the Court of Queen's Bench for the said *William White, Richard Talboys, William Bell* and *Richard Heydon,* shall be, and is hereby, reversed: And it is further ORDERED, That the Plaintiff *Matthew Ashby* do recover his Damages by the Jury assessed in the Queen's Bench, and also do recover the further Sum of Ten Pounds for his Costs in this Behalf sustained, by this Court to him adjudged.

L.J., XVII, 369.

135. *Ashby* v. *White:* resolutions of the House of Commons, 1704.

Resolved . . . That, according to the known Laws and Usage of Parliament, it is the sole Right of the Commons of *England,* in Parliament assembled (except in Cases otherwise provided for by Act of Parliament) to examine, and determine, all Matters relating to the Right of Election of their own Members.

Resolved . . . That, according to the known Laws and Usage of Parliament, neither the Qualification of any Elector, or the Right of any Person elected, is cognizable or determinable elsewhere, than before the Commons of *England,* in Parliament assembled, except in such Cases, as are specially provided for by Act of Parliament.

Resolved . . . That the examining, and determining, the Qualification, or Right of any Elector, or any Person elected to serve in

Parliament, in any Court of Law, or elsewhere than before the Commons of *England*, in Parliament assembled (except in such Cases as are specially provided for by Act of Parliament) will expose all Mayors, Bailiffs, and other Officers, who are obliged to take the Poll, and make a Return thereupon, to Multiplicity of Actions, vexatious Suits, and insupportable Expenses, and will subject them to different and independent Jurisdictions, and inconsistent Determinations in the same Case, without Relief.

Resolved . . . That *Matthew Ashby*, having, in Contempt of the Jurisdiction of this House, commenced and prosecuted an Action at Common Law against *William White*, and others, the Constables of *Aylesbury*, for not receiving his vote at an Election of Burgesses, to serve in Parliament for the said Borough of *Aylesbury*, is guilty of a Breach of the Privilege of this House.

Resolved . . . That who ever shall presume to commence or prosecute any Action, Indictment, or Information, which shall bring the Right of Electors, or Persons elected to serve in Parliament, to the Determination of any other Jurisdiction, than that of the House of Commons (except in Cases especially provided for by Act of Parliament) such Person and Persons, and all Attorneys, Solicitors, Counsellors and Serjeants at Law, soliciting, prosecuting, or pleading in any such Case, are guilty of a high Breach of the Privilege of this House.

C.J., XIV, 308.

136. *Ashby* v. *White:* resolutions of the House of Lords, 1704.

It is Resolved, by the Lords Spiritual and Temporal in Parliament assembled, That, by the known Laws of this Kingdom, every Freeholder, or other Person having a Right to give his Vote at the Election of Members to serve in Parliament, and being willfully denied or hindered so to do, by the Officer who ought to receive the same, may maintain an Action in the Queen's Courts against such Officer, to assert his Right, and recover Damages for the Injury.

It is Resolved . . . That the asserting, that a Person, having Right to give his Vote at an Election, and being hindered so to do by the Officer who ought to take the same, is without Remedy for such Wrong by the ordinary Course of Law, is destructive of the Property of the Subject, against the Freedom of Elections, and manifestly tends to encourage Corruption and Partiality in Officers who are to make

Returns to Parliament, and to subject the Freeholders and other Electors to their arbitrary Will and Pleasure.

It is Resolved . . . That the declaring *Matthew Ashby* guilty of a Breach of Privilege of the House of Commons, for prosecuting an Action against the Constables of *Aylesbury*, for not receiving his Vote at an Election, after he had, in the known and proper Methods of Law, obtained a Judgement in Parliament for Recovery of his Damages, is an unprecedented Attempt upon the Judicature of Parliament, and is, in Effect, to subject the Law of *England* to the Votes of the House of Commons.

It is Resolved . . . That the deterring Electors from prosecuting Actions in the ordinary Course of Law, where they are deprived of their Right of voting, and terrifying Attornies, Solicitors, Counsellors, and Serjeants at Law, from soliciting, prosecuting, and pleading, in such Cases, by voting their so doing to be a Breach of Privilege of the House of Commons, is a manifest assuming a Power to control the Law, to hinder the Course of Justice, and subject the Property of *Englishmen* to the arbitrary Votes of the House of Commons.

L.J., XVII, 534.

137. *Paty's Case,* 1704.

Regina *vers.* Paty et alios.

Paty and four others were committed by the speaker of the house of commons, by virtue of an order of that house; and upon a *habeas corpus* to bring them before this court, the warrant was returned, which follows *in haec verba: Martis 5 die Decembris* 1704. By virtue of an order of the house of commons of *England* in parliament assembled this day made, these are to require you forthwith upon sight hereof to receive into your custody the body of *John Paty,* who, as it appears to the house of commons, is guilty of commencing and prosecuting an action at law against the late constables of *Aylesbury,* for not allowing his vote in the election of members to serve in parliament, contrary to the declaration, in high contempt of the jurisdiction, and in breach of the known privileges of this house; and him in safe custody to keep, during the pleasure of the said house of commons; for which this shall be your warrant. Given under my hand this fifth of *December anno Domini* 1704. To the keeper of her majesty's gaol of *Newgate,* or his deputy. This warrant was signed *Robert Harley*. This *habeas corpus* was moved for on the last *Monday* but one in the term, and the court . . . put off delivering their opinion till *Monday*, which was the last day of the term, and then all *seriatim* delivered their opinions. I did not hear very well, but the substance of what was said, as I apprehended was to the following effect.

. . . POWELL justice . . . said, he had had but a short time to consider of a cause of this consequence: that it was the first cause of this nature, that had ever been before this court; . . . He said, the court could not judge of the return: First, because they were committed by another law, and consequently we cannot discharge them by that law, by which they were not committed. There is a *lex parliamenti*, for the common law is not the only law in this kingdom; and the house of commons do not commit men by the common law, but by the law of parliament. Consider the judicature of parliament. The house of lords have the power of judicature by the common law upon writs of error, but they cannot proceed originally in any cause. But they proceed too in another manner in case of their own privileges, and therein the judges do not assist, as they do upon writs of error; and their proceeding in that case is by the *lex parliamenti*. So the commons have also a power of judicature, but that is not by the common law, but by the law of parliament, to determine their own privileges; and it is by this law that these persons are committed. He said, this court might judge of privilege, but not contrary to the judgement of the house of commons, which yet we must do in this case, if we discharge the prisoners from their imprisonment, which is the only judgement the house of commons can give, upon their determination, that these persons have been guilty of a breach of their privileges.

. . . But if they should discharge these persons, that are committed by the house of commons for a breach of privilege, this would be to take upon themselves directly to judge of the privileges of parliament. This want of jurisdiction in the court cures all the faults in the commitment; though if that were to be debated, there ought to be a difference taken between a commitment for a crime, and for a contempt. And as to that objection to the warrant, that it was to detain the prisoners during the pleasure of the house of commons, that he said was the constant form of warrants by the house. It is objected, that in bringing these actions the prisoners have done nothing but what the lords have adjudged they may do, and the house of lords is the supreme judicature of the kingdom. As to that, he said, that if this commitment were for that reason an excess of jurisdiction, that court could not remedy it, but it ought to be remedied by conference, and that was the proper remedy, where the parliament assumes an excessive jurisdiction . . . Upon conferences the reasons upon which the houses act will appear, and if the commons have no reason for what they do, it is to be presumed they will never be chosen again; and if the lords are in the wrong, the other house will not rest till all is set right again.

HOLT chief justice said, that the legality of the commitment depended upon the vote recited in the warrant; and for his part he thought the prisoners ought to be discharged, though in this his opinion he was so unfortunate as to go contrary to the act of the house of commons, and the opinion of all the rest of the judges of *England*, whose assistance they had desired, and there had been a meeting for that purpose. He said, that this was not such an imprisonment as the freemen of *England* ought to be bound by; for that this, which was only doing a legal act, could not be made illegal by the vote of the house of commons; for that neither house of parliament, nor both houses jointly, could dispose of the liberty or property of the subject; for to this purpose the queen must join: and that it was in the necessity of their several concurrences to such acts, that the great security of the liberty of the subject consisted. He said, that the first matter, which was laid as a breach of privileges, was none: . . . because one might file an original against a parliament-man, and continue it down, without breach of privilege. And that it should be so is of absolute necessity, in order to save the statute of limitations . . . and consequently the commencing an action against the constables of *Aylesbury* is no breach of privilege. As to prosecuting the action, which was the second matter; he said, it was uncertain what sort of prosecuting they meant. For prosecuting might be only continuing the original, which as was said before, would be no breach of privilege, . . . The third thing is, the persons the action is brought against, *viz.* the constables of *Aylesbury*; now it does not appear, that the constables of *Aylesbury* have any privilege, and if they have any, it ought to have been set out, because *qua* constables of *Aylesbury*, they have no more privilege than the constables of *St. Martin's in the Fields*. The fourth matter, he said, was for bringing an action at common law for not allowing his vote in the election of members to serve in parliament. Now to bring an action against a person, who is not privileged, he said was no offence, though no action would lie in this case, or though the matter upon which the action was grounded was false . . . A man who brings an action against another, who is not a privileged person, is not to have his action stopped, especially if he has a good cause for action, which that the plaintiffs in this case have, appears by the reversal of the judgment of this court in *domo procerum* in the case of *Ashby vers. White*. And this action, which was brought in this case, appears by the description of it in the vote of the house of commons, to be for the same cause of action that that was. I will suppose, that the bringing such actions was declared by the house of commons to be a breach of their privilege; but that declaration will not make that a breach of privilege that was not so before. But if they have any such privileges they ought to shew precedents of it. The privileges of the house of commons are well known, and are founded upon the law of the land, and are nothing but the law. As we all know they have no privilege in the cases of breaches of the peace. And if they declare themselves to have privileges, which they have no legal claim to, the people of *England* will not be estopped by that declaration. This privilege of theirs concerns the liberty of the people in a high degree, by subjecting them to imprisonment for the infringement of them, which is what the people cannot be subjected to without an act of parliament. As to what was said, that the house of commons are judges of their own privileges, he said, they were so, when it comes before them. And as to the instances cited, where the judges have been cautious in giving any answer in parliament in matters of privilege of parliament; he said, the reason for that was, because the members know probably their own privileges better than the judges. But when a matter of privilege comes in question in *Westminster-hall* the judges must determine it, as they did in *Binyon's* case. Suppose these actions against the constables of *Aylesbury* had gone on, and the defendants had pleaded this privilege; we must have determined, whether there were any such privilege or no.

. . . That the bringing this action is no breach of the privilege of the house of commons, appears by the judgment in the case of *Ashby* and *White*, in the argument of which case before the house of lords, this argument of the privilege of the house of commons was insisted on. Besides if the bringing of this action was a breach of the privilege of the house of commons, why was not *Ashby* committed, when he first brought the action; but the suffering him to go on with this action is an argument, that this pretence of privilege is a new thing. *Ashby* recovered in his action, and these men have followed his steps, and yet they are here said to have acted in breach of the privilege of the house of commons. I shall say nothing to the case of *Ashby* and *White*, because the reasons upon which that judgment was given are printed. He said, the bringing of this action is said to be in high contempt of the jurisdiction of the house of commons; but that he said, could not be, because neither house of parliament could hold plea in any action; and besides, the defendants might wave their privilege. He said, he made no question of the power of the house of commons to commit; they might commit any man for offering an affront to a member, or for a breach of privilege; nay they might commit for a crime, because they might impeach . . . He said, both houses of parliament were bound by the law of the land, and in their actions were obliged to pursue it.

Lord Raymond, Reports of Cases (4th ed., 1790), vol. II, p. 1105.

138. John Wilkes and the No. 45 *North Briton*: Pratt discharges Wilkes, 1763.

L.C.J. PRATT . . . said . . .

The third matter insisted upon for Mr Wilkes is, that he is a member of parliament, (which has been admitted by the king's serjeants) and intitled to privilege to be free from arrests in all cases except treason, felony, and actual breach of the peace; and therefore ought to be discharged from imprisonment without bail; and we are all of opinion that he is intitled to that privilege, and must be discharged without bail. In the case of the Seven Bishops, the Court took notice of the privilege of parliament, and thought the bishops would have been intitled to it, if they had not judged them to have been guilty of a breach of the peace; for three of them, Wright, Holloway, and Allybone, deemed a seditious libel to be an actual breach of the peace, and therefore they were ousted of their privilege most unjustly. If Mr. Wilkes had been described as a member of parliament in the return, we must have taken notice of the law of privilege of parliament, otherwise the members would be without remedy, where they are wrongfully arrested against the law of parliament. We are bound to take notice of their privileges as being part of the law of the land. . . . We are all of opinion that a libel is not a breach of the peace. It tends to the breach of the peace, and that is the utmost, . . . But that which only tends to the breach of the peace cannot be a breach of it. Suppose a libel be a breach of the peace, yet I think it cannot exclude privilege; because I cannot find that a libeller is bound to find surety of the peace, in any book whatever, nor ever was, in any case, except one, viz. the case of the Seven Bishops, where three judges said, that surety of the peace was required in the case of a libel. Judge Powell, the only honest man of the four judges, dissented; and I am bold to be of his opinion, and to say, that case is not law. But it shews the miserable condition of the state at that time. Upon the whole, it is absurd to require surety of the peace or bail in the case of a libeller, and therefore Mr. Wilkes must be discharged from his imprisonment.

S.T., xix, 989.

139. John Wilkes and the No. 45 *North Briton*: resolutions of the House of Commons, 1763–4.

(I) 15 NOVEMBER 1763

Mr Chancellor of the Exchequer informed the House, that he was commanded by the King to acquaint the House, that His Majesty having received Information that *John Wilkes* Esquire, a Member of this House, was the Author of a most seditious and dangerous Libel, published since the last Session of Parliament; He had caused the said *John Wilkes* Esquire to be apprehended, and secured, in order to his being tried for the same by due Course of Law: And Mr. *Wilkes* having been discharged out of Custody by the Court of *Common Pleas*, upon Account of his Privilege as a Member of this House; and having, when called upon by the legal Process of the Court of *King's Bench*, stood out, and declined to appear, and answer to an Information which has since been exhibited against him by His Majesty's Attorney General for the same Offence: In this Situation, His Majesty being desirous to show all possible Attention to the Privileges of the House of Commons, in every Instance wherein they can be supposed to be concerned; and at the same Time thinking it of the utmost Importance not to suffer the Public Justice of the Kingdom to be eluded, has chosen to direct the said Libel, and also Copies of the Examinations upon which Mr. *Wilkes* was apprehended and secured, to be laid before this House for their Consideration: And Mr. Chancellor of the Exchequer delivered the said Papers in at the Table.

Resolved, Nemine contradicente, That an humble Address be presented to His Majesty, to return His Majesty the Thanks of this House for His most gracious Message, and for the tender Regard therein expressed for the Privileges of this House; and to assure His Majesty that this House will forthwith take into their most serious Consideration, the very important Matter communicated by His Majesty's Message. . . .

Resolved, That the Paper intituled, "The *North Briton* No. 45" is a false, scandalous, and seditious Libel, containing Expressions of the most unexampled Insolence and Contumely towards His Majesty, the grossest Aspersions upon both Houses of Parliament, and the most audacious Defiance of the Authority of the whole Legislature; and most manifestly tending to alienate the Affections of the People from His Majesty, to withdraw them from their Obedience to the Laws of the Realm, and to excite them to traitorous Insurrections against His Majesty's Government.

Resolved, That the said Paper be burnt by the Hands of the common Hangman.

C.J., xxix, 667.

(2) 24 NOVEMBER 1763

The Question being put, That Privilege of Parliament does not extend to the Case of writing and publishing seditious Libels, nor ought to be allowed to obstruct the ordinary Course of the Laws, in the speedy and effectual Prosecution of so heinous and dangerous an Offence;

The House divided
The Yeas went forth

| Tellers for the Yeas, | { Mr *Morton*
 Mr *Oswald* } | 258 |
| Tellers for the Noes, | { Mr *Onslow*
 Mr *Hussey* } | 133 |

So it was resolved in the Affirmative.

C.J., xxix, 675.

(3) 19 JANUARY 1764

Resolved, That it appears to this House that the said *John Wilkes* Esquire is guilty of Writing and Publishing the Paper, intituled, "The *North Briton*, No. 45," which this House has voted to be a false, scandalous and seditious Libel, containing Expressions of the most unexampled Insolence and Contumely towards His Majesty, the grossest Aspersions upon both Houses of Parliament, and the most audacious Defiance of the Authority of the whole Legislature; and most manifestly tending to alienate the Affections of the People from His Majesty, to withdraw them from their Obedience to the Laws of the Realm, and to excite them to traitorous Insurrections against His Majesty's Government.

Resolved, That the said *John Wilkes*, Esquire be, for his said Offence, expelled this House.

C.J., XXIX, 723.

140. John Wilkes and the No. 45 *North Briton* : resolution and protest in the House of Lords, 1763.

29 NOVEMBER 1763

And it being moved, "To agree with the Commons in the said Resolution:"[1]

The same was objected to.

After long Debate thereupon;

The Question was put, "Whether to agree with the Commons in the said Resolution?"

It was resolved in the Affirmative.

Dissentient. [17 Peers]

Because we cannot hear, without the utmost Concern and Astonishment, a Doctrine advanced now for the First Time in this House, which we apprehend to be new, dangerous, and unwarrantable; *videlicet*, That the Personal Privilege of both Houses of Parliament has never held, and ought not to hold, in the Case of any Criminal Prosecution whatsoever; by which, all the Records of Parliament, all History, all the Authorities of the gravest and soberest Judges, are entirely rescinded; and the fundamental Principles of the Constitution, with regard to the Independence of Parliament, torn up, and buried under the Ruins of our most established Rights. . . .

The Law of Privilege, touching Imprisonment of the Person of Lords of Parliament, as stated by the Two Standing Orders, declares generally, "That no Lord of Parliament, sitting the Parliament, or within the usual Times of Privilege of Parliament, is to be imprisoned or restrained without Sentence or Order of the House, unless it be for Treason or Felony, or for refusing to give Security for the Peace, and Refusal to pay Obedience to a Writ of *Habeas Corpus*."

. . .

[1] See No. **139** (2).

The Resolution of the other House, now agreed to, is a direct Contradiction to the Rule of Parliamentary Privilege laid down in the aforesaid Standing Orders, both in Letter and Spirit.

... The First Objection is to the Generality of this Resolution, which, as it is penned, denies the Privilege to the supposed Libeller, not only where he refuses to give Sureties, but likewise throughout the whole Prosecution from the Beginning to the End; so that, although he should submit to be bound, he may notwithstanding be afterwards arrested, tried, convicted, and punished, sitting the Parliament, and without Leave of the House; wherein the Law of Privilege is fundamentally misunderstood, by which no Commitment whatever is tolerated, but that only which is made upon the Refusal of Sureties, or in other excepted Cases, of Treason or Felony, and the *Habeas Corpus*.

If Privilege will not hold throughout in the Case of a Seditious Libel, it must be, because that Offence is such a Breach of the Peace for which Sureties may be demanded; and if that be so, it will readily be admitted, that the Case comes within the Exception; "Provided always, that Sureties have been refused, and that the Party is committed only till he shall give Sureties."

But this Offence is not a Breach of the Peace; it does not fall within any Definition of a Breach of the Peace, given by any of the good Writers upon that Subject; all which Breaches, from Menace to actual Wounding, either alone or with a Multitude, are described to be, Acts of Violence against the Person, Goods or Possession, putting the Subject in fear by Blows, Threats, or Gestures ...

But, if a Libel could possibly by any abuse of Language, or has anywhere been, called inadvertently a Breach of the Peace; there is not the least Colour to say, that the Libeller can be bound to give Sureties for the Peace, for the following Reasons:

Because none can be so bound unless he be taken in the actual Commitment of a Breach of the Peace, striking, or putting some one or more of his Majesty's Subjects in Fear.

Because there is no Authority, or even ambiguous Hint, in any Law Book, that he may be so bound.

Because no Libeller, in Fact, was ever so bound.

Because no Crown Lawyer, in the most despotic Times, ever insisted he should be so bound, even in the Days when the Press swarmed with the most invenomed and virulent Libels, and when the Prosecutions raged with such uncommon Fury against this Species of

Offenders; when the Law of Libels was ransacked every Term; when Loss of Ears, perpetual Imprisonment, Banishment, and Fines of Ten and Twenty Thousand Pounds, were the common Judgments in *The Star Chamber*; and when the Crown had assumed an uncontrollable Authority over the Press.

This Resolution does not only infringe the Privilege of Parliament, but points to the Restraint of the Personal Liberty of every common Subject in these Realms; seeing that it does in Effect affirm, that all men, without Exception, may be bound to the Peace for this Offence.

By this Doctrine, every Man's Liberty, privileged as well as un-privileged, is surrendered into the Hands of a Secretary of State: *He* is by this Means empowered, in the first Instance, to pronounce the Paper to be a seditious Libel, a Matter of such Difficulty that some have pretended it is too high to be intrusted to a Special Jury of the First Rank and Condition: *He* is to understand and decide by himself the meaning of every *Innuendo*: *He* is to determine the Tendency thereof, and brand it with his own Epithets: *He* is to adjudge the Party guilty, and make him Author or Publisher, as he sees good; and, lastly, *He* is to give Sentence, by committing the Party . . .

From what has been observed, it appears to us, that the Exception of a seditious Libel from Privilege is neither founded on Usage or written Precedents; and therefore this Resolution is of the First Im-pression: Nay, it is not only a new Law narrowing the known and ancient Rule, but it is likewise a Law *ex post facto, pendente Lite, et ex Parte*, now first declared to meet with the Circumstances of a parti-cular Case: And it must be further considered, that this House is thus called upon to give a Sanction to the Determinations of the other, who have not condescended to confer with us upon this Point, till they have prejudged it themselves. . . .

It is not to be conceived that our Ancestors, when they framed the Law of Privilege, would have left the Case of a Seditious Libel (as it is called) the only unprivileged Misdemeanour: Whatever else they had given up to the Crown, they would have guarded the Case of supposed Libels, above all others, with Privilege, as being most likely to be abused by outrageous and vindictive Prosecutions.

But this great Privilege had a much deeper Reach; It was wisely planned, and hath hitherto, through all Times, been resolutely maintained.

It was not made to screen Criminals, but to preserve the very Being and Life of Parliament; for, when our Ancestors considered, that the

Law had lodged the great Powers of Arrest, Indictment and Information, in the Crown, they saw the Parliament would be undone, if,
during the Time of Privilege, the Royal Process should be admitted
in any Misdemeanour whatsoever; therefore they excepted none:
Where the Abuse of Power would be fatal, the Power ought never
to be given, because Redress comes too late.

A Parliament under perpetual Terror of Imprisonment can neither
be free, nor bold, nor honest; and, if this Privilege was once removed,
the most important Question might be irrecoverably lost, or carried,
by a sudden Irruption of Messengers, let loose against the Members
Half an Hour before the Debate. . . .

If the Severity of the Law touching Libels, as it hath sometimes been
laid down, be duly weighed, it must strike both Houses of Parliament
with Terror and Dismay.

The Repetition of a Libel, the Delivery of it unread to another, is
said to be a Publication; nay the bare Possession of it has been deemed
criminal, unless it is immediately destroyed, or carried to a Magistrate.

Every Lord of Parliament then, who hath done this, who is falsely
accused, nay who is, though without any Information, named in the
Secretary of State's Warrant, has lost his Privilege by this Resolution,
and lies at the Mercy of that Enemy to Learning and Liberty, *the
Messenger of the Press.*

For these, and many other forcible Reasons, we hold it highly
unbecoming the Dignity, Gravity, and Wisdom, of the House of
Peers, as well as their Justice, thus judicially to explain away and
diminish the Privilege of their Persons, founded in the Wisdom of
Ages, declared with Precision in our Standing Orders, so repeatedly
confirmed, and hitherto preserved inviolable, by the Spirit of our
Ancestors; called to it only by the other House on a particular Occasion and to serve a particular Purpose, *ex post facto, ex Parte et pendente Lite* in the Courts below.

L.J., xxx, 426.

141. Act allowing civil suits against members and their servants at any time, 1770.

*An Act for the further preventing delays of justice by reason of privilege
of parliament.*

Whereas *the several laws heretofore made for restraining the privilege of
parliament, with respect to actions or suits commenced and prosecuted at*

any time from and immediately after the dissolution or prorogation of any parliament, until a new parliament should meet, or the same be reassembled; and from and immediately after an adjournment of both houses of parliament for above the space of fourteen days, until both houses should meet or assemble; are insufficient to obviate the inconveniences arising from the delay of suits by reason of privilege of parliament; whereby the parties often lose the benefit of several terms: for the preventing all delays the King or his subjects may receive in prosecuting their several rights, titles, debts, dues, demands, or suits, for which they have cause; be it enacted . . . That from and after the twenty-fourth day of *June* one thousand seven hundred and seventy, any person or persons shall and may, at any time, commence and prosecute any action or suit in any court of record, or court of equity, or of admiralty, and in all causes matrimonial and testamentary, in any court having cognizance of causes matrimonial and testamentary, against any peer or lord of parliament of *Great Britain*, or against any of the knights, citizens, and burgesses, and the commissioners for shires and burghs of the house of commons of *Great Britain* for the time being, or against their or any of their menial or any other servants, or any other person intitled to the privilege of parliament of *Great Britain*; and no such action, suit, or any other process or proceeding thereupon, shall at any time be impeached, stayed, or delayed, by or under colour or pretence of any privilege of parliament.

II. Provided nevertheless, and be it further enacted . . . That nothing in this act shall extend to subject the person of any of the knights, citizens, and burgesses, or the commissioners of shires and burghs of the house of commons of *Great Britain* for the time being, to be arrested or imprisoned upon any such suit or proceedings.

10 Geo. III, c. 50: *S.L.*, XXVIII, 358.

142. The Middlesex elections: resolutions of the House of Commons, 1769.

(1) 3 FEBRUARY 1769

And a Motion being made, and the Question being put, That *John Wilkes*, Esquire, a Member of this House, who hath at the Bar of this House, confessed himself to be the Author and Publisher of what this House is resolved to be an insolent, scandalous, and seditious Libel;

and who has been convicted in the Court of King's Bench, of having printed and published a seditious Libel, and Three obscene and impious Libels; and, by the Judgment of the said Court, has been sentenced to undergo Twenty-two Months Imprisonment, and is now in Execution under the said Judgment, be expelled this House. The House divided ... So it was resolved in the Affirmative [219–137].

Ordered, That Mr. Speaker do issue his Warrant to the Clerk of the Crown, to make out a new Writ for the Electing of a Knight of the Shire to serve in this present Parliament for the County of *Middlesex*, in the room of *John Wilkes*, Esquire, expelled this House.

C.J., XXXII, 178.

(2) 17 FEBRUARY 1769

Ordered, That the Deputy Clerk of the Crown do attend this House immediately, with the Return to the Writ for electing a Knight of the Shire to serve in this present Parliament for the County of *Middlesex*, in the room of *John Wilkes*, Esquire, expelled this House.

And the Deputy Clerk of the Crown attending, according to Order; The said Writ and Return were read.

A Motion was made, and the Question being proposed, That *John Wilkes*, Esquire, having been, in this Session of Parliament, expelled this House, was, and is, incapable of being elected a Member to serve in this present Parliament;

The House was moved, That the Entry in the Journal of the House, of the 6th Day of *March*, 1711[1], in relation to the Proceedings of the House, upon the Return of a Burgess to serve in Parliament for the Borough of *King's Lynn* in the County of *Norfolk*, in the room of *Robert Walpole*, Esquire, expelled the House, might be read.

And the same was read accordingly.

The House was also moved, that the Resolution of the House, of *Friday* the 3rd Day of this Instant *February*, relating to the Expulsion of *John Wilkes*, Esquire, then a Member of this House, might be read.

And the same being read accordingly;

An Amendment was proposed to be made to the Question, by inserting after the Word "House" these Words, "for having been the Author and Publisher of what this House hath resolved to be an insolent, scandalous, and seditious Libel; and for having been convicted in the Court of King's Bench, of having printed and published a seditious Libel, and Three obscene and impious Libels; and having,

[1] O.S.

by the Judgment of the said Court, been sentenced to undergo Twenty-two months Imprisonment, and being in Execution under the said Judgment."

And the Question being put, That those Words be there inserted; The House divided . . . [102–228]
So it passed in the Negative.

Then the Main Question being put, That *John Wilkes*, Esquire, having been, in this Session of Parliament, expelled this House, was, and is, incapable of being elected a Member to serve in this present Parliament; The House divided . . . [235–89]
So it was resolved in the Affirmative.

A Motion being made, That the late Election of a Knight of the Shire to serve in this present Parliament for the County of *Middlesex*, is a void Election;

A Member in his Place, informed the House, that he was present at the last Election of a Knight of the Shire to serve in this present Parliament for the said County; that there was no other Candidate than the said Mr *Wilkes*; that there was no Poll demanded for any other Person, nor any Kind of Opposition to the Election of the said Mr *Wilkes*.

Resolved, That the late Election of a Knight of the Shire to serve in this present Parliament for the County of *Middlesex*, is a void Election.

Ordered, That Mr. Speaker do issue his Warrant to the Clerk of the Crown, to make out a new Writ for the Electing of a Knight of the Shire to serve in this present Parliament for the County of *Middlesex*, in the room of *John Wilkes*, Esquire, who is adjudged incapable of being elected a Member to serve in this present Parliament, and whose Election for the said County has been declared void.   C.J., xxxII, 228.

(3) 15 APRIL 1769

Then the question being put, That *Henry Lawes Luttrell*, Esquire, ought to have been returned a Knight of the Shire to serve in this present Parliament for the County of *Middlesex*;

The House divided.
The Yeas went forth.

| Tellers for the Yeas, | { Mr. *Onslow*
 Mr *Edmonstone* } 197 |
| Tellers for the Noes, | { Mr. *Thomas Townshend*, Junior,
 Mr. *Montagu* } 143 |

So it was resolved in the Affirmative.

Ordered, That the Deputy Clerk of the Crown do amend the Return for the County of *Middlesex*, by rasing out the name of *John Wilkes*, Esquire, and inserting the Name of *Henry Lawes Luttrell*, Esquire, instead thereof.

C.J., xxxii, 387.

143. The Middlesex elections: Lords' protest, 1770.

2 FEBRUARY 1770

Then it was moved, "To resolve, That the House of Commons, in the Exercise of its Judicature in Matters of Election, is bound to judge according to the Law of the Land, and the known and established Laws and Custom of Parliament, which is Part thereof."

It was resolved in the Negative.

Dissentient

1st, Because the Resolution proposed was in our Judgment highly necessary to lay the Foundation of a Proceeding, which might tend to quiet the Minds of the People, by doing them Justice, at a Time when a Decision of the other House, which appears to us inconsistent with the Principles of the Constitution, and irreconcileable to the Law of the Land, has spread so universal an Alarm, and produced so general a Discontent, throughout the Kingdom.

2ndly, Because, although we do not deny that the Determination on the Right to a Seat in the House of Commons is competent to the Jurisdiction of that House alone, yet when to this it is added, that whatever they, in the Exercise of that Jurisdiction, think fit to declare to be Law, is therefore to be so considered, because there lies no Appeal, we conceive ourselves called upon to give that Proposition the strongest Negative; for, if admitted, the Law of the Land (by which all Courts of Judicature, without Exception, are equally bound to proceed) is at once overturned, and resolved into the Will and Pleasure of a Majority of One House of Parliament, who, in assuming it, assume a Power to over-rule at Pleasure the fundamental Right of Election, which the Constitution has placed in other Hands, those of their Constituents: and if ever this pretended Power should come to be exercised to the full Extent of the Principle, the House will be no longer a Representative of the People, but a separate Body, altogether independent of them, self-existing and self-elected.

3rdly, Because, when we are told that Expulsion implies Incapacity; and the Proof insisted upon is, that the People have acquiesced in the Principle, by not re-electing Persons who have been expelled; we equally deny the Position as false, and reject the Proof offered, as in no Way supporting the Position to which it is applied; we are sure the Doctrine is not to be found in any Statute or Law-Book, nor in the Journals of the House of Commons, neither is it consonant with any just or known Analogy of Law; and as not re-electing would, at most, but infer a Supposition of the Electors Approbation of the Grounds of the Expulsion, and by no Means their Acquiescence in the Conclusion of an implied Incapacity; so, were there not One Instance of a Re-election after Expulsion but Mr. *Woolaston's*, that alone demonstrates that neither did the Constituents admit, nor the House of Commons maintain, Incapacity to be the Consequence of Expulsion; even the Case of Mr. *Walpole* shews, by the first Re-election, the Sense of the People, that Expulsion did not infer Incapacity; and that Precedent too, (which is the only One of an Incapacity), produced as it was under the Influence of Party Violence in the latter Days of Queen *Anne*, in so far as it relates to the Introduction of a Candidate having a Minority of Votes, decides expressly against the Proceedings of the House of Commons, in the late *Middlesex* Election . . . .

6thly, Because, upon the Whole, we deem the Power which the House of Commons have assumed to themselves, of creating an Incapacity, unknown to the Law, and thereby depriving, in Effect, all the Electors of *Great Britain* of their valuable Right of Free Election, confirmed to them by so many solemn Statutes, a flagrant Usurpation, as highly repugnant to every essential Principle of the Constitution as the Claim of Ship-money by King *Charles* the First, or that of suspending and dispensing Power by King *James* the Second; this being, indeed, in our Opinion, a suspending and dispensing Power assumed and exercised by the House of Commons against the ancient and fundamental Liberties of the Kingdom. [Signed by 42 peers].

Then the main Question was put, "That any Resolution of this House, directly or indirectly, impeaching a Judgment of the House of Commons in a Matter where their Jurisdiction is competent, final, and conclusive, would be a Violation of the Constitutional Rights of the Commons, tends to make a Breach between the Two Houses of Parliament, and leads to general Confusion."

It was resolved in the Affirmative.

L.J., XXXII, 417.

144. The Middlesex elections: resolutions expunged from the Journals, 1782.

3 MAY 1782

The House was moved, That the Entry in the Journal of the House, of the 17th Day of *February* 1769, of the Resolution, "That *John Wilkes*, Esquire, having been in this Session of Parliament expelled this House, was and is incapable of being elected a Member to serve in this present Parliament," might be read.

And the same being read accordingly;

A Motion was made, and the Question being put, That the said Resolution be expunged from the Journals of this House, as being subversive of the Rights of the whole Body of Electors of this Kingdom;

The House divided. . . .

So it was resolved in the affirmative.

· · ·

Ordered, That all the Declarations, Orders, and Resolutions of this House, respecting the Election of *John Wilkes*, Esquire, for the County of *Middlesex*, as a void Election, the due and legal Election of *Henry Lawes Luttrell*, Esquire, into Parliament for the said County, and the Incapacity of *John Wilkes*, Esquire, to be elected a Member to serve in the said Parliament, be expunged from the Journals of this House, as being subversive of the Rights of the whole Body of Electors of this Kingdom.

And the same was expunged, by the Clerk, at the Table, accordingly.

C.J., xxxviii, 977.

145. Parliamentary reporting: Commons resolution, 1738.

13 APRIL 1738

Resolved, That it is an high Indignity to, and a notorious Breach of the Privilege of, this House, for any News Writer, in Letters, or other Papers (as Minutes, or under any other Denomination), or for any Printer or Publisher of any printed News Paper, of any Denomination, to presume to insert in the said Letters or Papers, or to give therein any Account of, the Debates, or other Proceedings, of this House, or any Committee thereof, as well during the Recess as the Sitting of Parliament; and that this House will proceed with the utmost Severity against such Offenders. C.J., xxiii, 148.

146. Commons resolution: to arrest Brass Crosby, 1771.

27 MARCH 1771

Resolved, That *Brass Crosby*, Esquire, Lord Mayor of the city of *London*, having discharged out of the Custody of One of the Messengers of this House *J. Miller* (for whom the News Paper, intituled, "*The London Evening Post*, from *Thursday, March 7*, to *Saturday, March 9, 1771*," purports to be printed, and of which a Complaint was made in the House of Commons, on the 12th Day of this Instant *March*, and who, for his Contempt, in not obeying the Order of this House, for his Attendance on this House upon *Thursday* the 14th Day of this Instant *March*, was ordered to be taken into the Custody of the Serjeant at Arms, or his Deputy, attending this House, and who, by Virtue of the Speaker's Warrant, issued under the said Order, had been taken into the Custody of the said Messenger) and having signed a Warrant against the said Messenger, for having executed the said Warrant of the Speaker, and having held the said Messenger to Bail for the same, is guilty of a Breach of the Privilege of this House. . . .

. . . Then the main Question . . . being put, That *Brass Crosby*, Esquire, Lord Mayor of the City of *London*, and a Member of this House, be, for his said Offence, committed to the Tower of *London*;. . .

So it was resolved in the Affirmative.

Ordered, That Mr. Speaker do issue his Warrants accordingly.

C.J., xxxiii, 289.

147. De Grey refuses *Habeas Corpus* to Brass Crosby, 1771.

L.C.J. DE GREY . . . The writ by which the lord mayor is now brought before us, is a Habeas Corpus at common law, for it is not signed *per statutum*. It is called a prerogative writ for the king; or a remedial writ: and this writ was properly advised by the counsel for his lordship, because all the judges (including Holt) agreed, that such a writ as the present case required, is not within the statute. This is a writ by which the subject has a right of remedy to be discharged out of custody, if he hath been committed, and is detained contrary to law; therefore the Court must consider, whether the authority committing, is a legal authority. If the commitment is made by those who have authority to commit, this Court cannot discharge or bail the party committed; nor can this Court admit to bail, one charged or committed in execution. Whether the authority committing the lord mayor, is a legal

245

authority or not, must be adjudged by the return of the writ now before the Court. The return states the commitment to be by the House of Commons, for a breach of privilege, which is also stated in the return; and this breach of privilege or contempt is, as the counsel has truly described it, threefold; discharging a printer in custody of a messenger by order of the House of Commons; signing a warrant for the commitment of the messenger, and holding him to bail; that is, treating a messenger of the House of Commons as acting criminally in the execution of the orders of that House. . . . The House of Commons, without doubt, have power to commit persons examined at their bar touching elections, when they prevaricate or speak falsely; so they have for breaches of privilege; so they have in many other cases. . . . This power of committing must be inherent in the House of Commons, from the very nature of its institution, and therefore is part of the law of the land. They certainly always could commit in many cases. In matters of elections, they can commit sheriffs, mayors, officers, witnesses, etc. and it is now agreed that they can commit generally for all contempts. All contempts are either punishable in the Court contemned, or in some higher court. Now the parliament has no superior court; therefore the contempts against either house can only be punished by themselves. . . .

In the case of the Aylesbury men,[1] the counsel admitted, lord chief justice Holt owned, and the House of Lords acknowledged, that the House of Commons had power to commit for contempt and breach of privilege. Indeed, it seems, they must have power to commit for any crime, because they have power to impeach for any crime. When the House of Commons adjudge anything to be a contempt, or a breach of privilege, their adjudication is a conviction, and their commitment in consequence, is execution; and no court can discharge or bail a person that is in execution by the judgement of any other court. The House of Commons therefore having an authority to commit, and that commitment being an execution, the question is, what can this court do? It can do nothing when a person is in execution by the judgement of a court having a competent jurisdiction: in such case, this court is not a court of appeal.

It is objected, 1. That the House of Commons are mistaken, for they have not this power, this authority; 2. That supposing they have, yet in this case they have not used it rightly and properly; and 3. That

[1] See No. 137.

the execution of their orders was irregular. In order to judge, I will consider the practice of the courts in common and ordinary cases. I do not find any case where the courts have taken cognisance of such execution, or of commitments of this kind: there is no precedent of Westminster-hall interfering in such a case. . . . How then can we do anything in the present case, when the law by which the lord mayor is committed, is different from the law by which he seeks to be relieved? He is committed by the law of parliament, and yet he would have redress from the common law. The law of parliament is only known to parliament men, by experience in the House. Lord Coke says, every man looks for it, but few can find it. The House of Commons only know how to act within their own limits. We are not a court of appeal. We do not know certainly the jurisdiction of the House of Commons. We cannot judge of the laws and privileges of the House, because we have no knowledge of those laws and privileges. We cannot judge of the contempts thereof: we cannot judge of the punishment thereof.

I wish we had some code of the law of parliament; but till we have such a code, it is impossible we should be able to judge of it. Perhaps a contempt in the House of Commons, in the Chancery, in this court, and in the court of Durham, may be very different; therefore we cannot judge of it, but every court must be sole judge of its own contempts. Besides, as the court cannot go out of the return of this writ, how can we enquire as to the truth of the fact, as to the nature of the contempt? We have no means of trying whether the lord-mayor did right or wrong. This court cannot summon a jury to try the matter. We cannot examine into the fact. Here are no parties in litigation before the court. We cannot call in any body. We cannot hear any witnesses, or depositions of witnesses. We cannot issue any process. We are even now hearing *ex parte*, and without any counsel on the contrary side. Again, if we could determine upon the contempts of any other court, so might the other courts of Westminster-hall; and what confusion would then ensue! none of us knowing the law by which persons are committed by the House of Commons. If three persons are committed for the same breach of privilege, and applied severally to different courts, one court perhaps would bail, another court discharge, a third re-commit.

Two objections have been made, which I own have great weight; because they hold forth, if pursued to all possible cases, consequences of most important mischief. 1st, It is said, that if the rights and privileges of parliament are legal rights, for that very reason the Court must take notice of them, because they are legal. And 2ndly, If the law of parliament is part of the law of the land, the judges must take cognizance of one part of the law of the land, as well as of the other. But these objections will not prevail. There are two sorts of privileges which ought never to be confounded; personal privilege, and the privilege belonging to the whole collective body of that assembly. . . .

At present, when the House of Commons commits for contempt, it is very necessary to state what is the particular breach of privilege; but it would be a sufficient return, to state the breach of privilege generally. This doctrine is fortified by the opinion of all the judges, in the case of Lord Shaftesbury, and I never heard this decision complained of till 1704. Though they were times of heat, the judges could have no motive in their decision, but a regard to the laws. The houses disputed about jurisdiction, but the judges were not concerned in the dispute. As for the present case, I am perfectly satisfied, that if Lord Holt himself were to have determined it, the lord-mayor would be remanded. In the case of Mr. Murray, the judges could not hesitate concerning the contempt by a man who refused to receive his sentence in a proper posture. All the judges agreed, that he must be remanded, because he was committed by a court having competent jurisdiction. Courts of justice have no cognizance of the acts of the houses of parliament, because they belong 'ad aliud examen.' I have the most perfect satisfaction in my own mind in that determination. Sir Martin Wright, who felt a generous and distinguished warmth for the liberty of the subject; Mr. Justice Denison, who was so free from connexions and ambition of every kind; and Mr. Justice Foster, who may truly be called the Magna Charta of liberty of persons, as well as fortunes; all these revered judges concurred in this point: I am therefore clearly and with full satisfaction of opinion, that the lord-mayor must be remanded.

S.T., XIX, 1146.

148. Speaker recognises 'newswriters', 1803.

24th [May, 1803]. Settled with the Serjeant-at-Arms and Mr Ley that the gallery door should be opened every day, if required, at twelve; and the Serjeant would let the housekeeper understand that the "newswriters" might be let in in their usual places (the back row of the gallery), as being understood to have the order of particular Members, like any other strangers.

Diary & Correspondence of Charles Abbot, Lord Colchester (1861), vol. I, p. 421.

VIII. PROCEDURE

Parliamentary procedure, developed under the Tudors and Stuarts, seems to have undergone little change in this period, although the subject requires further investigation. Rules and customs which had emerged during the struggle against prerogative were faithfully adhered to in the fight against influence, and their enforcement greatly assisted in preventing parliament from becoming completely subservient to the Court or utterly unresponsive to the people. As Arthur Onslow put it, the 'terms of proceeding' were a 'protection to the minority, against the attempts of power' (**149**). One or two changes are illustrated in the documents. In Anne's reign Standing Orders No. 66 (**150**) and No. 67 (**151**) were adopted: the former to prevent the House from having to consider, and perhaps yield to, petitions for money from private persons, and the latter to ensure a full examination of financial proposals. Another change was in the method of considering election petitions. Till 1770 they were usually tried by the Committee of Privileges and Elections (**94, 96, 98, 99, 104**), (which any member could attend) and decided on party lines. It was a method, as Dodington said (**82**), whereby a majority could 'fortify and increase themselves'. A more judicial approach was encouraged by Grenville's Act of 1770, already referred to (**123**), which introduced a method of trying disputed returns by a committee elaborately chosen by ballot, and which, according to Hatsell, was 'one of the noblest works for the honour of the House of Commons and the security of the constitution that was ever devised by any minister or statesman'.[1]

In the elaboration and enforcement of the *lex et consuetudo Parliamenti*, much depended on the emergence first of a non-royal, then of a non-partisan, Speaker. The House indicated its objections to a royal nominee in 1695, when they rejected Littleton (**152**). Henceforth the Speaker was chosen by the majority in the House, and this vote at the beginning of the session became an important indication to the ministers of the strength of the various parties (**108**). However, this did not produce an independent Speaker, any more than there existed an independent House of Commons. His control of procedure made him a key figure in the eighteenth-century system of Court control over parliament, and for the bulk of this period he is the nominee of the ministers. Until 1742 he even sometimes held ministerial office, and spoke in committee. It was fortunate that during the most stable

---

[1] Cited by W. Holdsworth, *History of English Law*, vol. x, p. 549 n.

period of the system the chair was held by Arthur Onslow, who all sides agreed made an outstanding contribution to the dignity and impartiality of the office (**149, 153**). Even the opposition to Walpole conceded that he had, 'by a certain decency of behaviour, made himself many personal friends in the minority'.[1] He held the office for thirty-three years (1727–61), setting an important precedent in 1742 by resigning the valuable post of Treasurer of the Navy. On his retirement he was awarded a pension of £3,000, at the request of his colleagues (**153**). His successors continued his practice of not holding ministerial office, and an Act of Parliament of 1790 placed them financially above the political battlefield by granting the Speaker a salary of £6,000 a year and disabling him from holding any office of profit, during pleasure, under the crown (**154**). Nevertheless, complete impartiality was not fully achieved in this period. With Onslow's retirement, we enter another period of violent political warfare in which successive Speakers joined the troops: Fletcher Norton (1770–80), for example, in the opposition to George III, and Addington (1789–1801) in his support. Speaker Abbot (1802–17) was so outspoken in his views against Catholic Relief that he was almost formally censured by the House (1813), after a debate in which it is clear that opinion was hardening against partisanship in a Speaker. After this there was more progress towards impartiality; though there were set-backs, and the standards set by Onslow were not achieved again till the days of Shaw Lefevre (1839–57).

By this time the conservative devotion to traditional forms was out of date. The eighteenth-century procedure, owing to its 'historic origin', was the '*procedure of opposition*',[2] appropriate in a period when minority rights needed safeguards against majority power, when parliament still regarded itself principally as a check on the Court, and scantiness of legislation permitted a leisurely time-table; but unsuitable at a time of vast legislative programmes under government leadership. Only the beginnings of reform are seen in this period. In 1806 a new rule was made requiring that notice of all motions, except those of a purely routine nature, had to be given at least a day before they were to be brought up. And about the same time, the House began to reserve one or two days each week for government business.[3]

149. Parliamentary rules of procedure.

It is very much to be wished, that the rules, which have been from time to time laid down by the House, for the preservation of decency and order, in the debates and behaviour of Members of the House, could

---

[1] See p. 106.
[2] J. Redlich, *Procedure of the House of Commons* (1908), vol. I, p. 57.
[3] *Ibid.*, p. 70.

be enforced, and adhered to more strictly than they have been of late years: It certainly requires a conduct, on the part of the Speaker, full of resolution, yet of delicacy: But, as I well remember that Mr Onslow did in fact carry these rules into execution, to a certain point, the fault has not been in the want of rules, or of authority in the Chair to maintain those rules, if the Speaker thought proper to exercise that authority. . . .

. . . All these rules I but too well remember that Mr Onslow endeavoured to preserve with great strictness, yet with civility to the Members offending; though I do not pretend to say, that his endeavours always had their full effect. Besides the propriety, that in a Senate composed of Gentlemen of the first rank and fortune in the country, and deliberating on subjects of the greatest national importance—that, in such an assembly, decency and decorum should be observed, as well as in their deportment and behaviour to each other, as in their debates—Mr Onslow used frequently to assign another reason for adhering strictly to the rules and orders of the House;— He said, it was a maxim he had often heard, when he was a young man, from old and experienced Members, "That nothing tended more to throw power into the hands of the Administration, and those who acted with the majority of the House of Commons, than a neglect of, or departure from, these rules—That the terms of proceeding, as instituted by our ancestors, operated as a check and control on the actions of Ministers; and that they were, in many instances, a shelter and protection to the minority, against the attempts of power."

J. Hatsell, *Precedents of Proceedings in the House of Commons* (3rd ed., 1796), vol. II, p. 220.

150. Standing Order, No. 66, 1713.

HOUSE OF COMMONS PROCEEDINGS, 11 JUNE 1713

The Resolution of the 11th of *December*, in the Fifth Year of the Queen, being read; *viz.*

"*Resolved*, That this House will receive no Petition for any Sum of Money relating to publick Service, but what is recommended from the Crown;"

Ordered, That the said Resolution be declared to be a Standing Order of the House.

C.J., XVII, 417.

151. Standing Order, No. 67, 1707.

HOUSE OF COMMONS PROCEEDINGS, 29 MARCH 1707

Resolved, That this House will not proceed upon any Petition, Motion, or Bill for granting any Money, or for releasing, or compounding, any Sum of Money owing to the Crown, but in a Committee of the whole House; and that the same be declared to be a standing Order of the House.

C.J., xv, 367

152. House of Commons rejects a royal nominee for Speaker, 1695.

HOUSE OF COMMONS PROCEEDINGS, 14 MARCH 1695

. . . Mr Comptroller of his Majesty's Household [Wharton] stood up, and spake as followeth:

Mr Jodrell

I am commanded by the king to inform this House, That the late Speaker, *Sir John Trevor*, hath sent him Word, That his Indisposition does so continue upon him, that he cannot further attend the Service of the House, as Speaker: And further commanded me to say, That there may be no Delay in the publick Proceedings, he does give Leave to this House to proceed to the Choice of a new Speaker.

Sir, The Filling of That Chair is the highest Station any Commoner of *England* can be called to; but, however honourable it is, the Toil and Difficulties of it are so great, that I believe there is no reasonable Man that hears me, but would be rather glad to have it supplied by any Man than himself: And therefore, I shall, without fear of displeasing any Person, out of so many who are qualified to serve you, to nominate ——

Upon this he was interrupted by a great Noise in the House, crying No, No, No:

And several Gentlemen stood up, to speak to Order.

Exceptions were taken by several Members, That it was contrary to the undoubted Right of the House, of choosing their own Speaker, to have any Person, who brought a Message from the King, to nominate one to them.

Notwithstanding, the Comptroller stood up again, and named Sir *Thomas Littleton*; which was seconded by Sir *Henry Goodrick*.

Whereupon arose a Debate:

And another Person, viz. *Paul Foley* Esquire, was proposed by Sir *Christopher Musgrave*, and seconded by the Lord *Digby*.

And, after a long Debate, in relation to both the Persons, the Question was put by the Clerk, That Sir *Thomas Littleton* take the Chair of this House as Speaker.

The Clerk declared the Yeas had it.

The House was divided.

The Yeas on the Right Hand.

And the Noes on the Left.

The Tellers were appointed by the Clerk; *viz.*

  For the Yeas:

James Chadwick Esquire: 146.

  The Teller for the Noes:

Colonel *Granville*   179.

So it passed in the Negative.

Then the Second Question being about to be put, Mr. *Foley* stood up to speak; but the House would not hear him; but ordered the Clerk to put the Question, That *Paul Foley* Esquire take the Chair of this House as Speaker.

It was Resolved, *Nemine contradicente.*

Upon which, *Mr Foley* made his Excuse in his Place; which was not admitted by the House.

He was conducted to the Chair by the honourable Colonel *Granvill*, and the honourable *Henry Boyle* Esquire.

And, upon the first Step of the Chair, after some Pause, he made a Speech to the House again, to excuse himself.

Which not being allowed, he sat down.

C.J., XI, 272.

153. Arthur Onslow as Speaker.

March 18 [1761] The Commons resolved, *nem. con.* "That the Thanks of this House be given to Mr Speaker, for his constant and unwearied attendance in the chair, during the course of above thirty-three years, in five successive parliaments; for the unshaken integrity and steady impartiality, of his conduct there; and for the indefatigable pains he has, with uncommon abilities, constantly taken, to promote the real interest of his king and country, to maintain the honour and dignity of parliament, and to preserve inviolable the rights and privileges of the Commons of Great Britain . . ."

The Commons next resolved, *nem. con.* "That an humble Address be presented to his Majesty, humbly to beseech his Majesty, that he will be graciously pleased to confer some signal mark of his royal favour upon the right hon. Arthur Onslow, esq., Speaker of this House, for his great and eminent services performed to his country, for the space of 33 years and upwards; during which he has, with such distinguished ability and integrity, presided in the chair of this House: and to assure his Majesty, that whatever expence his Majesty shall think proper to be incurred upon that account, this House will make good the same to His Majesty."

P.H., xv, 1013.

154. The Speaker's salary, 1790.

An act for the better support of the dignity of the speaker of the house of commons; and for disabling the speaker of the house of commons for the time being from holding any office or place of profit, during pleasure, under the crown.

Most gracious Sovereign.

We your Majesty's most dutiful and loyal subjects, the commons of *Great Britain*, in parliament assembled, being desirous of making provision for enabling the speaker of the house of commons for the time being more effectually to support the dignity of the said office, and the expence necessarily attending the same; and having resolved that, for that purpose, the lords commissioners of the treasury should be authorised to direct, from time to time, a sum to be issued at the exchequer, which, together with the fees and allowances of five pounds *per* day, now payable on account of the said office, may amount to the clear yearly sum of six thousand pounds, do therefore most humbly beseech your Majesty that it may be enacted . . . [The speaker's secretary to deliver to the treasury, at the times herein mentioned, an account of the fees received, and sums due or received of the allowance to the speaker out of the civil list.]

II [If the fees, and the sum received or due to the speaker from the civil list, within any of the periods before-mentioned, shall exceed 1,500 £. the excess to be carried to the account of the next quarter, &c.]

III [If the fees and allowance from the civil list, for the quarter ending April 5, 1790, shall be less than 1,500 £. the deficiency to be made good from the supplies for 1790;]

IV [and thereafter from the consolidated fund.]

V [After previous appropriations out of the consolidated fund, the payments under this act to have preference, &c.]

VI And be it further enacted, That the several sum and sums of money directed by this act to be issued to the speaker of the house of commons, for the purpose of completing the clear sum of one thousand five hundred pounds, shall be free and clear from all taxes, impositions, and other publick charges whatever; and that the speaker of the house of commons for the time being shall be free and clear of all taxes, impositions and publick charges, in respect of such sums, any thing contained in any law or statute to the contrary thereof in anywise notwithstanding.

VII And be it enacted by the authority aforesaid, That the speaker of the house of commons for the time being shall not hold or enjoy, in his own name, or in the name of any person or persons in trust for him or for his benefit, any office or place of profit under the crown during pleasure.

30 Geo. III, c. 10: S.L., xxxvii, 11.

CHAPTER 4

LOCAL GOVERNMENT

One sentence from the Webbs' great work on local government graphically brings out the difficulty of adequately illustrating this subject, except in a number of volumes. 'If a single highly evolved organisation had, at all the various stages of its development from the Lord's Court of a rural Manor right up to the most fully developed Municipal Corporation, been successively photographed for the information of future generations, these different pictures could hardly have represented the several stages more strikingly than do the hundreds of distinct local authorities simultaneously existing in the eighteenth century.'[1] This teeming variety was the result of a number of circumstances. Firstly, the organs of local government had originally been superimposed on the medieval ones without abolishing them; secondly, the Civil War and the Revolution had freed them from central control; and, thirdly, they were thus able to adapt themselves as the economic and social changes of the eighteenth century gave them new tasks to perform. The result was, as Halévy said, that 'England was a museum of constitutional archaeology where the relics of past ages accumulated'[2]—as well as a building-site for new structures. The principal units alluded to in this chapter, the parish, the county, the manor and the borough, carried out the tasks set them by the common and statute law free from any control save that provided by action in the courts, initiated by the crown, or by a private person, or by another local government unit. For, of all the institutions of the period, local government was the least characterised by Montesquieu's separation of powers. Administration and legislation were carried out under judicial forms by presentment and indictment. Roads were repaired, bridges maintained, the poor relieved, drunkenness suppressed, grazing regulated, factory smoke abated, markets run and streets scavenged by a process whereby duties were imposed by law on private individuals, public officials or local communities, and punishments meted out by the courts for neglect to carry them out. Thus local autonomy, though great, was not complete, and it was further modified by the very real control exercised through the social homogeneity of the men who ran all the eighteenth-century institutions; and by the delicate nexus of interests typified, for example, by the importance attached by the First Lord of the Treasury to the instructions sent (by the Bishop of Winchester as Lord of the Manor of Taunton) to the

[1] S. and B. Webb, *The Manor and the Borough* (1908), p. 203.
[2] E. Halévy, *History of the English People in the 19th Century* (1949), vol. I, p. 111.

mayor of the borough that he would choose such men for the jury as would choose such men as constables as would distribute the local charity to poor voters of the right political colour (155).

And, if there was little control from above, there was even less from below. The county bench, the borough corporation, the parish vestry and the manor court, each at its own level, was generally in the hands of an oligarchy which usually renewed itself by co-optation. Even where democratic forms existed there was little popular control, and much power was vested in these cliques to do good or evil. The circumstances, the times, and above all the personalities of the local leaders produced every shade of result from the enterprising benevolence of Liverpool through the torpor of Leicester to the corrupt rule of the political 'boss', Joseph Merceron, in Bethnal Green. The success of the best proves the adequacy of the institutions in the early part of the period, but, as the eighteenth century was turned upside-down by the increasingly rapid economic, social and political change, even the most stream-lined of vestry committees and the most benevolent of reforming J.P.s proved less and less able to cope with the colossal problems these changes brought. The industrial and agrarian revolutions broke up the social links between landlord and tenant, and between master and man, which had once given reality to the political power of the J.P.s in the countryside and the mayor and aldermen in the town. The accompanying rise in population and its shift in location massed people together in areas where, as it happened, the local government arrangements were at their most primitive, leaving many, more sophisticated corporations with nothing to do except return Members of Parliament. Moreover, the new classes, the industrialists and the workers, found themselves excluded from the vestry, the town-hall and the bench by social, political and religious exclusiveness; and at the same time these classes were having their discontents formulated into political theories by radicals under the impact of the American and French Revolutions. Thus by the end of this period the time is ripe for the wholesale rationalisation of local government based on such new principles as democratic control by ratepayers, the use of contractors and paid experts, national uniformity and control from Whitehall. One by one, these new principles can be seen emerging during the period, partly under the stimulus of Acts of Parliament, but mainly by a process of local self-help in the extension, legally or extra-legally, of existing powers. One or two Acts laid new duties on the old machinery; stacks of private statutes created new *ad hoc* bodies like Turnpike Trusts, Boards of Guardians of the Poor, Commissioners of Sewers and Improvement Commissioners; while private citizens formed thief-taking associations without parliamentary authority. Here and there we see the new methods tried out: the justices sitting in special sessions at regular times and places; the vestries appointing committees; contractors and salaried professionals paid out of the rates replacing the annual, unpaid, compulsory service of amateurs; bridges being maintained by surveyors instead of being presented at the sessions after they have fallen into the river. But such improvements depended mainly on local initiative, and sometimes were made by the authorities simply to shift responsibility. Salaried officials, moreover, could be just as corrupt and inefficient as their masters. And, in any case, these changes only scratched the surface, for any thorough overhaul of local government was not to be expected from the unreformed House of Commons: that was the work of the next century.

155. Interdependence of local and central government, 1754.

DUKE OF NEWCASTLE TO DR. HOADLY[1]

Claremont Augt 9 1754.

SIR

As I know your Zeal for His Majesty's Service, & for the Whig Cause, I take the Liberty to trouble you with the Enclosed Request from the Friends of the Government at Taunton. Lord Egremont and the Whigs there, have recommended Mr Maxwel a very honest worthy Man, and a particular Friend of Mine to represent That Town upon the present Vacancy. You will see by the Enclosed Paper, (which was given me by Mr. Maxwel,) The Favor we ask of you, and I hope there will be no Inconvenience in the granting it. The present Agent or Steward, is represented to be a Friend to the Opposite Interest, & not to have made a true Representation to the Bishop of Winchester of the State of the Case. It is said, That what is now asked by our Friends, was formerly the constant Practice; If so, I am persuaded you will give Orders, to have it put upon the Old Foot. Or, If there should not be any great Objection to what is asked, I shou'd be extreamly obliged to you, If you wou'd grant it; For I think, It might be of great Service to my Friend Mr. Maxwel. If I should have been mistaken, and that it is Dr. Hoadley Your Brother, who is Clerk of the Castle; I must beg you would excuse me, & convey My Request to your Brother, & support it with your good Offices. I am, S^r, with great Truth & Regard

Your Most obedient humble Servant

HOLLES NEWCASTLE.

---

[1] Son of Benjamin Hoadly, Bishop of Winchester.

Memorandum from Taunton

The Constables of the Borough of Taunton, are chosen by a Jury impannell'd at a Court held by D.r Hoadley, as Clerk of the Castle of the Manor of Taunton Deane—or His Deputy, of which Manor the Bishop of Winchester is Lord.

These Constables have the Distribution of the Money belonging to the Poor of the Borough of Taunton, called Feoffee Money, which is never less than about 40 Pounds a Year, Sometimes £100 £150 or £200 a Year, according as the Lives drop, & Purchases are made. Which Money is now given away, to those Poor Voters, that oppose the Government Interest. The Clerks of the Castle, for many Years back, used to compliment the Mayor of Taunton for the Time being, with nominating this Jury, 'till the Death of Mr Dyke; when Dr Hoadley was by His Father the present Bishop of Winchester appointed Clerk in His Room, ever since which Time, the Bishop's Steward has held the Courts, & named the Jury Himself. Which have always consisted of Persons in direct Opposition to the Whig Interest;—Lord Egremont applied two years following to The Bishop, and desired He would give The Mayor Leave to name the Jury which The Bishop granted and gave Orders accordingly, but by Persuasions & other Misrepresentations of the Steward & others He was prevailed on, to alter His Mind both Times, tho' it's very certain, that the affairs of the Hundred, have no Connection with those of the Borough; & consequently it can be no Detriment, to His Lordship's Interest to grant the above Favour.

If, through the Duke of Newcastle or otherwise, you could at this Juncture prevail on Dr Hoadley, & The Bishop, to give the Steward absolute Orders, to hold the Court at the Time, the Mayor would appoint, & impannell the Jury to consist of the Persons undernamed it would add great strength to the Whig Cause.—

[24 Names follow]

Add. MSS. 32736, ff. 186–9.

I. THE PARISH

The ecclesiastical parish became the basic unit of local government in Tudor times. From then on, an ever-increasing burden of duties was laid on it by Tudor and Stuart legislation, while at the same time, especially in the south, it gradually absorbed many of the functions previously performed by the manor. It work was done by four principal officers: the churchwarden, the overseer of the poor, the surveyor of the highways, and the petty constable. The churchwarden was mainly responsible for the fabric of the church, the collection of the church rate, and the morals of the parishioners (**156**). The overseer performed the increasingly onerous tasks of relieving various kinds of pauper (**157, 158, 159**); passing vagrants through the parish (**160**) and preventing them from settling there without a settlement certificate (**161**); or litigating with other parishes over the same problem (**162**). The surveyor inspected the roads, presented them to the J.P.s, supervised their repair and collected fines and rates. His duties are detailed in the Act of 1691 (**163**). The constable took his orders from the high constable, and was the chief executive officer of the local justices (**164**). These four were assisted by a variety of lesser officials who were appointed for special or miscellaneous duties, and who, like the constable, had in earlier times been appointed at the court-leet or court-baron of the manor. The beadle (**165**) was typical of this class, but there were many others, such as the ale-conner, the scavenger, the hayward, and the field-keeper (**166**). The principal officers were chosen annually from among the leading inhabitants of the parish, the church-wardens by the vestry and the incumbent, the other three by the J.P.s. The offices were unpaid and compulsory, though they could be performed by deputies; and in most villages their holders, along with the incumbent and one or two of their social equals (farmers, millers, inn-keepers and so on), quietly ran the local affairs in the vestry, making their own appointments, choosing their successors, under the supervision of the local J.P.s. A smaller number of villages had an 'open' vestry, which closely supervised the ac-tivities of the officers and wielded a certain amount of democratic control. In Steeple Aston we see a vestry making bye-laws for the cultivation and grazing of the open-fields and common, choosing fieldsmen for the following year, and hiring a field-keeper (**166**). (This is another example of a parish taking on the functions of the manor.) Later in the period, when pauperism had reached such gigantic proportions, we find villages in Essex agreeing to-gether to set up a joint workhouse under a contractor (**167**). In London and the industrial areas, mainly because the tasks imposed on these unwilling, unpaid, temporary amateurs were too great (the substantial inhabitants avoiding office by paying fines), corruption and inefficiency were the result. The extreme case is perhaps Bethnal Green, where the open vestry came under the domination of a political 'boss' and 'racketeer', Joseph Merceron (**168**). It did not seem to matter whether the vestry was open or close: corruption and waste or integrity and efficiency could be found in each. According to the Webbs, St George's, Hanover Square, was the best-run parish in England. It was a close vestry, inhabited mostly by nobility and gentry, who wanted the parish well managed for their own comfort, and who were above parish corruption, having bigger fish to fry. And for the most efficient open vestry, using all the modern techniques of democratic control by ratepayers over parish officers, the appointment of salaried experts, the auditing of accounts, the choosing of standing committees for day-to-day supervision, and the formulation of enlightened policies, the same authors award the palm to Liverpool (**169**).

156. A churchwarden's accounts, 1765.

Feb: 16	Paid for a fox.	0:	1: 0.
	2 Ringing Days.	0:	6: 0.
	To fox's head.	0:	1: 0.
	Journey to Rumford twice to the Visitation	0:	10: 0.
	Paid for Sitation &c.	1:	0: 6.
March 29	Paid for Bread and wine	0:	2: 6.
	Paid for Bellrope	0:	5: 0.
	Paid John Hoge for Quarter Sarley	0:	12: 6.
	Paid for washing and mending ye Sorplis	0:	3: 0.
	Paid Ropers Bill	0:	19: 6.
	Paid Wacklin Bill	2:	16: 0.

MS. Minutes, West Thurrock (Essex) Churchwarden's Accounts.

157. An overseer's accounts, 1724 and 1731.

1724

For Removing Francis Poulton from Mr Garnetts Barne to Weston beyond Boldock being soe Rotten of ye pox as not able to walk or ride and for all charges and other expences 1 9 3

For ye Crying out and Lyeing Inn of Ann Dun of Rippon at Thos Raggs 1 17 6

Charges concerning Peter Simons being very ill and not willing to walk or ride but in a Cart to Hendon from ye Harrow in Wood Street . . . . – 16

providing for Jonas Eylet in his illness and phissek &c . 2 4 2

To the Widdow Bigg of Wood Street for nursing and takeing care of Mary Green found famished on ye Forest &c 5^s 3^d expended ab^t hir funeral 7^s 9^d . . . . . – 12 6

To five Naked Turkey Gally Slaves in their way home . 2 6

To nursing and providing for John Tood when ill of ye smallpox and maintaining him till well enough to remove from White Chaple to Walthamstowe wth apothecaryes Bills, Britches, hatt and shooes 2 11 9

To two poor women cast on our Essex Coast Ready to cry out . . . . − 1 3

To passing of 9 poor Naked Gally Slaves . . . . − 2 9

To the Widdow Poxon for cureing sev^rall parishioners &c. 2 − −

1731

To Dame Duck being lame . . . . . . − 1 6

To Mrs Mills at the House of Correction for maintaneing Bess Gray . . . . 4 − −

To Mr. Blean the surgion for setting old Phoebys arm . 3 3 0

To for laying out old Phoeby 1^s and to the Bearers 4^s . − 5 0

To Abraham Lawrence at twice he being lame . . . − 4 0

To charges to getting him into the Hospitali . . . − 6 3

To Mr Garnet what he disbursed for a poore woman in Noads Barne . . . . − 12 −

To D^o for a horse and cart to carry Dame Duck to the hospitall − 2 6

To Harewood at 3 severall tymes when her child was hurt p. falling into ye fire . . . . − 7 6

To Boram at severall tymes when his familly had the small pox 2 2 6

To Andrew Thornton a parishoner of Coggishall when sick of small pox 2 6

Barnes, p. 21.

158. Vestry minutes, 1737.

Jan: 10 1737.

Att a Vestery then held By the in Habatance of West Thorack it was then a gread by a great Mayjolotry of the Said Parish of West Thorack that Eliz. Burn a poor Child belong to the Said Parish of West Thorack Should be furthwith Be Bound out as an aprentece to Thos. Godsafe it being the farme turn now to take on that he now rents of Captⁿ Grantham.

John England Church Worden.
Jeremiah: Jones. Overseer.
Love Perrey. Constabel.

MS. Minutes, West Thurrock with Purfleet (Essex).

159. Vestry minutes, 1801.

(1)

West Thurrock Novr 9th 1801.

I do hear by Agreed to pay to the Church Warden or Overseers of the Parish of West Thorock The Sum of Fifteen Pound In consequence of Ann Martin haveing Sworn Child to me William Stokes, before L. Button Esqr The Parish of West Thorock are willing to release me the s^d William Stokes from any further demand upon payment of the Like sum of Fifteen Pound . . .

I William Stokes, Now pay down Into the hands of J. Button Overseer the Sum of Nine Pound Five Shillings and Sixpence, In part of payment—

And I William Stokes so hearby pledge my Word, for the further payment of the Sum of Five Pound, Fourteen Shillings and Sixpence to make up the s^d Sum of Fifteen Pound: Too be paid On or before twelve Calander Months from the date hereof— If not paid I stand liable to be taken up for the s^d Sum of Five pounds 14 Shillings & 6^d.—due to the S^d Parish of West Thorock

I hereby Sign My Name

In the Presence of John Button Overseer
　　　　　　　　　Jere: Townsend Overseer
　　　　　　　　　Jacob: Green Constable
　　　　　　　　　The Mark of Will: Stokes X.

MS. Minutes, West Thurrock (Essex).

(2)

At a Vestry held at the Poor House the 8th of Decr 1801.
Present Mr Clarkson, Mr Joyner
Mr Townsend Overseer Mr Button Overseer

Resolved In Consequence of William Stokes Marrying Ann Martin who is with Child by him he is now willing to marry her if the Parish will give him £2–14–6 after he is marryed—agreed—also agreed to pay him £9: 5: 6 which is now in Mr Curtis's hands

MS. Minutes, West Thurrock with Purfleet (Essex).

160. Removal certificate, 1790.

To Thomas Lawrence, a constable in the City of London, and also to all constables and other officers of the Peace whom it may concern to receive and convey. And to the Churchwardens, Chapel Wardens or Overseers of the Poor, of the Parish of Walthamstow in the County of Essex, or either of them to receive and obey.

Whereas Martha King was apprehended in the Parish of St. Mary Le Bow in this City as a rogue and vagabond, wandering abroad, lodging in the open air and not giving a good account of herself, and upon examination of the said Martha taken before me upon oath (which examination is hereunto annexed) it doth appear that the last legal settlement of the said Martha is in the said parish of Walthamstow. These are therefore to require you the said Thomas to convey the said Martha to the Parish of St. Mary White Chapel in the County of Middlesex, that being the first parish in the next Precinct through which she ought to pass, in the direct way to the said parish, to which she ought to be sent, and to deliver her to the Constable or other officer, of such first parish in such next precinct, together with this pass and Duplicate of the examination of the said Martha taking his receipt for the same. And the said Martha to be thence conveyed on in like manner to the said parish of Walthamstow there to be delivered to some Church Warden, Chapel Warden, or Overseer of the Poor to be provided for according to law. And you the said Church Wardens, Chapel Wardens and Overseers of the poor are hereby required to receive the said Martha and provide for her as aforesaid. Given under my hand and seal this 16th day of April in the year of our Lord 1790.

BRASS CROSBY

London   The Examination of Martha King a vagabond ap-
to wit   prehended in the said City and brought before me
            one of his Majesty's Justices of the Peace for the
said City. Taken this 16th day of April 1790

Who on her oath saith, that her mother informed her and which Information she believes to be true that her said mother lived in the parish of Walthamstow in the County of Essex where her said mother was legally settled and that she this examinant hath not since obtained a subsequent settlement to this Examinant's knowledge and belief.

The Mark × of
Martha King

Sworn the Day and year first above written before me

BRASS CROSBY.

Barnes, preface, pp. 3-4.

161. Settlement certificate, 1717.

We, James Matthews, Richd Kirkham, Thos Skingle, Robt Woolley, Churchwardens and Overseers of the Parish of Walthamstow in the County of Essex do hereby own and acknowledge Mary Lawrance to be an Inhabitant legally settled in the Parish of Walthamstow aforesaid. In witness whereof we have hereunto set our hands and seals the twentieth day of March in the year of our Sovereign King George by the grace of God of Great Britain, France and Ireland, Defender of the Faith, etc. Annoq. Dom. 1717.

Attested by   James Matthews
                    Richard Kirkham   Churchwardens

                    Tho. Skingle
                    the mark + of   Overseers
                    Richard Wolle

To the Churchwardens and Overseers of the Poor of the Parish of Woodford in the County of Essex or any or either of them.

We whose names are hereunto subscribed, Justices of the Peace of the County of Essex aforesaid, do allow of the Certificate above written

Dated the 22nd Day of Aprill, Anno Dom 1717

JO. CONYERS.
R. DENNETT.

Barnes, preface, p. 3.

162. A disputed settlement, 1810.

At a Vestry held at the Fox & Goose on thursday the 20th of Sep. 1810.

Present Mr Snowden, Mr Curtiss, Mr Clarkson, Mr C. Selsdon, Mr Button, Mr Joyner Mr Skinner—

265

To consult relative to a notice that has been sent by the Church Wardens & Overseers of the Parish of Buckland in the county of Dorset—

To appeal against an Order of F. I. H. Wollaston & Charles Tower, Two of his Majesty's Justices of the Peace, for the County of Essex, Concerning the removal of Ann Portis Widow and her 3 children.— It was agreed that Mr Wall of Brentwood should be informed of the above business immediately & that he attend at the Quarter Sessions at Chelmsford on behalf of the Parish of West Thorock.

MS. Minutes, West Thurrock (Essex).

163. A Highways Act, 1691.

An act for the repairing and amending the highways, and for settling the rates of carriage of goods.

Whereas the free and easy intercourse and means of conveying goods and merchandizes from one market-town to another, contributes very much to the advancement of trade, increase of wealth, and raising the value of lands, as well as to the ease and convenience of the subject in general; for which ends therefore divers good and necessary laws have been heretofore made for the enlarging, repairing, and amending the highways and common roads of this kingdom: notwithstanding which laws, the same are not in many parts sufficiently amended and repaired, but remain almost impassable; all which is occasioned, not only by reason of some ambiguities in the said laws, but by want of a sufficient provision to compel the execution of the same; for remedy whereof:

II. [All laws about highways to be put in execution.]

III. And be it further enacted . . . That from henceforth, upon the six and twentieth day of *December* in every year, unless that day shall be *Sunday*, and then on the seven and twentieth, the constables, headboroughs, tythingmen, churchwardens, surveyor or surveyors of the highways, and inhabitants in every parish, shall assemble together, and the major part of them as are so assembled shall make a list of the names of a competent number of the inhabitants in their parish, who have an estate in lands, tenements, or hereditaments, in their own right or their wives, of the value of ten pounds by the year, or a personal estate of the value of one hundred pounds, or are occupiers or tenants of houses, lands, tenements, or hereditaments, of the yearly value of thirty pounds, if any such there be, or if there be no such persons in the parish, then the said list to be of the most sufficient inhabitants of such parish; and shall return such list unto two or more of the justices of the peace in or near the division of the county in which their parish lies, at a special sessions to be held for that purpose within the said division, . . . and the said justices shall then and there, out of the said lists, according to their discretion, and the largeness of the parish, by warrant under their hands and seals, nominate and appoint one, two or more, as they think fit and approve of, being of like sufficiency as aforesaid, to be surveyor or surveyors of the highways of every parish within the division, or for any hamlet, precinct, liberty, tything, or town, of and in the same division for the year ensuing which nomination and appointment shall, by the constables, headboroughs, tythingmen, or surveyor of the highways for the time being, or some of them, be notified to the person or persons so nominated, chosen, and appointed by the said justices, within six days after such nomination, by serving him or them with the said warrant or warrants, or by leaving the same, or a true copy thereof, at his or their houses, or usual places of abode; and from thenceforth the person or persons, so nominated and appointed, shall be surveyor or surveyors of the highways for the parish, town, village, hamlet, precinct, or tything, for which he shall have been so nominated, chosen, and appointed, for the year ensuing. . . .

VIII. And be it . . . enacted . . . That every surveyor of the highways, appointed as in and by this act is directed, shall within fourteen days next after his first acceptance of the said office, and so from time to time every four months, during his being surveyor, take a view of all the roads, common highways, watercourses, bridges, causeways, and pavements within the parish, town, village, hamlet, precinct, or tything, for which he is appointed surveyor, that are to be repaired by the said parish, [etc.] . . . and shall make a presentment upon oath, in what state and condition he finds the same respectively, to some justice of the peace of the same division, if then resident there, otherwise to some neighbouring justice of the peace for the said county, . . . and what defaults or annoyances they shall find in any of the said highways, causeways, bridges, ditches, hedges, trees, watercourses, drains, or gutters, next adjoining to the same, they shall from time to time, the next *Sunday* immediately after sermon ended, give publick notice of the same in the parish church, and if the same shall not be removed, repaired, and amended, within thirty days after such notice given, that then the said surveyor or surveyors of the said highways shall within thirty days remove, repair, and amend the same, and dispose of the same annoyances to and for the repair of the said highways; and the said surveyor and surveyors shall be reimbursed what charges and expences they shall be at in so doing, by the parties who should have done the same; and in case the said parties shall upon demand refuse or neglect to pay the said surveyors their said charges, then the said surveyors shall apply him or themselves to any justice of the peace within the division of the county wherein such highway is, and in default thereof, to any neighbouring justice for the said county, and upon his or their making oath before such justice of the notice to the defaulter in manner aforesaid (which oath the said justice is impowered and required to administer) that then the said surveyors shall be repaid all such their charges as shall be allowed to be reasonable by the said justice. . . .

XIV. *And whereas in pursuance of the statute made in the fifth year of the reign of the late Queen* Elizabeth, *many parishes and places are oftentimes presented upon the knowledge and view of a justice of peace, or otherwise, for not repairing and amending their highways, and the fines imposed and set on such presentments, and other fines and issues for not repairing and amending the highways, are returned into the court of* Exchequer, *or other courts, and such fines and issues against such parishes for not amending their highways, are levied on some particular inhabitants of such parishes or places, and there being no provision made for the making of a rate to reimburse such particular inhabitants;* be it therefore . . . enacted . . .,

That no fine, issue, penalty, or forfeiture, shall hereafter be returned into the court of *Exchequer,* or other court, but shall be levied and paid into the hands of the surveyors of such parish or place, to be applied towards the repair and amendment of such highway; and that if any fine, penalty or forfeiture, imposed on any parish or place for not repairing the highways, shall hereafter be levied on any one or more of the inhabitants, of such parish or place, that then such inhabitant or inhabitants shall make his or their complaint to the justices of the peace at their special sessions, and the said justices, or any two of them, are hereby impowered and authorized, by warrant under their hands and seals, to cause a rate to be made, according to the form and manner aforesaid, for the reimbursing such inhabitant or inhabitants the monies so levied on him or them as aforesaid, which rate so made and confirmed by two justices, as aforesaid, shall be collected and levied by the surveyor or surveyors of the highways of such parish or place so presented or indicted as aforesaid, and the said surveyor or surveyors, shall within one month next after making and confirming the rate aforesaid, pay unto the inhabitant or inhabitants such money so levied on him or them as aforesaid.

XVII. [Justices may in sessions order an assessment to be made, to repair the ways]

XVIII. [Assessment not to exceed 6d in the pound.]

3 & 4 Will. & Mary, c. 12: S.L., IX, 146.

164. High and petty constables, 1797.

FORM USED BY THE HIGH CONSTABLE OF THE COUNTY OF ESSEX AND ISSUED TO THE LOCAL CONSTABLES OF THE BEACONTREE HUNDRED

Essex   To the constable of the parish of . . .

By virtue of a Precept directed to me from two of His Majesty's Justices of the Peace for this County, these are to require you respectively, to give Notice to, and warn your respective Highway Surveyors, to take a View of the Highways, Causeways, Hedges, Ditches and Bridges within your respective Parishes and Wards, and make their personal Appearance before such of His Majesty's Justices of the Peace for this County, as shall be present at a special sessions to be holden at the Angel Inn; at Great Ilford, on Saturday the 22nd day of July 1797 by eleven o'Clock in the Forenoon, and then and there upon oath present the state and condition thereof; and you are respectively (the night before the said meeting) to make general Privy Search throughout your respective Parishes and Wards, for all Rogues, Vagabonds and Sturdy Beggars, and apprehend and bring all such to the said meeting; and you are also to set and keep strict Watch and Ward within your respective Parishes and Wards, and at the Time and Place aforesaid, return in Writing the Names of all unlicensed Ale housekeepers, and all Disorders in licensed Alehouses, with the names of all idle, disorderly and riotous Livers; and you are then and there to present all other Things presentable by Virtue of and under your office, and you are to give the Justices of the Peace for this County, living within your respective Parishes and Wards, Notice of the said Meeting in writing.

JOSEPH MARKBY, High Constable.

Barnes, preface, p. 4.

165. The office and duties of the beadle, 1779.

He is constantly to attend the Vestrys and diligently to execute all the orders he may receive therefrom and is to leave notice in writing at the residence within the parish of the Majesty's Justice of the peace, the churchwardens and overseers of the poor and of all such Inhabitants who have served or pay^d the fine for being excused from serving the office of churchwarden specifying the place where and time when such Vestry is to be holden notwithstanding the same notice may be given in the Church.

He is constantly to attend on Sundays during the time of Divine service to prevent Boys from playing in the Churchyard or other disorderly matters, and to be aiding and assisting the Constable at all times in takeing up Beggars and other disorderly persons, to execute the orders of the Churchwardens and Overseers of the poor for the time being in aiding and assisting the Constable to secure such persons as to the said Churchwardens and Overseers may be thought within the meaning of the present or any future acts of Parliament for the better or more speedily recruiting his Majestys forces.

He is to attend to and procure the passing of all Vagrants, paupers, &c., and diligently to search for and produce to the Vestry or to the Overseers of the Poor once within every quarter of a year at the least a true list of all persons suspected of keeping disorderly houses, of all who receive Inmates, with the names of such inmates, and of all persons who may now do, or may hereafter come to reside in any cottage within the parish not having a sustificate from their legal place of settlement, and he is to do every matter and thing in his power that can be reasonably required of him as the servant and messenger of the Vestry, churchwardens and overseers of the poor for the time being. . . .

N.B.—The rules of the Vestry clerk and beadle were approved by Anthony Todd and Peregrine Bertie, esq^{rs}, two of his Majesty's Justices of the peace.

Barnes, p. 70.

166. Vestry bye-laws, 1762.

ARTICLES AGREED UPON BY THE INHABITANTS OF STEEPLE ASTON

Jany. 5th, 1762.

1st. We agree to lay down Saintfoin in the Furlong called Slater-Lot to Pudding edge to be mounded by the Yard Land. No horse or sheep to be turn'd in under the Penalty of twenty shillings for every head of cattle for each offence. No person to turn to his Plow to damage his Neighbour, if detected to pay five chillings.

2. We agree to sow one Hundred of Clover-seed in Barley Field, to be bought by the Constable, every Person to pay according to the Yard Land.

. . .

6. We agree to put in Field-men to see that no Person overstock, and they shall be obliged to count the sheep twice every year under Penalty of twenty shillings. The sheep to be counted once between ye first day of May and the twentieth day of May, the other time between the first day of November and the twentieth of ye said month.

. . .

1762   At a Vestry held in the Parish Church of Steeple Aston the
Jan 5   5th January 1762, it was agreed to appoint Richard Fox, Jacob Watson and William Wing to be Fieldsmen for one year from this day.
Present at this Vestry

(sd) J. Noel, Rector. Richd. Fox. Jacob Watson.
William Wing. Will Wing. William Preston.

Agreed by the Vestrey that Thos. Dean is Hired to look after the field; to look after the Crowes and Cach the moulds if he can: and to look after the moulds at Headon way, Dean headge and Slaterfoot that is now laid down Sandfine. And it [is] further agreed that the field men now appointed shall be all agreed to lett Thos. Dean the field keeper know when the field shall be stocked. Thos. Dean agrees to keep the field at the Yearly sum of foure pounds and ten shillings and ye sd Thos. Dean is to find his own powder and shot all the time he keep the sd field, and if the said Thos. Dean neglects or refuses to do His Duty He shall forfitt to the fieldmen now apointed the sume of twenty shillings to be reducted out of the sume above menchoned and

if the said fieldsmen should neglect to pay the sd Thos. Dean when he
has proformed his above contract they agree to pay him the sd Thos
Dean the sume of twenty shillings over & above the agreed wages as
Witness I have set our hand this 7 day of Novr. 1763.

 THOMAS DEAN.

Quoted by A. Ballard in *Oxfordshire Archaeological Society Report* (Banbury, 1913), pp. 140–4.

167. A joint workhouse for three parishes, 1803.

At a Vestry held the 22nd day of April 1803 ———

Resolved that "as it appears to me that the Poor of our Parish would
be better managed and our own rates be lessened by taking the management of them away from the present Contractor, and that it would
be altogether more satisfactory to us to do so, and that as the House at
present occupied by the poor is likely to be more expensive than
necessary" that proper notice be given to Mr Green and to the other
parishes concerned for determining the Contract. The Parish at the
same time wish most completely to express that they have uniformly
experienced great satisfaction in the heretofore agreement with the
Parishes of Alvely & Stifford, and have only to lament that the late
innovations have, in great measure, led to this resolution.

W. MURGATROYD. Vicar
JAMES PECT.
JAMES GILLBIE etc.

MS. Minutes, West Thurrock, 1803.

168. Bethnal Green: a corrupt open vestry, c. 1800.

The Rev. *Joshua King*, called in, and Examined.

You are a clergyman of the parish of Bethnal-Green?—The Rector
of that parish.

How long have you held that situation?—About seven years.

Do you principally reside there?—Yes, I do, and discharge all the
duties myself.

Is it a very large parish?—It consists of a population of about 40,000,
generally the lowest description of people; the overflowing population
out of Spitalfields have settled in that parish.

As clergyman of the parish, you have felt it your duty to make
yourself acquainted, as far as lay in your power, with the state and
condition of the Police?—Surely.

What is that?—I am sorry to say that it is most deplorable; every Sunday morning, during the time of Divine Service, several hundred persons assemble in a field adjoining the church-yard, where they fight dogs, hunt ducks, gamble, enter into subscriptions to fee drovers for a bullock; I have seen them drive the animal through the most populous parts of the parish, force sticks pointed with iron up the body, put peas into the ears, and infuriate the beast, so as to endanger the lives of all persons passing along the streets. . . .

Do they ever drive the bullock across the church-yard?—Yes; about two months ago, during the time of Divine Service, to the great consternation of the congregation, a bullock was hunted in the church-yard; and although Mr. Merceron, a Magistrate for the county, the beadles, and Mr. Merceron's clerk, who is a constable, were present; I cannot learn, that they took any steps to put a stop to so wanton and disgraceful an outrage; on the contrary, I have reason to believe, that the officers of my parish frequently connive at and sanction such practices. . . .

Did you ever speak to Mr. Merceron, or to any of the Magistrates, or lay any special complaint before the Bench of Magistrates?—I complained to Mr. Merceron, about five years ago, of the disgraceful practice of bullock-hunting, and expressed a wish to be in the commission of the peace, that I might more effectually prevent such practices. Upon that occasion, Mr. Merceron declared that there was no kind of amusement he was so fond of as bullock-hunting, and that in his younger days he was generally the first in the chase; he discouraged me at the same time from entertaining any hopes of getting into the commission, by saying, no person could be appointed unless he was recommended by the other Magistrates; and that if any other Magistrate was necessary for the district, he should take care to recommend his friend Mr. Timmings, and not me.

. . . Are you at all acquainted with the condition in which the public-houses are in, in your parish, whether they are orderly or disorderly? —Some of them I apprehend are very disorderly, and I cannot but think that great blame is imputable to the acting magistrates for the district, for not suppressing the licences of such houses.

. . . What are the particular houses the names of which you have learnt?—There are three that have been particularly pointed out; the one is the Sun in Slater-street, the Three Sugar Loaves in St. John-street, and the Seven Stars in Fleet-street. . . .

Do you know anything as to the mode in which those houses are held, or who is the proprietor, or with whom they deal, that would lead you to think that any protection would be given them against such complaints, if they had been made?—The three houses I have mentioned belong to property of which Mr. Merceron is rent gatherer; he took a lease of the latter house, that is of the Seven Stars, in the year 1788, and afterwards underlet it to Messrs. Hanburys; that the Three Sugar Loaves are in Messrs. Hanburys trade. . . .

Is there any personal difference between you and Mr. Merceron?— Nothing, except what has arisen from a disapprobation of his official conduct; he is the treasurer of the parish, has ammassed a large fortune without any ostensible means; takes care to elect the most ignorant and the lowest characters, on whom he can depend, to fill all parochial offices, and to audit his accounts; when I say elect, I mean that his influence is so extensive in the parish, that whoever he nominates, the vestry is sure to sanction and appoint.

Has there been a considerable opposition to that influence within your own memory, by the parishioners?—Yes, there has; and indeed I am told that previous to my coming into the parish, the same op-position was manifested; that for the last 25 years, the respectable part of the parish have been contending with him for a successful examina-tion of his accounts, and have never succeeded; with the assistance of the Dissenters, with whom he has identified himself, and the publicans who dare not withhold their support, he bears down all opposition; a grant of upwards of 12,000 £ from Parliament, during a time of great distress in the parish, in the year 1800, passed through his hands for the relief of the out-door poor, which I have reason to believe was not applied to the purpose for which it was intended, nor is it satisfactorily accounted for.

What reason have you to believe that?—I have got an extract, which I have made from the parish register, in which it appears to have been audited, and I have been informed, that he pretended he had mislaid or lost his vouchers, and not a single voucher was pro-duced; Mr. Mitford, jun. was, I believe, sent down by Government, to inquire how the money had been expended; I am not aware how far he was satisfied. I have brought with me an extract from the parish register, purporting to be an audit of the account; that 505 £ which appears at the bottom, remained in his hands about two years; there was then a little disturbance in the parish, and it was brought forward and paid to the Poor's Rate account. . . .

Were you not strong enough in the vestry to force him to an account?—By no means; I will state what occurred a very short time ago:—In order to prevent investigation, I have seen him instigate his creatures to riot and clamour, even within the walls of the church; he has taken his stand on the church steps, and proposed three times three huzzars, taking his hat off and being the foremost in the shout; so successful was he on that occasion, that lately he has adjourned all public vestry meetings to the church-yard, where a mob has collected to support him. He instigated that mob, at a late meeting, to attack a person of the name of Shevill, who, had he not taken refuge in my house, would probably have fallen a sacrifice to their fury. . . .

Is Mr. Merceron popular among the lower classes of the inhabitants in your parish?—Universally abhorred; but having the collection of rents to a very considerable extent, and a number of houses of a very small description in the parish, and as he can command the publicans by being a licensing Magistrate, and having been a commissioner of the property tax, and sitting on all appeals with respect to the assessed as well as parochial Taxes, he has had an opportunity of most despotically tyrannizing over the parish.

Do you know, whether the parish officers pay a regular attention to keeping the streets orderly and quiet at night?—Considering the description of population, I think they are as orderly as can be expected.

By whom are the constables named?—Every officer in the parish is appointed by Mr. Merceron, and all obey his mandates. . . .

Minutes of Evidence before the Select Committee of the House of Commons on the State of the Police of the Metropolis (1816), p. 151.

169. Liverpool: an efficient open vestry, 1802.

At the Annual Vestry [of Liverpool] in the parochial chapel of St. Nicholas and Our Lady, on Easter Tuesday, the 20th April 1802, the following report from the Parish Committee, stating the various acts done by them since their appointment, and recommending others to the notice of their successors, was presented and read by the Vestry Clerk:—

. . . For the sake of order the Committee will begin with the duty imposed upon them on the day of their appointment, and that will be best done by adverting to the resolutions of the last Annual Vestry. At that Vestry the arguments for and against the rating of shipping by name, and of personal property in general, so as to do equal justice to the inhabitants of every denomination, and give universal satisfaction, ended in the following resolution:—Mr Leigh moved, 'That it be an instruction to the Churchwardens and Overseers to assess stock in trade, of which ships are a part, after a reasonable rate.' Mr Stanistreet moved as an amendment, 'That the Churchwardens and Overseers learn from the merchants whether they admit shipping to be rateable, and if so, that the amount of the rate be fixed by arbitration; but if the merchants do not admit the liability of shipping, that the rate be in future laid so as to include shipping, under the opinion of counsel, in order ultimately to enforce the payment;' and the motion, as amended, being seconded by the Rev. Samuel Renshaw, Rector of the Parish, was carried.

In consequence of this resolution, a meeting of the Committee was held on the 28th April, when it was unanimously agreed that a limited number of their body should be deputed to carry it into effect, experience having shown that where a multiplicity of general business is left to be transacted by a numerous body, the whole is greatly accelerated by a division of its members into smaller ones for specific and special purposes, under the control of the body at large. With this view the deputation, and a select number of the merchants, had a conference on the first day of June, when it was not admitted by the merchants that their shipping in the docks, or at the port of Liverpool, were rateable within the parish of Liverpool, and therefore so much of the resolution of the Vestry as directs the amount of the proposed rate on the merchants to be determined by arbitration in the event of their admitting their liability has not been carried into effect. The Committee, having no alternative, immediately adopted the mode of taxation directed by the Vestry, in which, though shipping be not named, yet in the measure of taxation, the profits that arise therefrom, as a species of personal property, are included. In the accomplishment of this rate, on the basis of equal justice between the merchants and the tradesmen, much time was necessarily bestowed by the Committee; and though their meetings on this particular occasion were thirty in number, yet, from the difficulties with which the subject abounded, it was not before the month of November that the rate for the year's service was completed and allowed. The acts of the Committee at each meeting from 28th April to the month of November inclusively, your Committee have caused to be minuted in a book, kept for this purpose only, which is now on the table for inspection.

The next subject in the order of time which the Committee have to lay before the Vestry, is their proceedings upon another resolution of the last Vestry, founded on the motion of Dr. Currie, in effect that a house for the reception of paupers labouring under fever and other infectious diseases be immediately erected on the open space of ground belonging to the parish, south of the workhouse, under the direction of the Parish Committee and the physicians of the Infirmary and Dispensary . . . Reasons, however, of great weight having since occurred to abandon that situation, your Committee, under the advice of the Faculty, purchased a field to the eastward of the workhouse, and an hospital for the reception of paupers in case of fever, upon an economical plan to answer the end proposed, is now building upon it, under the direction of the Committee and the Faculty of the two institutions. The expense of this building is calculated at £5000, and hitherto has been borne by the rate for the poor, because the use of it is to be confined to persons of that description; and as upon the whole there will be a very considerable saving to the Parish by the proposed establishment, and as it will also tend to the decrease of fever in the town, the Committee flatter themselves the Vestry will approve the step they have taken in thus departing from the strict letter of the resolution, and by expending the sum of £1200 in the purchase of land, a part only of which is at present necessary for the intended hospital. The minutes of the Committee's proceedings at their meetings on this business are also entered in a book kept for this purpose only, and are now on the table for inspection.

The Committee having now stated their proceedings upon the acts of the Vestry, it remains for them, in conformity with the sentiments they have already expressed, to lay before the public such other matters as have come under their direction, some of which, they are sorry to be obliged to say, will fall to the lot of their successors in office to be completed. The first is the dispute between the Parish and the Corporation of Liverpool respecting the rates on the dock and town duties, which now amount to a very large sum, no less than £12,000—a sum, however, which the Committee have every reason to hope will shortly be recovered by the judgement of the magistrates, to whom, by the resistance of the Corporation, the Churchwardens have been compelled to apply for redress. The giving judgement upon the application has hitherto been deferred at the request of the solicitor for the Corporation, who was not then armed with sufficient proof to sustain his clients' opposition to the rate, but as the time required for that purpose has now elapsed, it only remains for the magistrates again to meet to form their decision on the claim, a meeting which has hitherto been prevented by the absence of Mr Dawson. . . .

Your Committee, upon mature consideration of the attention and labour necessary to be employed in the well discharging of the duties of the several officers following, and by way of stimulus to each to exert himself the more, have increased their salaries—Mr. Simmon's, from £200 to £210 & Mr. Lewis's, from £80 to £100; the Government Collector's, from £80 to £100; the Sextons of the parish churches, £20 each. They have increased the salary of the Rev. Mr. Kidd, the Chaplain of the Workhouse, to 30 guineas per annum. . . .

The next subject brings the Committee's address nearly to a close, and it is a subject in which, as a body representing the inhabitants out of Vestry, they feel a particular interest. Collectively and individually they have seen with satisfaction the exemplary lives and characters of their worthy Rectors; but while they are thus gratified they cannot help expressing their concern that, comparatively with the income of other Rectors in the vicinity, whose cures bear no proportion to theirs, the salaries and fees annexed to their vocation have, for a series of years, continued to remain so low, in a parish, too, where the rates are under those of every other place in the kingdom. It is upon the conviction of the Committee that the salaries of the Rectors are inadequate to their high situation and deserts, and are no rewards for the pains bestowed by them in the exercise of their religious duties, that they have unanimously resolved to submit to the consideration and justice of the Vestry the following reasonable propositions:—

1st, That the income of the Reverend the Rectors of Liverpool is inadequate to their services and the duties of their high office.

2nd, That it be referred to the Committee to be this day appointed to make such a reasonable addition to the income of the Rectors out of the rate to be levied for the churches and clergy, as such Committee shall think proper.

3rd, That the Committee be authorised to review the Table of Fees and Church Dues, established in 1733, not only as to Rectors, but also to Churchwardens, Clerks, and Sextons, and to make therein such reasonable alterations in their favour as the law will warrant and the Committee shall think just between them and the Parish.

S. and B. Webb, *The Parish and the County* (1906), p. 137.

II. THE COUNTY

The machinery of the parish (and of the manor) was under the close supervision of the justice of the peace. The expansion of his responsibilities in Tudor and Stuart times involved the attenuation of the activities of the other, sometimes much older, county offices, and these latter will be dealt with first. The most important man in the county was the Lord Lieutenant, who was usually the *custos rotulorum* as well. Appointed by the king, he was usually a great nobleman, and a member of the Privy Council. He commanded the county military forces, appointing the deputy-lieutenants and other officers, but performed few local government functions. Nevertheless, he was the key figure in any grip the central government had on the localities. He was important occasionally to deal with civil strife (**170, 171**), but he was vital constantly to wage the party war. Increasingly, as the century progressed, the J.P.s were appointed on his recommendation (**172**). He was thus the fountain of patronage as far as the localities were concerned, and the head of a vast 'interest' as far as the ministers were concerned. An idea of the importance the politicians attached to him can be gained from observing the dismissals of Lords Lieutenant that sometimes accompanied changes of administration; and from noticing the interest that both sides (especially the Tories) took in the appointment of county officers. The ancient office of sheriff had faded to a ceremonial shadow. He was still appointed annually by the crown, though he had long ago been displaced by the justice of the peace, just as the county court had been displaced by the quarter sessions, though it was still in the former that the sheriff returned the two knights of the shire. He was also responsible for the county gaol.

We must now turn to 'the most important and the most ubiquitous organ of local government':[1] the justice of the peace. Acting in the court of quarter sessions, these officers had taken over the work previously carried out by the county court, and, acting in pairs or more in petty sessions, that of the hundred court and sheriff's tourn. Over two centuries of statutes had placed such a wide variety of judicial and administrative work on their shoulders that it is impossible to give more than a few hints of it in the documents. In the quarter sessions, held at least four times a year, apart from trying a vast number of criminal cases (**173**), they administered the laws concerning bridges (**174, 183**), roads (**175, 176**), gaols (**177**), houses of correction (**178**), wages, prices, licensing of traders, and so on. And this administration was carried out under judicial forms: that is to say, individuals, or communities, or their officers, would be presented by the grand jury, or a high constable, or a J.P. 'on his own view', and tried before the petty jury for neglect of some local government duty imposed on them by the law. Many problems

[1] W. Holdsworth, *History of English Law* (1938), vol. x, p. 128.

could be dealt with by two or more J.P.s only, either meeting at their convenience in one of their houses or at an inn; or, as later became common, holding petty sessions at regular intervals in the divisions of the county roughly corresponding to the old hundreds. Here, among other things, they appointed overseers of the poor and allowed their accounts, signed settlement certificates (161), appointed surveyors of the highways, fixed the highway rate (163), apart from trying a host of minor offences or committing them for the quarter sessions. Similarly, many offences could be summarily tried by one justice 'on his own view'. He could enter an alehouse and there and then fine a drunkard five shillings or put him in the stocks for six hours (179). A gambler could be fined from five to twenty shillings or given a month's hard labour; and a butcher killing on a Sunday might have to pay six and eightpence. The single justice also had his vital part to play in the general administration of local government: he could order a parish to relieve a pauper (180); or present an impassable highway or damaged bridge at the quarter sessions.

The looseness of central control left much to local initiative, and thus produced wide variations in the quality of the magistracy, from justices like the Rev. Richard Burn on the one hand to those like Joseph Merceron on the other, with the majority somewhere in between. Though generalisation is difficult, one can see a steady improvement in their efficiency as the century progressed. With certain exceptions (like the notorious Middlesex bench) there was a tendency for them to rise in social status (172), and to be appointed more on grounds of administrative ability than political allegiance. The clergy, who became socially acceptable during this period, also began to appear on the bench, and more frequently as the century progressed. This also had a good effect. The improvement in the justices is reflected in the steps they took, partly under legislative pressure, but mostly on their own initiative, to modernise the medieval machinery they had to operate. An example of statutory help is the Act of 1739 giving them powers to levy a general rate (181). And for their own convenience, they gradually separated their judicial from their administrative work. At quarter and petty sessions, for example, it became the custom to deal in public with judicial matters like criminal cases or disputes connected with the presentation of roads and bridges, but to appoint staff, or issue regulations for the running of a house of correction, in private afterwards. Specialisation of function can be seen in the increasing use made of special sessions, like the brewster sessions (182) and highway sessions (163) held at regular intervals. More use was made of contracting (183, 184); salaried experts like the county treasurer (185), master of the house of correction (178), or the surveyor of bridges (186); and special committees (185). But what the Webbs call 'the most remarkable constitutional development of county government between 1689 and 1835' was the growth of the 'provincial legislature', the famous Speenhamland decisions being a good example (**187**). In addition, of course, the magistrates took a leading part in acquiring and using the special powers provided by parliament in the *ad hoc* bodies, to which a section is devoted later. This improvement did not take place everywhere. The Middlesex bench deteriorated in quality as its problems grew worse. The quarter sessions actually led the way in most of the modernising developments so far mentioned; it was in duties allotted to double and single justices that the trading justices (who kept away from the quarter sessions) grew fat on London vice. But law and order in the Metropolis was a vital concern of the central government; and their intervention took the form, first, of paying a certain magistrate (like Henry Fielding) a salary out of the Secret Service account, and, later, of setting up in 1792 seven new public offices (on the lines of Bow Street) with stipendiary magistrates and paid constables (**188**). Although these measures helped to eliminate the trading justices, they only touched the fringe of the gigantic problem of adjusting medieval machinery to modern problems; and the tangled confusion of communities, officials and powers in the Metropolis was reproduced, as industrialisation and the 'massing of men'[1] developed, all over the country.

170. The Lord Lieutenant, 1690.

After our very hearty Commendations to your Lop^Hp. whereas there is cause to suspect that in this time of publick danger. Their Maties Enemies may be conspiring against the Government. And the necessity of the present juncture,[2] Requiring that this Kingdome be speedily put into the best Condition of Defence that may be with the least inconvenience, We do therefore by Her Maties Express Command, pray and Require your Lop^Hp forthwith to Direct your Deputy Lieutenants to cause one halfe of the Militia Horse within your Lieutenancy, to be Raised, and to continue together for Twelve daies from the time of their being so Raised, And withall, to take care that the other halfe of the said Militia Horse, be put into the best posture that may be, in Order to be likewise Raised at the end of the said Twelve Daies, if her Matie shall so think fit. And we do further Pray and Require your Lop^Hp to give the necessary Directions within your said Lieutenancy for the securing all such Papists and other persons whom you shall have reason to suspect to be disaffected to the Government as may probably be active against it in case of an Insurrection or

---

[1] The Webbs' phrase.
[2] The battle off Beachy Head had taken place two days before.

Invasion. And of your Lop^Hp's proceedings herein, and of the Condition of the said Militia Horse, we exspect a speedy account for Her Ma^{ies}: Information. And so we bid you Lop^Hp very heartily farewell. From the Council Chamber in Whitehall the Second day of July 1690—

Your Lop^Hps very Loving Friends
[signed by 15 Privy Councillors]

Add. MSS. 40166, f. 66.

171. Deputy-lieutenant and High Constable, 1745.

March 28. 1745.

Whereas a Warrant is Isued out from the Debuty Leivetenants That is to say Jasper Kinsman Esq. Stifford Thos Lennard Barrett Esqr of Avely Henery Talbot Esqr of North Ockendon all of ye County of Essex to Mr. Richd Hyden High Constable of ye Hun^d of Chafford in ye said County and by an Order from ye Said Mr. Richd Hyden, Diret^d to Our Parish of West Thoreck to keep a Watch Day and Night upon susspition of an Invasion wee parishioners do Mutally Agree this 27 Day of Decmber 1745 at a publick Vestry to keep Watch Day and Night according to ye Said Order as Wittness our Hands as Under Writting.

God preserve his Majesty King George the Duke of Cumberland and all the Royal Family

John: England	Churchwarden
Ann Doggart	Overseer
Benj^e Cass	Constable
	etc.

MS. Minutes, West Thurrock, Essex.

172. Appointment of justices, 1807.

COUNTY HALL DERBY. EPIPHANY SESSIONS 1807

His Grace the Duke of Devonshire, the Lord Lieutenant of the County, having with his usual attention to the Magistracy referred to the present Bench, through the Clerk of the peace, the question of introducing Mr. Thos. Hassall into the Commission of the peace; the Justices now assembled, in obedience to His Grace's request to receive their opinions in writing, find it their duty to state that, though the

good sense & unexceptional character of Mr. Hassall are fully acknowledged by some of them who have had opportunities of knowing him,
his situation in life does not seem to entitle him to a place in the Commission of the peace of this county, conformably to those regulations
under which his Grace's consideration has applied and guarded it.
They hold that any departure from them in any instance however
unexceptional in itself, would unavoidably open the way to others
which might not be so, to the injury of that weight and consequence
of the Magistracy in the public mind on which its efficacy so materially
depends. They recollect similar objections to similar applications;
and they cannot consistently with precedent, or with their deliberate
judgment on a review of the rules and usages hitherto observed here,
recommend the admission of Mr. Hassall into the Commission of the
peace.

In thus submitting their unanimous opinion they beg to offer to
His Grace The Lord-Lieutenant their respectful acknowledgments of
that confidence with which he has honoured them, and his obliging
consideration of their wishes and satisfaction. Cox, II, 301.

173. The Commission of the Peace.

George the third, by the grace of *God*, of the united kingdom of *Great
Britain* and *Ireland*, king, defender of the faith, To *A. B. C. D.* &c,
greeting.

Know ye that we have assigned you jointly and severally and every
one of you our justices to keep our peace in our county of W. And to
keep and cause to be kept all ordinances and statutes for the good of
the peace, and for preservation of the same, and for the quiet rule and
government of our people made, in all and singular their articles in
our said county (as well within liberties as without) according to the
force form and effect of the same; And to chastise and punish all
persons that offend the form of those ordinances or statutes, or any one
of them, in the aforesaid county, as it ought to be done according to
the form of those ordinances and statutes; And to cause to come before
you, or any of you, all those who to any one or more of our people
concerning their bodies or the firing of their houses have used threats,
to find sufficient security for the peace, or their good behaviour, towards us and our people; and if they shall refuse to find such security,
then confine them in our prisons until they shall find such security to
cause to be safely kept.

We have also assigned you, and every two or more of you (of whom any one of you aforesaid A. B. C. D. &c. we will shall be one) our justices to inquire the truth more fully, by the oath of good and lawful men of the aforesaid county, by whom the truth of the matter shall be the better known, of all and all manner of felonies, poisonings, inchantments, sorceries, arts magic, trespasses, forestallings, regratings, ingrossings, and extortions whatsoever; and of all and singular other crimes and offences, of which the justices of our peace may or ought lawfully to inquire, by whomsoever and after what manner soever in the said county done or perpetrated, or which shall happen to be there done or attempted; and also of all those who in the aforesaid county in companies against our peace, in disturbance of our people, with armed force have gone or rode, or hereafter shall presume to go or ride; And also of all those who have there lain in wait, or hereafter shall presume to lie in wait, to maim or cut or kill our people; And also of all victuallers, and all and singular other persons, who in the abuse of weights and measures, or in selling victuals, against the form of the ordinances and statutes or any one of them therefore made for the common benefit of *England*, and our people thereof, have offended or attempted, or hereafter shall presume in the said county to offend or attempt; And also of all sheriffs, bailiffs, stewards, constables, keepers of gaols, and other officers, who in the execution of their offices about the premises or any of them have unduly behaved themselves, or hereafter shall presume to behave themselves unduly, or have been or shall happen hereafter to be careless, remiss, or negligent in our aforesaid county; And of all and singular articles and circumstances, and all other things whatsoever, that concern the premises or any of them, by whomsoever and after what manner soever in our aforesaid county done or perpetrated, or which hereafter shall there happen to be done or attempted in what manner soever; And to inspect all indictments whatsoever so before you or any of you taken or to be taken, or before others late our justices of the peace in the aforesaid county made or taken, and not yet determined; and to make and continue processes thereupon against all and singular the persons so indicted, or who before you hereafter shall happen to be indicted until they can be taken, surrender themselves, or be outlawed; And to hear and determine all and singular the felonies, poisonings, inchantments, sorceries, arts magic, trespasses, forestallings, regratings, ingrossings, extortions, unlawful assemblies, indictments aforesaid, and all and singular other the premises, according to the laws and statutes of *England*, as in the like case it has been accustomed, or ought to be done; And the same offenders and every of them for their offences by fines, ransoms, amerciaments, forfeitures, and other means as according to the law and custom of *England*, or form of the ordinances and statutes aforesaid it has been accustomed, or ought to be done, to chastise and punish.

Provided always, that if a case of difficulty upon the determination of any the premises before you or any two or more of you shall happen to arise then let judgement in no wise be given thereon before you or any two or more of you, unless in the presence of one of our justices of the one or other bench, or of one of our justices appointed to hold the assizes in the aforesaid county.

And therefore we command you and every of you, that to keeping the peace, ordinances, statutes, and all and singular other the premises, you diligently apply yourselves; and that at certain days and places which you or any such two or more of you as is aforesaid shall appoint for these purposes into the premises ye make inquiries; and all and singular the premises hear and determine, and perform and fulfil them in the aforesaid form, doing therein what to justice appertains, according to the law and custom of *England*; Saving to us the amerciaments, and other things to us therefrom belonging.

And we command by the tenor of these presents our sheriff of W. that at certain days and places, which you or any such two or more of you as is aforesaid shall make known to him, he cause to come before you or such two or more of you as aforesaid so many and such good and lawful men of his bailiwick (as well within liberties as without) by whom the truth of the matter in the premises shall be the better known and inquired into.

Lastly, We have assigned you the aforesaid A. B. keeper of the rolls of our peace in our said county; And therefore you shall cause to be brought before you and your said fellows, at the days and places aforesaid, the writs, precepts, processes, and indictments aforesaid, that they may be inspected, and by a due course determined as is aforesaid.

In witness whereof we have caused these our letters to be made patent. Witness ourself at Westminster, &c.

Burn, III, 5.

174. Quarter Sessions: Grand Jury presentment of a bridge, 1748.

DERBYSHIRE QUARTER SESSIONS, 1748

We the Grand Jury of the Lord the King & the body of this County at the General Quarter Sessions of the Peace held in & for the said County this 10th day of January 1748 do present a certain Horse Bridge over the River Dove lying in the said County called Aston Bridge to be so much out of Repair as to be in danger of immediate falling. And we present & say if there was a Carrier Bridge erected at the same place it would be of utmost utility to this County and absolutely necessary to be done for the safety of Passengers the Passage over the said River there being very much used by Travellers from many parts of the Kingdom but more especially by the Subjects of our said Lord the King residing in this County & ye Neighbouring County. And Us the Jurors aforesaid do further present that it is altogether unknown to us nor can we find that any Persons lands Tenements or Body Politic ought of right or by ancient custom repair the same or any part hereof

> Witness our hands

> Tho: Wagstaff [& 13 other jurors]

Cox, II, 223.

175. Petty Sessions: presentment of a parish for an impassable road, 1695.

The presentment of Chief Constables of the Hundred of Winstree. At our Petty Sessions held at Colchester . . . we had no presentments come to our hands from our Petty Constables, therefore we have nothing to present as to their part; but as to our part we present the parish of East Donyland for a piece of road called by the name of Roomand Hill . . . being unpassable for carts, and some of the horse-road very bad likewise. So we have nothing more to present but our service to the Honourable Jury.

> John Tye,
> Richard Stone, } Constables.

15th January 1694. (O.S.)

Essex Quarter Sessions Archives, 1695 (Sessions Bundle 8), printed in S. and B. Webb, *Parish and County* (1906), p. 46, note 5.

176. Quarter Sessions: a highway rate ordered, 1713.

DERBYSHIRE QUARTER SESSIONS ORDERS FOR EASTER, 1713

Whereas the inhabitants of Ashborne in this County have made it appear to this Court that they have already done their six days work apeice towards the repairing of their Highwaies (pursuant to the act of Parliamt in that case made & provided) &c it proveing insufficient to amend the same This Court doth order & it is hereby ordered that the sum of six pence in the pound be raised by Assessmt for & towards the repairing & amending thereof.

Cox, II, 230.

177. Quarter Sessions: the county gaol, 1716.

SHROPSHIRE QUARTER SESSIONS, JULY 1716

Upon complaint made to this Court by Joan Crumpton, Widow, Gaoler for the County Gaol of this County of Salop, Complayning of severall Irregularities and Misbehaviours of the prisoners in the said Gaol, and that they frequently send for Strong Liquors out of the town into the Gaol, Sitt upp late, gett Drunk, and very often Insult and Abuse the said Gaoler and her Servants, and disturb other Prisoners. And doe pretend that the Garretts and Severall of the other Rooms (if ye Prisoners find their own beds) are free from paying anything to the said Gaoler, and has thrown out the Gaolers bed out of some of the Rooms and have putt in their own bedds, and doe refuse to pay anything for the same, and doe lock up the Doors and keep the Gaoler out of severall of the Rooms pretending that they have a Right so to doe. And also complayning that some of the Prisoners That have bedds of their own in the Gaol doe take other Prisoners to lye with them, and take money of the Prisoners for their lodging, and thereby exclude the said Gaoler from having any benefit from the said prisoners, and by several rude and ill practises and behaviours of the said prisoners doe deprive the said Gaoler from making any Advantage of the said Gaol, Altho' the said Gaoler hath abt. Seventy prisoners for Debt belonging to the said Gaol, and hath given great Security for the said Gaol and is att great Expense in keeping Servants and persons to look after the said prisoners and Gaol. This Court, taking this matter into Consideration, and upon reading the former Orders made by this Court for the settling of the Gaol and the Rates for Lodging for the said prisoners, hath thought fitt and doth hereby order that the Rates for Lodging shall be as followeth (that is to say): That threepence per week be paid for every prisoner that lyeth in the Comon Garretts which Garretts are those in that syde of the Gaol which are next the Raven and joyn to the House of Correction and doe lye over the Kitchin and the Room now used for the Chappell, and in all other Garretts where the prisoners lye on their own bedds one Shilling per week, and if any prisoners lye two or more in a bedd to pay one Shilling per week each, and if any prisoners lye in the Garretts on the Gaoler's bedd, to pay one Shilling, Sixpence each person as if he lay in any other Room, one pair of Stairs, the Comon Garrett only excepted; and the former Order to stand ratifyed and Confirmed to pay the same rates in all other Rooms in the said Gaol as is mentioned in the said former orders, except what is hereby particularly altered and directed. And further that the said Gaoler, her under Gaoler, Turnkey, and Servants doe likewise take care of and prevent all mutinies and disorders that may happen in the said Gaol for the future, and in order thereto to prevent Strong Liquors to be brought into the prisoners in ye said Gaol to disorder them and breed Mutines and disturbances.

Offley Wakeman, *Shropshire County Records* (Shrewsbury, 1901), vol. II, p. 26.

178. Quarter Sessions: appointment of the Master of the House of Correction, 1711.

DERBYSHIRE QUARTER SESSIONS ORDERS, 1711

This day on Reading the Petitions from the Gentlemen and Freeholders in the Hundred of High Peake returning their thanks to this Court for the Order of the last General Quartr Sessions of the Peace for this County whereby a house of Correccion was appointed and Ordered to be Erected at Tidswell in this County and that William Shore of the said Towne should be Master and keeper thereof, and praying that a Competent yearely Sallery might be allowed, to the said William Shore, for the Same; And it now on debate of the premises, appearing to this Court, that the Law cannot so effectually be put in Execution without the said House of Correction, And the said William Shore haveing behaved himselfe honestly and dilligently in the said office since the last Sessions. It is this day Unanimously Ordered by this Court that the Order of the said last Generall Quarter Sessions for ye Erecting and appointing of the said house of Correction, and the said William Shore keeper or Master thereof, shall be & is hereby confirmed, And this Court doth further Order and appoint that the sd William Shore Shall & is hereby allowed twenty pounds and for the same to Comence and begin from the said last General Quarter Sessions, being the tenth day of April last past, And the Treasurer of this County is hereby Ordered & appointed, from tyme to tyme, out of the County Treasure to pay the same.

Cox, II, 34.

179. The single justice: a form for conviction of drunkenness.

Westmorland. Be it remembered, that on the —— day of —— in the year of our Lord ——, at the parish of —— in the county of ——, I J. P. esquire, one of the justices of our lord the king assigned to keep the peace in and for the said county, and also to hear and determine divers felonies, trespasses, and other misdemeanours in the said county committed, personally saw one A. O. of the parish of —— aforesaid, labourer, drunk, contrary to the form of the statutes in that case made and provided: Whereupon it is considered and adjudged by me the said justice, that the said A. O. be convicted, and he is by me accordingly hereby convicted of the offence of being drunk, upon my own view as aforesaid, according to the form of the statutes in that case made and provided: And I do hereby adjudge that the said A. O. for the said offence hath forfeited the sum of 5s. to be paid and distributed as the law directs. In witness whereof I the said justice to this present conviction have set my hand and seal, the day and year above written.

Burn, I, 77,

180. The single justice: Poor Relief ordered, 1719.

[4 May 1719]

To the Constable and Churchwarden and others, the Overseers of the poor of the Parish of Burton Joyce.

Greeting:

Whereas complaint hath been made unto me Sir Thos. Parkyns Bart., one of his Majesty's Justices of the Peace . . . that Geo. Merston of your town who appears to Me to be an Inhabitant legally settled in your s^d Parish is in Great need and Poverty and likely to perish for want of Employment to maintain himself and family.

These are therefore in His Majesty's Name to command you the Ch. Warden etc., . . . to set ye said George Merston on work or pay unto him Two shillings weekly forth and out of your Publick Levey for ye use of ye Poor made . . . etc. . . . otherwise to come before me and show cause to the contrary. Hereof faill not at your peril.

W. E. Tate, *The Parish Chest* (Cambridge, 1951), p. 229.

181. The County Rate: Act of 1739.

An act for the more easy assessing, collecting and levying of county rates.

[Preamble recites a number of statutes authorising the levying of rates for repairing bridges and highways, for building and repairing gaols, for building and maintaining houses of correction, for relieving the poor in hospitals and almshouses, for relieving prisoners and setting them on work, for punishing rogues and vagabonds and sending them "whither they ought to be sent."]

. . . and whereas it is apparent that the manner and methods prescribed by the said several acts for collecting some of the rates are impracticable, the sums charged on each parish in the respective divisions being so small, that they do not by an equal pound rate amount to more than a fractional part of a farthing in the pound on the several persons thereby rateable; and if possible to have been rated, the expence of assessing and collecting the same would have amounted to more than the sum rated: and whereas many and great doubts, difficulties and inconveniences have arisen in making and collecting other of the said rates; therefore that the good ends and purposes of the said several statutes may be answered, and the several sums of money thereby intended to be raised may effectually be collected, with as much ease and certainty, and as little expence as can be to the parties obliged by the said laws to pay the same; be it therefore enacted . . . That . . . the justices of the peace in that part of *Great Britain* called *England*, within the respective limits of their commissions, at their general or quarter sessions, or the greater part of them then and there assembled, shall have full power and authority, from time to time, to make one general rate or assessment for such sum or sums of money as they in their discretions shall think sufficient to answer all and every the ends and purposes of the before recited acts, instead and in lieu of the several separate and distinct rates directed thereby to be made, levied and collected; which rate shall be assessed upon every town, parish or place . . . in such proportions as any of the rates hereto-

fore made in pursuance of the said several acts have been usually assessed; and the several and respective sums so assessed upon each and every town, parish or place . . . shall be collected by the high constables of the respective hundreds and divisions, in which any town, parish or place doth lie, in such manner, and at such times, as is herein after directed. . . .

VI. And be it further enacted . . . That the respective high constables shall, and they are thereby required, at or before the next general or quarter sessions respectively after they or any of them shall have received such sum or sums of money, to pay the same into the hands of such person or persons (being resident in any such county, riding, division, city, liberty, or place, where such rates shall be respectively made) whom the said justices shall at their respective general or quarter sessions, or the greater part of them then and there assembled, appoint to be the treasurer or treasurers (which treasurer or treasurers they are hereby authorized and impowered to nominate and appoint) such treasurer or treasurers first giving sufficient security in such sums as shall be approved of by the said justices at their respective general or quarter sessions, or the greater part of them then and there assembled, to be accountable for the several and respective sums of money which shall be respectively paid to them in pursuance of this act, and to pay such sums of money as shall be ordered to be paid by the justices in their general or quarter sessions, and for the due and faithful execution of the trusts reposed in him or them; and all and every such sum or sums of money as shall be paid into his or their hands by virtue of and in pursuance of this act, shall be deemed and taken to be the publick stock; and the said treasurer or treasurers shall and are hereby required to pay so much of the money in their hands to such person or persons as the said justices at their respective general or quarter sessions or the greater part of them then and there assembled, shall by their orders from time to time direct and appoint, for the uses and purposes to which the publick stock of any county, city, riding, division, or liberty, is or shall be applicable by law.

VII. [Treasurers to keep books of entries, and to account upon oath.]

XIII. And be it further enacted . . . That no part of the money to be raised and collected in pursuance of this act shall be applied to the repair of any bridges, gaols, prisons, or houses of correction, until presentments be made by the respective grand juries, at the assize, great sessions, general gaol delivery, or general or quarter sessions of the peace held for any county, riding, division, city, town corporate, or liberty, of the insufficiency, inconveniency, or want of reparation of their bridges, gaols, prisons, or houses of correction.

XIV. And be it further enacted . . . when any publick bridges, ramparts, banks, or cops, or other works, are to be repaired at the expence of any county, riding, hundred, division, liberty, or town corporate; it shall and may be lawful to and for the justices of the peace at their general or quarter sessions respectively, or the greater part of them then and there assembled, if they think proper and convenient, after presentment to be made as aforesaid of the want of reparation of such bridges, ramparts, banks, or cops, to contract and agree with any person or persons for rebuilding, repairing, and amending of such bridges [etc] . . . as shall be within their respective counties [etc] . . . and all other works which are to be repaired and done by assessment on the respective counties [etc] . . . for any term or terms of years, not exceeding seven years, at a certain annual sum, payment, or allowance for the same; such contractor or contractors giving sufficient security for the due performance thereof, to the respective clerk of the peace for the time being, or the town clerk, high bailiff, or chief officer of any city, town corporate, or liberty; and that such justices at their respective general or quarter sessions shall give publick notice of their intention of contracting with any person or persons for rebuilding, repairing, and amending the bridges . . . and other works aforesaid; and that such contracts shall be made at the most reasonable price or prices which shall be proposed by such contractors respectively; and that all contracts when agreed to, and all orders relating thereto, shall be entered in a book, to be kept by the respective clerk, high bailiff, or chief officer of any city, town corporate, or liberty for that purpose; who is and are hereby required to keep them amongst the records of such county, city, town corporate, or liberty, to be from time to time inspected at all seasonable times by any of the said justices within the limits of their commissions; and by any person or persons employed or to be employed by any parish, township, or place, contributing to the purposes of this act, without fee or reward. . . .

12 Geo. II, c. 29: *S.L.*, XVII, 316.

182. Brewster Sessions: a form for an alehouse licence.

Westmorland, ⎫ At a general meeting of his majesty's justices of
East Ward. ⎭ the peace for the said county, acting within the
division of the *East Ward* aforesaid, in the county aforesaid, holden
at —— in and for the said division, for licensing persons to keep inns
and alehouses the —— day of *September* in the —— year of the reign
of our sovereign lord *George* the third, of the United Kingdom of
Great Britain and *Ireland*, king, defender of the faith, and so forth, and
in the year of our Lord ——.

We his majesty's justices of the peace for the said county, whose
hands and seals are hereunto set, (whereof one is of the *quorum*,) assembled at the said general meeting, do allow and license *A.B.* yeoman,
at the sign of —— in —— within the divison and county aforesaid, to
keep a common alehouse or victualling house, and to utter and sell
victuals, beer, ale, cyder, and other exciseable liquors, to be drank in
the same house wherein he now dwelleth, and not elsewhere, for one
whole year, from the 29th day of this present month of *September*,
and no longer; so as the true assize in bread, beer, ale, and other
liquors, hereby allowed to be sold, be duly kept; and no unlawful game
or games, drunkenness or any other disorder, be suffered in his house,
yard, garden, or backside; but that good order and rule be maintained
and kept therein, according to the laws of this realm, in that behalf
made. Given under our hands and seals the day and year first above
written.

Burn, I, 68.

183. Quarter Sessions: a bridge contractor appointed, 1753.

NORTH RIDING QUARTER SESSIONS ORDERS [I MAY 1753]

. . . whereas Tho. Davison, Lyonel Vane, Will. Sutton, and Richard-
son Ferrand, Esquires, and the Rev. John Emerson, Clerk, five Justices
of the County Palatine of Durham, and Tho. Skottowe, Esq., a Justice
of the North Riding, have, by a report in writing under their hands,
dated April 28th last, this day delivered into this Court, set forth
that they had that day met and viewed the repairs and condition of the
great bridge over the river Teas at Yarm, and that sundry repairs
are now necessary to be done for the support and preservation of the
said bridge, a particular of which said repairs are mentioned in their
said report, and the said Justices having in their said report set forth

that it will in their judgments be for the interests of the said county of Durham and for the said Riding to determine a contract now subsisting with John Bennyson, mason, for the keeping of the said bridge in repair (the said Bennyson being advanced in years and desirous to have the same contract determined) and that the present and future repairs of the said bridge be done under the direction and inspection of two neighbouring Justices of each county, and that the annual sum of £8. 5. 2 payable to the repairs of the said bridge be for the future paid by the Bridgewardens of Yarm into the hands of a person who will be responsible for the same, in order to be and remain a fund for repairing the said bridge, it being apprehended that a less sum will yearly defray the expence after the repairs now wanted and in the said report mentioned are done: it is therefore Ordered that the said contract be determined, and that such security as the said Bennyson entered into for the performance thereof be delivered up to him to be cancelled, and that any two Justices of the Division of Langbarugh in conjunction with two or more of the Durham Justices make such contracts or agreements, and such Orders for the doing and finishing not only the repairs in the said report mentioned, but also all future repairs of the said bridge as to them shall seem meet: and this Court doth also Order that the said annual payment shall from time to time be paid without deduction by the said Bridgewardens into the hands of David Burton of Yarm, gent^n, who hath agreed to give proper security for the same, and that the said Justices to whom the said repairs are referred may be at liberty to direct the application of the said sum towards the said repairs as they shall think fit, and that they from time to time make their report to this Court, not only of the expence of making the reparations in the said report mentioned, but also of the annual disbursements attending the repairs of the said bridge, to the end that the Court may be acquainted with the state and condition of the said bridge, and of the proper application of the said annual sum left for the repairs thereof, until this Court shall think fit to make further Order therein.

Atkinson, IX, 222.

184. Quarter Sessions: contract for transporting convicts, 1788.

SHROPSHIRE QUARTER SESSIONS, APRIL 1788

Advertisement for Shrewsbury General Evening Post and the St. James' Chronicle.

"Any person willing to contract with the Justices of the Peace for the County of Salop for the Removal of the Convicts from Shrewsbury Gaol on Board such Vessell as His Majesty shall be pleased to appoint to receive them at so much pr. Man pr. Mile are desired to send in their Proposals . . ."

Offley Wakeman, Shropshire County Records (Shrewsbury, 1901), vol. III, p. 28.

185. Quarter Sessions: committee appointed to audit the County Treasurer's accounts, 1709.

DERBYSHIRE QUARTER SESSIONS ORDER

Whereas Mr. John Wright was some tyme since made Treasurer of the County and hath this present Sessions produced his account in Court, in order to be passed and allowed, this Court do therefore order and it is hereby ordered that the same be viewed inspected and referred to Thomas Cotchett, Samuel Pole, Henry Gilbert, and Michael Burton, Esqrs, or any two of them, who are desired to report the same next sessions with their judgments and opinions therein under ye hands of any two or more of ym.

Cox, I, 120.

186. Quarter Sessions: bridge surveyors appointed, 1754.

NORTH RIDING QUARTER SESSIONS ORDERS [8 OCTOBER 1754]

Ordered that, Mr. Will Brown of Heaning and Mr. Matthew Ward, jun^r., of Crakehall, shall be jointly Surveyors of all bridges within the North Riding lyable to be repaired or rebuilt at the expence of the same, and that they shall be allowed the yearly salary of £20, to be paid by the Thr^r. at every General Qu. Sessions, at four equal payments in the year, and the several C.C^s[1] for the said Riding are hereby Ordered from time to time to give notice to the said Surveyors, or either of them, of the want of repairs of the several bridges within their several Divisions; Ordered that the several C.C^s be continued their salary of 10s. a year for looking after the county bridges, and that they do from time to time give notice to Will Brown or Mr Math. Ward whenever any bridge within their several Divisions is out of repair. . . .

Atkinson, IX, 229.

[1] County Constables.

187. Quarter Sessions: the Speenhamland Resolutions, 1795.

BERKSHIRE, *to wit*

At a General Meeting of the Justices of this County, together with several discreet persons assembled by public advertisement on Wednesday the 6th of May, 1795, at the Pelican Inn in Speenhamland, (in pursuance of an order of the last Court of General Quarter Sessions) for the purpose of rating Husbandry Wages, by the day or week, if then approved of,

Present

CHARLES DUNDAS, ESQ; *in the Chair,*

Rev. John Craven,	Henry Deane, Esq.
Rev. George Watts,	John Whitcomb, Esq.
Rev. Jas. Morgan, D.D.	William Walker, Esq.
Edward Thornhill, Esq.	Wm. Henry Price, Esq.
John Blagrave, Esq.	W. Wiseman Clarke, Esq.
Rev. Henry Sawbridge,	John G. Ravenshaw, Esq.
Rev. — Wilson,	Thomas Slack, Esq.
Rev. Edward Townsend,	John Croft, Esq.
Rev. Richard Coxe,	

Resolved Unanimously, that the present state of the Poor does require further assistance than has been generally given them.

Resolved, that it is not expedient for the Magistrates to grant that assistance by regulating the Wages of Day Labourers, according to the directions of the Statutes of the 5th Eliz. and 1st James: But the Magistrates very earnestly recommend to the Farmers and others throughout the county, to increase the Pay of their Labourers in proportion to the present Price of Provisions; and agreeable thereto, the Magistrates now present have unanimously Resolved, That they will, in their several divisions, make the following calculations and allowances for relief of all poor and industrous Men and their families, who to the satisfaction of the Justices of their Parish, shall endeavour (as far as they can) for their own support and maintenance:

That is to say,

When the Gallon Loaf of Second Flour, weighing 8 lb. 11 ozs. shall cost 1s.

Then every poor and industrous Man shall have for his own support 3s. weekly, either produced by his own or his family's labour, or an allowance from the poor rates, and for the support of his Wife and every other of his family, 1s 6d.

When the Gallon Loaf shall cost 1s. 4d.

Then every poor and industrous Man shall have 4s. weekly for his own, and 1s. and 10d for the support of every other of his family.

And so in proportion, as the price of Bread rises or falls, (that is to say) 3d. to the Man, and 1d. to every other of the family, on every 1d. which the loaf rises above 1s.

By order of the Meeting,

W. BUDD, Deputy Clerk of the Peace.

Reading Mercury and Oxford Gazette, May 11, 1795.

188. Act establishing public offices and stipendiary magistrates in the Metropolis, 1792.

An Act for the more effectual administration of the office of a Justice of the peace in such parts of the counties of Middlesex *and* Surrey *as lie in and near the Metropolis, and for the more effectual prevention of felonies*

. . . be it enacted . . . That it shall and may be lawful for his Majesty to cause seven several publick offices to be established in or near the following places, namely, the parishes of *Saint Margaret Westminster, Saint James Westminster, Saint James Clerkenwell, Saint Leonard Shore-ditch, Saint Mary Whitechapel,* and *Saint Paul Chadwell,* in the County of *Middlesex,* and at or near *Saint Margaret's Hill,* in the borough of *Southwark,* in the county of *Surrey,* and at each of the said publick offices to appoint three fit and able persons, being justices of the peace for the said county of *Middlesex,* and the county of *Surrey* respectively, to execute the office of a justice of the peace, together with such other justices of the peace for the said counties respectively, as may think proper to attend.

II. And be it further enacted . . . That one or more of the said justices so to be appointed as aforesaid shall diligently attend at each of the said public offices every day, from ten of the clock in the morning until eight of the clock in the evening, and at such times and places as shall be found necessary; and that two of the said justices, so to be appointed as aforesaid, shall in like manner attend together at each of the said offices, from eleven of the clock in the forenoon until one in the afternoon, and from six of the clock in the evening until eight of the clock in the evening of every day: provided always, That the attendance of one of the said justices may be supplied, during the hours at which the attendance of two is required as aforesaid, by any other justice of the peace for the said counties of *Middlesex* or *Surrey* respectively.

III. [After establishment of the offices, no fees to be taken, except at them, by any justice for Middlesex, &c. on penalty of £100. But not to extend to fees for licensing alehouses under 26 Geo. 2. c. 31 or taken at the publick office in Bow Street, &c.]

VIII. And be it further enacted . . . That it shall and may be lawful for his Majesty, his heirs and successors, by and with the advice of his or their privy council, to direct the salaries hereinafter mentioned to be paid to the justices so appointed to attend each of the said seven publick offices, for their time and trouble, and such further sums for their expences in the said offices, and for the payment of clerks, peace officers, and others therein employed, in such manner as to his Majesty, his heirs and successors, by and with the advice of his or their privy council, shall seem meet: provided always, That the yearly salary paid to each of the justices shall be four hundred pounds, clear of all taxes and deductions whatever: provided also, That the whole charges attending any one of the said offices (the said salaries being included) shall not exceed the annual sum of two thousand pounds. . . .

XV. And be it further enacted . . . That the justices to be appointed as aforesaid shall, in their respective offices, as soon as conveniently may be after their appointment, retain and employ a sufficient number of fit and able men, whom they are hereby authorised and impowered to swear in, to act as constables for preserving the peace and preventing robberies and other felonies, and apprehending offenders against the peace within the said counties of *Middlesex* and *Surrey* respectively, as well by night as by day; which said constables, so appointed and sworn as aforesaid, shall have all such powers and authorities, privileges and advantages, as any constable duly appointed now has, or hereafter may have, by virtue of any law or statute now made, or hereafter to be made, and shall obey all such lawful commands as they shall from time to time receive from the said justices, for the apprehending offenders, or otherwise conducting themselves in the execution of their said office or employment. . . .

XVII. *And whereas divers ill-disposed and suspected persons, and reputed thieves, frequent the avenues to places of publick resort, and the streets and highways, with intent to commit felony on the persons and property of his Majesty's subjects there being, and although their evil purposes are sufficiently manifest, the power of his Majesty's justices of the peace to demand of them surities for their good behaviour hath not been of sufficient effect to prevent them from carrying their evil purposes into execution;* be it enacted That [Constables &c. may apprehend any suspicious person, and convey him before a justice, and if it shall appear upon oath that he is a reputed thief, &c. he shall be deemed a rogue within 17 Geo. 2. c. 5. Persons thinking themselves aggrieved may appeal to the quarter sessions. If conviction be affirmed, the justices may proceed as might have been done if the party had been committed. Punishments not to exceed imprisonment to hard labour for six months.]

XVIII. Provided also, and be it . . . enacted . . . That nothing in this act contained shall extend, or be construed to extend, to deprive the mayor and commonalty and citizens of the city of *London*, of any rights, privileges, or jurisdictions which they have heretofore lawfully claimed, exercised, or enjoyed, within the town and borough of *Southwark*, and the liberties thereof, or to prevent the mayor of the city of *London* for the time being, and such of the aldermen of the said city who have borne the office of mayoralty, and the recorder of the said city for the time being, from acting as justices of the peace within the said town and borough of *Southwark*, and the liberties thereof, in such and the like manner as they could or might have done in case this act had not been made.   32 Geo. III, c. 53: *S.L.* XXXVII, 591.

III. THE MANOR

In some parts of England, particularly the North, the manor or township retained sufficient vigour to play the role performed elsewhere by the parish. Its work was carried out in the court-baron and court-leet, of distinct origin and function, but merged into one by the eighteenth century, except in the minds of lawyers. The court-baron, originally the private court of the lord of the manor, met under the presidency of the lord or his steward, attended by the tenants, some of whom formed the homage or jury. It settled local disputes; regulated the agriculture, the market, the docks, or whatever else had grown on the estate; and appointed officers to administer its bye-laws: the reeve, the bailiff, the beadle, hayward, clerk of the market, leather sealer and so on. The court of Chipping Norton (the lordship of which belonged to the bailiffs and burgesses of the borough of

Chipping Norton) may be seen functioning in a rural context in the middle of the period (**189**). The court-leet, in origin a franchise enabling the lord's tenants to avoid attending the sheriff's tourn, met under the presidency of the steward, to deal with local criminal cases (presented by the jury); to appoint officers, like the constable, the ale-conner and so on; and to make bye-laws mainly for dealing with 'nuisances'—a category which could be extended to include practically every aspect of local government. The court-leet of Manchester has been chosen to illustrate the activities of these courts in urban surroundings (**190**). Here the steward selected the jury, which chose the borough reeve (i.e. the mayor), the constables, the ale-conners, scavengers, etc., and so it can easily be imagined how the local industrial aristocracy maintained a grip on the town, which they governed very efficiently, taking powers by local Acts for the appointment of commissioners (which they dominated (**202**)), and successfully resisting the attacks of the open vestry of the parish, which wanted democratic control.

189. The court-baron of Chipping Norton, 1764.

The Borough of Chipping Norton in the County of Oxford.

At a COURT BARON and view of Frankpledge of the Bailiffs and Burgesses of the Borough of Chipping Norton aforesaid Lords of the said Manor held at Chipping Norton in the said Borough, the 22nd day of October 1764 before John Wakefield, Deputy Steward there.

Free Suitors there.
John Bulley, Robert Brown, Charles Heynes.
NAMES OF THE HOMAGE.
[19 names]

ORDERS made in the Court Baron as follows.

(1) That the Great Common below the Town be heyned from all manner of Cattle on the 13th day of February next, every offender for every offence contrary to this order to incur a penalty of Ten shillings to the Lords of this Manor and one shilling to the Drivers or Person that shall impound the cattle or present the offender.

(2) That the said Common shall be broke on the 2nd day of May next and not before, and then not till after sunrising. (Penalty 2s. 6d. to Lords, and 1s to Drivers &c.)

. . .

(4) That no person shall put any cattle upon any commonable place within this Manor but what are Parishioners (except the officer of the Excise). And no parishioner unless he is a householder (Penalty a guinea per head to the Lords and 2s. 6d per head to the Drivers).

(6) That no cow or heifer shall go on any Commonable place within this Manor without Knobs on their horns. Penalty, 2s. to the Lords for each horn that shall be unknobbed and 1s. to the Drivers, provided that if they are put on again within four days after notice given, it shall not be deemed an offence.

. . .

(12) That no pig shall go on any Commonable Place within this Manor till after Harvest and not then unless ringed. (Penalty 2s. to the Lords and 6d to the Drivers)

. . .

(20) That Parishioners only do take or carry away any dung from off any Commonable Place within this Manor and they upon their heads or backs only. (Penalty, 2s. 6d. to the Lords and 2s. 6d. to Informer.)

(21) That the Jury do meet between the hours of two and three in the afternoon on the day the Great Common is broke and go round the said Common and examine the mounds and if any person's mounds shall appear insufficient they shall be proceeded against as the law directs.

. . .

(23) That no person do milk any beast in any Public Street within this Borough (Market and Fair days excepted). (Penalty 5s. to the Lords and 2s. 6d. to the Informer.)

. . .

WE PRESENT

Richard Money, John Kilby for Constables. Sworn.

Thomas Guy, Wm. Banbury, Thomas Brooker for Tythingmen. Sworn.

John Insall, John Claydon for Clerks to the Market. Sworn.

Thomas Brookes, Bellman and Beadle, and to receive 40s. for serving the office of Beadle, if he does his duty to the satisfaction of next year's Jury.

William Hyett, Thomas Edgington for Drivers. Sworn.

Stephen Marshall, Leather Sealer.

Richard Robinson, for forestalling this Market the 17th of this inst., by buying three couples of live fowls near one hour before the Market Bell rung.

Quoted by A. Ballard in *Oxfordshire Archaeological Society Report* (Banbury, 1913), p. 134.

190. The court-leet of Manchester, 1734 and 1805.

MANOR OF MANCHESTER
WITH ITS MEMBERS IN THE COUNTY PALATINE
OF LANCASTER

[23 Oct., 1734]

The Court Leet or View of Pledge of Sir Oswald Mosley Barron^t Lord of the Manor aforesaid Held at Manchester aforesaid on Wednesday the Twenty Third day of October in the Eighth Year of the Reign of our Sovereign Lord George the Second of Great Brittain ffrance and Ireland King Defender of the ffaith And in the year of our Lord One Thousand Seven Hundred and Thirty ffour before William Radcliff Gentl Steward And also ffrancis Mosley Gentleman Deputy Steward of the said Court ...

We the Jury of this Leet Upon the Presentment of the Market Lookers for ffish and fflesh do Amerce (To witt) James Green of Stockport for Exposeing to Sale unmarketable Beef the Sume of fforty Shillings.

John Sidebotham of Stockport for the Same Offence Thirty Shillings.

Upon the Presentment of the Market Lookers ffor White Meats for the Deansgate We do Amerce Robert Buckley of Chetwood for one Gill Short of Measure Two Shillings.

William Aldred of Olfeild Lane for one Pint Short of Measure Two Shillings.

Upon Presentment of the officers to Prevent Engrossing fforestalling and Regrateing We do Amerce James Rogers of Ashton for Buying and Takeing out of the Market One Load of Wheat before Twelve of the Clock on the Market Day One Shilling Also we do Amerce Margaret Kettle for the Same Offence One Shilling Also Mary Birch for buying and Takeing in the Same Manner Three Loads of Wheat Three Shillings. ...

Upon Presentment of the Scavengers for Barnstreet We the Jury of this Leet do Amerce the ffollowing Persons to witt Thomas Darlington, Thomas Penkethman, William Rogers, Benjamin Wright, Widow Lowe, and Mathew Pickford for Refuseing and Neglecting to Sweep and keep Clean the Street over against their Respective Courts Twelve pence each. . . .

[13 May 1805]

. . .

Also that a certain Street called Milk Street in this Manor is out of repair and a great Nuisance to all persons passing and repassing in and along the same And the Jurors aforesaid do present that the Proprietors of the Theatre Royal within this Manor and Peter Caygill of this Manor are owners of certain Messuages or other buildings in or adjoining to the said Street and by reason thereof the said Jurors do present that the said Proprietors of the said Theatre Royal and the said Peter of right ought to repair and amend the said Street or such part or parts thereof as appertain to them or any of them to repair in respect of such his or their said Messuages or other Buildings whereupon it is considered that the said Proprietors of the said Theatre Royal and the said Peter be in Mercy.

The Jurors aforesaid upon their Oaths aforesaid do further present that William Joule of this Manor Cotton Spinner on the first day of May Instant was and from henceforth hitherto hath been and still is possessed of a certain Cotton ffactory or Building situate in or near Long Mill Gate within this Manor and of a ffurnace thereunto belonging and being so possessed thereof the said William on the said first day of May and on divers other days and times since with fforce and arms in the Manor aforesaid did burn and cause and procure to be burnt large quantities of Coal and did thereby then and there wrongfully and injuriously make and cause and procure to be made divers large quantities of smoke and soot which at the said several times then issued from the said ffurnace and the Chimney belonging thereto into and upon the Dwelling-houses of divers of his Majesty's liege subjects within the said Manor and into and upon divers Streets and Common Highways there to the great Damage and common Nuisance of the Inhabitants of the said Manor and of all other his Majesty's subjects passing and repassing in and through the said Streets and Common Highways whereupon it is considered that the said William be in Mercy.

J. P. Earwaker, *Court Leet Records of the Manor of Manchester* (Manchester, 1888), vol. VII, pp. 29, 34; vol. IX, p. 220.

There were some two hundred municipal boroughs, whose defining characteristic consisted in the fact that their chief officers were *ex officio* justices of the peace. This feature erected them into liberties where the officers of the county could not function. (Some of the boroughs were counties in themselves.) They may be regarded as the end-product of a development which stretches from the manor through the various stages of manorial borough. The latter were communities which had acquired one or more of the characteristics of the municipal borough, without attaining its essential one: the Commission of the Peace. From the endless variety of these only one or two types can be mentioned. Beccles was governed by the Portreeve, Surveyors and Commonalty of Beccles Fen, a chartered corporation which, during this period, gradually extended its power from simply regulating the fen to administering the town itself. Birmingham was governed by a court-leet in which the lord had virtually no power. At Alnwick the government was shared between the 'Chamberlains, "Four-and-Twenty", and "Common Gild" of the Freemen on the one hand, and on the other the Court Leet and Court Baron of the Earl of Northumberland'.[1] In the municipal boroughs, some form of corporate body, such as the mayor, 12 aldermen and 30 common-councilmen of Bristol (**195**), had acquired by charter or prescription most if not all of the following kinds of jurisdiction: control of the court-baron type over common land (**191**), markets, docks and so on, and over the appointment of officers like beadles, haywards and herdsmen; control of the court-leet type over minor criminal offences, over the suppression of 'nuisances' (**192**), over the appointment of constables, ale-conners, bread-weighers, etc. (**193, 194**); control over trade and industry derived from gild origins; and, above all, the powers of the commission of the peace which we have seen exercised in the counties in quarter sessions, petty sessions, and by single justices. In a few boroughs these powers were exercised by a Common Hall consisting of the whole body of the freemen. In a few more the aldermen and councillors were elected by the freemen: for example, in the City of London, which we shall examine in more detail later. In the great majority, however, the typical oligarchical rule had established itself (**195**) and the freemen were of no importance. Their economic significance had largely disappeared in the laissez-faire atmosphere of the time, and, in any case, corporations could nullify their influence either by restricting their number or by granting the freedom to large numbers of non-residents.[2] Oligarchical or not, the mayor and his brethren took a smaller and smaller part in local government as time went on. This develop-

---

[1] S. and B. Webb, *The Manor and the Borough* (1908), pp. 187 ff.
[2] See No. **98**.

ment was due mainly to the creation of *ad hoc* bodies, and to the gradual concentration of all the work, judicial, administrative and legislative, into the hands of that small group of the corporation who were J.P.s by reason of their office: the mayor, the ex-mayors, the aldermen, the recorder, the steward, and so on. It was a process analogous to the concentration of power in the hands of the magistrates in the counties; and was similarly accompanied by the emergence of modern techniques, such as the separation of judicial, administrative and legislative business, the appointment of committees, the use of contractors and salaried officials. In the meantime, the main body of the corporation contented itself with managing the corporate property (**196**), applying its charities to its friends, relations and political supporters, and doing nothing for the benefit of the town. It regarded its privileges and its property as entirely its own concern, beyond the reach of anyone, not even parliament, to interfere; and gradually became more and more isolated from the public it was supposed to serve (**195**). Some corporations, indeed, only existed to perform one function: the election of two burgesses for the House of Commons; and after that had been eliminated in 1832 there was really nothing in existence for the commissioners of 1835 to investigate.

191. Leicester: Common Field Regulations, 1800.

31st March 1800.

Ordered that the Consent of the Common Hall be given, & it hereby is given to all the Tenants of Lands in the South fields to set their Lands there, or any part thereof, this present year, with early Potatoes, Peas or Beans—provided such Tenants in the following Year sow a Crop of Corn thereon, & in the year succeding that year suffer such land to remain fallow—And that on the next year afterwards they lay down all such land in a husbandlike manner with grass seeds upon another Crop of Corn. Provided also that nothing in this order extend or be construed to extend to release such Tenants from the Obligation of their Covenants enter'd into by their leases in future years or in those years beyond the privileges & permission usually allowed.

MS. Hall Book, Borough of Leicester.

192. Leicester: nuisances, 1746.

14 April 1746

Ordered that Mr Mayor the Aldermen and the Chamberlains or any five or more of them do as soon as Conveniently they can view the ditch in the Church Gate against Saint Margaretts Church, the Lane by the Meeting house & the Pipes which carry the water out of Mr

Stanleys Meadow near the Castle Mill to see what is necessary to be done to them so that they may report their Opinion thereof at the next Hall.

MS. Hall Book, Borough of Leicester.

193. Leicester: appointment of bellmen, 1706.

8th Day of October 1706

It is ordered at this Hall that Nicholas Swingler & John Yates shall be Bellmen to goe nightly through this Burrough from tenn of the clock at Night till six of the clock in the morning to be removeable at the pleasure of the Mayor for the time being and that the Corporation shall provide Bells to be paid for by the Chamberlaines & to be allowed in their accounts And that each of the said Bellmen shall have a coat bought for them by the Mayor for the time being the price not to exceed 4s. a yard and a small Badge of Silver with the Town Arms put upon the sleeve of each Coat and two Staves the said Bells Coats Badges & Staves to be taken away & Bellmen removed by the Mayor & Justices for the time being or the more part or greater number of them upon any misdemeanour.

MS. Hall Book, Borough of Leicester.

194. Leicester: appointment of watchmen, flesh-tasters, etc., 1748.

23 Dec. 1748

Ordered that the Sum of Twenty Pounds be paid by the Chamberlains out of the Town Stock unto such Person or Persons as shall apprehend and take any housebreaker or housebreakers within the Borough so as the Person or Persons so apprehended and taken shall discover his her or their Accomplice or Accomplices that then and in such case the person or persons that shall make such discovery as aforesaid shall not only be Intitled to the said Sum of £20 but also to his Majestys Pardon in case the same can be procured by the Corporation.

Ordered that the Aldermen of each Ward within this Borough shall appoint such a Nightly Watch within his ward as he shall think proper until the first day of March next and that each such Watchman shall not have above One shilling for each Night he shall so watch and that the same be paid weekly by the Chamberlains of the said Borough.

Ordered that the Flesh Tasters, Searchers and Sealers of Hide and Tallow, Searchers and Sealers of Leather, Fish Tasters and Ale Tasters which were appointed to serve the last year be continued for the year ensuing.

MS. Hall Book, Borough of Leicester.

195. Oligarchical government in Bristol, 1755.

[15 January 1755]

DEBATE ON THE BRISTOL NIGHTLY-WATCH BILL

SIR JOHN PHILIPPS: . . . by the unfortunate and singular form of government established in the city of Bristol, the magistrates are quite independent of their fellow-citizens, either as to their being chosen into office, or as to their continuance in power after being chosen. To illustrate this, I must beg leave to give a short account of their present form of government; and shall first observe, that the chief power is lodged in a court, which consists of a mayor, 12 aldermen, and 30 other common-council men, in all 43 persons. The mayor is chosen annually, not by the citizens as in other corporations, but by the majority of the other members of this court, all of whom, after being once chosen, continue for life, or during their good behaviour. When any one of the aldermen dies, or is removed, a new alderman is chosen from among the common-council men, not by the citizens of any ward or precinct, but by the majority of the other aldermen; and when any one of the thirty common council men dies, a new common-council man is chosen, not by the citizens of any ward or precinct, but by the majority of the said court, that is to say, by the majority of the mayor, aldermen, and common-council men. In this court is lodged the power to make by-laws for the good government of the city, and to enforce those laws by pains, punishments, penalties, fines, and amerciaments; and the mayor and aldermen are not only justices of the peace, but of oyer and terminer and general gaol delivery, within the said city. Then with regard to their officers, the recorder is always to be an alderman, is chosen by the majority of the said court of common-council and continues during life, or good behaviour: and their two coroners, their town-clerk, and the steward of their sheriffs-court, are all chosen in the same manner, and for the same time: their two sheriffs indeed are chosen annually, but in the choice of them the citizens have nothing to do, for they are chosen by the court of common-council only; so that this court has not only the power of chusing all their magistrates and officers, but by some of their old charters it seems likewise to have a power of removing any one of them, for what the majority of it may think proper to call a misbehaviour in office; for with respect to the aldermen, the power of removing or deposing an alderman is expressly granted to the mayor

and aldermen by some of their old charters; and as all their old jurisdictions, powers, and privileges, are confirmed by queen Anne's
charter, this power, and likewise the exclusive jurisdiction of the court
of common-council seems to be confirmed. . . .

P.H., xv, 471.

196. Leicester: improvements, 1747.

March 21 1747.

Ordered that Humphrey Whorstalls house, Cokers Kitchen, Guard-
house & the Piazza be all pulled down and a new Gainsborow built
on or near as conveniently may be to the place where those buildings
stand according to the plan delivered in by Mr Mayor at the last Hall
and that the Shambles and Shops in the Saturday Market be likewise
pulled down and a new Shambles with a Vault under them be made
under the said Gainsborow and that the expense of building the said
Gainsborow and of pulling down the aforesaid Buildings be paid by
the Chamerlains for the time being and allowed them again in their
accounts, and that Mr John Westley shall buy in all the materials
Direct all the Workmen that shall be made use of about the buildings
and see that they perform the same as they ought to do And that for
his Care & Trouble . . . therein he shall be allowed twelve pence in
the pound for all money that shall be laid onto both for the erecting
and pulling down of the said buildings (Except only for such Joiners
and Carpenters work as he shall do and performe) And that the Chamberlains shall nominate the Workmen and direct where the materials
for erecting the said Buildings shall be bought.

MS. Hall Book, Borough of Leicester.

V. CITY OF LONDON

The outstanding example of the retention of the democratic element in the
government of a borough was the City of London. It is possible here to
indicate only the bare bones of its complex structure and exciting history.
There are four principal governing bodies to consider. The first, the Court
of Common Hall, consisted of the mayor and about eight thousand livery-
men belonging to the eighty-nine guilds and companies. The second, the
Court of Aldermen, consisted of the mayor and twenty-five aldermen, elected
for life by the freemen ratepayers of the twenty-six wards into which the
City was divided for administrative purposes. The senior aldermen (later all
of them) were justices of the peace. The third body, the Court of Common

Council, consisted of the mayor, twenty-five aldermen and about two hundred citizens elected annually by the freemen ratepayers. The aldermen and common councillors were elected by the fourth body we have to consider, the Court of Wardmote. There were twenty-six of these, one in each ward.[1] This court also elected the ward beadle, the ward clerk, the constables, the scavengers and the questmen (the members of the inquest of the ward). It was thus responsible for the detailed administration of the City, that is to say, for the enforcement of the compulsory service of the citizens, any delinquencies being searched out by the inquest and presented to the court (197).

In the early part of the period, the court of aldermen was the effective central governing body of the City, with the court of common council acting in an advisory capacity. Each alderman was the 'captain of his ward', and with his ward councillors supervised the performance by the citizens of their personal obligations to watch, cleanse and light the streets, serve their turn as constable, and so on. In the main, the court of aldermen represented the interests of the great financial houses, and were therefore supporters of the government. The court of common council, representing lower levels in the business world, was usually linked up with the opposition, that is to say, it was Tory or Jacobite in the early part of the period, and Radical later. There were naturally struggles between the two, and the principal object of the aldermen at first was to get themselves recognised as a kind of second chamber, with powers of veto over the acts of the court of common council. This was possible owing to the vagueness of the statute which restored the City's privileges in the Revolution settlement; and, thanks to Walpole, the aldermen got their way by Act of Parliament in 1725.[2] They maintained this dominating position till a second revolution occurred in 1746,[3] when, thanks to the Pelhams, the *status quo* was restored. From this time on, the administration of the City was slowly transformed. The court of common council became the real executive power, leaving the aldermen to concentrate on their purely judicial business. As the years went on, it extended its influence into the wards, superseding the ancient system of personal service run by the courts of wardmote by the more modern method of salaried experts controlled by itself. By the end of the period, it had a real grip on every detail of City administration, and it had achieved it by the usual method of extending its existing powers and acquiring new ones by Act of Parliament. By now it was administering a revenue bigger than that of all the other boroughs put together, and there were, of course, plenty of perquisites for all concerned, from the lord mayor downwards. On the other hand, the magistracy was not corrupt; and by eighteenth-century standards this enormous conglomeration of volatile people was efficiently governed.

The success of this ratepayers' democracy was of prime importance, far

---

[1] See also No. 203. [2] 11 Geo. I, c. 18. [3] 19 Geo. II, c. 8.

beyond the efficient paving and lighting of the streets of its precincts; for the City of London forms part of the history of England. Its role in the Revolution has been noticed[1]; and its influence on day-to-day politics was increasingly vital all through the period. Apart from the times when its citizens came out on the streets, the centre of this activity was the Court of Common Hall, about which little has been said so far. This body of livery-men selected two of the aldermen who had been sheriffs, and from this pair the court of aldermen chose one to be the lord mayor. Common Hall also elected the sheriffs and the chamberlain (among others); and returned four members of parliament whom it expected to represent its point of view as delegates. It was here that were fought out the battles between aldermen and liverymen, between Court and Country, Whigs and Jacobites, Tories and Radicals. The City led the agitation in the late 1760's and 1770's. Earlier, the liverymen had tended to be exploited by opposition politicians for their own purposes; but with emergence of John Wilkes the City became a power in the land in its own right[2]; and with its four M.P.s, its pamphlets, its resolutions and remonstrances (198), and its street demonstrations, it helped to make and break governments to the end of this period. It really was, to use Herbert Butterfield's term, 'a separate estate of the realm'.[3]

197. An alderman's charge to the Inquest of the Ward.

Ye shall truly inquire if any person keep any bawdy house, gaming house or other house of ill-fame; or keep an ale-house, or victualling house, or sell beer or ale without a licence. Also, if any Freeman against his oath made, conceal, cover, or colour the goods of foreigners by which the King may in anywise lose, or the franchises of this City be emblemished. Also, if any officer, by colour of his office, do extortion to any man. Also, if any man encroach, or take of the common ground of this City. Also, if any common way or common course of water be foreclosed or letted, that it may not have its course as it was wont, to the annoyance of the Ward, and by whom it is done. Ye shall diligently make search and inquiry whether there be any vintner, inn-holder, ale-house keeper, or any other person or persons whatsoever, within this Ward that do use, or keep in his, her or their house or houses any measures which be unsealed, and by law not allowed to sell wine, beer, ale or other liquors thereby, and whether any of them do sell by any measures not sealed. Also, if any persons within this Ward do sell any goods, wares, and merchandises by false scales,

---

[1] See Nos. 4 and 5. [2] See Chapter 3, part VI, p. 208.
[3] H. Butterfield, *George III, Lord North and the People* (1949), p. 181.

weights and measures. Also, forasmuch as it is thought that divers and many persons dwelling within the Liberties of this City daily occupy as Freemen, whereas indeed they be none, nor never were admitted into the Liberties of this City; ye shall therefore require every such person dwelling within this Ward, whom ye shall suspect of the same, to show you the copy of his Freedom, under the seal of the office of the Chamberlain of the said City; and such as ye shall find without their copies, or deny to show their copies, ye shall write and present their names in your Indentures. Also, if any dwelling within this Ward which do offer or put to sale any wares or merchandises in the open streets or lanes of this City, or go from house to house to sell the same, commonly called hawkers Also, if any have fraudulently or unduly obtained the Freedom of this City. Ye shall assemble yourselves twice, or oftener if need require, so long as ye shall continue of this Inquest, and present the defaults which ye shall find to be committed concerning any of the articles of your charge, to the end due remedy may be speedily applied and the offenders punished as occasion shall require.

An Inquiry into the Nature and Duties of Inquest Jurymen, by a Citizen (1824), quoted by S. and B. Webb, *The Manor and the Borough* (1908), p. 595.

198. Common Hall address to George III, 1770.

TO THE KING'S MOST EXCELLENT MAJESTY

The humble Address, Remonstrance, and Petition, of the Lord Mayor, Aldermen, and Livery of the City of London, in Common Hall assembled.

(Presented at St. James's, on Wednesday, the 14th of March, 1770.)

May it please your Majesty,

We have already, in our petition, dutifully represented to your Majesty, the chief injuries we have sustained: we are unwilling to believe that your Majesty can slight the desires of your people, or be regardless of their affection, and deaf to their complaints. Yet their complaints remain unanswered, their injuries are confirmed; and the only judge removeable at the pleasure of the crown has been dismissed from his high office for defending in parliament the laws and the constitution.

We therefore venture once more to address ourselves to your Majesty, as to the father of your people; as to him who must be both able and willing to redress our grievances; and we repeat our application with the greater propriety, because we see the instruments of our wrongs, who have carried into execution the measures of which we complain, more particularly distinguished by your Majesty's royal bounty and favour.

Under the same secret and malign influence, which, through each successive administration, has defeated every good, and suggested every bad, intention, the majority of the House of Commons have deprived your people of their dearest rights.

They have done a deed more ruinous in its consequences than the levying of ship-money by Charles the First, or the dispensing power assumed by James the Second. A deed, which must vitiate all the future proceedings of this parliament: for the acts of the legislature itself can no more be valid without a legal House of Commons than without a legal prince upon the throne. . . .

Under James the Second they complained that the sitting of parliament was interrupted, because it was not corruptly subservient to his designs: We complain now, that the sitting of this parliament is not interrupted, because it is corruptly subservient to the designs of your Majesty's ministers. Had the parliament under James the Second been as submissive to his commands as the parliament is at this day to the dictates of a minister, instead of clamours for its meeting, the nation would have rung, as now, with outcries for its dissolution. . . .

Since, therefore, the misdeeds of your Majesty's ministers in violating the freedom of election, and depraving the noble constitution of parliaments, are notorious, as well as subversive of the fundamental laws and liberties of this realm; and since your Majesty, both in honour and justice, is obliged inviolably to preserve them, according to the oath made to God and your subjects at your coronation; we, your Majesty's remonstrants, assure ourselves, that your Majesty will restore the constitutional government and quiet of your people by dissolving this parliament, and removing those evil ministers for ever from your councils.

Signed by order,

JAMES HODGES, Town Clerk.

Annual Register (1770), Appendix to the Chronicle, p. 199.

VI. *AD HOC* BODIES

In the modernisation of local government in the eighteenth century, in the equipment of it with new techniques to deal with new problems, the greatest influence was that of the *ad hoc* bodies. General legislation, to deal with a problem (like the roads or the police) for the country as a whole, was rarely politically possible in this period. Instead, large numbers of statutes were passed setting up commissions to carry out specific tasks in specific areas. The Webbs calculated that there were probably in existence in the eighteenth century 100 commissioners of sewers, 125 guardians of the poor, 300 improvement commissioners and 1100 turnpike trusts. These numbers, together with the length and verbosity of the statutes concerned, would have rendered the task of illustrating them impossible, had they not possessed certain common characteristics. The commissioners of sewers, to regulate the draining of land liable to be flooded by the sea or rivers, are not included here. They were ancient institutions erected to solve the problems posed by nature; while in the documents we must limit ourselves to those mainly eighteenth-century authorities created to tackle difficulties produced by human beings. The Acts setting up incorporated guardians of the poor differed from the rest in that they usually conferred the new powers on the existing authorities, the parish or the borough, instead of creating new ones (**199**). On the other hand, all the powers to maintain roads by collecting tolls were, after 1711, conferred on specially created bodies called turnpike trusts, though these might have an *ex officio* element in their composition (**200**). Before 1711, the justices of the peace had usually received these powers; just as in Devon, for example, in 1758 the justices were given powers to contract for the repair of bridges without waiting for presentment by a grand jury (**201**). Local communities were usually able to acquire these powers without much difficulty, though there might be successful local opposition. The statutes creating improvement commissioners tell the same story. The new powers were sometimes given to the vestry or the corporation; but usually (and especially after 1748) they were granted to specially created bodies of commissioners, with the existing authorities having *ex officio* membership (**202**). These commissioners provided services like paving, lighting, cleansing, watching, suppression of nuisances, and so on; and the commissioners of Manchester went to the lengths in 1824 of acquiring powers to set up a gas-works. The Manchester commissioners were unusual in being well controlled by the existing local authority.[1] Normally, these bodies provided the essential local services alongside the complete inertia of the corporations. Sometimes, even, the inhabitants got together in private association without acquiring special powers from parliament, like,

---

[1] See p. 300.

for example, the various prosecution societies which were formed to maintain law and order imperfectly upheld by the local and central authorities till the reforms initiated by Peel (203).

199. Norwich: Incorporated Guardians of the Poor, 1711.

An Act for erecting a Workhouse in the City and County of Norwich for the better Imployment and maintaining the Poor there.

WHEREAS it is found by Experience that the Poor in the City of Norwich and County and Liberties of the same do daily multiply and Idleness Laziness and Debauchery amongst the meaner Sort do greatly increase for want of Workhouses to set them to work and a sufficient Authority to compel them thereto as well to the Charge of the Inhabitants and Grief of the charitable and honest Hous-holders of the said City as the great Distress of the Poor themselves for which sufficient Redress hath not yet been provided. For remedy whereof be it enacted . . . That . . . there be and shall be a Corporation to continue forever within the City of Norwich and County of the same and the Liberties thereof consisting of the several Persons herein after mentioned (that is to say) of the Mayor Recorder and Steward Justices of the Peace Sheriffs and Aldermen of the said City for the Time being and of Thirty two other Persons to be chosen out of the most honest discreet and charitable Inhabitants of the said City and County and Liberties thereof in the Four great wards in the said City and the Towns and Out-Parishes in the County of the said City (that is to say) Eight out of every of the said great Wards and of such other charitable Persons as shall be elected and constituted Guardians of the Poor of the said City in such Manner as is herein after expressed.

II. And the said first Thirty two Persons shall be elected on the Third Day of May next ensuing or within Three days after an Assembly of the said City for that Purpose to be held by the Votes of the Mayor Sheriffs Citizens and Commonalty in Common Council assembled or of the major Part of them then present.

. . .

VII. And for the better governing the said Corporation the said Mayor Recorder Steward Justices of the Peace Sheriffs Aldermen and Guardians or the major Part of them whereof the said Mayor for the Time being or his Deputy to be one shall have and hereby have Authority to meet on the Seventh Day of May next ensuing in the Guildhall in the Market Place of the said City or in some other convenient Place and shall on that Day or any other Day or Time that to them shall seem convenient elect and constitute out of and from amongst themselves the several Officers following (that is to say) One Governor One Deputy Governor One Treasurer and Twenty Assistants to continue in the said Office for One Year.

. . .

XII. [The said Court empowered to raise Money, not exceeding £5,000, for buying or erecting Workhouses, &c.; and also for the Maintenance and Employment of the Poor therein, or within the Care of the said Corporation.]

. . . The Mayor and Justices of the Peace of and for the said City and County for the Time being which said Mayor and Justices or any Two of them may and are hereby required to grant and issue out their Warrant under their Hands and Seals thereby to authorize and require the Church Wardens and Overseers of the Poor or such Person or Persons as the said Guardians shall appoint out of every respective Parish Town Hamlet and Precinct in the said City and County or Liberties thereof to rate and assess the said Sum or Sums of Money on the respective Inhabitants and on every Parson and Vicar and on all and every the Occupiers of Lands Houses Tenements Tythes Impropriate Appropriation of Tythes and on all Persons having and using Stocks and Personal Estates in the said respective Parishes . . . or having Money out at Interest in equal Proportions as near as may be according to their several and respective Values and Estates. . . .

XVI. And be it further enacted . . . That the said Corporation shall have the Care and provide for the Maintenance of all the Poor of the said City or County and Liberties thereof of what Age or Sex soever they be which are or ought to be by Law relieved and provided for by their respective Parishes there except such as shall be otherwise sufficiently provided for by the charitable Gifts of other Persons or in Hospitals or Almshouses within the said City already erected or to be erected. . . .

XVII. And that it shall and may be lawful to and for the said Governor Deputy Governor and Assistants or any Three of them whereof the said Governor Deputy Governor to be One by Warrant under their Hands and Seals to be directed to the Constables of or in the said City and County or any or either of them or to such Person or Persons as shall be appointed by the Guardians to apprehend or cause to be apprehended any Rogues Vagrants or Sturdy Beggars or idle lazy or disorderly Persons within the said City and County and Liberties thereof and to cause them to be conveyed kept and set to work in the said Workhouses Hospitals or Houses of Correction for any Time not exceeding Three Years. . . .

10 Anne, c. 15: S.R., ix, 583.

200. Cambridgeshire: Turnpike Trust, 1738.

An Act for Repairing part of the Road from London *to* Cambridge, *beginning at the End of the Parish of* Foulmire *in the said County, next to* Barley *in the County of Hertford, and ending at the Pavement in* Trumpington Street, *in the Town of* Cambridge.

Whereas that Part of the great and ancient Road, leading from *London* to *Cambridge*, which lies in the several Parishes of *Foulmire, Thriplow, Newton, Harlston, Hawkston,* and *Trumpington,* in the County of *Cambridge,* and in the Liberty and Town of *Cambridge,* to the end of the Pavement in *Trumpington Street* in the said Town of *Cambridge,* about Seven Miles in length, is become very ruinous, and at many times of the Year almost impassable, by reason of the great Quantity of Provisions continually conveyed for the Use of the City of *London,* and other great and heavy Loads daily drawn through the same, insomuch that it is become very dangerous to all Persons travelling that way, and the said Conveyances are become very difficult; and for that ordinary Course appointed by the Laws and Statutes of this Realm is not sufficient for the effectual Repairing the same, neither are the Inhabitants of the Parishes, in which the said ruinous Places . . . do lie, of Ability to repair the said Road, except some other Provisions be made for the raising Monies towards putting the same into good and sufficient Repair: For remedy whereof, and to the intent the same may forthwith be effectually repaired, and from Time to Time hereafter kept in good and sufficient repair . . . be it Enacted . . . That for the Surveying, Ordering, Repairing, and keeping in Repair, that Part of the said Road . . . it shall be in the Power of Sir *Thomas Hatton* [followed by 49 other names] . . . the Vice Chancellor of *Cambridge* for the Time being, the Mayor of *Cambridge* for the Time being, who are hereby nominated and appointed Trustees for putting this Act in Execution, and the survivors of them; and they, or any Five or more of them, or such Person or Persons as they, or any Five of them shall authorize and appoint, shall and may erect or cause to be erected a Gate or . . . Turnpike . . . in or cross any Part or Parts of the said Road, and to receive and take (before they shall be permitted to pass through the same) the Tolls following, *Videlicet,* For every Coach, Berlin, Chaise, Chariot, or Calash, drawn by Four or more Horses, the Sum of One Shilling; For every Coach . . . drawn by Two Horses, the Sum of Six Pence; for every Chaise or Calash drawn by One Horse only, the Sum of Three Pence; For every Waggon, the Sum of One Shilling; for every Cart or other Carriage, the Sum of Six Pence; For every Horse, Mare, Gelding, Ass or Mule, not drawing, the Sum of One Peny; For every Score of Oxen or Neat Cattle, the Sum of Four Pence, and so in proportion for any greater or lesser Number, exceeding Four; For every Score of Calves and Hogs, the Sum of Two Pence, and so in proportion for any greater or Lesser Number, exceeding Four; which said respective Sum or Sums of Money shall be demanded and taken in the Name of, or as a Toll: . . .

III. Provided also, That during the Continuance of this Act, all Coaches . . . and Passengers on Horseback, shall pass and repass Tollfree, on the Day or Days there shall be an Election for a Knight or Knights of the Shire, to serve in Parliament for the said County of *Cambridge*; Any Thing herein contained to the contrary notwithstanding.

IV. And be it further enacted . . . That they the said Trustees, or any Five or more of them, by Writing under their Hands and Seals, shall and may, from Time to Time, choose and appoint One or more fit Person or Persons, to be Receiver or Receivers . . . of such Money, in the Name of such Toll, as shall be Due and Payable by Virtue of this Act; and also One or More fit Person or Persons, to be Surveyor or Surveyors, to see the Condition of the said Road, and to see that the same be repaired, and that the Monies raised or to be raised, and expended, by Virtue of this Act, be duly applied;

IX. [Trustees may borrow Money on the Toll, at 5 £ *per Cent.*]

. . .

XVII. And be it further Enacted . . . That it shall and may be lawful for the said Trustees . . . to compound or agree with any of the

Parishes, to which the said Road doth belong, for a certain Sum of Money, or otherwise by the Year, as the said Trustees or any Five or more of them shall think reasonable, in lieu of the Statute-Work to be done by such Parish or Parishes as aforesaid. . . .

11 Geo. II, c. 14: *Public General Acts*, XXXVI, 287.

201. Devon: justices acquire special powers over bridges, 1758.

An Act for the more easy and speedy repairing of Publick Bridges within the County of Devon.

WHEREAS by an Act passed in the Twelfth Year of the Reign of His present Majesty, intituled, *An Act for the more easy assessment collecting, and levying of County Rates*; it is enacted, That no Part of the Money to be raised and collected in pursuance of the said Act, shall be applied to the Repair of any Bridges, until Presentment shall be made by the respective Grand Juries at the Assize, Great Sessions, General Gaol Delivery, or General or Quarter Sessions of the Peace held for any County, Riding, Division, City, Town-Corporate, or Liberty, of the Insufficiency, Inconveniency, or want of Repairations of the Bridges: And whereas until such Presentments have been made, the Justices of the Peace have no Power at their General or Quarter Sessions to contract and agree for rebuilding, repairing, and amending the same, or any other Works which are to be repaired and done by Assessment on their respective Counties [etc], and then only for any Term or Terms of Years, not exceeding Seven Years, in such Manner as by the said Act is directed: And whereas by frequent Accidents and sudden unforeseen Decays which happen to Bridges by Floods and Stormy Weather, Frost and otherwise; which need immediate Repairs: and for want of which it has happened that several Bridges or great Parts of them have been thrown down or carried away before the same can be presented according to . . . the said Act, and for want of Powers in the Justices of Peace to contract with Persons for repairing . . . the said County Bridges before they are in Decay or are presented, great Inconveniences . . . have arisen to His Majesty's Subjects Travelling in the County of *Devon*, and very large and unnecessary Expences . . . have afterwards been paid . . . out of the said County Rates, the greatest Part of which might have been by a timely Repair prevented, if any Person had been by Contract obliged to keep, repair, and support the said County Bridges, when and as often as the same have been needful; be it therefore enacted ... That ... it shall ... be lawful for the Justices of the Peace in ... *Devon*, at their General or Quarter Sessions ... to contract ... with any Person ... for supporting, maintaining ... any ... of the Bridges, Ramparts, Banks, Cops, and Wearings thereunto belonging, and the Highways and Causeways adjoining to the Ends of any Bridges ... for any Term or Terms of years not exceeding Twenty one Years, at a certain annual Sum ...; such Contract or Contracts to be made ... although the said Bridges ... shall not at the Time ... have been presented ...; and that such Justices at their respective General or Quarter Sessions, shall give publick Notice of their Intention of contracting ... for rebuilding ... the Bridges ...; and that such Contracts shall be made at the most reasonable Price or Prices which shall be proposed by such Contractors respectively ...

31 Geo. II, c. 47: *Road Acts*, VI, 115.

202. Manchester and Salford: Improvement Commissioners, 1765.

An Act for Cleansing and Lighting the Streets, Lanes, and Passages, within the Towns of Manchester *and* Salford, *in the County Palatine of* Lancaster; *and for providing Fire Engines and Fire Men; and for preventing Annoyances within the said Towns.*

Whereas the Town of Manchester, in the County Palatine of Lancaster, is a large populous, and trading Town, and the Town of Salford lying contiguous thereto, is also a populous and trading Town: and whereas it would tend greatly to the Safety, Preservation, and Benefit of the Inhabitants of the said several Towns respectively, if the Streets, Lanes, and Passages, thereof respectively were kept clean and properly lighted, and if the said Towns were kept free from Nuisances and Annoyances, and other Matters and Things endangering the Lives, Healths, or Properties of such Inhabitants; and if sufficient Engines and able Men were kept and employed for the Estinguishment of Fires which may happen within the said Towns respectively: ... be it enacted ... That from and after the passing of this Act, James Bayley, [14 names follow] Esquires: Roger Sedgwick Bachelor of Physick, the Reverend the Warden and Fellows of the College of Christ in Manchester, for the time being; the Borough Reeves and Constables of the Towns of Manchester and Salford for the time being; James Allen [and 61 other names] . . . Gentlemen, shall be, and they are hereby constituted and appointed Commissioners for putting this Act into Execution: And when any of the Commissioners herein named, or at any Time to be elected in pursuance of this Act, (except the Borough Reeves and Constables of the said Towns of Manchester and Salford respectively for the time being, who are to be Commissioners ex officio) shall die, or remove out of the said Townships to dwell, or refuse to act, or be rendered incapable of being a Commissioner, or acting as said, as is herein after-mentioned, it shall and may be lawful for the remaining Commissioners, at any Meeting in pursuance of this Act, or any Nine or more of them at such Meeting assembled, to nominate, elect, and appoint, a fit Person or Persons, inhabiting within One of the said Townships, and being an Owner, Proprietor, or Occupier, of a House or Houses, Warehouses, or other Buildings, or some other Tenement within the said Townships, or One of them, of the clear yearly Value of Thirty Pounds over and above all Taxes and Reprizes, to supply the Place or Places of him or them so dying, removing, or refusing to act, or being rendered incapable of acting, as herein after is mentioned. . . .

And be it further enacted by the Authority aforesaid, That it shall and may be lawful for the said Commissioners, from time to time, at any of their Meetings to be held in pursuance of this Act, or any Nine or more of them at such Meeting assembled, to nominate and appoint such and so many Scavengers, Rakers, or Cleansers of the Streets, Lanes, Passages, and Publick Places, Keepers and Lighters of Lamps, Keepers and Managers of Fire Engines, and so many able bodied Men, not exceeding Fifty, to be Firemen within the said Townships, and so many Clerks, Treasurers, and other Officers, as they shall think proper. . . .

And be it further enacted by the Authority aforesaid, That all and every Person or Persons, inhabiting within the Towns of Manchester and Salford, or either of them (so far as the Commissioners so assembled, or any Nine or more of them, shall by publick Notice to be given by the Bell-men or public Cryers of the said Towns respectively, direct) shall, from and after the said fifth Day of July, sweep and cleanse, or cause to be swept and cleansed, the Streets, Causeways, Lanes, and Passages, within the said Townships respectively, before or on the Side of their respective Houses, Warehouses, Shops, Stables, and other Buildings (not being Dead Walls) to the Middle of such Streets, Cause-

ways, Lanes, and Passages, Twice in every Week; that is to say, Every
Monday and Friday, between the Hours of Eight and Twelve, or
upon such other Days, and at such other Times, as the said Commissioners so assembled as aforesaid, or any Nine or more of them, shall
appoint, and collect and put together the Dirt and Soil in the said
Streets, Causeways, Lanes and Passages, with the least Obstruction
to the Way, Road, and Passage, therein respectively that may be, to
the End the same may be ready for the Scavenger to carry away, upon
Pain of forfeiting Five Shillings for every Offence or Neglect; and the
Scavenger or Scavengers, or other Officer or Officers, to be from time
to time appointed for that Purpose, shall, and be and they are hereby
required to sweep and cleanse, or cause to be swept and cleansed, the
Street or Place within the said Town of Manchester, commonly called
The Market Place, and also the Street or Place there commonly called
The Shambles; and before all void Houses, Dead Walls, void or waste
Grounds and Places, Churches, Churchyards, Chapels, Meeting-
houses, the School called The Free School, the College or Hospital,
and other publick Buildings within either of the said Towns, and also
the Bridge called Salford Bridge, at such Times as shall be appointed
by the said Commissioners so assembled as aforesaid, or any Nine or
more of them, and collect and put together the Dirt and Soil thereof,
in the Manner aforesaid, to the End the same may be ready for loading
and carrying away, upon Pain of forfeiting Five shillings for every
Offence or Neglect; and no Person or Persons whosoever shall throw,
cast, or lay, or cause, permit, or suffer, to be thrown, cast, or laid, any
Ashes, Rubbish, Dust, Dirt, Dung, or other Filth or Annoyance whatsoever, in any Street, Causeway, Lane, Passage, Churchyard, Water-
course, or into the River Irwell, at any Place within the said Towns of
Manchester or Salford.

And it is hereby further enacted . . . That it shall and may be lawful
to and for the said Commissioners, or any Nine or more of them, from
time to time, at any of their said Meetings, to contract with any
Person or Persons, for a sufficient Number of Lamps, necessary to be
fixed and set up in the said Towns respectively, and for Iron Posts, and
other Materials, needful for fixing the same, from time to time, and
for finding and providing the said Lamps with all Requisites, and for
lighting, supporting, attending, and repairing, the same; and also
with any Person or Persons, to be and act as Scavenger or Scavengers,
to carry away the Dust and Soil of the Streets, Lanes, and Public

Passages, in the said Towns respectively, according to the Purpose of this Act; and also with any Person or Persons to make, and finish, and repair, and keep in Order, One or more Fire Engine or Fire Engines, or to buy or procure such Fire Engine or Fire Engines, together with a sufficient number of Leathern Buckets, and other Matters and Things relating thereto, as the said Commissioners so assembled, or any Nine or more of them, at any such Meeting, shall think meet and proper; and to purchase, lease, or otherwise to agree for, a proper and convenient Place or Places for the Keeping of the said Fire Engine or Engines, and Buckets, and other Things relating thereto: And the said Commissioners, so assembled . . . are hereby also authorized, impowered, and required, to put to the best Bidder, or otherwise sell or dispose of all such Dung, Dirt, or Manure, as shall arise in the said Streets, Causeways, Lanes, . . ., or be collected carried or laid together, and by such Scavenger or Officer, for that Purpose, taken or carried away as aforesaid; and to apply the Money arising therefrom for the Purposes in this Act mentioned, or such of them as they shall think proper.

. . .

And be it further enacted . . . That it shall and may be lawful for the said Commissioners . . ., at any of their Meeting or Meetings aforesaid, yearly and every Year, or oftener, if they shall think proper, to state, set down, and ascertain, what Sum and Sums of Money shall be raised by Taxation and Assessment, in the manner herein after mentioned, by and out of the said Townships of Manchester and Salford respectively, so far as they the said Commissioners . . . shall at any such Meeting . . . direct the Taxation and Assessment to be and extend within each of the said Towns, for defraying the Expences of passing, and from time to time putting, this Act, or any Part or Parts thereof, in Execution, so that the whole Money they shall so ascertain to be raised, either by One Rate or Assessment, or different Rates or Assessments, shall not exceed in the Whole, in the First Year, the Sum of One Shilling in the Pound, nor afterwards, in any One Year, the Sum of Six Pence in the Pound, for every Pound for which the Houses, Buildings and other Tenements, to be taxed or rated by virtue of this Act, shall for the time being be rated in value to the Land Tax . . .

5 Geo. III, c. 81: *Local Acts*, XIII, 855.

203. Billingsgate Ward: voluntary association for military training, 1780.

[10 July 1780]

At a General Meeting of the Inhabitants of this Ward [Billingsgate], held at *Butchers-Hall* this Day, in consequence of public Summonses left at each House, in order to receive the Report of the Committee appointed to carry into Execution the Resolutions of the several Ward-meetings, held before the Worshipful *Thomas Sainsbury*, Esq; Alderman of the said Ward, from the Eighth to the Eighteenth Day of *June* last; it was agreed, 'That an Association should be formed from the Inhabitants for learning the Military Exercise for the Protection of their Neighbours and their own Property, by the Exertion of every effectual legal Method in the Assistance of the Civil Power, for the Preservation of the public Peace of this City, by guarding it against those alarming Dangers to which it lately stood exposed.'

In Obedience to his Majesty's Proclamations, and in respectful Compliance with the several Orders and Recommendations from the Lord Mayor, the Courts of Aldermen, Common Council, and Lieutenancy of the City of *London*, the Inhabitants of this Ward having solicited to be called together by their worthy Alderman, and being excited by a noble Zeal for rescuing the Honour of the City from farther Disgrace, assembled at the above Hall, at Six o'Clock in the Afternoon, on *Thursday* the Eighth Day of *June* (when great Danger was apprehended from the [Gordon] Rioters returning from their Depredations in the *Borough*), and unanimously resolved, That they would immediately arm and associate themselves for the Protection of the Ward; and that the Alderman, Deputy, and Common Council, with Twelve other responsible Inhabitants, should be a Committee for conducting the said Business. To the Honour of the Inhabitants, it is hereby declared, that, in less than *Three Hours* after the Resolution was formed, upwards of Sixty of them did actually arm themselves as Militia-men and *free Citizens*; and under the Command of the Officers of the Militia, duly appointed by the Commissioners of Lieutenancy for the said City, did patrole the Streets, Lanes, &c. in the said Ward; examined whether all the Public Houses had regularly conformed to the Order of the Court of Aldermen; saw that the Constables and Watchmen attended closely to their Duty; took up several suspected Persons that were found lurking in the Ward, and pursued several others: by which

Means, no Riots, Tumults, or Disturbances have happened to annoy the Peace of the said Ward during, or since the Commencement of, the late horrid Outrages, which threatened the Destruction of all Laws and all Government.

. . .

The Utility of such an Association being thus evidently demonstrated, the following Committee was unanimously appointed to prepare a Plan, and to carry it into Execution, upon the above laudable Principles, for the common Safety of the Ward:

> David Evans, *Chairman*
> William Deane, *Treasurer* . . .
> [Ten Names follow.]

Quoted in L. Radzinowicz, *History of English Criminal Law* (1956), vol. II, p. 467.

CHAPTER 5

THE CHURCH

The successful efforts of the religious and political leaders in 1688 and 1714 to preserve 'their religion, liberties and properties'[1] resulted in a century of harmonious alliance between Church and State. There were, of course, initial difficulties in the reigns of William and Mary and Anne—all part of the fierce party contentions of that period—but with the Protestant Succession safely achieved the Church thankfully took possession of the field, after over a century and a half of bitter warfare on both its flanks, and proceeded to enjoy the fruits of victory for as long as the eighteenth-century constitution survived. During that period, to use Burke's phrase, 'the Church and the State' were 'one and the same thing, being different integral parts of the same whole'.[2] However, towards the end of this period, the new economic, social and philosophical forces which were undermining eighteenth-century politics forced the Church also to come to terms with the new world of the nineteenth century.

Before 1714, religion was still right at the heart of politics, and the Church could still quite genuinely be regarded as 'in danger'. On the one hand, the Whigs feared the overthrow of the 'happy establishment' from the Roman Catholic side; and, on the other, the Tories trembled at the growth of dissent, which they blamed on the Toleration Act. One result was the stricter enforcement, on occasion, of anti-Catholic legislation, and additions to it in times of national emergency (204). Another was the passing by the Tories in the days of their triumph of the Occasional Conformity Act (205) and the Schism Act (206). The former (like the Sacheverell Clause in reverse) was partly intended to place local government, and thus parliamentary elections, exclusively in the hands of Anglican Tories; while the latter would have dried up Nonconformity at its source. Such measures, however, were not typical of the liberal-minded eighteenth century. While the penal legislation was left on the statute-book to quieten the fears of the Anglican public, its enforcement was exceedingly lax. Roman Catholics were for the most part unmolested (207); and Dissenters holding public office had an annual Indemnity Act passed for their benefit from 1727 onwards (208). Later in the century the attitude towards those outside the Anglican communion became even more liberal. In 1778 Savile's Act (209) took away from Roman Catholics the disabilities that had been imposed on

[1] See No. 2, p. 10.
[2] 'Speech on the Petition of the Unitarians', in *Works* (1792–1827), vol. v, p. 353.

them in 1700; and in 1779 dissenting ministers and teachers were relieved from subscribing to certain of the Thirty-nine Articles to which subscription had been made compulsory by the Toleration Act (**210**). However, the French Revolution and the personal hostility of the monarchs (**211**)[1] delayed the achievement of equal civil status till 1828 and 1829.

While it thus dictated a non-vindictive peace to its former enemies, the Church of England became more fully integrated into public life than at any time before or since. One possible cause of division within its ranks was eliminated in the early stages. The convocation of Canterbury, which was allowed to meet occasionally between 1689 and 1717, became the scene of such violent disputes between the two Houses (in which the Lower House advanced radical programmes designed to give convocation legislative parity with parliament, and to free the Lower House from the control of the bishops) that the government closed it down. It ceased to transact business between 1717 and 1855. In this, the Hanoverians were only following the precedent set by Charles II and James II, for convocation had lost its *raison d'être* as far as governments were concerned when it waived its privilege of taxing itself in 1664.

If the suspension of convocation masked any disaffection among the lower clergy, the policy of post-Revolution governments towards church preferment was designed to crush it out of existence. It was a question of showing the clergy on which side their bread was buttered; and the means were provided by the mass of benefices at the disposal of those in power, the easy acceptance of pluralism, the practice of translating bishops up the steep ladder of preferment, and the value of the prizes at the top (**212**). The ejection of the Non-jurors provided the opportunity to fill their places with more complaisant clerics; and, from that time on, what Lord Cowper preached (**213**), and Gibson (**214**) and Newcastle (**215**) practised, geared the 'great engine of power'[2] to the great machine of 'influence' operated by succeeding governments. Ecclesiastical preferment depended on political allegiance: as Gibson described his policy, 'the persons whom I recommended to the favour of the Court, were such, as besides their known affection to the established Church, were also known to be well affected towards the administration in the State'.[3] Utility to the Court on the part of a cleric of talent could mean the rapid promotion enjoyed by a Hoadly (**216**)[4]; independence of mind could condemn a Watson to remain on the first rung of the ladder for the rest of his life (**217**). And so it remained till the early nineteenth century, when promotion in the Church (like that in the civil service and the armed forces) gradually became politically neutral. And the

---

[1] See also No. **77**, p. 133.
[2] George III's phrase: R. R. Sedgwick, *Letters from George III to Lord Bute* (1939), p. 212.
[3] Quoted by N. Sykes, *Edmund Gibson* (Oxford, 1926), p. 408.
[4] See also No. **155**, p. 258.

meticulous care with which not only kings and their ministers, but also their allies and opponents among the nobility and gentry, supervised all ecclesiastical appointments in their gift returned a double bonus, direct and indirect, which we must now examine.

In the first place, the clergy could render valuable service to the party that sponsored them. Though they did not often speak, the bishops were always valuable (218), and often vital, with their votes (219) and their proxies (220) in the House of Lords. As Sykes' analysis shows, for example, thirteen of the bishops of William's appointment voted with the Whigs for the rejection of the Occasional Conformity Bill of 1703, with only two on the other side; while in 1718 ten of Anne's nominees voted with Tories against the repeal of the Occasional Conformity Act itself, with only three on the other side.[1] After a period of Whig office, the picture changes again, and a speaker in the House of Commons could declare that 'the Bishops cling all together to advance any proposition that had a Court air'.[2] Outside parliament, their literary talents were exploited by both Court and Country (217, 221, 26, 83); and each bishop in his diocese was at the centre of a network of 'interests' of first importance in parliamentary elections (222). When the Bishop of Chichester wrote to the Duke of Newcastle during the campaign for the important election of 1734: 'I did before I left Chichester, signify my desire to my friends in behalf of the old members; who I think can't lose it at the next election',[3] he was performing a function in his see similar to that of a Lord Lieutenant in his shire. The lower clergy in their turn pulled their weight. George Selwyn described them as follows: 'The clergy are as so many turnspits ready to be put into the wheel, and to turn it round as the Minister pleases'.[4] This gives the essence of the situation, if allowance is made for the exaggeration to be expected from Selwyn and for the fact that many of the clergy were trying to turn the wheel in the other direction, on behalf of the opposition.

Political spade-work by the clergy was only one of the advantages that political leaders derived from the control of clerical preferment. Like other forms of patronage, it was also used to reward and punish politicians themselves. As the Bishop of Killala advised Mrs Clayton in 1730, it was necessary to 'render ecclesiastical preferments of the same use to their Majesties with civil employments'.[5] For every member of the nobility and gentry was fostering the career of at least one cleric, whether he was a younger son just coming down from Cambridge, or their chaplain, or a poor relation, or the tutor of their children, or their pamphleteer, or their old headmaster.

---

[1] N. Sykes, *Church and State in England in the 18th Century* (Cambridge, 1934), pp. 34–5.
[2] H.M.C. Egmont, *Diary of the First Lord Egmont* (1923), vol. I, p. 153.
[3] Add. MSS. 32688, f. 135.
[4] H.M.C., *Carlisle* (1897), p. 83.
[5] K. Thomson, *Memoirs of Viscountess Sundon* (1847), vol. II, p. 9.

And bishops, cathedral chapters and landed proprietors, and ministers like Newcastle, were constantly inundated with requests for clerical appointments, usually sent in when the present holders had only just taken to their sick-beds (223); and the delicate task of adjusting all these claims, of showing just the right amount of favouritism here, of administering just the correct portion of punishment there, often drove Newcastle to despair, especially when, as was usually the case, the whole business was bedevilled by the personal predilections of the monarch (215, 224).

Thus a procedure of preferment was adopted which, as Gibson described it in his day, brought 'the body of the clergy and the two Universities, at least to be easy under a Whig Administration',[1] and which kept their lay patrons toeing the line also. While such a system reduced the temperature of religious animosity, it naturally failed to act as a tonic on the general health of the Church. 'A religious langour fell over England',[2] producing increasing tolerance, it is true, but also all the vices associated with patronage: 'pluralities, non-residence, the neglect of their cures, the irregularities in the lives of the Clergy, which were too visible'.[3] Owing to their attendance in the House of Lords, for example, and owing to the difficulties of travel at that time, the bishops spent most of the year in London (225). Though there was certainly nothing new in this—bishops had always played their part in affairs of state—nevertheless, conscientious churchmen as many of them were, they could not avoid letting the supervision of their see take second place. Of the three basic responsibilities of the episcopacy, ordination presented the least problem, for if the candidates could not be ordained during the bishop's summer residence in his diocese, they could go up to London, or by means of Letters Dimissory be ordained by a neighbouring bishop. The other two duties, visitation of the clergy and confirmation of the laity, were usually carried out together during the summer residence every third year: and, given the shortness of the time, the size of the dioceses, the difficulties of transport, and the age and infirmities of some of the bishops,[4] even the utmost zeal (and there was no lack of it (226)) could not have produced a performance satisfactory in our eyes; though, as Sykes points out, 'in respect of numbers confirmed and the frequency of confirmation circuits, the Hanoverian Church may challenge comparison with any century of its predecessors'.[5] (227). Similar remarks could be made about the lower clergy in the performance of their duties: for example, the celebration of Holy Communion (228). However, if most of the clergy were content to conform

---

[1] Quoted by N. Sykes, *Edmund Gibson*, p. 408.

[2] W. E. H. Lecky, *History of England* (1925), vol. I, p. 363.

[3] G. Burnet, *History of His Own Time* (Edinburgh, 1753), vol. v, p. 198.

[4] Hoadly's lameness, for example, forced him to preach on his knees, walk with crutches, and ride only in a chaise.

[5] N. Sykes, *Church and State*, p. 132 (on whose researches I have leaned heavily in this chapter).

to the low standards of their age, 'there were in many country villages clergy-men of distinguished learning and piety, who were, as it were, buried alive among the vicious and the ignorant and in a manner excluded from all the comfort of social life'.[1] These carried out their duties assiduously like the Rev. William Cole (229). The historian has no means of calculating the effects of such a personal influence till it reaches the dimensions of the Evangelical movement of the later part of the century (241).

Political activity was not the only cause of absenteeism, for pluralism also inevitably created this evil among the bishops and the middle ranks of the clergy. It was normal practice for bishops to hold other benefices *in commendam*—usually, among others, the deaneries and prebends of cathedral churches. The heavy expenses which bishops had to meet on first taking over their charges made such a recourse inevitable, at least to tide them over the first year or so; and in the case of the poor bishoprics the *commendams* had to be permanent. From 1768 to 1782, for example, Newton held the deanery of St Paul's (worth about £2,000 a year) along with the see of Bristol (worth about £450 a year) (225). The holder of another 'little bishopric', Watson of Llandaff (worth about £450 a year), required a number of other benefices to make his life an economic proposition (230); and Sykes calculates that, out of his thirty-four years' tenure of that wild bishopric, Watson spent twenty-five in residence on the shores of Lake Windermere.[2]

Episcopal pluralists were only a fraction of the total number of clergy holding more than one benefice. The law as it stood till the reforms of the eighteen-thirties was based on the Statute of 1529[3] and the Canons of 1604. While it forbade the holding together of two incompatible benefices (i.e. those having the cure of souls), it allowed a whole army of exceptions. For example, spiritual members of the king's council were allowed three incompatible benefices; the king's chaplains an unlimited number; the chaplains of the royal family and of the spiritual and temporal nobility two each. And the size of this breach is better appreciated when it is noted that archbishops and dukes were allowed six chaplains each, marquesses and earls five each, and so on down the scale. Other exceptions were the brothers and sons of temporal lords, all doctors and bachelors of divinity, doctors of law and bachelors of canon law of the British universities whose degrees were not of grace—all of whom were allowed to hold two benefices in plurality. Add to this the provision in the Act of Henry VIII that 'no deanery, archdeaconry, chancellorship, treasureship, chantership, or prebend in any cathedral or collegiate church, nor parsonage that had a vicar endowed, nor any benefice perpetually appropriate' was to be interpreted as

---

[1] *The Contempt of the Clergy Considered* (1739), quoted by N. Sykes, *Edmund Gibson*, p. 212.
[2] *Church and State*, p. 377.　　　　　　　[3] 21 Hen. VIII, c. 13.

having the cure of souls, and the total amount of pluralism can be seen in its proper dimensions.[1] It represented an enormous fund out of which the nobility and gentry provided for their relations and dependants (215, 223, 224, 231). And this is the sector of the Church which fostered the fashionable and political clergy so much decried by contemporary reformers and later critics. These were the clergy who cast their eyes upwards—towards the leaders of society—and not only encouraged the 'trifling manners' of the upper classes (232), but also were incapable of preventing the spread of 'enthusiasm' among the lower (233). These were the parsons who regarded their livings as sinecures, who drew the income and paid curates a small stipend to perform the duties—thus creating one of the greatest scandals of the time, the mass of poor clergy (234). As one of the great lay supporters of the Evangelical revival, William Wilberforce, expressed it in the House of Commons in 1806, 'What would be said if a captain of a man of war should receive all the salary and emoluments belonging to the ship, and, living upon shore, should appoint a deputy to perform the duties of the ship, at a very low salary?'[2]; and he was not the only reformer who addressed himself to this problem in the early nineteenth century (235).

Another defect which received the attention of reformers was the lack of churches in over-populated areas. The Church was one of the many institutions of the Age of Reason which needed rationalisation. Like parliamentary constituencies and municipal boroughs, parish churches were not distributed in accordance with the needs of an age being rapidly transformed by economic and demographic change (236). As a bishop of London put it, 'the fluctuations in manufactures and commerce . . . have had the effect of transferring large masses of the people from districts well-planted with churches to places altogether unprovided with the means of religious worship'.[3] While there were legal difficulties about erecting new Anglican churches in existing parishes, the Nonconformists had no such obstacle; and thus, as the Earl of Harrowby told the Lords in 1810, 'the inhabitants might prefer the church of England, but that church shut her doors against them' (236).

And they were the same people against whom the existing structure of society also shut its doors: the products of the Industrial Revolution. And it was at these that the Wesleys (237) and George Whitefield (238) aimed their sermons, earning, not unnaturally, the criticism of the official Church (239). Constrained to evangelise outside the parochial structure of the Church of England, and destined later to secede from it, the Methodists also contracted out of the intellectual temper of Latitudinarianism, the code of churchmanship prevalent in this period. In reaction against the sectarian

---

[1] See Sykes, *Church and State*, chap. 4, for a full explanation of this subject.
[2] *P.D.*, VI, 924.
[3] W. Howley, Bishop of London, *Charge Delivered to the Clergy of London* (1818), p. 16.

animosities of the previous period, and under the influence of the philosophical consequences of the scientific revolution, the typical men of latitude frowned upon religious enthusiasm. Christianity for them was plain and simple. The rational nature of the Supreme Being could be deduced from the rule of law in nature around them. God was the Father of all mankind, and it was the chief duty of His children to behave with brotherly affection towards one another. Forms of church government and ceremonial worship were unimportant compared with the ethical principles common to all who believed in Christianity, which were the simple duties that all men living in society owed their fellow men. 'If keeping the seventh day holy were only a human institution,' wrote Addison in *The Spectator*, in 1711, 'it would be the best method that could have been thought of for the polishing and civilising of mankind';[1] and this view is developed in a homely manner by the late-seventeenth-century divine, Tillotson, whose sermons were best-sellers in the eighteenth century (240). But to the Methodists and the Evangelicals (241), the church prudent was cold and prosaic, all of a piece with absentee sinecurists and political bishops. The latter set their face against the Evangelical revival (242), and against all proposals for church reform. Accompanied by the rest of the eighteenth-century institutions, and fortified by fears of the overthrow of all they held dear, both spiritually and materially, which were engendered in England by the French Revolution, they successfully delayed radical change till the period covered by these documents was over.

204. Anti-Catholic legislation, 1700.

An act for the further preventing the growth of popery.

Whereas there has beene of late a much greater Resort into this Kingdom than formerly of Popish Bishops Priests and Jesuits and they doe very openly and in insolent Manner affront the Laws and daily endeavour to pervert His Majesties naturall borne Subjects which has beene occasioned by Neglect of the due Execution of the Laws already in Force For preventing the further Growth of Popery and of such treasonable and execrable Designes and Conspiracies against His Majesties Person and Government and the Established Religion as have lately as well as frequently heretofore been brought to Light and happily defeated by the wonderfull Providence of God Be it enacted ... That ... all and every Person and Persons who shall apprehend and take One or more Popish Bishop Priest or Jesuite and prosecute him or them soe apprehended and taken untill he or they be convicted

---

[1] Quoted by Sykes, *Church and State*, p. 231.

of saying Mass or of exerciseing any other Part of the Office or Function of a Popish Bishop or Priest within these Realmes shall have and receive from the Sheriff or Sheriffs of the County where such Conviction shall be made (without paying any Fee for the same) for every such Offender soe convicted the Summe of One hundred Pounds . . .

III. And for a further Remedy against the Growth of Popery over and beyond the good Laws already made Be it further enacted by the Authority aforesaid That if any Popish Bishop Priest or Jesuit whatsoever shall say Masse or exercise any other Part of the Office or Function of a Popish Bishop or Priest within these Realmes or the Dominions thereunto belonging or if any Papist or Person makeing Profession of the Popish Religion shall keepe Schoole or take upon themselves the Education or Government or Boarding of Youth in any Place within this Realme or the Dominions thereto belonging and such Person or Persons being thereof lawfully convicted that then every such Person shall on such Conviction be adjudged to perpetuall Imprisonment in such Place or Places within this Kingdome as the King by Advice of His Privy Council shall appoint

IV. And be it alsoe further enacted . . . That . . . if any Person educated in the Popish Religion or professing the same shall not within Six Months after he or she shall attaine the Age of Eighteene Yeares take the Oaths of Allegiance and Supremacy and alsoe subscribe the Declaration sett downe and exprest in an Act of Parliament [30 Car. II, stat 2] . . . intituled An Act for the more effectuall preserveing the Kings Person and Government by disabling Papists from sitting in either House of Parliament to be by him or her made repeated and subscribed in the Courts of Chancery or Kings Bench or Quarter Sessions of the County where such Person shall reside every such Person shall in respect of him or herselfe only and not to or in respect of any of his or her Heires or Posterity be disabled and made incapable to inherit or take by Discent Devise or Limittation in Possession Reversion or Remainder any Lands Tenements or Hereditaments within this Kingdome of England Dominion of Wales or Towne of Berwick upon Tweed And that during the Life of such Person or untill he or she doe take the said Oaths and make repeate and subscribe the said Declaration in Manner as aforesaid the next of his or her Kindred which shall be a Protestant shall have and enjoy the said Lands Tenements and Hereditaments without being accountable for the Profitts by him or her received during such Enjoyment thereof as aforesaid but in case of any wilfull Wast ... the Party disabled his or her Executors and Administrators shall and may recover Treble Damages ... And every Papist or Person makeing Profession of the Popish Religion shall be disabled and is hereby made incapable to purchase either in his or her owne Name or in the Name of any Person or Persons to his or her Use or in Trust for him or her any Mannors Lands Profitts out of Lands Tenements Rents Termes or Hereditaments ...

V. Provided alwaies That nothing in this Act contained shall be construed to extend to any Popish Priest for saying Masse or officiating as a Priest within the Dwelling House of any Forreigne Minister residing here soe as such Priest be not one of His Majesties naturall borne Subjects nor naturalized within any of His Kingdomes or Dominions and soe as the Name of such Priest and the Place of his Birth and the Forreigne Minister to whom he shall belong be entred and registred in the Office of the Principall Secretary of State.

VI. And whereas by an Act made in the Third Yeare of King James the First intituled An Act to prevent and avoid Dangers which may grow by Popish Recusants whosoever shall be convicted of sending or causing to be sent any Child or any other Person under their Government into Parts beyond the Seas out of the Kings Obedience to the Intent that such Child or Person soe sent should be educated in the Romish Religion contrary to the said Act is to forfeite One hundred Pounds One Halfe to the King's Majesty and the other Halfe to him that shall sue for the same For the greater Incouragement and Reward of those who shall discover such Offenders Be it enacted ... That the said Summe of One hundred Pounds shall be to the sole Use and Benefitt of him or her who shall discover and convict any Person soe offending ...

VII. And to the end that the Protestant Children of Popish Parents may not in the Life times of such their Parents for want of fitting Maintenance be necessitated in complyance with their Parents to imbrace the Popish Religion contrary to their Owne Inclinations Be it enacted ... That ... if any such Parent in order to the compelling such his or her Protestant Child to change his or her Religion shall refuse to allow such Child fitting Maintenance suitable to the Degree and Ability of such Parent and to the Age and Education of such Child then upon Complaint thereof made to the Lord High Chancellor of England or Lord Keeper of the Great Seale or Commissioners for the Great Seale for the Time being It shall be lawfull for the said Lord Chancellor Lord Keeper or Commissioners to make such Order therein as shall be agreeable to the Intent of this Act.

11 Will. III, c. 4: S.R., VII, 586.

205. Occasional Conformity Act, 1711.

An act for preserving the protestant religion, by better securing the Church of England, as by law established; and for confirming the toleration granted to protestant dissenters by an act, intituled, An act for exempting their Majesties' protestant subjects, dissenting from the Church of England, from the penalties of certain laws, and for supplying the defects thereof; and for the further securing the protestant succession, by requiring the practisers of the law in North Britain to take the oaths, and subscribe the declaration therein mentioned.

I. Whereas an act was made in the thirteenth year of the reign of the late King Charles the Second [13 Car. II, St. 2. c. 1.] . . . and another act was made in the five and twentieth year of the reign of late King Charles the Second [25 Car. II, c. 2.] . . . both which acts were made for the security of the Church of England as by law established: Now for the better securing the said Church, and quieting the minds of her Majesty's protestant subjects dissenting from the Church of England, and rendering them secure in the exercise of their religious worship, as also for the further strengthening of the provision already made for the security of the succession to the crown in the House of Hanover. Be it enacted . . . That if any Person or Persons . . . either Peers or Commoners who have or shall have any office or offices Civil or Military or receive any Pay, Salary, Fee or Wages by reason of any Patent or grant from or under Her Majesty or any of Her Majesty's Predecessors or of Her Heirs or Successors . . . or if any Mayor, Alderman, Recorder, Bailiff, Town Clerk, Common Council Man or other Person bearing any office of Magistracy . . . who by the said recited acts . . . are obliged to receive the Sacrament of the Lord's Supper according to the rites and usage of the Church of England . . . shall at any time after their Admission into their respective offices . . . knowingly or willingly resort to or be present at any Conventicle, Assembly or Meeting . . . for the exercise of Religion in other Manner

than according to the Liturgy and Practice of the Church of England
... shall forfeit Forty Pounds to be recovered by Him or them that
shall sue for the same ... in any of her Majesty's Courts. ...

II. And be it further enacted That every Person convicted ... shall
be disabled from thenceforth to hold such office ... and shall be
adjudged incapable to bear any office or employment whatsoever. ...

III. Provided always and be it further enacted ... That if any Person
... who shall have been convicted ... shall after such Conviction
conform to the Church of England for the space of one year without
having been present at any Conventicle, Assembly or Meeting ... and
receive the Sacrament of the Lord's Supper according to the Rites
and Usage of the Church of England at least Three Times in the year
every such Person shall be capable of the grant of any the offices or
employments aforesaid.

[IV. Such persons conforming to make oath of Conformity and that
he has received the Sacrament.]

[V. Limits Prosecution to three months.]

[VI. Exempts offices of Inheritance from being made void, but requires a non-conforming Holder to appoint a Deputy.]

VII. And it is hereby further enacted ... That the toleration granted to
the protestant dissenters, by the act made in the first year of the reign
of King William and Queen Mary[1] ... shall be, and is hereby ratified
and confirmed, and that the same act shall at all times be inviolably
observed for the exempting of such protestant dissenters as are thereby
intended, from the pains and penalties therein mentioned.

VIII. And for rendering the said last-mentioned act more effectual
according to the true intent and meaning thereof; Be it further enacted
... That if any person dissenting from the Church of England, (not in
holy orders, or pretended holy orders, or pretending to holy orders,
nor any preacher or teacher of any congregation) who should have
been entitled to the benefit of the said last-mentioned act, if such
person had duly taken, made, and subscribed the oaths and declaration, or otherwise qualified him or herself as required by the said act,
and now is or shall be prosecuted upon or by virtue of any of the penal
statutes, from which protestant dissenters are exempted by the said

[1] No. 15.

act, shall at any time during such prosecution, take, make, and subscribe the said oaths and declaration, or being of the people called
Quakers, shall make and subscribe the aforesaid declaration, and also
the declaration of fidelity, and subscribe the profession of their christian
belief, according to the said act, or before any two of her Majesty's
justices of the peace, (who are hereby required to take and return the
same to the next quarter sessions of the peace, to be there recorded)
such person . . . is hereby entitled to the benefit of the said act, and
shall be thenceforth exempted . . . from all the penalties and forfeitures
incurred by force of any of the aforesaid penal statutes.

IX. And whereas it is or may be doubted whether a preacher or teacher
of any congregation of dissenting protestants, duly in all respects
qualified according to the said act, be allowed, . . . to officiate in any
congregation in any county, other than that in which he so qualified
himself, although in a congregation or place of meeting duly certified
and registered as is required by the said act; Be it . . . enacted . . .
That any such preacher or teacher, so duly qualified . . . is hereby
allowed to officiate in any congregation although the same be not in
the county wherein he was so qualified; provided that the said congregation, or place of meeting, hath been before such officiating duly
. . . registered . . . and such preacher or teacher shall, if required,
produce a certificate of his having so qualified himself, under the hand
of the clerk of the peace for the county or place where he so qualified
himself, which certificate such clerk of the peace is hereby required to
make; and shall also before any justice of the peace of such county or
place where he shall so officiate, make and subscribe such declaration,
and take such oaths as are mentioned . . . if thereunto required.

X. And be it further enacted . . . That on or before the fifteenth day
of June next, all advocates, writers to the signet, notaries public, and
other members of the college of Justice, within . . . Scotland, . . . are
hereby obliged to take and subscribe the oath appointed by the act
of the sixth year of her Majesty's reign [6 Anne, c. 14] . . . before the
lords of session of the aforesaid part of her Majesty's kingdom; except
such of the said persons who have already taken the same: And if any
of the persons aforesaid do . . . refuse to take and subscribe the said
oath, as aforesaid, such persons shall be *ipso facto* adjudged . . . disabled
in law to . . . exercise in any manner his said employment or practice.

XI. And be it further enacted . . . That in all time coming no person

. . . shall be admitted to the employment of advocate, writer to the signet, notary public, or any office belonging to the said college of Justice, until he . . . have taken and subscribed the aforesaid oath, in manner as is above directed.

10 Anne, c. 6: *S.R.*, IX, 551.

206. Schism Act, 1714.

An Act to prevent the growth of schism, and for the further security of the Churches of England and Ireland as by law, established.

Whereas by an act of parliament [13 and 14 Car. II, c. 4] . . . *and whereas notwithstanding the said act, sundry papists and other persons dissenting from the church of* England, *have taken upon them to instruct and teach youth as tutors or schoolmasters, and have for such purpose openly set up schools and seminaries, whereby, if due and speedy remedy be not had, great danger might ensue to this church and state: for the making the said recited act more effectual, and preventing the danger aforesaid, be it enacted* . . . That every person or persons who shall, . . . keep any public or private school or seminary, or teach and instruct any youth as tutor or schoolmaster, within that part of *Great Britain* called *England*, the dominion of *Wales*, or town of *Berwick* upon *Tweed*, before such person or persons shall have subscribed so much of the said declaration and acknowledgement, as is before recited, [in 13 and 14 Car. II, c. 4] and shall have had and obtained a licence from the respective archbishop, bishop, or ordinary of the place, under his seal of office (for which the party shall pay one shilling, and no more over and above the duties payable to Her Majesty for the same) and shall be thereof lawfully convicted, upon an information, presentment or indictment, in any of Her Majesty's courts of record at *Westminster*, or at the Assizes, or before justices of *Oyer* and *Terminer*, shall and may be committed to the common gaol . . . there to remain without bail or mainprize for the space of three months, to commence from the time that such person or persons shall be received into the said gaol.

II. Provided always, . . . That no licence shall be granted by any archbishop, bishop, or ordinary, unless the person or persons who shall sue for the same, shall produce a certificate of his or their having received the sacrament according to the usage of the Church of *England*, in some parish church, within the space of one year next before the grant of such licence, under the hand of the minister and one of the church-wardens of the said parish, nor until such person or persons shall have taken or subscribed the oaths of allegiance and supremacy,[1] and abjuration, as appointed by law, and shall have made and subscribed the declaration against transubstantiation, contained in the act [25 Car. II, c. 2.] . . . intituled, *An act for preventing dangers which may happen from popish recusants*, before the said archbishop, bishop or ordinary, which said oaths and declarations, the said archbishop, bishop or ordinary, are hereby empowered to administer and receive; and such archbishops, bishops, and ordinaries, are required to file such certificates, and keep an exact register of the same . . .

III. And be it further enacted . . . That any person who shall have obtained a licence . . . and subscribed the oaths, as above appointed, and shall at any time after, during the time of his or their keeping any public or private school or seminary, or instructing any youth as tutor or schoolmaster, knowingly or willingly, resort to, . . . any conventicle, . . . within *England*, *Wales*, or town of *Berwick* upon *Tweed*, for the exercise of religion in any other manner than according to the liturgy and practice of the Church of *England*, or shall . . . be present at any meeting . . . although the liturgy be there used, where Her Majesty (whom God long preserve) and the Elector of *Brunswick*, . . . shall not there be prayed for in express words, according to the liturgy of the Church of *England*, except where such particular offices of the liturgy are used, wherein there are no express directions to pray for Her Majesty and the royal family, shall . . . thenceforth be incapable of keeping any public or private school or seminary, or instructing any youth as tutor or schoolmaster.

IV. And be it further enacted . . . That if any person licenced, as aforesaid, shall teach any other catechism than the catechism set forth in the book of common prayer, the licence of such person shall from thenceforth be void, and such person shall be liable to the penalties of this act.

V. And be it further enacted . . . That it shall . . . be lawful, to and for the bishop of the diocese, or other proper ordinary, to cite any person or persons whatsoever, keeping school or seminary, or teaching without a licence, as aforesaid, and to proceed against, and punish such person or persons by ecclesiastical censure, subject to such appeals as in

[1] See No. **10**, pp. 29–30.

cases of ordinary jurisdiction; this act or any other law to the contrary notwithstanding.

VI. Provided always, that no person offending against this act, shall be punished twice for the same offence.

VII. [No second prosecution shall be made while a former is depending.]

VIII. Provided always, That this act, . . . shall not extend, . . . to any tutor teaching or instructing youth in any college or hall, within either of the universities of . . . *England*, nor to any tutor who shall be employed by any nobleman or noblewoman, to teach his or her own children, grand-children or great-grand-children only, in his or her family; provided such tutor, . . . do in every respect qualify himself according to this act, except only in that of taking a licence from the bishop.

IX. Provided also, That the penalties in this act shall not extend to any foreigner, or alien of the foreign reformed churches, allowed, . . . by the Queen's Majesty, her heirs or successors, in *England*, for instructing or teaching any child or children of any such foreigner or alien only, as a tutor or schoolmaster.

X. Provided always, . . . That if any person who shall have been convicted, as aforesaid, . . . shall, after such conviction, conform to the Church of *England*, for the space of one year, . . . and receive the sacrament of the Lord's Supper according to the rites and usage of the Church of *England* at least three times in that year, every such person or persons shall be again capable of having and using a licence to teach school, or to instruct youth as a tutor or schoolmaster, her or they also performing all that is made requisite thereunto by this act.

XI. [Persons conforming after conviction, to make oath of their having conformed.]

XII. Provided always, That this act shall not extend, . . . to any person, who as a tutor, or schoolmaster, shall instruct youth in reading, writing, arithmetic, or any part of mathematical learning only, so far as such mathematical learning relates to navigation, or any mechanical art only, and so far as such reading, writing, arithmetic or mathematical learning shall be taught in the *English* tongue only.

XIII. . . . Be it therefore enacted . . . That all . . . the remedies, provisions, and clauses, in and by this act . . . shall attend . . . to *Ireland*, in as full and effectual manner, as if *Ireland* had been expressly named and mentioned in all and every the clauses in this act.

13 Anne, c. 7: S.R., IX, 915.

207. Lax administration of Penal Laws, 1710.

June 22, 1710

ACCOUNT OF THE STATE IN WHICH THE ROMAN CATHOLICS EXIST AT PRESENT IN REGARD TO THE EXERCISE OF THEIR RELIGION IN THESE THREE KINGDOMS OF ENGLAND, SCOTLAND, AND IRELAND.

Regarding the First.

Every one knows very well the many and rigorous laws, which, from the time of Queen Elizabeth to the present, have always been passed by the Parliaments of this Kingdom against the Roman Catholics, and that all of them are in force; and thus it only remains to discover if the Government carries them out.

But this is certain, that out of all of them only two are in use, that is the one making the Catholics pay double Taxes, and the one which prevents them from taking Civil or Military offices without taking the oaths, which are contrary to the Religion they profess. But as regards the exercise of their religion itself, they enjoy complete freedom, since without any fear or inconvenience they go to make their devotions in the Chapels of the Ministers of the Catholic Princes; and there is no person of distinction who wishes and is able to keep a Chaplain, either in the City or in their Country Houses, who does not keep one, without the Government making any inquiry about it, unless it is for other different reasons.

It is true, however, that at the time of the last trouble that took place in this Court between the Anglicans and the Presbyterians on account of Doctor Sacheverel's Sermon, Parliament, in which the latter have a majority, made a proposal to Her Britannic Majesty, to secure themselves against all those who do not take the two oaths, and who are called Non-jurors, that is the oath of Fidelity to the present Government, and the oath of Abjuration of the Prince of Wales, in such a way that, since the Catholics were amongst this number on account of firmly refusing principally the second (of which we shall speak in more detail below), although they had not taken part in the

340

Cause for which Parliament was setting up such careful arrangements, the Queen could not except them from the Proclamation, by which she ordered the execution of the penal laws against all Non-jurors, when for the same reason all were suspected of being ill-affected. With all this, the Minister of the Emperor, and the Minister of His Majesty of Portugal soon made an appeal to the ministers of this Court, although they knew well that the Queen's Proclamation was directed not so much against the Catholics as against the Anglican Non-jurors, and of that they were assured by the Secretaries of State, but that at the same time no distinction could be made between former and the latter; but that from this no great prejudice would result against them. As in fact it happened, because not even a single one left London, and only a few, and these were of low estate, were called to take these oaths, without any other purpose than to make them pay forty Shillings, which is the penalty for those who refuse for the first time. So that a week later no one talked any more about these matters, or persecution, if it can be called that. . . .

As a proof that the spirit of persecuting Catholics does not rule here, it is enough to say that, four miles from London, in a very public and frequented place, a kind of Convent of Nuns maintains itself with its own Church and Chaplain, where likewise are boarded many Girls having their education, without any obstacle from the government, although it is known to them and to everybody. In the Baths, where so many people from the other Provinces assemble, a Benedictine monk has resided for many years, who keeps what is like a public chapel for the Catholics of the City, and for the others, who go over there to use the medicinal properties of those waters, without there being anyone to worry them. . . .

P.R.O. 31/9/101 (with covering letter from D. Luigi da Cugna to Em. Sig. Card. Paolucci). Translated from the Italian by the Editor.

208. Indemnity Act, 1727.

An Act for indemnifying Persons, who have omitted to qualify themselves for Offices and Imployments, within the time limited by Law, and for allowing further time for that purpose; and for repealing so much of Two Acts of Parliament therein mentioned, as requires Persons to qualify themselves to continue in Offices or Imployments for the space of Six Months, after the Demise of His Majesty, His Heirs, or Successors.

Whereas divers Persons, who, on Account of their Offices, Places, Imployments, or Professions, or any other Cause or Occasion, ought to have taken and subscribed the Oaths, or the Assurance respectively appointed to be taken by such Persons, in and by an Act made in the First Year of the Reign of His late Majesty King George the first, of Glorious Memory [intituled, *An Act for the further security of His Majesty's Person and Government, and the Succession of the Crown in the Heirs of the late Princess Sophia, being Protestants, and for extinguishing the Hopes of the Pretended Prince of Wales, and his open and secret Abettors*] or to have qualified themselves according to an Act made in the Twenty fifth Year of the Reign of King Charles the Second [intituled, *An Act for preventing Dangers which may happen from Popish Recusants*] by receiving the Sacrament of the Lord's Supper, according to the usage of the Church of England, and making and subscribing the Declaration against Transubstantiation therein mentioned, have through ignorance of the Law, absence, or some unavoidable Accident, omitted to take and subscribe the said Oaths of Assurance, or otherwise to qualify themselves, as aforesaid, within such time, and in such manner, as in and by the said Acts respectively, or by any other Act of Parliament in that behalf made and provided, is required, whereby they may be in danger of incurring divers Penalties and Disabilities: For quieting the Minds of His Majesty's Subjects, and for preventing any Inconveniences, that might otherwise happen by means of such Omissions, Be it enacted . . . That all and every Person and Persons, who shall, on or before the Twenty eighth Day of *November*, in the year of our Lord, One Thousand seven hundred and twenty eight, take and subscribe the said Oaths and Assurance respectively . . . and also receive the Sacrament of the Lord's Supper, according to the Usage of the Church of England, and make and subscribe the said Declaration against Transubstantiation . . . shall be, and are hereby indemnified, freed, and discharged of, from and against all Penalties, Forfeitures, Incapacities, and Disabilities incurred, or to be incurred, for or by reason of any former Neglect or Omission of taking or subscribing the said Oaths or Assurance, or receiving the said Sacrament, or making and subscribing the said Declaration respectively . . .

. . . Provided always, that this Act, or any thing herein contained, shall not extend, or be construed to extend, to restore or entitle any Person or Persons to any Office, Imployment, Benefice, Matter, or Thing whatsoever, already actually avoided by Judgment of any of

His Majesty's Courts of Record or already filled up or enjoyed by another Person, but that such Office, Imployment, Benefice, Matter, or Thing so avoided, or filled up, or enjoyed as aforesaid, shall be and remain in and unto the Person or Persons, who is or are now entitled by Law to the same, as if this Act had never been made.

1 Geo. II, c. 23: *Public General Acts*, XXXIX, 659.

209. Catholic Relief Act, 1778.

An act for relieving his Majesty's subjects professing the popish religion from certain penalties and disabilities imposed on them by an act, made in the eleventh and twelfth years of the reign of King William *the Third, intituled,* An Act for the further preventing the growth of popery.[1]

Whereas it is expedient to repeal certain provisions in an act of the eleventh and twelfth years of the reign of King William *the Third, intituled* An act for the further preventing the growth of popery, *whereby certain penalties and disabilities are imposed on persons professing the popish religion;* . . . be it enacted; . . . That so much of the said act as relates to the apprehending, taking, or prosecuting, of popish bishops, priests, or jesuits; and also so much of the said acts as subjects popish bishops, priests, or jesuits, and papists, or persons professing the popish religion, and keeping school, or taking upon themselves the education or government or boarding of youth, within this realm, or the dominions thereto belonging, to perpetual imprisonment; and also so much of the said act as disables persons educated in the popish religion, or professing the same, under the circumstances therein mentioned, to inherit or take by descent, devise, or limitation in possession, reversion, or remainder, any lands, tenements, or hereditaments, within the Kingdom of *England*, dominion of *Wales*, and town of *Berwick upon Tweed*, and gives to the next of kin, being a protestant, a right to have and enjoy such lands [etc.] . . .; and also so much of the said act as disables papists, or persons professing the popish religion, to purchase any manors, lands, profits out of lands, tenements, rents, terms, or hereditaments, within the Kingdom of *England* [etc] . . . and makes void all and singular estates, terms, and other interests or profits whatsoever out of lands, to be made, suffered, or done, from and after the day therein mentioned, to or for the use or behoof of any such person or persons, or upon any trust or confidence, mediately or immediately,

[1] No. 204.

343

for the relief of any such person or persons; shall be, and the same, and every clause and matter and thing herein-before mentioned, is and are hereby repealed.

. . .

IV. Provided also, That nothing herein contained shall extend, or be construed to extend, to any person or persons, but such who shall, within the space of six calendar months after the passing of this act, or of accruing of his, her, or their title, being of the age of twenty-one years, or who, being under the age of twenty-one years, shall, within six months after he or she shall attain the age of twenty-one years, or being of unsound mind, or in prison, or beyond the seas, then within six months after such disability removed, take and subscribe an oath in the words following:

I, A. B. do sincerely promise and swear, That I will be faithful and bear true allegiance to his majesty King George the Third, and him will defend, to the utmost of my power, against all conspiracies and attempts whatever that shall be made against his person, crown, or dignity; and I will do my utmost endeavour to disclose and make known to his Majesty, his heirs and successors, all treasons and traitorous conspiracies which may be formed against him or them; and I do faithfully promise to maintain, support, and defend, to the utmost of my power, the succession of the crown in his Majesty's family, against any person or persons whatsoever; hereby utterly renouncing and abjuring any obedience or allegiance unto the person taking upon himself the stile and title of Prince of Wales, in the life time of his father, and who, since his death, is said to have assumed the stile and title of King of Britain, by the name of Charles the Third, and to any other person claiming or pretending a right to the crown of these realms; and I do swear, that I do reject and detest, as an unchristian and impious position, That it is lawful to murder or destroy any person or persons whatsoever, for or under pretence of their being hereticks; and also that unchristian and impious principle, that no faith is to be kept with hereticks: I further declare, that it is no article of my faith, and that I do renounce, reject, and abjure, the opinion, that princes excommunicated by the pope and council, or by any authority of the see of Rome or by any authority whatsoever, may be deposed or murdered by their subjects, or any person whatsoever: and I do declare, that I do not believe that the pope of Rome, or any other foreign prince, prelate, state, or potentate, hath, or ought to have, any temporal or civil jurisdiction, power, superiority, or pre-eminence, directly or indirectly, within this realm. And I do solemnly, in the presence of God, profess, testify, and declare, that I do make this declaration, and every part thereof, in the plain and ordinary sense of the words of this oath; without any evasion, equivocation, or mental reservation whatever, and without any dispensation already granted by the pope, or any authority of the see of Rome, or any person whatever; and without thinking that I am or can be acquitted before God or man, or absolved of this declaration, or any part thereof, although the pope, or any other persons or authority whatsoever, shall dispense with or annul the same, or declare that it was null or void.

V. Provided always, . . . That nothing in this act contained shall extend, or be construed to extend, to any popish bishop, priest, jesuit, or schoolmaster, who shall not have taken and subscribed the above oath in the above words before he shall have been apprehended or any prosecution commenced against him.

18 Geo. III, c. 60: *S.L.*, XXXII, 152.

210. Dissenters' Relief Act, 1779.

An Act for the further Relief of Protestant Dissenting Ministers and Schoolmasters.

Whereas, by an Act[1] made in the first Year of the Reign of King William and Queen Mary . . . Persons dissenting from the Church of England, in holy Orders, or pretended holy Orders, or pretending to holy Orders, and Preachers or Teachers of any Congregation of Dissenting Protestants, are required, in order to be intitled to certain Exemptions, Benefits, Privileges, and Advantages, to declare their Approbation of, and to subscribe, the Articles of Religion mentioned in the Statute made in the thirteenth Year of the Reign of Queen Elizabeth (except as in the said Act, made in the first Year of the Reign of King William and Queen Mary, is excepted): And whereas many such Persons scruple to declare their Approbation of, and to subscribe the said Articles not excepted as aforesaid: For giving Ease to such scrupulous Persons in the Exercise of Religion, may it please your Majesty that it may be enacted; and be it enacted . . ., That every Person dissenting from the Church of *England*, and in holy Orders, or pretended holy Orders, or pretending to holy Orders, being a Preacher or Teacher of any Congregation of dissenting Protestants, who, if he scruple to declare and subscribe as aforesaid, shall take the Oaths, and make and

[1] Toleration Act. See No. **15**.

345

subscribe the Declaration against Popery, required by the said Act, in the first Year of the Reign of King *William* and Queen *Mary*, to be taken, made, and subscribed by Protestant Dissenting Ministers, and shall also make and subscribe a Declaration in the Words following; *videlicet,*

I A. B. do solemnly declare, in the Presence of Almighty God, that I am a Christian and a Protestant, and as such, that I believe that the Scriptures of the Old and New Testament, as commonly received among Protestant Churches, do contain the revealed Will of God; and that I do receive the same as the Rule of my Doctrine and Practice.

shall be and every such Person is hereby declared to be, intitled to all the Exemptions, Benefits, Privileges, and Advantages, granted to Protestant Dissenting Ministers by the said Act, made in the first Year of the Reign of King *William* and Queen *Mary*; by an Act[1] . . . and every such person, qualifying himself as aforesaid, shall be exempted from serving in the Militia of this Kingdom, and shall also be exempted from any Imprisonment, or other Punishment, by virtue of an Act [the Act of Uniformity] . . . for preaching or officiating in any Congregation of Protestant Dissenters, for the Exercise of Religion permitted and allowed by Law.

II. And be it further enacted by the Authority aforesaid, That no Dissenting Minister, nor any other Protestant dissenting from the Church of *England,* who shall take the aforesaid Oaths, and make and subscribe the above-mentioned Declaration against Popery, and the Declaration herein-before mentioned, shall be prosecuted in any Court whatsoever, for teaching and instructing Youth as a Tutor or Schoolmaster; any Law or Statute to the contrary notwithstanding.

III. Provided always, That nothing in this Act contained shall extend, or be construed to extend, to the enabling of any Person dissenting from the Church of *England* to obtain or hold the Mastership of any College or School of Royal Foundation, or of any other endowed College or School for the Education of Youth, unless the same shall have been founded since the first Year of the Reign of their late Majesties King *William* and Queen *Mary*, for the immediate Use and Benefit of Protestant Dissenters.

. . .

19 Geo. III, c. 44: *S.L.*, XXXII, 258.

[1] Occasional Conformity Act, See No. 205.

211. George III and Catholic emancipation, 1795.

GEORGE III TO THE LORD KENYON

Queen's House, March 7th, 1795.

... The following queries on the present attempt to abolish all distinctions in Religion in Ireland, with the intention of favouring the Roman Catholics in that Kingdom, are stated from the desire of learning whether this can be done, without affecting the Constitution of this Country; if not, there is no occasion to view whether this measure in itself be not highly improper.

The only laws which now affect the Papists in Ireland are the Acts of Supremacy and Uniformity, the Test Act, and the Bill of Rights. It seems to require very serious investigation how far the King can give His assent to a Repeal of any one of those Acts, without a breach of His Coronation Oath,[1] and of the Articles of Union with Scotland.

The construction put on the Coronation Oath by the Parliament at the Revolution seems strongly marked in the Journals of the House of Commons, when the Clause was proposed by way of Rider to the Bill establishing the Coronation Oath, declaring that nothing contained in it should be construed to bind down the King and Queen, their Heirs and Successors, not to give the Royal Assent to any Bill for qualifying the Act of Uniformity so far as to render it palatable to Protestant Dissenters, and the Clause was negatived upon a division. This leads to the implication that the Coronation Oath was understood at the Revolution to bind the Crown not to assent to any Repeal of any of the existing Laws at the Revolution, or which were then enacted, for the maintenance and defence of the Protestant Religion as by Law established.

If the Oath was understood to bind the Crown not to assent to the Repeal of the Act of Uniformity in favour of Protestant Dissenters, it would seem to bind the Crown full as strongly not to assent to the Repeal of the Act of Supremacy, or the Test Act, in favour of Roman Catholics.

Another question arises from the provisions of the Act limiting the Succession to the Crown, by which a forfeiture of the Crown is expressly enacted, if the King upon the Throne should hold communication, or be reconciled to the Church of Rome. May not the

---

[1] No. 13.

Repeal of the Act of Supremacy and the establishing the Popish Religion in any of the Hereditary Dominions, be construed as amounting to a reconciliation with the Church of Rome?

Would not the Chancellor of England incur some risk in affixing the Great Seal to a Bill for giving the Pope a concurrent Ecclesiastical Jurisdiction with the King?

. . .

H. Phillpotts (ed.), *Letters from His late Majesty to the late Lord Kenyon on the Coronation Oath etc.* (1827), p. 5.

212. Values of Church dignities, 1762.

A List of the Archbishops, Bishops, Deans, and Prebendaries. In England and Wales, in His Majesty's Gift. With the reputed Yearly Value, of Their respective Dignities. 1762.

ARCHBISHOP OF CANTERBURY

Doctor Thomas Secker
Value of the See

£
7000 a Year

DEAN OF CANTERBURY

Doctor William Friend
Value of the Deanry

£
900 a Year

There are Nine Prebends in the Cathedral of Canterbury, in His Majesty's Gift, and Three in the Archbishop of Canterbury.

. . .

Value of Each 350 £ a Year.

ARCHBISHOP OF YORK

Honble Dr. Robert Drummond.
Value of the See

£
4500 a Year.

DEAN OF YORK

Dr. John Fountain   £
Value of the Deanry   600 a Year

The Prebends in the Cathedral Church of York, and also the Prebends in the Cathedral Church of Southwell in the Diocese of York, are all in the Gift of the Archbishop of York.

. . .

BISHOP OF BRISTOL

Dr. Thomas Newton   £
Value of the See   450 a Year.

The Bishop holds in COMMENDAM the Residentiary of St. Pauls worth £800 a Year, & the Rectory of Bow worth £300 a Year.

. . .

BISHOP OF LONDON

Dr. Richard Osbaldeston
Dean of His Majesty's Chapel Royal   £
Value of the See   4000 a Year.

DEAN OF ST PAUL'S

Dr Frederick Cornwallis Lord Bishop of Lichfield & Coventry.
Value of the Deanry   1800 a Year.

Residentiaries of St. Paul's are

Dr Wilson, Dr Newton Lord Bishop of Bristol, and Dr Secker
Value of the Residentiaries   800 a Year.

. . .

BISHOP OF OXFORD

Dr John Hume
Value of the See   £
500 a Year

His Lordship holds in Commendam the Deanry of St Paul's,
worth   1800 a Year (sic)

DEAN OF OXFORD

Dr David Gregory
Value of the Deanry   900 a Year

THE CANONS OF CHRIST CHURCH, ARE,

Dr Philip Barton, Dr John Nicholl
Dr Edwd Bentham, Dr John Tottie   Value 400 a Year.
Dr Danl Burton, Honble S. —— Barrington

There are two Other Canonries in this Church, One is annexed to
the King's Professor in Divinity in Oxford; the other to the King's
Hebrew Professor In Oxford.

UNIVERSITY OF OXFORD
Professors

King's Professor of Physic   £
  Dr Kelly   200 a Year
King's Professor of Civil Law
  Dr Jenner   100 a Year
King's Professor of Modern History
  Mr Spence   300 a Year

. . . .

BISHOP OF LLANDAFF

Dr John Ewer, Canon of Windsor   £
Value of the See   500 a Year

. . .

213. Lord Cowper's advice to George I on ecclesiastical administration, 1714.

I have but one thing more humbly to represent to your Majesty, as the only, and, if I mistake not, a sure means to extinguish the being and the very name of party amongst us, that your Majesty would be pleased to use the utmost caution not to prefer any of those ecclesiastics whose known principles lead them to scruple the validity of a limitation of the right to the Crown by Act of parliament. There is sufficient number of the clergy of the Church of England, of the most learned and best livers, out of whom your Majesty may choose for all preferments that shall fall vacant, who are not the least tainted with those notions which, while they continue, will ever find matter for discontents and divisions in your Majesty's Kingdoms. But when once it is discerned that, by a steady and uninterrupted administration, no man who is known to hold opinions inconsistent with the very foundation of your Majesty's government can get into any of the Crown preferments in the Church, they who find themselves troubled with these inconvenient scruples will soon apply their thoughts and studies in good earnest to satisfy themselves, and then others, of the weakness of those errors, which will afterwards, in a little time, be confined to a few melancholy Non-jurors, who are the less dangerous for being known; and when the clergy are brought to be of one mind as to your Majesty's title, all differences in opinion among the laity on that head will soon vanish. But that part of the clergy who have always violently contended against excluding the next successor, though a Papist, will never own themselves to have been in the wrong while they find they have a fair chance for the best of the Church preferments without disavowing those errors, otherwise than by taking the oaths in form.

Lord Cowper, *An Impartial History of Parties* (1714), quoted in J. Campbell, *Lives of the Chancellors* (1846), vol. IV, p. 422.

214. Bishop Gibson's scheme for Church preferment, 1724.

PROMOTIONS BY DIOCESES.

Query. Considering the great number of ecclesiastical benefices which are in the gift of ye King, the Lord Chancellor and the Chancellor of the Duchy in all parts of England; how comes it to pass that in ye space of six and thirty years which have passed since the time of the Revolution, the clergy of England are not more attached to ye interest of ye Protestant succession and the Royal Family?

Answer. Because these promotions have not been so ordered and disposed of in such a way as to create a general dependence, and raise a general expectation among ye clergy; but have been bestowed uncertainly and as it were, by chance, and been understood to fall only to ye share of the favourites of particular persons in Power and Office; and by consequence have had no influence, nor raised any expectation, excepting in such favourites only. . . .

REMEDY.

A resolution to be taken and in a proper manner notified, that ye Parochial Livings in ye gift of the King, of the Lord Chancellor and of ye Chancellor of the Duchy, which are not given to Chaplains in Ordinary of ye King or to ye domestick chaplains of ye said Chancellors respectively, will be bestowed upon clergy officiating at ye time the vacancy happens, by virtue of institution or licence, within ye Diocese to which such benefice belongs; or to such persons in the two Universities as are natives of the Diocese and are in Holy Orders at ye time when ye vacancy happens.

RESULTS.

(1) This will make ye body of ye clergy of every diocese esteem all benefices of ye formentioned patronage which are within their dioceses, to be in effect their own property; and every one who thinks his condition may be bettered by any particular vacancy or vacancies in view, will have his eye upon them and put himself in proper methods to obtain them; whereas in ye present method of disposing of these favours, a benefice . . . raises no more expectation among ye clergy of ye diocese or even of the neighbourhood, where it lies, than if it were a hundred miles off and in any other diocese of England.

(2) The expectation being thus raised by vacancies in view, the clergy will take all proper methods to recommend themselves to such of ye nobility and gentry as are in ye interest of the government, and are known to have credit above; and the Bishops of the several dioceses who are now for the most part in the interest of the Government, and who will be consulted of course concerning ye characters and behaviour of ye clergy who shall be candidates, will be much more regarded by their clergy and have a greater influence over them in all

matters relating to ye service of ye Government. Especially ye young clergy, who either remain in ye Universities, or are come fresh from it to curacies, and have no preferment and who are generally most noisy against ye Government, will then become expectants of favour from the Crown upon ye prospect of particular vacancies in their eye. And as ye smaller benefices in ye gift of ye Seals are very numerous and dispersed all over the nation, and though small, are certain, and more desirable than curacies; this would undoubtedly create a great dependence upon ye Government as well among the younger clergy of every diocese, as among the natives thereof in ye two Universities. If it be said that care may be taken without any such limitation to particular dioceses, to bestow ye promotions of ye crown upon such persons only as are known to deserve well of ye Government, ye answer is; that it is not the bestowing the benefice when vacant from whence ye great benefit arises to ye Government, inasmuch as that is a favour only to one single person . . . but it is from ye raising a fixed and certain expectation of something directly and immediately within their view, to which the clergy of that diocese are particularly entitled; and from the regard that is paid them by ye Crown in appropriating the favours to them in particular and securing them against the inroads of foreign competitors. In order to keep up the expectations it seems to be a good rule, not to promise any benefice before it comes actually vacant. . . .

[This scheme was ordered to be put into operation by the King (6 May 1724) but was successfully opposed by the new Lord Chancellor *King* in the following year]

Quoted by N. Sykes, *Edmund Gibson* (Oxford, 1926), App. B, p. 399.

215. The Duke of Newcastle as 'Ecclesiastical Minister', 1754.

DUKE OF NEWCASTLE TO LORD HALIFAX

Newcastle House, Augt 18th, 1754

. . . I enter very fully into the Reasons, which may induce Your Lordship earnestly to wish the Promotion of Mr. Davis to a Prebend of Canterbury. I am sorry to find, Your Lordship will not as readily enter into the Difficulties, (not to say the Impossibility,) of my doing it at present. I should hope, however, from your Justice, & Candour, that when you have weigh'd what I shall here represent to you, your Lordship will no longer accuse me of Want of Friendship for you.

I honor, & esteem you, for your publick Qualities—I love you (If you will give me Leave to say so, & to do so,) for your private ones. But that Honor, & that Love, can't make me force the King to do what He may be disinclin'd to; or justify me, in breaking my Word to others, whom I may neither honor, or love, one quarter so much as I do you. Your Lordship is mistaken, if you think, I can do what I please. The King has His own Way of thinking, & acting, in the Disposal of Preferments, and particularly Ecclesiastical ones. It was from this Cause, that a great Number of Ecclesiastical Preferments were undispos'd of, for near Two Years. It was from His Maj$^{ty's}$ own Determination, that my Lord Chancellor could not obtain, to this Day, an Exchange only for His Friend, & Neighbour, Dr Barnard, of the City, (a most valuable, & Eminent Clergyman,) from a Prebend of Norwich to one of Windsor.

This is the Cause, with other Reasons, why Mr Carter, a most zealous Whig Clergyman, and Magistrate in Suffolk, espous'd by the Duke of Grafton, and Father in Law to the Earl of Rochford, Brother in Law to Mr Drake of the East India Company, & zealously insisted upon by Both; Has not, in upwards of Seven Years Sollicitation obtain'd a Prebend in the King's Gift. My Lord Bath has in vain sollicited also for a very meritorious, & able man, Dr Newton of the City. Had it been in my Power, I can assure Your Lordship that above Half, if not all, of the Persons abovemention'd, would have been provided for long before now. And yet Your Lordship is pleased to suppose it my Determination that the Duke of Dorset's Friend should succeed Dr Shuckford. If it is in my Power, It must be my Wish, or I should be the most false of all Men. When I was last at Hanover, there was a Vacancy of a Prebend of Canterbury. The Duke of Dorset; My Lord Abergavenny, for his own Uncle, Dr Tatton; And Dr. Head, Deputy Clerk of the Closet, were Sollicitors. The King was pleased, of Himself, to give it, after a Year & Half, to My Lord Abergavenny's Uncle. The Duke of Dorset was extremely mortified at it; that, in his own County, (where there was then a contested Election, in which His Grace had a great, meritorious & expensive Share,) His Recomm^n. of Mr Curtis, (an active, & zealous Man, in the Cause,) should be set aside. His Grace was not well pleased with me; For indeed He had a Right to My Assistance, as He had given a Bishopric in Ireland to a

Cambridge Friend of Mine, in Expectation of this Preferment for Mr Curtis. This being the Case, I must assist Mr Curtis preferably to Everybody. Dr Head has Pretensions of His own, as having long serv'd the King, as Clerk of the Closet. Those Pretensions are strongly back'd by the Arch. BP. of Canterbury; and are Such in themselves, as, I have long given Dr Head Reason to think, I should not oppose. My Lady Pembroke, thro' My Lady Yarmouth, is a warm, and angry Sollicitor for your Friend, Mr Dampier. I can say no more, than I have formerly done;—I will do it the first Moment I can. I will lay Your LordP's Request, in the best Manner before the King; And, tho' It should not succeed now, I hope it may not be long before It will, in case of other Vacancies.

Add. MSS. 32736, f. 182.

216. The career of Bishop Hoadly.[1]

But now it may not be amiss to digress a little, and to give some account of bishop *Hoadley*, our once famous writer of controversy, and to observe how preferment, or the hopes of it, alters and corrupts the mind of men: I call him and the rest of his brethren, in this paper, *bishops*, as legally such; without determining whether he, or those others who have so often, and so notoriously, broken the canons of the apostles, and the known laws of *Christianity*, both in their coming in, and behaviours afterwards, can be esteemed *Christian Bishops* or not. Now in the year 1711, after I had published my four volumes of *Primitive Christianity Reviv'd*, we had a meeting at Mr *Benjamin Hoadley*'s (that was his name then, and I do but transcribe my own account from *The Life of Dr Clarke*, first edition, page 28, 29.) who, upon our debate about the genuineness of the *Apostolical Constitutions*, thus declared his mind, "That without entering into dispute, whether these *Constitutions* were really genuine and apostolical, or not, he was for receiving them, as much better than what was already in the church." After five years, in 1716, Mr *Hoadley* was made bishop of *Bangor*. At which time, I told his lordship, that he had now 500 £. [it proved 800 £.] a year, to keep the [primitive] *Christian* Religion out of *England*. And, I think, that he has since he was made a bishop, (for he was a much better man before,) abundantly verified my prediction. In the first place, he took the bishoprick of *Bangor*, and the 800 £. a year, which was intended to maintain a resident bishop in that diocese,

[1] See also Nos. 221, 231.

and this for six intire years together, without ever seeing that diocese in his life, to the great scandal of religion. He then became a great writer of controversy, one of the most pernicious things to true *Christianity* in the world, as well as disagreeable to the peaceable temper of a good *Christian*. And, indeed, this *Bangorian Controversy* seemed, for a great while, to engross the attention of the publick: altho' when a great friend of mine, of ability, and at other time of inclination, to employ his time better, had once acknowledged to the very learned Mr *Wasse*, who was his friend also, that he was reading the *Bangorian Controversy*, he was justly called no other than a *reptile* for his pains. After this, bishop *Hoadley* was removed from the bishop-rick of *Bangor* to that of *Hereford*; and from *Hereford* to *Salisbury*; and from *Salisbury* to *Winchester*. He also, with others of his brethren, raises an estate out of the revenues of the church, for his own family; and with the rest of his brethren, 'till lately, left his diocese almost every year, to approve himself a political bishop in the house of lords . . .

> *Memoirs of the Life and Writings of Mr William Whiston*, written by himself (1753), vol. I, p. 208.

217. The career of Bishop Watson, 1782.

. . . the Duke of Rutland wrote to me at Yarmouth—that he had *determined to support Lord Shelburne's administration*, as he had received the most positive assurances, that the independency of America was to be acknowledged, and the wishes of the people relative to a parliamentary reform granted. He further told me, that the bishopric of Landaff, he had reason to believe, would be disposed of in my favour if *he asked it;* and desired to know, whether, if the offer should be made, I would accept it. I returned for answer that I conceived there could be no dishonour in *my accepting a bishopric* from an administration which he had previously *determined* to support; and that I had expected Lord Shelburne would have given me the bishopric without application, but that if I must owe it to the interposition of some great man, I had rather owe it to that of His Grace than to any other.

On Sunday, July 21st, I received an express from the Duke of Rutland, informing me that he had seen Lord Shelburne, who had *anticipated* his wishes, by mentioning me for the vacant bishopric *before he had asked it*. I kissed hands on the 26th of that month, and was received, as the phrase is, *very graciously*; this was the first time that I had ever been at St. James's.

In this manner I did acquire a bishopric. But I have no great reason to be proud of the promotion; for I think I owed it not to any regard, which he who gave it me, had to the zeal and industry with which I had for many years discharged the functions, and fulfilled the duties, of an academic life, but to the opinion which, from my Sermon, he had erroneously entertained, that I was a warm, and might become an useful partisan. Lord Shelburne, indeed, had expressed to the Duke of Grafton his expectation, that I would occasionally write a pamphlet for their administration. The Duke did me justice in assuring him, that he had perfectly mistaken my character; that though I might write on an abstract question, concerning government or the principles of legislation, it would not be with a view of assisting any administration.

I had written in support of the principles of the Revolution, because I thought those principles useful to the state, and I saw them vilified and neglected; I had taken part with the people in their petitions against the influence of the Crown, because I thought that influence would destroy the constitution, and I saw that it was increasing; I had opposed the supporters of the American war, because I thought that war not only to be inexpedient, but unjust. But all this was done from my own sense of things, and without the least view of pleasing any party: I did, however, happen to please a party, and they made me a bishop. I have hitherto followed, and shall continue to follow, my own judgment in all public transactions; all parties now understand this, and it is probable that I may continue to be Bishop of Landaff as long as I live. . . .

Anecdotes of the Life of Richard Watson, Bishop of Landaff, written by himself (1818), vol. I, p. 150.

218. Bishops in the House of Lords.

And now having given some account of several of our present bishops, and almost all of them political bishops also, who spend so much of their time, not in their own dioceses, where they ought both to live and die, but in the capital city, and in parliament: it may be worth our while to take some notice how little good they do there, either to learning, morality, or religion; they being too well known to be little better than tools of the court, to merit better bishopricks, by voting as they are directed; which they seldom fail to do. Yet has there

lately been two cases, when the business they were to do was so pro-
digiously gross, one of which was the last gin bill, (which gin is, by
one of the best judges, estimated to kill no fewer than 100,000 poor
people in *Europe* every year, and, by some examples I have known, I
deem that estimate not very extravagant) that not one single bishop
could be prevailed on to vote for it: nay, some of them were too
unusually bold, as to speak against it. Now what was the consequence
of this unanimous opposition? why the bill went through the house of
lords notwithstanding; and stands as an act of parliament, assented to
by the *lords spiritual*, as well as *temporal*, at this day. Which thing puts
me in mind of an answer the lord *Carteret* made sometime since to
bishop *Hare*, who, when he complained of the hard words that lord
had given some of the bishops in a speech in the house of lords, put
him in mind, that his lordship might one day be a minister of state
himself, and might then want the bishops votes. This lord replied,
"If I want you, I know how to have you." The meaning of which
words are easily understood, without a comment. In short, I cannot
but esteem bishops in the house of lords to be the very greatest grievance of *christianity* now in these Kingdoms, and utterly contrary to
the laws of the gospel.

> *Memoirs of the Life and Writings of Mr. William Whiston*, written by himself (1753),
> vol. I, p. 235.

219. Duke of Newcastle as the bishops' 'whip', 1767.

DUKE OF NEWCASTLE TO THE BISHOP OF WORCESTER

Claremont, June 9, 1767

MY DEAR, & CONSTANT GOOD FRIEND,

... The House of Lords are adjourned to Wensday Se'nnight the
17th Inst, when The Dividend Bill of the E.I. Company comes on, by
Order; & other Business of Consequence will be before us, as long as
the Parliament sits. It is the Earnest Wish of My Lord Mansfield, &
all our Friends, That The House may be well attended. It is particularly Incumbent upon the Bishops to be There; For the Duke of
Bedford, with His usual Sincerity & Frankness, owned, That the
Reason, He hoped That The House would adjourn to The Wensday,
& not to The Monday, or Tuesday, which was much contended for,
was, That, as Trinity Sunday was the General Ordination Day, It
would be difficult for The Bishops to return to Parliament before

Wensday; and His Grace wished to have the Attendance of all The Bishops. This Reason prevailed so strongly with The House, That Wensday was immediately order'd . . .

I am, My Dear Old Friend,
Ever & Unalterably Your's
HOLLES NEWCASTLE

P.S. The Lamprey is excellent.

Add. MSS. 32982, f. 266.

220. The Archbishop of Canterbury's proxy, 1734.

DR J. LYNCH, DEAN OF CANTERBURY, TO NEWCASTLE

Lambeth Jan: 15th 1733/4

MAY IT PLEASE YOUR GRACE.

When I return'd from Y^r Grace this Morning to Lambeth I found the Archbishop [Wake] extremely Ill with a violent Fit of the Stone & Gravel, & neither fit nor inclined to give Attention to any Business, & indeed I assure Your Grace if I had an Affair of the utmost consequence to have transacted with Him today, I could not have done it. However when I return from Canterbury (for wch Place I purpose to set out to morrow) I will do my best endeavour's to Persuade My Lord Archbishop to Oblige Your Grace both in appointing a Proxy for ye next Session of Parliament & in fixing upon the Bishop of Durham for ye Person; tho' if Her Majesty & Your Grace will please to recollect what I had the honour to say to you both upon this subject, was only that I would endeavour to Persuade ye Archbishop if the Court at any time was hard press'd in any particular point to make a Proxy, to serve them in that Vote.

I am with all possible Respect
My Lord Your Grace's most obliged & most
obedient Humble Servt

J. LYNCH.

Add. MSS. 32689, f. 142.

221. Hoadly as Whig pamphleteer, 1709.[1]

[13 December 1709]

. . . some members took occasion to speak in favour of Mr Hoadly, whose principles were more agreeable to the sense of the majority of

[1] See also Nos. 216, 231.

that House; and who, in several writings, had vindicated the Revolution. Upon which it was resolved, "That the rev. Mr Benjamin Hoadly, rector of St. Peter's Poor, London, for having often justified the principles on which her majesty and the nation proceeded in the late happy Revolution, had justly merited the favour and recommendation of this House.

2. That an humble Address be presented to her majesty, that she would be graciously pleased to bestow some dignity in the church on Mr Hoadly, for his eminent services both in the church and state". This Address having been presented to the queen, she answered, "That she would take a proper opportunity to comply with their desires:" Which, however, she never did.

P.H., VI, 807.

222. The clergy and parliamentary elections, 1733.

DR LYNCH, DEAN OF CANTERBURY, TO NEWCASTLE

Lambeth Oct. 17th 1733

MAY IT PLEASE YOUR GRACE

I was my self this morning (when the letter Your Grace was pleas'd to Honour me with was brought here) with the Gentleman for whom My Lord Archbishop [Wake] intends the Living of Ringmer, who very readily promis'd me to serve Mr Pelham & Mr Butler with His Vote & Interest at the next Election, & I make no question He will be very punctual in the Performance of His Promise, this I beg leave to assure Your Grace (tho' I do not at all distrust Him) His future Friendship with me shall certainly Stand or Fall according to His Behaviour at the next Election in Sussex; I shall likewise recommend to Him, when He goes down, to take His Measures in these Affair's from the Gentleman Your Grace is pleas'd to direct Him too; & I beg leave to return my Thank's for Him (as I doubt not when He comes to know it he will do for Himself) for yr. Grace's Goodness in promising Him Your Countenance & Regard, I hope, & make no question but He will always so behave Himself as yᵗ Your Grace shall think fit to continue it to Him.

Yʳ are several other Clergymen in Sussex whom My Lord Archbishop at one time or other, has had an opportunity of Preferring, tho' many of yᵐ I know are Persons' whom Your Grace or some of Your Family Recommended to My Lord, & they I suppose will be gratefull enough to Serve the Interest Your Grace espouses, yet if y^r be any whom the Archbishop has oblig'd of w^m Your Grace is doubtfull, if your Grace be pleased to let me be inform'd of them, I am sure My Lord Archbishop will cause His Secretary to write to them in the most pressing term's to desire Y^r Vote & Interest for These Gentlemen.

I have ye Honour to assure Your Grace that I am with all possible Respect & Regard

> May it Please Your Grace
>> Your Grace's
>>> Most Dutyfull
>>>> & Most obedient Humble Servt
>>>>> J. LYNCH.

Add. MSS. 32688, f. 516.

223. The Duke of Newcastle receives a testimonial, 1760.

[Received June 15th, 1760]

TO HIS GRACE THE DUKE OF NEWCASTLE

FIRST LORD OF THE TREASURY

We beg leave to recommend to Your Grace Dr Bray, Fellow of Exeter College in Oxford; who has for many years been a Tutor of the College and is a person of learning, and Exemplary Character, & as one who has distinguished his zeal, upon all proper Occasions for the present happy establishment; and in particular was eminently service-able to the Whig Interest in the last County Election, which was attended with some prejudice to his private circumstances. And being convinced that it would be of real and important service, to the cause of Loyalty in the University, to reward a person of His Known Abilities and experienced attachment to the Government: And having the greatest reason to expect his future services in a Situation near us; we most earnestly desire, that your Grace would be pleased to recom-mend him to his Majesty, for the next Vacant Canonry of Christ Church

(D of)	Marlborough
(Lord)	Harcourt
,,	Macclesfield
,,	Parker.

Add. MSS. 32907, f. 237.

224. The Duke of Newcastle turns down an application, 1760.

DUKE OF NEWCASTLE TO REV. MR. FRED. HARVEY

Newcastle House June 9th: 1760

SIR,

I had yesterday the favour of your Letter, and am obliged to acquaint you, that I have received such strong applications from the Townshend Family, the Walpoles, and all the nobility, & first Gentlemen, in the county of Norfolk, in favour of Mr Edwd Townshend, Son to the late Lord Townshend, to succeed to the Deanery of Norwich, and my near Relation to the Townshend Family, and the Regard, which must be paid to the Gentlemen of Norfolk, in which County this Preferment is, are such, that It will be impossible for me to avoid recommending Mr Townshend to the King, and employing any credit I may have, in support of it.

Mr Townshend has been so long in The King's Service, and His Father had so much merit to this country, and to this Royal Family that I believe His Majesty will be very desirous to oblige Mr Townshend upon this occasion.

I have been thus particular, that you may see the State of this case in the light, in which It is—I shall be very glad of an opportunity of shewing you with how much Truth, & Respect,

I am Sir, &c:

HOLLES NEWCASTLE.

Add. MSS. 32907, f. 90.

225. Deans and Chapters neglect their duties.

But though the Bishop was forced to desist from his attendance on the public service at St. Pauls,[1] yet he was not under the like necessity at Bristol; as his call thither was in the summer season, and he was as it were two different creatures in summer and winter. From the time that he was first made Bishop, he constantly went to Bristol every summer, and usually stayed there the three months intervening between his last residence at St. Pauls and the next following; and when he was no longer able to go St. Pauls, he continued at Bristol for four or five months, and went to church as often as his health and the weather would permit. . . . by living and residing there so much, he

[1] His chest was weak.

was in hopes that his example would have induced the other members of the church to perform also their part, and to discharge at least their statutable duties. The deanery is worth at least 500 £. a year, and each prebend is worth about half that sum, and their estates are capable of good improvement: and for these preferments the residence usually required is three months for the Dean, and half that time for each Prebendary. But alas! never was church more shamefully neglected. The Bishop has several times been there for months together, without seeing the face of Dean, or Prebendary, or any thing better than a Minor Canon. The care and management of the church was left to Mr Camplin, Precentor or Senior Minor Canon, and to the Sexton. His example having no kind of effect, he remonstrated several times, that their preferments deserved a little better attendance, as they would well bear the expense of it; their neglect was the more conspicuous and culpable, being in the second city in the Kingdom; that their want of residence was the general complaint not only of the city, but likewise of all the country; that great numbers resorted every year to the Wells, and generally came, at least on a Sunday, to see the Cathedral; that they were astonished at finding only one Minor Canon both to read and to preach, and perhaps administer the sacrament ...

Life of Dr. Thomas Newton, written by himself, in *Lives of Dr. E. Pocock, Dr. Z. Pearce, Dr. T. Newton and Rev. P. Skelton* (1816), vol. II, p. 169.

226. Bishop Burnet: a conscientious prelate.

[written by Nov. 30, 1710.]

... and soon after the Prince was put in the Throne, I was made Bishop of Salisbury.

I WAS NAMED TO BE BISHOP OF SALISBURY.

When I saw that was resolved on I set my selfe seriously to form a method how I would behave my selfe in that station. I spent a whole week in retirement and sat up the whole night before I was Consecrated. I set my selfe to examine all the sins of my former life and to renew my mournings for them I run over all the thoughts I had at any time entertained of the duty of Bishops and made solemne vows to God to put them in practise. I resolved never to indulge loseness or luxury nor to raise fortunes to my children out of the revenues of the Church. I resolved to abstract my selfe from Courts and secular affairs as much as was possible, and never to engage in the persecuting of any of what side soever on the account of differences of religion, and to dedicate my selfe to the functions belonging to the Order, preaching, catechising, confirming, and ordaining and governing the Clergy in the best manner I could. Thus I studied to prepare myself for taking that character upon me. I told all this to the Queen who was much pleased with it, and added only her desire that my wife should wear plain clothes suteable rather to what became a Bishop's wife, than to her education, in which she found a very steady and entire compliance with so reasonable a command.

. . .

I WENT TO MY DIOCESSE TO DO MY DUTY THERE.

But now I was to go into my Diocesse, and for that end I formed my designs thus; I resolved to preach constantly every Lord's day and also to preach the weekly lecture at Salisbury. I resolved to go round my Diocesse about three weeks or a moneth once a year, preaching and confirming every day from Church to Church. I resolved thus once in three years besides the formality of the Trienniall Visitation to go round to all the chieffe parts of my Diocesse and to hold conferences with my Clergy upon the chieffe heads of Divinity, in which in a discourse of about two hours length I opened all that related to the head proposed, and encouraged them to object or propose questions relating to the subject. In this I continued till I published my Explanation of the Articles, and then I did not think it necessary to continue those conferences any longer. I found the Clergy were not much the better for them, and false stories were made and believed of what I delivered in those conferences; and tho as I went round I kept an open table to all the Clergy, yet nothing could mollify their aversion to a man that was for tolleration and for treating the Dissenters with gentlenes. I continued still to go about preaching and confirming, so that I have confirmed and preached in 275 Churches of my Diocesse, and 10 or 12 times in all the market touns and considerable places. I look upon confirmation if rightly managed as the most effectual mean possible for reviving Christianity, but I could never prevail with the greater part of my Clergy to think of any other way of preparing their youth to it but to hear them repeat their catechism, they did not study to make them consider it as the becoming a Christian by an act

of their own. I have now setled upon a method in which I intend to
continue as long as God continues my strength to execute it. I stay a
week in a place where every morning I go and preach and confirm
in some Church within 6 or 7 mile of the place, and then at 5 a clock
after evening praier I catechise some children and explain the whole
Catechisme to them, so that I go thro it all in six daies and confirm
there next Lord's day, and make presents to the value of about a crown
a child to all whom I catechised, and I have them all to dine with me
on the Lord's day. This seems to be the most profitable method I can
devise both for instructing as well as provoking the Clergy to catechise much, and for setting a good emulation among the younger
sort to be well instructed. I have likewise set up a school for 50 poor
children at Salisbury who are taught and clothed at my charge, and
to whom I go once a moneth and hear 10 of them repeat such Psalms
and parts of the New Testament as I prescribe, and give them 18 pence
a piece for reward, this is a mean to keep them in good order. I set
my selfe to encourage my Clergy not only by my going often about
among them and by assisting them kyndly in all their concerns, but
by a large share of my income with which I have relieved their neces-
sities. I never renewed a lease but I gave a considerable share of the
fine either to the Minister of the Parish, or if he was well provided to
some neighbooring charity, so that I can reckon 3000 lib. given by
me in larger sums among them besides smaller ones that occurre
daily . . . .

I looked on Ordinations as the most important part of a Bishop's
care and that on which the law had laid no restraints, for it was absolutely in the Bishop's power to ordain or not as he judged a person
qualified for it, and so I resolved to take that matter to heart. I never
turned over the examining those who came to me for orders to a
Chaplain or an Archdeacon, I examined them very carefully my selfe.
I began allwaies to examine them concerning the proof of the Christian
religion and the authority of the Scriptures and the nature of the Gospell
Covenant in Christ; if they understood not these aright I dismissed
them, but upon a competent understanding of these I went thro the
other parts of Divinity and soon saw into the measure of their knowledge. One defect run through them all, even those who could not be
called ignorant, they read the Scriptures so little that they scarce knew
the most common things in them, but when I was satisfied that they
had a competent measure of knowledge, I directed the rest of my

discourse to their consciences and went thro all the parts of the Pastorall Care to give them good directions and to awaken in them a right sense of things. I pressed them to imploy their time in praier, fasting and meditation and in reading carefully the Epistles to Timothy and Titus. I spoke copiously to them every day for four daies together upon these subjects, sometimes to them alltogether and some times singly. I referred the examining them in Greek and Latin to the Archdeacon and brought them to a publick examination in the Chapterhouse before the Dean and Prebendaries. As for their moralls we were forced to take that implicitly from the Testimonialls signed by the Clergy in whose neighbourhood they had lived, in which I have found such an easiness of signing these, that unlesse I knew the men I grew to regard them very little. This was the best method that in the present state of our affairs I could take, yet I found it so defective and so farre short of a due exactnes that I must confesse the Ordination weeks were much dreaded by me and were the most afflicting part of the whole year and of the whole Episcopall duty. . . . Thus I laid my plan and have now followed it executing it almost 22 years.

H. C. Foxcroft, *A Supplement to Burnet's History of My Own Time* (Oxford, 1902), p. 497.

227. Confirmation, 1722.

WHITE KENNETT TO WAKE, 18 JULY 1722

I have entered on my stages of confirmation, and began at Uppingham in Rutland, within which county they have had no confirmation these forty years. The numbers as taken by one of my attendents were 1700 and odd. I appoint it on Sundays after noon, because the good folk have their best clothes and horses to spare; otherwise we should have very few upon these dripping days when they must wait upon their hay and corn. I intend constantly to preach myself in the morning and to have evening prayer over before 3, and to spend the remainder of the day in that office. I had not done at Uppingham till after ten at night.

N. Sykes, *Church and State in England in the 18th Century* (Cambridge, 1934), p. 119.

228. Holy Communion, 1741.

[A CHARGE DELIVERED TO THE CLERGY OF OXFORD, 1741]

But besides increasing the Number of your Communicants, it were very desirable, that they who do communicate should do it more frequently. In the three first Centuries the Eucharist was everywhere celebrated weekly, and in many Places almost daily. Decay of Piety occasioned an Injunction in the Sixth, that every Christian should receive thrice in the Year; which was reduced in the Thirteenth, perhaps with a bad Intention, to once. Our Church requires thrice *at the least:* which evidently implies, that more than thrice is hoped for. And indeed each Person will scarce be able to communicate so often unless the Communion be administered oftener. But besides, it is appointed to be every Lord's Day in Cathedral and Collegiate Church, and Part of the Office for it is read every Lord's Day in every Church, for an Admonition of what it were to be wished the People could be brought to. This indeed at best must be a Work of Time; but one Thing might be done at present in all your Parishes, as God be thanked, it is in most of them: a Sacrament might easily be interposed in that long Interval between *Whitsuntide* and *Christmas*: and the usual Season for it, about the Feast of St *Michael*, (when your People having gathered in the Fruits of the Earth have some Rest from their Labours, and must surely feel some Gratitude to the Giver of all Good) is a very proper Time. And if afterwards you can advance from a quarterly Communion to a monthly one, I make no Doubt but you will.

B. Porteus and G. Stinton (eds.), Works of Thomas Secker (Dublin, 1775), vol. v, p. 323.

229. Rev. William Cole: a conscientious parson, 1766.

Thursday, 20 [March, 1766] Cold & dry. Wrote to Mr. Masters & Mr. Uffendale. I went in my Chaise to Eaton to pray by the wife of Robert King; from thence to West Blecheley on the same Errand to the wife of Robert Mollard, very ill with a Cancer on her Thigh; from thence to Robert Ashby, who is better, but I prayed by him, I did also with Wm. Bradbury who was very ill of a Consumption. I wrote to Mr. Etheridge of Simpson, Brother-in-Law to Farmer Turner, who died at West Blecheley yesterday of the Small Pox, to let him be put into the Grave this Evening, & I would read the Burial Service over him to morrow: as hardly any of the Parish had had the Distemper, & few of the Clergy could be got to bury him: as even those who had had it themselves, were afraid of carrying the Infection to their Wives & Children. He readily assented to my Proposal: Mrs. Willis so alarmed, that she went out of the Parish for a week or two.

Friday, 21. Dry & cold, but fine. The Carpenters here. After Matins, I read the Burial Service over the half-filled up Grave of

Mr. Turner. Mrs. Holt & her Daughter, Mrs. Goodwin, drank Tea & Coffee with me. Mr. Tomkins of Newton grafted 2 Trees in my Garden.

. . .

Sunday, 23. Snow & Cold. At Matins Mr. Emerton, Mr. Crane & Jonathan Daniel dined with me. At Vespres, when I catechised the Children. Lent my pretty Dun Horse to Mrs. Holt to fetch her Son from Eton Schole.

Monday, 25. Cold & Snow. At Matins. Baptised Robert the Son of Mr. Purcell of E[a]ton, whose Wife died in Childbed of it this Day. Message from Mr Barton to meet him to morrow at Dinner at Stanton Barry at Mr. Shipton's & to go to Sherington with him at Night; but it snowed too hard to go out anywhere. Mun Holt came from Eton, & brought me some Colly-Flower Plants.

Tuesday, 25. Great Snow. At Matins. The Annunciation of our Lady. Letter from Mrs Barton with their Address in Holles Street, Cavendish Square, they going to Town next week for 6 weeks.

Wedn: 26. Great Snow & cold. It snowed all Day. No Church.

Thursd: 27. Great Snow on the Ground. No going to Church; however, I buried Mrs. Purcell in the Afternoon. Mr. Cartwright, with his Friends Messrs Ashurst & Maxwell prevented going to Town yesterday, went to Day in worse Weather. I sent my 2 French wigs to my London Barber to alter them, they being made so miserably I could not wear them.

Good Friday, [28] Fine & frosty. At Matins.

Saturday, 29. Fine Day. At Matins: after which I went to see Mrs Willis & to offer her to administer the Holy Sacrament to her to morrow, as she was always used to come to Church, & especially at these Times. She chose to stay 'till Whitsuntide, as it might occasion other People to make the same Request. Paid a Levy & half to the Poor of Fenny-Stratford, £1. 15. od. to Mr. Stevens, who utterly refused to make any Satisfaction for the damage he had done me last Hay Time. Mr Pitts drank Tea with me.

Easter Day, 30. Tolerable fine Day. After Service, when I administered the Holy Sacrament to about 40 People, I went to do the same to Dame Mollard & Wm. Bradbury, in my Chaise, at the other end of the Town. Anne Keburn dined in the kitchen with Wm. Wood, Tansley & John Holdom, whose Father's Horses I had. After

Vespers I drank Tea with Mr. & Mrs Willis, he coming from Mr Bland's at Berkhampsted yesterday, where he had been placed on his being taken from Eton Schole, where they could do nothing with him. Little Rain at Night.

Monday, 31. Fine Day, but windy. After Matins I chose Mr Broughton my Church-Warden for Blecheley, & we chose Mr Ric: Lane for F. Stratford & Mr Purcell for Eaton: & Wm Daniel Overseer of the Poor. We were told of Mr Leicester's Design of cho[o]sing a Chapel Warden for F. Str: in the Afternoon. I went to Mrs Willis to know if she approved of Mr Stevens's paying Mr Leicester the 20sh. for last year's St Martin's Sermon: she said, no.

F. G. Stokes, *The Blecheley Diary of the Rev. William Cole* (1931), p. 26.

230. Pluralism and non-residence, 1808.

LETTER TO THE ARCHBISHOP OF CANTERBURY, MAY 18, 1808

... The logical maxim, *sublatâ causâ tolitur effectus*, is applicable to the non-residence of the clergy and to the poverty of stipendiary curates. The principal cause of both these evils, is the allowing the clergy to hold more livings than one. Take away pluralities, and there will be few stipendiary curates. Build at the public expense parsonage-houses, and there will be few non-resident clergy. If it be not thought right to build parsonage-houses at the public expense, let the livings, where houses are wanted, be sequestered, both in this country and Ireland, as they become vacant; and with the aid of Queen Anne's bounty, in addition to the monies arising from the sequestrations, let parsonage houses be provided at the expense of the church itself.

Pluralities are become necessary on account of the poverty of the greater part of the parish-churches and chapels. This poverty arises from the appropriations and the impropriations which were improvidently granted at the Reformation, but which ought not now to be disturbed. What is wanted to make up the small benefices to at least 100 £ a-year, must be supplied from the public grants. ... I cannot help thinking that the provision of two thousand a-year, which I possess from the church, is a case full in point.

It arises from the tithes of two churches in Shropshire, of two in Leicestershire, of two in my diocese, of three in Huntingdonshire, on all of which I have resident curates; of five more as appropriations to the bishoprick, and of two more in the Isle of Ely, as appropriations to the archdeaconry of Ely. I mention not this as a matter of complaint, but as a proof how little palliations will avail in amending the situation of the stipendiary curates.

I have the honour, &c.

R. LANDAFF.

Anecdotes of the Life of Richard Watson, Bishop of Landaff, written by himself (1818), vol. II, p. 347.

231. Ecclesiastical patronage, 1760.

THE DUKE OF NEWCASTLE TO BISHOP HOADLY[1]

Claremont May 31st 1760

... The Rule, which I have laid down to Myself, in all Recommendations, which I have ever made to the Crown, has been, First, To recommend None, whom I did not think most sincerely well affected to His Majesty, and His Government, and, to the Principles upon which It is founded; and in this, I believe, I have been as seldom mistaken, as ever anybody was, in such a Course of years. Some few, & very Few, Instances must be excepted; the Reasons of which may have arose from unavoidable Necessity, occasioned by the Circumstances of the Times. The next Rule has been, To recommend none, whose Character as to Vertue, & Regularity of Life, would not justify it; and I flatter myself, That the present Vacancies are filled with Such, as will meet with your Lordship's Approbation, as answering in Every particular, the Rule I have laid down for my Conduct in this Respect.

Dr Friend is made Dean of Canterbury, who has received the greatest Marks of your Lordship's Approbation, & Favor. His Canonry of Christ Church is given to Dr Tottie Arch Deacon of Worcester, a most deserving man in Every Respect; And who has distinguished Himself, ever since He came into the World, by His Zeal for the Government. Dr Shipley Dean of Winchester one more nearly connected with your Lordship, His Canonry is given at the Earnest Recommendation of the Arch Bishop of Canterbury to Dr Burton, who was long Chaplain to His Grace; and whose particular Qualification for that Preferment, The Archbishop had a long opportunity of knowing. The Canonry of Windsor, vacant by poor Mr Blacowe, who was placed there, as a Reward for His great Merit upon a particular Occasion, is given to Dr Barnard, the Present deserving

---

[1] See also Nos. 216, 221.

Master of Eton School, where, by His Principles in Government, and His other great Talents, He has been, and is, able to do the Publick great Service. All These Dispositions were so strongly pressed by The King's Friends, and Servants, and were so right, & proper in themselves, that they could not, in My Opinion, have been resisted, without great Inconvenience to His Majesty's Service.

Add. MSS. 32906, f. 387.

232. The fashionable clergy.

But while I defend and *honour* the *Profession*, I mean not to flatter the *Professors* [the clergy]. As far, therefore as the Influence of their Conduct and Knowledge can be supposed to affect the *national Capacity*; so far, they seem falling into the same unmanly and effeminate Peculiarities, by which their Contemporaries are distinguished—Such of them, I mean, as have Opportunity of conversing with what is called *the World*, and are supposed to make a Part of it. In their Conduct they *curb not*, but *promote* and encourage the trifling Manners of the Times: It is grown a fashionable Thing, among these Gentlemen, to despise the Duties of their Parish, to wander about, as the various Seasons invite, to every Scene of false Gaiety, to *frequent* and *shine* in all *public* Places, their own *Pulpits* excepted.

Or if their Age and Situation sets them above these puerile Amusements, are we not to lament, that, instead of a manly and rational Regard to the Welfare of Mankind, the chief Employment of many a clerical life is, to slumber in a *Stall*, haunt *Levees*, or follow the gainful Trade of *Election-jobbing*?

> Rev. J. Brown, *Estimate of the Manners and Principles of the Times* (7th ed., 1758), vol. 1, p. 84.

233. Adam Smith on the clergy.

... The church of England in particular has always valued herself, with great reason, upon the unexceptionable loyalty of her principles. Under such a government the clergy naturally endeavour to recommend themselves to the sovereign, to the court, and to the nobility and gentry of the country, by whose influence they chiefly expect to obtain preferment. They pay court to those patrons, sometimes, no doubt, by the vilest flattery and assentation, but frequently too by cultivating all those arts which best deserve, and which are therefore most likely to gain them the esteem of people of rank and fortune; by their knowledge in all the different branches of useful and ornamental learning, by the decent liberality of their manners, and by the social good humour of their conversation, and by their avowed contempt of those absurd and hypocritical austerities which fanatics inculcate and pretend to practise, in order to draw upon themselves the veneration, and upon the greater part of men of rank and fortune, who avow that they do not practise them, the abhorrence of the common people. Such a clergy, however, while they pay their court in this manner to the higher ranks of life, are very apt to neglect altogether the means of maintaining their influence and authority with the lower. They are listened to, esteemed and respected by their superiors; but before their inferiors they are frequently incapable of defending, effectually and to the conviction of such hearers, their sober and moderate doctrines against the most ignorant enthusiast who chuses to attack them.

A. Smith, *Wealth of Nations* (Cannan's ed., 1950), vol. II, p. 292.

234. Absentee clergy and stipendiary curates, 1803.

Jany. 27th [1803] ... how do I pity the poor unfortunate, who enters into an office so solemn, as a mere profession, or business! What up-hill drudgery & how tedious must the several services appear, when not the *heart*, but the *lips* only are engaged! It is to be feared that there are too many of this unhappy sort. Some unwary youths aspire to the profession, as what is styled "a genteel one." To others their friends & relations dictate this, strongly seconding their cruelly unkind suggestions with the immediate possession of "handsome preferment" from family, or friendly patronage. These are your "master-men," who do their duty by proxy, haggling with poor curates, till they can find those who will starve with fewest symptoms of discontent.

As to the fine gentlemen themselves, they are far more anxious to attain the fame of being "excellent shots", giving the "view halloo", well-mounted in the field, & being "in at the death"—than raising their voices in the desk or pulpit, or feeding the flock, whom they are eager to fleece.

In this I rejoice, as one of the services most acceptable to my own feelings, which I have rendered as a tutor—I have diverted many young men, of this description, from the Church, & recommended the Army, in which I doubt not but they will appear to proper advantage. As to those who court this *genteel* profession, with no other prospect but of being "journeymen"—"soles"—not "upper-leathers"—which is (being interpreted), poor curates—they are truly to be pitied. If they regard present circumstances, without "having respect with the recompense of future reward," they would, I am sure, do better for themselves, & for their families, by making interest for upper-servants' places in a genteel family, than by being mere "*soles or understrappers*" in the Church. A journeyman in almost any trade or business, even a bricklayer's labourer, or the turner of a razor-grinder's wheel, all circumstances considered, is generally better paid than a stipendiary curate.

O. F. Christie (ed.), Diary of the Revd. William Jones (1929), p. 148.

235. Poverty among curates, 1810.

[18 June 1810]

EARL OF HARROWBY: ... He thought also, that some further regulations were necessary respecting the salaries of curates; that no curate ought to be permitted to act on a living where the incumbent was non-resident (except in the case of the infirmity of the incumbent) without a license from the bishop, specifying the salary he was to receive; and that, in livings below a certain value, the salary should be the whole income of the living. The present practice, according to which the non-resident incumbents, of livings of 50£. 60£. or 70£. a year, put into their own pockets a portion of this wretched pittance, and left much less than the wages of a day-labourer for the subsistence of their curates, appeared to him far from creditable to the parties concerned, and calculated to degrade the character of the Church. Many instances came within his own knowledge, in which parishes were served for 20£. or even for 10£. per annum, and in which, of course, all they knew of their clergyman was the sound of his voice in the reading desk, or pulpit, once a week, a fortnight, or a month. This must also be the case where curates are permitted to serve more than two churches. An abuse which he thought required to be prevented.

P.D., XVII, 765.

236. Lack of churches in manufacturing areas, 1810.

[18 June 1810]

EARL OF HARROWBY . . . In many places, particularly in those which the increase of commercial and manufacturing wealth, had, of late years, raised from villages to towns, there was a great want of places of worship. There was no want, he believed, of religious disposition: for, in these places, chapels of every species of dissenting worship, were rising year after year by subscription. In the present state of the law, or at least according to the present mode of executing it, there was great difficulty in obtaining permission to erect an additional place of worship, according to the church of England, within the limits of an existing parish. The inhabitants, therefore, had no choice. They might prefer the church of England, but that church shut her doors against them; they had therefore no option, but either to neglect divine worship entirely, or to attend it in a form which they did not so well approve. He was rejoiced for one, that many should accept the latter alternative. The consequence, however, was inevitable; their attendance upon a place of dissenting worship, gradually led to a complete separation from the established church. This was an evil daily increasing, and which required speedy and effectual remedy.

P.D., XVII, 765

237. Wesley defends itinerant preaching, 1739.

[LETTER TO A FRIEND QUOTED IN JOURNAL, II JUNE 1739]

As to your advice that I should settle in College, I have no business there, having now no office, and no pupils. And whether the other branch of your proposal be expedient for me, viz., 'To accept of a cure of souls,' it will be time enough to consider, when one is offered to me.

But, in the mean time, you think I ought to sit still; because otherwise I should invade another's office, if I interfered with other people's business, and intermeddled with souls that did not belong to me. You accordingly ask, 'How is it that I assemble Christians who are none of my charge, to sing psalms, and pray, and hear the Scriptures expounded?' and think it hard to justify doing this in other men's parishes, upon Catholic principles.

Permit me to speak plainly. If by Catholic principles you mean any other than Scriptural, they weigh nothing with me: I allow no other rule, whether of faith or practice, than the Holy Scriptures: But on scriptural principles, I do not think it hard to justify whatever I do. God in Scripture commands me, according to my power, to instruct the ignorant, reform the wicked, confirm the virtuous. Man forbids me to do this in another's parish; that is, in effect, to do it at all; seeing I have now no parish of my own, nor probably ever shall. . . .

Suffer me now to tell you my principles in this matter. I look upon all the world as my parish; thus far I mean, that, in whatever part of it I am, I judge it meet, right, and my bounden duty, to declare unto all that are willing to hear, the glad tidings of salvation. This is the work which I know God has called me to; and sure I am, that his blessing attends it.

John Wesley, Works (1872), vol. I, p. 201.

238. Whitefield and the Kingswood colliers, 1739.

Saturday, Feb. 17 [1739] . . . About one in the afternoon, I went with my brother Seward, and another friend to Kingswood, and was most delightfully entertained by an old disciple of the Lord. My bowels have long since yearned towards the poor colliers, who are very numerous, and as sheep, having no shepherd. After dinner, therefore, I went upon a mount, and spoke to as many people as came unto me. They were upwards of two hundred. Blessed be God that I have now broken the ice! I believe I never was more acceptable to my Master than when I was standing to teach these hearers in the open fields. Some may censure me; but if I thus pleased men, I should not be the servant of Christ.

. . .

Tuesday, July 10 . . . Dined today with my honoured fellow labourer, Mr Wesley, and many other friends at Two Mile Hill, in Kingswood; and preached afterwards to several thousand people and colliers, in the school-house, which has been carried on so successfully, that the roof is ready to be put on. The design, I think, is good. Old as well as young are to be instructed. A great and visible alteration is seen in the behaviour of the colliers. Instead of cursing and swearing, they are heard to sing hymns about the woods; and the rising generation, I hope, will be a generation of Christians.

W. Wale (ed.), George Whitefield's Journal (1905), pp. 209, 298.

239. Bishop Gibson on the Methodists, 1744.

II . . . this new Sect of *Methodists* have broken-through all these provisions and Restraints; neither regarding the Penalties of the Laws which stand in full Force against them, nor embracing the Protection which the Act of *Toleration* might give them in Case they comply'd with the Conditions of it. And if this be not open *Defiance* of Government, it is hard to say what is.

They began with Evening Meetings at private Houses; but they have been going on, for some Time, to open and appoint *publick Places* of Religious Worship, with the same Freedom, as if they were warranted by the Act of *Toleration*. And, not content with that, they have had the Boldness to preach in the *Fields* and other open Places, and by publick Advertisements to invite the *Rabble* to be their Hearers; notwithstanding an express Declaration in a Statute (22 Car. II, c. 1.) against assembling in a FIELD, by Name.

. . .

IV. But notwithstanding such open Inroads upon the National Constitution; these Teachers and their Followers affect to be thought Members of the *National* Church, and do accordingly join in *Communion* with it; though in a *Manner* that is irregular, and contrary to the Directions laid down in the Rubrick before the *Communion*-Service; which is established by the Act of Uniformity.

. . .

V. But now these wholsom Rules are not only broken-through, but notoriously *despised* by the new sect of *Methodists*; who leaving their own Parish-Churches where they are known, come from several Quarters, in very *great Numbers*, to receive the Communion at *other* Churches, where they are not known; and between whom and the Minister there is no Manner of Relation.

This is a Practice which may justly be complained of by the Ministers of the Churches to which they resort in that irregular Manner; as it puts such Ministers under the Difficulty, either of rejecting *great Numbers* as unknown to them, or administering the Sacrament to *great Numbers*, of whom they have no knowledge.

. . .

Part II.

Besides the many *Irregularities* which are justly charged upon these Itinerant Preachers, as Violations of the Laws of Church and State; it may be proper to enquire, whether the Doctrins they teach, and those Lengths they run, *beyond* what is practised among our *Religious Societies*, or in any other Christian Church; be a Service or a Disservice to Religion? To which Purpose, the following Queries are submitted to Consideration.

Query 1. Whether Notions in Religion may not be heighten'd to such *Extremes*, as to lead *some* into a Disregard of Religion it self, through Despair of attaining such exalted *Heights*?

. . .

Qu. 2. Whether the Enemy of Mankind may not find his Account in their carrying Christianity, which was design'd for a Rule to *all* Stations and *all* Conditions; to such *Heights* as make it fairly practicable by *a very few* in Comparison, or rather by *none*?

Qu. 3. Whether, in particular, the carrying the Doctrin of *Justification by Faith alone* to such a Heighth, as not to allow, that a careful and sincere Observance of *Moral Duties* is so much as a *Condition* of our Acceptance with God, and of our being justified in his Sight; whether this, I say, does not naturally lead People to a *Disregard* of those Duties, and a low Esteem of them; or rather to think them no Part of the Christian Religion?

Qu. 4. Whether a due and regular Attendance on the publick Offices of Religion, paid by good Men in a serious and composed Way, does not better answer the true Ends of Devotion, and is not a better Evidence of the Co-operation of the Holy Spirit, than those sudden Agonies, Roarings and Screamings, Tremblings, Droppings-down, Ravings and Madnesses; into which their Hearers have been cast; according to the Relations given of them in the Journals referr'd to?[1]

. . .

Qu. 7. Whether a *gradual* Improvement in Grace and Goodness, is not a better Foundation of Comfort, and of an Assurance of a Gospel New Birth, than that which is founded on the Doctrin of a *sudden* and *instantaneous* Change; Which if there be any such Thing, is not easily

[1] Wesley's and Whitefield's.

377

distinguished from *Fancy* and *Imagination*; the Workings whereof we may well suppose to be more *Strong* and *powerful*, while the Person considers himself in the State of one who is admitted as a *Candidate* for such a Change, and is taught in due Time to expect it?

Qu. 8. Whether, in a Christian Nation, where the Instruction and Edification of the People is provided-for, by placing Ministers in *certain Districts,* to whom the Care of the Souls within those Districts is regularly committed; It can be for the Service of Religion, that Itinerant Preachers run up and down from Place to Place, and from County to County, drawing after them confused Multitudes of People, and leading them into a *Disesteem* of their own Pastors, as less willing or less able to instruct them in the Way of Salvation: An Evil, which our Church has wisely provided against in the Ordination of a Priest, by expressly limiting the Exercise of the Powers conferred upon him, of preaching the Word of God, and administering the Holy Sacraments, *to the Congregation where he shall be lawfully appointed thereinto.* . . .

Qu. 10. Whether it be for the Service of Religion to discourage People from reading Archbishop Tillotson's Sermons, and the *whole Duty of Man*; to whom our Methodists might have added many more of our best Writers after the Restoration. For, all these (together with explaining the whole Work of our Redemption by Christ) endeavour'd to turn the Minds of People to the Practice of *Moral Duties,* and to cure them of that Madness and Enthusiasm into which they had been led by the Antinomian Doctrins and others of the like Tendency, during the Times of Anarchy and Confusion.

> E. Gibson, *Observations upon the Conduct and Behaviour of a Certain Sect usually distinguished by the Name of Methodists* (2nd ed., 1744), pp. 4–13.

240. A sermon by Tillotson.

I JOHN V. 3

. . . And his commandments are not grievous

One of the great prejudices which men have entertain'd against the Christian Religion is this, that it lays upon men *heavy burthens and grievous to be born,* that the Laws of it are very strict and severe, difficult to be kept, and yet dangerous to be broken; That it requires us to govern and keep under our passions, and to contradict many times our strongest inclinations and desires, *to cut off our right hand* and *to pluck out our right eye,* to *love our enemies,* to *bless them that curse us,* to *do good to them that hate us,* and *to pray for them that despitefully use us and persecute us;* to forgive the greatest injuries that are done to us, and to make reparation for the least that we do to others, to be contented with our condition, patient under sufferings, and ready to sacrifice our dearest interests in this world, and even our very lives, in the cause of God and Religion: All these seem to be *hard sayings* and *grievous commandments.*

For the removal of this prejudice I have chosen these words of the Apostle, which expressly tell us the contrary, that *the Commandments of God are not grievous.*

. . . Now if I can make these three things evident;

I. The Laws of God are reasonable, that is, suitable to our nature and advantageous to our interest. . . . He hath commanded us nothing in the Gospel that is either unsuitable to our reason, or prejudicial to our interest; nay, nothing that is severe and against the grain of our nature, but when either the apparent necessity of our interest does require it, or an extraordinary reward is promis'd to our obedience. . . .

. . .

II. We are not destitute of sufficient power and strength for the performing of God's commands. Had God given us Laws but no power to keep them, his commandments would then indeed have been grievous. 'Tis true we have contracted a great deal of weakness and impotency by our wilful degeneracy from goodness, but that grace which the Gospel offers to us for our assistance is sufficient for us.

. . .

III. We have the greatest encouragement to the observance of God's Commands. Two things make any course of life easy; present pleasure, and the assurance of a future reward. Religion gives part of its reward in hand, the present comfort and satisfaction of having done our duty; and for the rest, it offers us the best security that Heaven can give.

. . .

But are there no difficulties then in Religion? Is every thing so plain and easy? Are all the ways of virtue so smooth and even as we have here represented them? Hath not our *Saviour* told us, *that strait is the gate and narrow is the way that leads to life, and few there be that find it*? Matt. 7. 14. Does not the *Apostle* say *that through much tribulation we must enter into the Kingdom of God*? Acts. 14. 22. And, *that all that will live godly in Christ Jesus shall suffer persecution*? And does not the *Scripture* everywhere speak of *striving*, and *wrestling*, and *running*, and *fighting*; of *labouring*, and *watching*, and *giving all diligence*? And is there nothing grievous in all this?

This is very material Objection; and therefore I shall be more careful to give a Satisfactory answer to it. And that I may do it the more distinctly be pleas'd to consider these *six* things. 1. That the suffering of persecution for Religion is an extraordinary case, which did chiefly concern the first Ages of Christianity. 2. That this discourse concerning the easiness of God's commands does all along suppose and acknowledge the difficulties of the entrance upon a religious course. 3. Nor is there any reason it should exclude our after-care and diligence. 4. All the difficulties of Religion are very much mitigated and allayed by hope and by love. 5. There is incomparably more difficulty and trouble in the ways of sin and vice than in the ways of Religion and Virtue. 6. If we do but put virtue and vice, a religious and a wicked course of life in equal circumstances; if we will but suppose a man as much accustomed and inur'd to the one as he has been to the other, then I shall not doubt to pronounce that the advantages of ease and pleasure will be found to be on the side of Religion. . . .

. . . If the same seriousness and industry of endeavour, which men commonly use to raise a fortune and advance themselves in the world, will serve to make a man a good man and to bring him to Heaven, what reason hath any man to complain of the hard terms of Religion? And I think I may truly say that usually less than this does it. . . . However this I am sure of, that if men would be as serious to save their immortal souls as they are to support these dying bodies; if they would but provide for eternity with the same solicitude and real care as they do for this life; if they would but seek Heaven with the same ardour of affection, and vigour of prosecution as they seek earthly things; if they would but love God as much as many men do the world, and mind godliness as much as men usually do gain; if they would but go to Church with as good a will as men ordinarily do to their Markets and Fairs, and be in as good earnest at their devotions as men commonly are in driving a bargain; if they would but endure some troubles and inconveniences in the ways of Religion with the same patience and constancy as they can do storms, and foul ways and mischances, when they are travelling about their worldly occasions; if they would but avoid bad company as men use to do cheaters, and reject the temptations of the Devil and the world as they would do the kind words and insinuations of a man they verily believe to have a design to over-reach them; I am confident that such a one could not fail of Heaven, and would be much surer of it upon these terms, than any man that doth all the other things could be of getting an estate, or of attaining any thing in this world.

J. Tillotson, *Works* (Dublin, 1739), vol. 1, p. 131.

241. The Evangelicals: defended by Charles Simeon, 1813.

To have some opportunities of meeting my people I considered as indispensable; for how could I know my sheep, if I did not see them in private; and how was it possible for me to visit so many at their own houses; and to find out all their different states and trials? If there were regular seasons for us to meet together ... I could learn .... whether any were in danger of being drawn away by the Dissenters, or were imbibing any erroneous tenets, or were acting in any respect unworthy of their holy profession. I am aware that even such societies as these are by many accounted irregular, and that very few of the governors of our Church would sanction them. Indeed it is a curious fact, that the establishing of such societies is generally supposed to indicate an indifference towards the Church, when it actually proceeds from a love to the Church, and a zeal for its interests. Were the Bishops acquainted with the ministers who are called Evangelical, they would soon see the importance, yea, and the absolute necessity of such meetings, not merely for the edification of the people, *but chiefly for the preservation of the Established Church.* The Dissenters in general, and the Methodists in particular, have such meetings; and they are found to be of the highest utility for the cultivation of mutual love, and for the keeping of their respective members in one compact body. Where nothing of that kind is established, the members of any church are only as a rope of sand, and may easily be scattered with every wind of doctrine, or drawn aside by any proselyting sectary. What influence can a minister maintain over his people, if he does not foster them as a brood under his wings? As to the idea of such meetings being contrary to our obligations as ministers of the Establishment, let any one read the Bishop's Charge to the Priest in the Ordination Service, and say, whether a clergyman can fulfil his duties without them? I am well persuaded he cannot; and experience proves that wherever there is an efficient ministry in the Church without somewhat of a similar super-intendence, the clergyman beats the bush, and the Dissenters catch the game: whereas, where such a superintendence is maintained, the people are united as an army with banners.

William Carus (ed.), *Memoirs of the Life of the Rev. Charles Simeon, M.A.* (1847), p. 138.

242. The Evangelicals: criticised by Bishop Randolph, 1810.

The duty of the Clergy is the more concerned in this, because the same general [French] revolution has caused, and in return receives increase from, the errors in religion which have arisen. These also have a share in our distractions. The infidelity which was studiously propagated at the beginning of these troubles, though it has since declined, and never had many followers compacted into any formidable body, yet has contributed to unsettle the minds of many, and to incline them to a dangerous licentiousness of opinion, or indifference in religion. The extreme into which others have run, shocked at this growing evil, has been equally prejudicial to sober and sound religion. Men have fought for separation, when the circumstances required the strictest union; and to rebuild the shaken faith of Christians on the fluctuating basis of enthusiasm; and to heal the wounds which Christian obedience had received from corruption of mind, profligacy of manner, and vitiousness of life, not by the evangelical doctrine and grace of re-pentance, as the Gospel teaches, but by new and unheard of conver-sions, the inventions of men of heated imaginations, or ambitious views. They have bewildered themselves and their followers in the mysteries and depths of Calvinism, in distrust or contempt of the simplicity of the Gospel. Hence has there been engendered a new schism, halting between the Church and dissension from it, which, while it professes to follow the purity of our Church, or even to refine upon it, is con-tinually undermining the establishment, and acts also occasionally at the head of the most discordant sects in opposition to it. By nothing more than this has the peace and credit of our Church been disturbed, whilst the most respectable ministers, if they enlist not themselves under this sect, are vilified by the uncharitable reflections and arrogant pre-tensions of these new Puritans.

J. Randolph, Bishop of London, *A Charge delivered to the Clergy of the Diocese of London* (1810), p. 11.

CHAPTER 6

LIBERTIES OF THE SUBJECT

The Revolution has been rightly revered as a landmark in the history of individual liberties. 'It is in the guarantee of these rights that the value of the Revolution consists; nor does the fact that we have enjoyed them so long diminish the importance of their origin.'[1] And our long enjoyment of them and, indeed, their enlargement, has been perhaps most of all due to another feature of the constitution which has its origin in 1688: the independence of the judiciary. The security of judges' tenure provided by the Act of Settlement,[2] coming as it did after the destruction of the prerogative courts in 1641, and clinched as it was by the statute of 1760 whereby the demise of the crown affected neither their office nor their salary, was regarded in the eighteenth century as the characteristic virtue of the English form of government by Englishmen and foreigners alike. It was, as George III put it, 'One of the best securities to the Rights and Liberties of my loving Subjects'[3]; a judgement in which Blackstone concurred in his trenchant manner (243). And one of its consequences was the establishment of 'perhaps the most distinctive, and certainly the most salutary, of all the characteristics of English constitutional law'[4]: the rule of law, which Dicey, in his classical analysis, described as having three chief features. 'We mean, in the first place, that no man is punishable or can be lawfully made to suffer in body or goods except for a distinct breach of the law established in the ordinary legal manner before the ordinary Courts of the land. In this sense the rule of law is contrasted with every system of government based on the exercise by persons in authority of wide, arbitrary, or discretionary powers of constraint ... We mean in the second place ... not only that with us no man is above the law, but (what is a different thing) that here every man, whatever be his rank or condition, is subject to the ordinary law of the realm and amenable to the jurisdiction of the ordinary tribunals. ... We may say,' thirdly 'that the constitution is pervaded by the rule of law on the ground that the general principles of the constitution (as for example the right to personal liberty, or the right of public meeting) are with us the result of judicial decisions determining the rights of private persons in particular cases brought before the Courts; whereas under many foreign con-

---

[1] D. Ogg, *England in the Reigns of James II and William III* (Oxford), 1955), p. 244.
[2] No. **21**, p. 59.
[3] *C.J.*, XXVIII, 1095.
[4] W. Holdsworth, *History of English Law* (1938), vol. x, p. 647.

stitutions the security (such as it is) given to the rights of individuals results, or appears to result, from the general principles of the constitution.'[1] Now a considerable proportion of the law defining the rights of the individual and delimiting the power of the state over him was constructed in the eighteenth century by the judges in their courts, sometimes with parliamentary help, and sometimes in the teeth of parliamentary hostility; and to the chief features of this we must now turn.[2]

243. Blackstone on the independent judiciary.

In this distinct and separate existence of the judicial power in a peculiar body of men, nominated indeed, but not removable at pleasure, by the crown, consists one main preservative of the public liberty; which cannot subsist long in any state, unless the administration of common justice be in some degree separated both from the legislative and also from the executive power. Were it joined with the legislative, the life, liberty, and property of the subject would be in the hands of arbitrary judges, whose decisions would be then regulated only by their own opinions, and not by any fundamental principles of law; which, though legislators may depart from, yet judges are bound to observe. Were it joined with the executive, this union might soon be an overbalance for the legislative. For which reason, by the statute of 16 Car. I. c. 10. which abolished the court of star-chamber, effectual care is taken to remove all judicial power out of the hands of the king's privy council; who, as then was evident from recent instances, might soon be inclined to pronounce that for law, which was most agreeable to the prince or his officers. Nothing therefore is more to be avoided, in a free constitution, than uniting the provinces of a judge and a minister of state.

W. Blackstone, *Commentaries on the Laws of England* (15th ed., 1809), vol. I, p. 268.

I. LIBERTY OF PERSON

'The most effectual protector of the liberty of the subject that any legal system has devised',[3] according to Sir William Holdsworth, was the writ of *Habeas Corpus*, the efficiency of which had been greatly improved by the Act of 1679.[4] A number of breaches still remained in the law, however, whereby personal liberty could be placed in jeopardy, and a good many of

---

[1] A. V. Dicey, *Law of the Constitution* (9th ed., 1939), pp. 188, 193, 195.
[2] For liberty of worship, see Chapter 1, pp. 6–7, and Chapter 5, pp. 325–6.
[3] *History of English Law*, vol. x, p. 658.
[4] 31 Car. II, c. 2.

these were plugged during this period. Since 1679 the writ had been circumvented by the requirement of excessive bail: this practice ceased after its condemnation in the Bill of Rights.[1] Two other weaknesses were not put right till the Habeas Corpus Amendment Act of 1816: the writ did not apply to cases other than detention on a criminal charge, and the courts had no power to examine the truth of the facts stated on the return to the writ by the gaoler. Nevertheless, the efficacy of the writ was proved daily, and perhaps this can best be illustrated by citing two unusual examples of its successful employment. In the first, the writ brought about not only the manumission of a negro slave, James Sommersett, who had been brought to England by his West Indian master, but also the opinion of Lord Mansfield that slavery was not recognised by the laws of England (244). In the second, Theobald Wolfe Tone, an Irish rebel who had been taken during the attempted French invasion of Ireland in 1798 and sentenced to death by court-martial, was released from military custody by the Irish Court of King's Bench, on the grounds that he was not a British soldier and therefore could not be tried under military law (245). 'When it is remembered that Wolfe Tone's substantial guilt was admitted, that the court was made up of judges who detested the rebels, and that in 1798 Ireland was in the midst of a revolutionary crisis, it will be admitted that no more splendid assertion of the supremacy of the law can be found than the protection of Wolfe Tone by the Irish Bench.'[2]

The power of the courts in defence of personal liberty against encroachments by the executive is also strikingly demonstrated in the cases resulting from the repressive activities of the Secretary of State against No. 45 *North Briton* and other opposition papers. These cases were decided against the government, and three of its powers were specifically condemned. Firstly, in *Leach* v. *Money*, Lord Mansfield denied the legality of general warrants. Along with Wilkes, Dryden Leach had been arrested by John Money and two other King's Messengers under a warrant for the apprehension of 'the authors, printers and publishers of a seditious and treasonable paper, intitled, The North Briton, No. 45' (246). As he was neither author, printer nor publisher, he was awarded £400 damages in the Court of Common Pleas. The case then came up before Lord Mansfield in the King's Bench on a writ of error, and he condemned the use of general warrants (247), though this particular point was not central to the case. Nevertheless, they were not used again after this time.

Secondly, in the case of *Entick* v. *Carrington*, Lord Chief Justice Camden denied power to the Secretary of State to commit persons to prison on any charge except treason. And, thirdly, in the same judgement he denied the

---

[1] See p. 28.
[2] A. V. Dicey, *Law of the Constitution* (9th ed., 1939), p. 294.

validity of a warrant to search, seize and carry away papers (**248**). John Entick, one of the authors of an opposition paper called *The Monitor*, had been arrested, had his house forcibly entered and his books and papers seized by Nathan Carrington and three other King's Messengers in November 1762, in pursuance of the warrant of the Secretary of State. He brought an action for trespass against them, which was eventually decided in his favour by Camden in the Court of Common Pleas. In the course of his judgement, the Lord Chief Justice demolished one by one the crown's arguments in favour of the Secretary of State's powers of arrest and seizure of papers. He could not arrest in virtue of his position as a member of the Privy Council, for an individual councillor had no power of arrest except in cases of treason. Neither did the Secretary of State possess the powers of a conservator or justice of the peace. The argument from long usage he scotched by showing that it was only proved as far back as the Revolution, and 'if the practice began then, it began too late to be law now.'[1] And, finally, he refused to accept the 'argument from state necessity, or a distinction that has been aimed at between state offences and others'. 'The common law', he said, 'does not understand that kind of reasoning, nor do our books take notice of any such distinctions.'[2]

If the courts thus had to clip the wings of the executive, they had no less trouble with the legislature—'for Englishmen are no more to be slaves to Parliaments, than to Kings', as Daniel Defoe wrote in 1701.[3] It has already been observed[4] that, on occasion, parliamentary privilege could be just as oppressive in the eighteenth century as royal prerogative had been in the seventeenth; and in a number of cases the courts demonstrated that the privileges of parliament were just as much under the rule of law as the rights of any other institution. In *Ashby* v. *White* (**133-136**) Holt showed that, while parliament was the sole judge of the use of its undoubted privileges, when the existence of a privilege was in question the courts must decide the issue. In *Paty's case* (**137**), Holt decided that if the House of Commons in arresting a person for a breach of privilege specified the nature of the breach, then the courts could examine the sufficiency of it and discharge the prisoner if it was insufficient. Of course, Holt was in the minority in these cases, and his views did not become generally accepted in the eighteenth century, least of all by the House of Commons. He had insisted that parliamentary privilege was part of the law, and that the law could not be changed by a House of Commons resolution; a point raised again in the case of *John Wilkes* (**138-140**) and in the controversy over the Middlesex Elections (**142-144**), and tacitly accepted after that.

---

[1] No. **248**, p. 396.   [2] No. **248**, p. 396.
[3] The last words of the *Legion Memorial* in *P.H.*, v, 1256.
[4] See Chapter 3, section VII.

244. *Sommersett's Case*, 1772.

LORD MANSFIELD.—On the part of Sommersett, the case which we gave notice should be decided this day, the Court now proceeds to give its opinion. I shall recite the return to the writ of Habeas Corpus, as the ground of our determination; omitting only words of form. The captain of the ship on board of which the negro was taken, makes his return to the writ in terms signifying that there have been, and still are, slaves to a great number in Africa; and that the trade in them is authorized by the laws and opinions of Virginia and Jamaica; that they are goods and chattels; and, as such, saleable and sold. That James Sommersett is a negro of Africa, and long before the return of the king's writ was brought to be sold, and was sold to Charles Steuart, esq. then in Jamaica, and has not been manumitted since; that Mr. Steuart, having occasion to transact business, came over hither, with an intention to return; and brought Sommersett to attend and abide with him, and to carry him back as soon as the business should be transacted. That such intention has been, and still continues; and that the negro did remain till the time of his departure in the service of his master Mr. Steuart, and quitted it without his consent; and thereupon, before the return of the king's writ, the said Charles Steuart did commit the slave on board the Anne and Mary, to safe custody, to be kept till he should set sail, and then to be taken with him to Jamaica, and there sold as a slave. And this is the cause why he, captain Knowles, who was then and now is, commander of the above vessel, then and now lying in the river of Thames, did the said negro, committed to his custody, detain; and on which he now renders him to the orders of the Court. We pay all due attention to the opinion of sir Philip Yorke, and lord chancellor Talbot, whereby they pledged themselves to the British planters, for all the legal consequences of slaves coming over to this kingdom or being baptized, recognized by lord Hardwicke, sitting as chancellor on the 19th of October, 1749, that trover would lie: that a notion had prevailed, if a negro came over, or became a Christian, he was emancipated, but no ground in law: that he and lord Talbot, when attorney and solicitor-general, were of opinion, that no such claim for freedom was valid; that though the statute of tenures had abolished villeins regardant to a manor, yet he did not conceive but that a man might still become a villein in gross, by confessing himself such in open court. We are so well agreed, that we

387

think there is no occasion of having it argued (as I intimated an intention at first,) before all the judges, as is usual, for obvious reasons, on a return to a Habeas Corpus. The only question before us is, whether the cause on the return is sufficient? If it is, the negro must be remanded; if it is not, he must be discharged. Accordingly, the return states, that the slave departed and refused to serve; whereupon he was kept, to be sold abroad. So high an act of dominion must be recognized by the law of the country where it is used. The power of a master over his slave has been extremely different, in different countries. The state of slavery is of such a nature, that it is incapable of being introduced on any reasons, moral or political, but only by positive law, which preserves its force long after the reasons, occasion, and time itself from whence it was created, is erased from memory. It is so odious, that nothing can be suffered to support it, but positive law. Whatever inconveniences, therefore, may follow from the decision, I cannot say this case is allowed or approved by the law of England; and therefore the black must be discharged.

S.T., xx, 80.

245. *Wolfe Tone's Case,* 1798.

. . . a motion was made in the Court of King's Bench by Mr. Curran, on an affidavit of Mr. Tone's father, stating that his son had been brought before a bench of officers, calling itself a court martial, and by them sentenced to death.

"I do not pretend to say," observed Mr. Curran, "that Mr. Tone is not guilty of the charges of which he was accused;—I presume the officers were honourable men;—but it is stated in the affidavit, as a solemn fact, that Mr. Tone had no commission under His Majesty, and therefore no court martial could have any cognizance of any crime imputed to him, while the Court of King's Bench sat in the capacity of the great criminal court of the land. In times when war was raging, when man was opposed to man in the field, courts martial might be endured; but every law authority is with me, while I stand upon this sacred and immutable principle of the constitution—*that martial law and civil law are incompatible;* and that the former must cease with the existence of the latter. This is not the time for arguing this momentous question. My client must appear in this court. *He is cast for death this day.* He may be ordered for execution while I address you. I call on the Court to support the law. I move for a *habeas corpus* to be directed to the provost marshal of the barracks of Dublin, and major Sandys to bring up the body of Mr. Tone.

Lord Chief Justice [Kilwarden].—Have a writ instantly prepared.

Mr. Curran.—My client may die while this writ is preparing.

Lord Chief Justice.—Mr. Sheriff, proceed to the barracks, and acquaint the provost-marshal that a writ is preparing to suspend Mr. Tone's execution; and *see that he be not executed.*

[The Court awaited in a state of the utmost agitation, the return of the Sheriff.]

Mr. Sheriff.—My lords, I have been at the barracks, in pursuance of your order. The provost-marshal says he must obey major Sandys. Major Sandys says he must obey lord Cornwallis.

Mr. Curran.—Mr. Tone's father, my lords, returns, after serving the Habeas Corpus: he says general Craig will not obey it.

Lord Chief Justice.—Mr. Sheriff; take the body of Tone into your custody. Take the provost-marshal and major Sandys into custody: and show the order of this Court to general Craig.

Mr. Sheriff (who was understood to have been refused admittance at the barracks) returns.—I have been at the barracks. Mr. Tone having cut his throat last night, is not in a condition to be removed. As to the second part of your order, I could not meet the parties.

[A French Emigrant Surgeon, whom General Craig had sent along with the Sheriff, was sworn.]

Surgeon.—I was sent to attend Mr. Tone this morning at four o'clock, his windpipe was divided. I took instant measures to secure his life, by closing the wound. There is no knowing, for four days, whether it will be mortal. His head is now kept in one position. *A sentinel is over him, to prevent his speaking.* His removal would kill him.

Mr. Curran applied for farther surgical aid, and for the admission of Mr. Tone's friends to him. [*Refused.*]

Lord Chief Justice.—Let a rule be made for suspending the execution of Theobald Wolfe Tone; and let it be served on the proper persons.

[The prisoner lingered until the 19th day of November, when he expired, after having endured in the interval the most excruciating pain.]

S.T., xxvii, 624.

246. *Leach* v. *Money*: the General Warrant, 1763.

George Montague Dunk, earl of Halifax, viscount Sunbury and baron Halifax, one of the lords of his majesty's most honourable privy council, lieutenant general of his majesty's forces, and principal secretary of state: these are in his majesty's name to authorize and require you (taking a constable to your assistance) to make strict and diligent search for the authors, printers and publishers of a seditious and treasonable paper, intitled, The North Briton, No. 45, Saturday April 23, 1763, printed for G. Kearsley in Ludgate-street, London, and them, or any of them, having found, to apprehend and seize, together with their papers, and to bring in safe custody before me, to be examined concerning the premisses, and further dealt with according to law: and in the due execution thereof, all mayors, sheriffs, justices of the peace, constables, and all other his majestys's officers civil and military, and loving subjects whom it may concern, are to be aiding and assisting to you, as there shall be occasion; and for so doing this shall be your warrant. Given at St. James's the 26th day of April, in the third year of his majesty's reign. DUNK HALIFAX.

To Nathan Carrington, John Money, James Watson, and Robert Blackmore, four of his majesty's messengers in ordinary.

S.T., XIX, 981.

247. *Leach* v. *Money*: Mansfield's judgement, 1765.

LORD MANSFIELD— . . . At present—as to the validity of the warrant, upon the single objection of the incertainty of the person, being neither named nor described—the common law, in many cases, gives authority to arrest without warrant; more especially, where taken in the very act: and there are many cases where particular acts of parliament have given authority to apprehend, under general warrants; as in the case of writs of assistance, or warrants to take up loose, idle, and disorderly people. But here, it is not contended, that the common law gave the officer authority to apprehend; nor that there is any act of parliament which warrants this case.

Therefore it must stand upon principles of common law.

It is not fit, that the receiving or judging of the information should be left to the discretion of the officer. The magistrate ought to judge; and should give certain directions to the officer. This is so, upon reason and convenience.

Then as to authorities—Hale and all others hold such an uncertain warrant void: and there is no case or book to the contrary.

It is said, 'that the usage has been so; and that many have been issued, since the Revolution, down to this time.'

But a usage, to grow into law, ought to be a general usage *communiter usitata et approbata*; and which, after a long continuance, it would be mischievous to overturn.

This is only the usage of a particular office, and contrary to the usage of all other justices and conservators of the peace.

There is the less reason for regarding this usage; because the form of the warrant probably took its rise from a positive statute; and the former precedents were inadvertently followed, after that law was expired.

Mr. Justice *Wilmot* declared, that he had no doubt, nor ever had, upon these warrants: he thought them illegal and void.

Neither had the two other judges, Mr. Justice Yates, and Mr. Justice Aston, any doubt (upon this first argument) of the illegality of them: for no degree of antiquity can give sanction to a usage bad in itself. And they esteemed this usage to be so. They were clear and unanimous in opinion, that this warrant was illegal and bad.

S.T., xix, 1026.

248. *Entick* v. *Carrington* : Camden's judgement, 1765.

LORD CHIEF JUSTICE CAMDEN . . . The power of this minister, in the way wherein it has been usually exercised, is pretty singular.

If he is considered in the light of a privy counsellor, although every member of that board is equally entitled to it with himself, yet he is the only one of that body who exerts it. . . .

To consider him as a conservator. He never binds to the peace, or good behaviour, which seems to have been the principal duty of a conservator; at least he never does it in those cases, where the law requires those sureties. But he commits in certain other cases, where it is very doubtful, whether the conservator had any jurisdiction whatever.

His warrants are chiefly exerted against libellers, whom he binds in the first instance to their good behaviour, which no other conservator ever attempted, from the best intelligence that we can learn from our books.

And though he doth all these things, yet it seems agreed, that he hath no power whatsoever to administer an oath or take bail.

This jurisdiction, as extraordinary as I have described it, is so dark and obscure in its origin, that the counsel have not been able to form any certain opinion from whence it sprang.

Sometimes they annex it to the office of secretary of state, sometimes to the quality of privy counsellor; and in the last argument it has been derived from the king's royal prerogative to commit by his own personal command.

Whatever may have been the true source of this authority it must be admitted, that at this day he is in the full legal exercise of it; because there has been not only a clear practice of it, at least since the Revolution, confirmed by a variety of precedents; but the authority has been recognized and confirmed by two cases in the very point since that period: and therefore we have not a power to unsettle or contradict it now, even though we are persuaded that the commencement of it was erroneous . . .

To proceed then . . . and consider the person in the capacity of a secretary of state . . . [Examination of the history and powers of the office.]

I have now finished all I have to say upon this head; and am satisfied, that the secretary of state hath assumed this power as a transfer, I know not how, of the royal authority to himself; and that the common law of England knows no such magistrate. . . .

. . . I come in my last place to the point, which is made by the justification; for the defendants . . . are under a necessity to maintain the legality of the warrants, under which they have acted, and to shew that the secretary of state in the instance now before us, had a jurisdiction to seize the plaintiff's papers. If he had no such jurisdiction, the law is clear, that the officers are as much responsible for the trespass as their superior.

This, though it is not the most difficult, is the most interesting question in the cause; because if this point should be determined in favour of the jurisdiction, the secret cabinets and bureaus of every subject in this kingdom will be thrown open to the search and inspection of a messenger, whenever the secretary of state shall think fit to charge, or even to suspect, a person to be the author, printer, or publisher of a seditious libel.

The messenger, under this warrant, is commanded to seize the person described, and to bring him with his papers to be examined before the secretary of state. In consequence of this, the house must be searched;

the lock and doors of every room, box, or trunk must be broken open; all the papers and books without exception, if the warrant be executed according to its tenor, must be seized and carried away; for it is observable, that nothing is left either to the discretion or to the humanity of the officer.

This power so assumed by the secretary of state is an execution upon all the party's papers, in the first instance. His house is rifled; his most valuable secrets are taken out of his possession, before the paper for which he is charged is found to be criminal by any competent jurisdiction, and before he is convicted either of writing, publishing, or being concerned in the paper.

This power, so claimed by the secretary of state, is not supported by one single citation from any law book extant. It is claimed by no other magistrate in this kingdom but himself; the great executive hand of criminal justice, the lord chief justice of the court of King's-bench, chief justice Scroggs excepted, never having assumed this authority.

The arguments, which the defendants' counsel have thought fit to urge in support of this practice, are of this kind.

That such warrants have issued frequently since the Revolution, which practice has been found by the special verdict; though I must observe, that the defendants have no right to avail themselves of that finding, because no such practice is averred in their justification.

That the case of the warrants bears a resemblance to the case of search for stolen goods.

They say too, that they have been executed without resistance upon many printers, booksellers, and authors, who have quietly submitted to the authority; that no action hath hitherto been brought to try the right: and that although they have been often read upon the returns of Habeas Corpus, yet no court of justice has ever declared them illegal.

And it is further insisted, that this power is essential to government, and the only means of quieting clamours and sedition.

These arguments, if they can be called arguments, shall be all taken notice of; because upon this question I am desirous of removing every colour or plausibility.

Before I state the question, it will be necessary to describe the power claimed by this warrant in its full extent.

If honestly exerted, it is a power to seize that man's papers, who is charged upon oath to be the author or publisher of a seditious libel; if oppressively, it acts against every man, who is so described in the warrant, though he be innocent.

It is executed against the party, before he is heard or even summoned; and the information, as well as the informers, is unknown.

It is executed by messengers with or without a constable (for it can never be pretended, that such is necessary in point of law) in the presence or the absence of the party, as the messengers shall think fit, and without a witness to testify what passes at the time of the transaction; so that when the papers are gone, as the only witnesses are the trespassers, the party injured is left without proof.

If this injury falls upon an innocent person, he is as destitute of remedy as the guilty: and the whole transaction is so guarded against discovery, that if the officer should be disposed to carry off a bank-bill, he may do it with impunity, since there is no man capable of proving either the taker or the thing taken.

It must not be here forgot, that no subject whatsoever is privileged from this search; because both Houses of Parliament have resolved, that there is no privilege in the case of a seditious libel.

Nor is there pretence to say, that the word 'papers' here mentioned ought in point of law to be restrained to the libellous papers only. The word is general, and there is nothing in the warrant to confine it; nay, I am able to affirm, that it has been upon a late occasion executed in its utmost latitude: for in the case of Wilkes against Wood, when the messengers hesitated about taking all the manuscripts, and sent to the secretary of state for more express orders for that purpose, the answer was, "that all must be taken, manuscripts and all." Accordingly, all was taken, and Mr. Wilkes's private pocket-book filled up the mouth of the sack.

I was likewise told in the same cause by one of the most experienced messengers, that he held himself bound by his oath to pay an implicit obedience to the commands of the secretary of state; that in common cases he was contented to seize the printed impressions of the papers mentioned in the warrant; but when he received directions to search further, or to make a more general seizure, his rule was to sweep all. The practice has been correspondent to the warrant.

Such is the power, and therefore one should naturally expect that the law to warrant it should be clear in proportion as the power is exorbitant.

If it is law, it will be found in our books. If it is not to be found there, it is not law.

The great end, for which men entered into society, was to secure their property. That right is preserved sacred and incommunicable in all instances, where it has not been taken away or abridged by some public law for the good of the whole. The cases where this right of property is set aside by positive law, are various. Distresses, executions, forfeitures, taxes, &c. are all of this description; wherein every man by common consent gives up that right, for the sake of justice and the general good. By the laws of England, every invasion of private property, be it ever so minute, is a trespass. No man can set his foot upon my ground without my licence, but he is liable to an action, though the damage be nothing; which is proved by every declaration in trespass, where the defendant is called upon to answer for bruising the grass and even treading upon the soil. If he admits the fact, he is bound to shew by way of justification, that some positive law has empowered or excused him. The justification is submitted to the judges, who are to look into the books; and if such a justification can be maintained by the text of the statute law, or by the principles of common law. If no such excuse can be found or produced, the silence of the books is an authority against the defendant, and the plaintiff must have judgment.

According to this reasoning, it is now incumbent upon the defendants to shew the law, by which this seizure is warranted. If that cannot be done, it is a trespass.

Papers are the owner's goods and chattels: they are his dearest property; and are so far from enduring a seizure, that they will hardly bear an inspection; and though the eye cannot by the laws of England be guilty of a trespass, yet where private papers are removed and carried away, the secret nature of those goods will be an aggravation of the trespass, and demand more considerable damages in that respect. Where is the written law that gives any magistrate such a power? I can safely answer, there is none; and therefore it is too much for us without such authority to pronounce a practice legal, which would be subversive of all the comforts of society. . . .

I come now to the practice since the Revolution, which has been strongly urged, with this emphatical addition, that an usage tolerated from the era of liberty, and continued downwards to this time through the best ages of the constitution, must necessarily have a legal commencement. Now, though that pretence can have no place in the question made by this plea, because no such practice is there alleged;

yet I will permit the defendant for the present to borrow a fact from the special verdict, for the sake of giving it an answer.

If the practice began then, it began too late to be law now. If it was more ancient, the Revolution is not to answer for it; and I could have wished, that upon this occasion the Revolution had not been considered as the only basis of our liberty.

The Revolution restored this constitution to its first principles. It did no more. It did not enlarge the liberty of the subject; but gave it a better security. It neither widened nor contracted the foundation, but repaired, and perhaps added a buttress or two to the fabric; and if any minister of state has since deviated from the principles at that time recognized, all that I can say is, that, so far from being sanctified, they are condemned by the Revolution.

. . . But still it is insisted, that there has been a general submission, and no action brought to try the right.

I answer, there has been a submission of guilt and poverty to power and the terror of punishment. But it would be strange doctrine to assert that all the people of this land are bound to acknowledge that to be universal law, which a few criminal booksellers have been afraid to dispute. . .

It is then said, that it is necessary for the ends of government to lodge such a power with a state officer; and that it is better to prevent the publication before than to punish the offender afterwards. I answer, if the legislature be of that opinion, they will revive the Licensing Act. But if they have not done that, I conceive they are not of that opinion. And with respect to the argument of state necessity, or a distinction that has been aimed at between state offences and others, the common law does not understand that kind of reasoning, nor do our books take notice of any such distinctions.

Serjeant Ashley was committed to the Tower in the 3rd of Charles 1st, by the House of Lords only for asserting in argument, that there was a 'law of state' different from the common law; and the Ship-Money judges were impeached for holding, first, that state-necessity would justify the raising money without consent of parliament; and secondly, that the king was judge of that necessity.

If the king himself has no power to declare when the law ought to be violated for reason of state, I am sure we his judges have no such prerogative.

Lastly, it is urged as an argument of utility, that such a search is a means of detecting offenders by discovering evidence. I wish some cases had been shewn, where the law forceth evidence out of the owner's custody by process. There is no process against papers in civil causes. It has been often tried, but never prevailed. Nay, where the adversary has by force or fraud got possession of your own proper evidence, there is no way to get it back but by action.

In the criminal law such proceeding was never heard of; and yet there are some crimes, such for instance as murder, rape, robbery, and house-breaking, to say nothing of forgery and perjury, that are more atrocious than libelling. But our law has provided no paper-search in these cases to help forward the conviction. . . .

If, however, a right search for the sake of discovering evidence ought in any case to be allowed, this crime above all others ought to be excepted, as wanting such a discovery less than any other. It is committed in open daylight, and in the face of the world; every act of publication makes new proof; and the solicitor of the treasury, if he pleases, may be the witness himself.

The messenger of the press, by the very constitution of his office, is directed to purchase every libel that comes forth, in order to be a witness. . . .

I have now taken notice of everything that has been urged upon the present point; and upon the whole we are all of opinion, that the warrant to seize and carry away the party's papers in the case of a seditious libel, is illegal and void.

S.T., XIX, 1045.

II. LIBERTY OF THE PRESS

Before the Revolution, the press had been controlled by the government by means of the Star Chamber and the Court of High Commission superimposed on the more detailed grip on the industry enjoyed by the Stationers' Company. This machinery, which existed mainly to control opinion but also partly to conform with the economic paternalism of the period, though overthrown in the Civil War, was in substance recreated by the ordinances of the Commonwealth and by the Licensing Acts of the later Stuarts. The last of these, of 1685, was renewed for two years in 1692; but a formidable opposition to the licensing system was steadily growing in this period, drawing its strength partly from the Whigs' revival of Milton's arguments and from the prevailing post-Revolutionary fear of economic activities by the state, but mainly from exasperation with the way the system was working in practice. The two last Licensers, Fraser and Bohun, were one after the other forced out of office, one for being too Whig and the other for being too Tory. Consequently, in 1695, the House of Commons voted against renewing the Act, a step which led to a conference with the Lords, who at first disagreed, but who were later convinced by the eighteen reasons drawn up by the Commons (249). This document condemned the Licensing Act, 'not as a thing essentially evil, but on account of the petty grievances, the exactions, the jobs, the commercial restrictions, the domiciliary visits, which were incidental to it'.[1] Thus the ancient apparatus for controlling opinion was allowed to collapse, a step which Macaulay considered 'has done more for liberty and for civilisation than the Great Charter or the Bill of Rights.'[2]

However, liberty of discussion, which is perhaps the basis of the all the other liberties, was not yet fully assured, for writers were still subject to a law of libel which still required considerable modification. Though we had the freest press in Europe, and though our scribes were far from mealy-mouthed in their attacks on governments, the State had greater reserves of power than today owing to two circumstances. One was the view taken by the lawyers in the early part of this period that any adverse comment on the government was libellous. Holt was quite clear about this in the case of *John Tutchin* in 1704 (250). The other was the view taken by most judges that it was for the jury to decide only upon two matters of fact: whether the document in question had been published, and whether it bore the meaning attributed to it in the indictment; while it was for the judges themselves to decide, as a matter of law, whether the writing was a libel. The only course open to a jury sympathetic to the defendant was to bring in a verdict of 'Not guilty' even when there was no doubt about the fact of publication. For example, Francklin, a printer of the *Craftsman*, was acquitted in 1729 by a jury chosen by a Tory sheriff. After 1730, however, the Special Juries Act of that year enabled judges of the courts at Westminster to swear in juries of a higher property qualification; and in the following year the conviction of Francklin was secured. In this case, Chief Justice Raymond repeated the historically correct opinion that it was for the judge to decide whether a writing was a libel, and he was followed by most authorities, including Lord Mansfield in the case of the *Dean of St. Asaph* in 1784 (251).

Developments in the second half of this period, however, were rendering the ideas of Holt, Raymond and Mansfield politically untenable, if legally correct. The great expansion of the press, and the mounting of the offensive against George III, produced clashes between newspapers and the government in which juries continued to resist the judges' directions and bring in verdicts of 'Not guilty', or 'Guilty of publishing only', as in the *Dean of St. Asaph's case*.[3] As Wedderburn said in the House of Commons in 1770,

[1] Lord Macaulay, *History of England* (1895), vol. II, p. 503.
[2] *Ibid.*   [3] See p. 404.

'so changeable is the nature of a libel, so much does it assume the nature of a cameleon, and suit its colour to the complexion of the times! in short its libellous quality is founded entirely on popular opinion'.[1] And in the reign of George III the law had become too alienated from public opinion and political theory to be properly enforceable; and, after a long struggle in which lawyers like Camden and Erskine and politicians like Fox were opposed by the majority of the bench, the law had to give way. This time it was at the behest of the legislature in the form of the Libel Act of 1792 (252), which declared the right of the jury to find a general verdict on the whole matter, and the right of the judge, according to his discretion, to give his directions to the jury, 'in like manner as in other criminal cases'. The defendant thus had the best of both worlds. And, if leaving the decision to the jury rendered the law uncertain, as Mansfield feared, then so was public opinion, and the jury was the best means of gearing the one to the changes the other. Moreover, juries were now more willing to convict, and thus the law became enforceable. On the other hand, Fox's Act represents a great gain to liberty, for juries were far less susceptible to executive pressure than the bench would have been, especially during the panic of the French Revolutionary and Napoleonic Wars.

In the same period, parliament in effect granted a further liberty to writers and publishers, though most reluctantly, as its privileges were involved. This was the right to report parliamentary proceedings, a subject which has already been treated in an earlier chapter.[2]

249. Commons' reasons for not renewing the Licensing Act, 1695.

And the Earl of *Bridgewater* reported, "That the Commons have agreed to all the Amendments made by their Lordships, except the Clause (A) to be added at the End of the Bill for reviving the Printing Act: to which they disagree, and give the Reasons following; (*videlicet,*)

"The Commons cannot agree to the Clause marked (A):

"1. Because it revives and re-enacts a Law which in no Wise answered the End for which it was made; the Title and Preamble of that Act being, "to prevent printing seditious and treasonable Books, Pamphlets, and Papers:" But there is no Penalty appointed for Offenders therein, they being left to be punished at Common Law (as they may be) without that Act; whereas there are great and grievous Penalties imposed by that Act, for Matters wherein neither Church nor State is any Ways concerned. . . .

[1] *P.H.*, XVI, 1288.   [2] See pp. 223-4, 244-9.

"3. Because that act prohibits printing any Thing before Entry thereof in the Register of the Company of Stationers (except Proclamations, Acts of Parliament, and such Books as shall be appointed under the Sign Manual, or under the Hand of a Principal Secretary of State); whereby both Houses of Parliament are disabled to order any Thing to be printed; and the said Company are empowered to hinder the printing all innocent and useful Books; and have an Opportunity to enter a Title to themselves, and their Friends, for what belongs to, and is the Labour and Right of, others.

"4. Because that Act prohibits any Books to be imported (without special License) into any Port in *England* (except *London*); by which Means the whole Foreign Trade of Books is restrained to *London*, unless the Lord Archbishop of *Canterbury* or the Lord Bishop of *London* shall, in Interruption of their more important Affairs in governing the Church, bestow their Time *gratis* in looking over Catalogues of Books, and granting licences; whereas the Commons think the other Ports of the Kingdom have as good Right as *London* to trade in Books, as well as other Merchandize.

"5. Because that Act leaves it in the Power, either of the Company of Stationers, or of the Archbishop of *Canterbury* and Bishop of *London*, to hinder any Books from being imported, even into the Port of *London*; for if One or more of the Company of Stationers will not come to the Custom-house, or that those Reverend Bishops shall not appoint any learned Man to go thither, and be present at the opening and viewing Books imported, the Custom-house Officer is obliged to detain them. . . .

"7. Because that Act prohibits any Custom-house Officer, under the Penalty of losing his Office, to open any Packet wherein are Books, until some or One of the Company of Stationers, and such learned Man as shall be so appointed, are present; which is impracticable, since he cannot know there are Books till he has opened the Packet.

"8. Because that Act confirms all Patents and Books granted, and to be granted; whereby the sole printing of all or most of the Classic Authors are, and have been for many Years past, together with a great Number of the best Books, and of most general Use, monopolized by the Company of Stationers; and prohibits the importing any such Books from beyond the Sea, whereby the Scholars in this Kingdom are forced, not only to buy them at the extravagant Price they demand, but must be content with their ill and incorrect Editions, and cannot have the more correct Copies which are published Abroad, nor the useful Notes of Foreigners or other learned Men upon them.

"9. Because that Act prohibits any Thing to be printed till licensed; and yet does not direct what shall be taken by the Licenser for such License; by Colour thereof, great Oppression may be, and has been, practised.

"10. Because that Act restrains Men bred up in the Trade of Printing and Founding of Letters from exercising their Trade, even in an innocent and inoffensive Way (though they are Freemen of the Company of Stationers), either as Masters or Journeymen; the Number of Workmen in each of these Trades being limited by that Act.

"11. Because that Act compels Master Printers to take Journeymen into their Service, though they have no Work or Employment for them. . . .

"15. Because that Act prohibits printing and importing, not only heretical, seditious, and schismatical Books, but all offensive Books, and doth not determine what shall be adjudged offensive Books; so that, without Doubt, if the late King *James* had continued in the Throne till this Time, Books against Popery would not [sic] have been deemed offensive Books.

"16. Because that Act subjects all Mens Houses, as well Peers as Commoners, to be searched at any Time, either by Day or Night, by a Warrant under the Sign Manual, or under the Hand of One of the Secretaries of State, directed to any Messenger, if such Messenger shall upon probable Reason suspect that there are any unlicensed Books there; and the Houses of all Persons free of the Company of Stationers are subject to the like Search, on a Warrant from the Master and Wardens of the said Company, or any One of them. . . .

"18. Lastly, There is a Proviso in that Act for *John Streater*, that he may print what he pleases, as if the Act had never been made; when the Commons see no Cause to distinguish him from all the rest of the Subjects of *England*."

After Debate,

The Question was put, "Whether this House will agree with the Commons, in leaving out the Clause (A)?"

It was Resolved in the Affirmative.

L.J., xv, 545.

250. *Tutchin's Case:* Holt's judgement, 1704.

HOLT, L.C.J.: Gentlemen of the jury, this is an information that is preferred by the queen's Attorney General against Mr. Tutchin, for writing and composing, and publishing, or causing to be writ, composed or published, several libels against the queen and her government; and all these that are set forth as libels, are entitled, The Observator, and they are in number six . . . [He quotes the offending passages]. So that now you have heard this evidence, you are to consider whether you are satisfied that Mr. Tutchin is guilty of writing, composing and publishing these libels. They say they are innocent papers, and no libels, and they say nothing is a libel but what reflects upon some particular person. But this is a very strange doctrine, to say, it is not a libel reflecting on the government, endeavouring to possess the people that the government is maladministered by corrupt persons, that are employed in such or such stations either in the navy or army.

To say that corrupt officers are appointed to administer affairs, is certainly a reflection on the government. If people should not be called to account for possessing the people with an ill opinion of the government, no government can subsist. For it is very necessary for all governments that the people should have a good opinion of it. And nothing can be worse to any government, than to endeavour to procure animosities, as to the management of it; this has been always looked upon as a crime, and no government can be safe without it be punished. . . .

S.T., XIV, 1125, 1128, 1129.

251. *Dean of St. Asaph's Case:* Buller's directions to the jury and Mansfield's judgement, 1784.

[The Rev. W. D. Shipley, Dean of St Asaph, was indicted for seditious libel, having published his brother-in-law's pamphlet in favour of parliamentary reform.]

Friday, August 6, 1784.

The Trial came on, at the assize at Shrewsbury, before the hon. Mr. Justice Buller. . . .

MR. JUSTICE BULLER:

Gentlemen of the Jury; This is an indictment against William Davies Shipley, for publishing the pamphlet which you have heard, and which the indictment states to be a libel.

The defendant has pleaded that he is not guilty; and whether he is guilty *of the fact* or not, is the matter for you to decide. . . .

You have been pressed very much by the counsel [Erskine for the Dean] and so have I also to give an opinion upon the question, whether this pamphlet is or is not a libel? Gentlemen, it is my happiness that I find the law so well and so fully settled that it is impossible for any man who means well to doubt about it; . . . the matter appears upon the record, and as such, it is not for me, a single judge sitting here at *nisi prius* to say, whether it is or is not a libel. Those who adopt the contrary doctrine forget a little to what lengths it would go; for if that were to be allowed. . . . you deprive the subject . . . of his appeal —you deprive him of his writ of error; for if I was to give an opinion here that it was not a libel, and you adopted that, the matter is closed for ever . . . whatever appears upon the record is not for our decision here, but may be the subject of further consideration in the court out of which the record comes; and afterwards, if either party thinks fit, they have a right to carry it to the dernier resort, and have the opinion of the House of Lords upon it; and therefore that has been the uniform and established answer not only in criminal but civil cases. . . .

You have been addressed by the quotation of a great many cases upon libels. It seems to me that that question is so well settled, that gentlemen should not agitate it again. . . . The very last case that has ever arisen upon a libel was conducted by a very respectable and honourable man, who is as warm a partisan, and upon the same side of the question, as the counsel for the defendant, and, I believe, of what is called the same party. He told the jury that there could be but three questions.

The first is, Whether the defendant is guilty of publishing the libel?

The second, Whether the innuendos or the averments made upon the record are true?

The third, which is a question of Law, Whether it is or is not a libel? Therefore, said he, the two first are the only questions which you have to consider: and this, added he, very rightly, is clear and undoubted law. It is adopted by me as clear and undoubted law, and it has been so held for considerably more than a century past. . . .

The Jury withdrew to consider of their verdict, and in about half an hour returned again into Court.

ASSOCIATE. Gentlemen, do you find the defendant Guilty or Not Guilty?

FOREMAN. Guilty of publishing *only*.

. . .

MR. JUSTICE BULLER. I believe that is a verdict not quite correct. . . .

[After a discussion between the Judge, and Erskine and the Jury]

The Associate recorded the Verdict. 'Guilty of publishing, but whether a libel or not the jury do not find.'

[Erskine, the Dean's counsel, applied for a new trial on the grounds of misdirection by the judge. This was heard in the Court of King's Bench on 15 November 1784. The next day] the EARL OF MANSFIELD, Lord Chief Justice, delivered himself as follows:

In this case of the King against Mr. Shipley, dean of St. Asaph, the motion to set aside the verdict, and to grant a new trial, upon account of the misdirection of the judge, supposes that upon this verdict (either as a general, or as minutes of a special verdict to be reduced into form), judgment may be given:—for if the verdict was defective, and omitted finding any thing within the province of the jury to find, there ought to be a *venire de novo*, and consequently this motion is totally improper; therefore, as I said, the motion supposes that judgment may be given upon the verdict; and it rests upon the objections to the direction of the judge. . . .

By the constitution the jury ought not to decide the question of law, whether such a writing, of such a meaning, published without a lawful excuse, be criminal; . . . therefore it is the duty of the judge to advise the jury to separate the question of fact from the question of law; and, as they ought not to decide the law; and the question remains entire upon the record, the judge is not called upon necessarily to tell them his own opinion. It is almost peculiar to the form of prosecution for libel, that the question of law remains entirely for the Court *upon record* . . . so that a general verdict, 'that the defendant is guilty,' is equivalent to a special verdict in other cases. It finds all which belongs to the jury to find; it finds nothing as to the question of the law. Therefore when a jury have been satisfied as to every fact within their province to find, they have been advised to find the defendant *guilty*, and in that shape they take the opinion of the Court upon the law. As to the last objection upon the *intent*: a criminal intent from doing a thing criminal in itself without a lawful excuse, is an inference of law, and a conclusive inference of law, not to be contradicted but by an excuse, which I have fully gone through. Where an *innocent act* is made criminal, when done with a particular intent, there the intent is a *material fact* to constitute a crime. This is the answer that is given to these three objections to the direction of the judge.

The subject matter of these three objections has arisen upon every trial for a libel since the Revolution, which is now near one hundred years ago. . . . During all this time, as far as it can be traced, one may venture to say, that the direction of every judge has been consonant to the doctrine of Mr. Justice Buller; and no counsel has complained of it by any application to the Court. . . .

. . . We must, as in all cases of tradition, trace backwards, and presume, from the usage which is remembered, that the precedent usage was the same. . . . I by accident (from memory only I speak now) recollect one where the *Craftsman* was acquitted; and I recollect it from a famous, witty, and ingenious ballad that was made at the time by Mr. Pulteney; and though it is a ballad, I will cite the stanza I remember from it, because it will show you the idea of the able men in opposition, and the leaders of the popular party in those days. They had not an idea of assuming that the jury had a right to determine upon a question of law, but they put it upon another and much better ground. The stanza I allude to is this:

> For Sir Philip well knows,
> That his *innuendos*
> Will serve him no longer
> In verse or in prose;

> For twelve honest men have decided the cause,
> Who are judges of fact, though not judges of laws.

It was the admission of the whole of that party: they put it right; they put it upon the *meaning* of the *innuendos*: upon *that* the jury acquitted the defendant: and they never put a pretence of any other power, except when talking to the jury themselves. . . .

Such a judicial practice in the precise point from the Revolution, as I think, down to the present day, is not to be shaken by arguments of general theory, or popular declamation. Every species of criminal prosecution has something peculiar in the mode of procedure; therefore general propositions, applied to all, tend only to complicate and embarrass the question. No deduction or conclusion can be drawn from what a jury *may* do, from the *form* of procedure, to what they *ought* to do upon the fundamental principles of the constitution and the reason of the thing, if they will act with integrity and good conscience.

The fundamental definition of trial by jury depends upon a universal maxim that is without an exception. Though a definition or maxim in law, without an exception, it is said, is hardly to be found, yet I take this to be a maxim without an exception: *Ad quaestionem iuris non respondent juratores; ad quaestionem facti non respondent judices.* . . .

. . . The constitution trusts, that, under the direction of a judge, they will not usurp a jurisdiction which is not in their province. They do not know and are not presumed to know the law; they are not sworn to decide the law; they are not required to decide the law. . . . But, further, upon the reason of the thing, and the eternal principles of justice, the jury ought not to assume the jurisdiction of the law. As I said before, they do not know, and are not presumed to know anything of the matter; they do not understand the language in which it is conceived, or the meaning of the terms. They have no rule to go by but their affections and wishes. . . . so the jury who usurp the judicature of the law, though they happen to be right, are themselves wrong, because they are right by chance only, and have not taken the constitutional way of deciding the question. It is the duty of the judge, in all cases of general justice, to tell the jury how to do right, though they have it *in their power* to do wrong, which is a matter entirely between God and their own consciences.

To be free, is to live under a government by law. The *liberty of the press* consists in printing without any previous license, subject to the consequences of law. The *licentiousness* of the press is *Pandora's* box, the source of every evil. . . .

Jealousy of leaving the law to the Court, as in other cases, so in the case of libels, is now, in the present state of things, puerile rant and declamation. The judges are totally independent of the ministers that may happen to be, and of the king himself. Their temptation is rather to the popularity of the day. . . .

In opposition to this, what is contended for? That the law shall be in every particular cause what any twelve men, who shall happen to be the jury, shall be inclined to think, liable to no review, and subject to no control, under all the prejudices of the popular cry of the day, and under all the bias of interest in this town, where thousands, more or less, are concerned in the publication of newspapers, paragraphs, and pamphlets. Under such an administration of law, no man could tell, no counsel could advise, whether a paper was or was not punishable.

I am glad I am not bound to subscribe to such an absurdity, such a solecism in politics.—Agreeable to the *uniform* judicial practice since the Revolution, warranted by the fundamental principles of the constitution, of the trial by jury, and upon the reason and fitness of the thing, we are all of opinion that this motion should be rejected, and this rule discharged.

S.T., XXI, 876.

252. Libel Act, 1792.

An act to remove doubts respecting the functions of juries in cases of libels.

Whereas doubts have arisen whether on the trial of an indictment or information for the making or publishing any libel, where an issue or issues are joined between the King and the defendant or defendants, on the plea of Not Guilty pleaded, it be competent to the jury impanelled to try the same to give their verdict upon the whole matter in issue: be it therefore declared and enacted ... That, on every such trial, the jury sworn to try the issue may give a general verdict of guilty or not guilty upon the whole matter put in issue upon such indictment or information; and shall not be required or directed, by the court or judge before whom such indictment or information shall be tried, to find the defendant or defendants guilty, merely on the proof of the publication by such defendant or defendants of the paper charged to be a libel, and of the sense ascribed to the same in such indictment or information.

II. Provided always, That, on every such trial, the court or judge before whom such indictment or information shall be tried, shall, according to their or his discretion give their or his opinion and directions to the jury on the matter in issue between the King and the defendant or defendants, in like manner as in other criminal cases.

III. Provided also, That nothing herein contained shall extend, or be construed to extend, to prevent the jury from finding a special verdict, in their discretion, as in other criminal cases.

IV. Provided also, That in case the jury shall find the defendant or defendants guilty, it shall and may be lawful for the said defendant or defendants to move in arrest of judgement, on such ground and in such manner as by law he or they might have done before the passing of this act; anything herein contained to the contrary notwithstanding.

32 Geo. III, c. 60: S.L., XXXVII, 627.

III. PETITIONS, PUBLIC MEETINGS, RIOTS AND REBELLIONS

The right of the subject to petition the king was guaranteed by the Bill of Rights[1]; and it was used, though not frequently in the early part of the period, as a means whereby the electorate and the people could represent their wishes to their rulers. But, as we have seen, the post-Revolutionary House of Commons could be just as oppressive as the pre-Revolutionary monarchy if the petitioners' recommendations were not to the taste of the majority of its members. The Kentish Petitioners, for example, in 1701 found themselves imprisoned and their petition stigmatised as 'scandalous, insolent, and seditious' (253). Petitioning became much more frequent with the opening of the Whig and Radical campaigns in the later part of the century. A number of petitions were presented during the Middlesex Elections crisis of 1769,[2] and many more appeared in the semi-revolutionary years of 1779-80.[2] From that time on, petitioning became more and more frequent, becoming a standard method of campaigning for such policies as parliamentary reform and the abolition of the slave-trade. The five-year period ending in 1789 produced 880 petitions to parliament; that of 1805 produced 1,026; that of 1815 produced 4,498; while in 1831 the figure had risen to 24,492.[3]

Petitioning becomes involved in the problem of the liberties of the subject because the preparation of a petition usually required a public meeting, and these also became much more common after 1769. 'In the eighteenth century the right of public meeting was as yet hardly envisaged as a constitutional right of the subject',[4] and the law on it was mainly developed in the nineteenth century. Blackstone, for example, has nothing to say about it. In other words, the law did not guarantee the right of public assembly, but did not deny it either, unless laws were infringed, in which case the meeting could become an unlawful assembly, or a riot, or a rebellion. It was the right and duty of magistrates, and of every citizen, to use reasonable force to suppress these, neither too much nor too little. The law on riot could become very severe. If a felony were committed, the rioters all could be treated as felons. And taking part in a riot to effect a public general object—for example, aiming to pull down *all* meeting-houses, as Dammaree was convicted of doing—could be construed as levying war against the king and therefore as treason (254). To the public mind this was a strained interpretation of the law, and in 1715 the Riot Act was passed, which clarified the subject (255). This provided that if twelve or more people 'being un-

---

[1] See p. 28.
[2] See p. 209.
[3] *Report from the Select Committee on Public Petitions* (1832), p. 10.
[4] W. Holdsworth, *History of English Law* (1938), vol. x, p. 701.

lawfully, riotously, and tumultously assembled together, to the destruction of the public peace' did not disperse within one hour of the reading of the proclamation by a magistrate ordering them to disperse, they should be guilty of felony. In addition, the Act indemnified those who injured or killed rioters while helping to disperse them. This arrangement proved much more suitable for dealing with disturbances than falling back on the clumsy weapon of constructive treason; and to those who helped in their suppression it also provided legal protection which had not always existed before, if the rioters had not gone so far as to commit a felony. However, the legal situation was still not perfectly clear, for during the course of the eighteenth century a misconception arose about the Riot Act: magistrates and the general public wrongly thought that it was illegal to call in the military to the aid of the civil power without reading the proclamation and waiting the hour. In riotous times, magistrates were reluctant to ask the soldiers to shoot for fear of placing themselves and the troops at the mercy of popular juries. During the riots over Wilkes in 1768, the juries were only too ready to find verdicts against officers and men who had only done their duty. The consequence was the failure of the magistrates and the government to take effective action against the mob during the first three days of the Gordon Riots, and the celebrated action of George III in sending in the troops, declaring: 'There shall be at all events one magistrate in the kingdom who will do his duty.'[1] He did this after a meeting of the Privy Council in which the Attorney-General, Wedderburn, gave it as his opinion that the Riot Act had not affected in any way the previous right and duty of magistrates and citizens to use the appropriate amount of force to suppress a disturbance. In the subsequent post-mortem in the House of Lords, Mansfield gave a very clear account of the law on the same lines (256).

In the same speech, Mansfield dealt with another aspect of the powers of the State to suppress riots and rebellions. Many lawyers believed that George III in 1780 had acted on his prerogative, on the theory that the Crown possessed an unlimited reserve of power to act in an emergency. Lord Hardwicke as Lord Chancellor had put forward this idea, for example, in 1739.[2] Lord Mansfield, on the other hand, expressed the view (which has since become accepted) that the government had simply acted on the powers that every citizen had to suppress a riot. Shortly after, Lord Thurlow said that the same principle applied even in cases of rebellion, like those of 1715 and 1745.[3] Some lawyers believed that the royal prerogative could be used to proclaim martial law, whereby the ordinary law was suspended and 'martial law' (i.e. what we call 'military law': the law put into force by the

---

[1] Lord Mahon, *History of England* (1854), vol. VII, p. 33.
[2] *P.H.*, x, 1383.
[3] *P.H.*, xxi, 736.

Mutiny Acts) applied to citizens as well as soldiers. What has since become accepted as the correct law on this subject was expressed by Lord Lough-borough (Wedderburn) in the case of *Grant* v. *Gould* (257). Grant had been sentenced by a court-martial to one thousand lashes on the bare back with a cat-o'-nine-tails for persuading two Foot Guards to desert and join the service of the East India Company. He prayed for a writ of prohibition in the Court of Common Pleas on the ground that he was not a soldier and therefore not subject to 'martial law'. Loughborough, in the course of his judgement, distinguished between martial law and what is now called 'military law'. The former, vague prerogative powers whereby the king could take whatever measures he pleased to restore order in a crisis, he denied existed in England. The latter, the positive law put into force by the Mutiny Acts, he recognised as essential, adding that the decisions of the courts-martial administering it could not be interfered with by the higher courts so long as they did not exceed their jurisdiction. A similar view of martial law was taken by the Irish Court of King's Bench in the case of *Wolfe Tone* (245).

253. The Kentish Petition, 1701.

[8 May 1701]

A petition from several Gentlemen of the County of *Kent* being offered to the House;

Ordered, That the said Petition he brought up to the Table.

And it was brought up accordingly.

And the House being informed, That several of the Gentlemen, who signed the said Petition, were at the Door, ready to own the same;

They were called in accordingly; *viz.*

Mr *William Colepeper*, Mr *Thomas Colepeper*, Mr *David Polhill*, Mr *Justinian Champneys*, and Mr *William Hamilton*:

And they, at the Bar owned the same Petition, and their Hands to the same.

And then they withdrew.

And the Petition was read, intituled, The humble Petition of the Gentlemen, Justices of the Peace, Grand Jury, and other Freeholders, at the General Quarter Sessions of the Peace holden at *Maidston*, in *Kent*, the 29th Day of *April* in the 13th Year of the Reign of our Sovereign Lord King *William* the Third; over *England*, etc.; setting forth, That they, deeply concerned at the dangerous Estate of this Kingdom, and of all *Europe*; and considering that the Fate of them, and their Posterity, depends on the Wisdom of their Representatives in Parliament; think themselves bound in Duty humbly to lay before this Honourable House, the Consequence, in this conjuncture, of a speedy Resolution, and most sincere Endeavour, to answer the great Trust reposed in their said Representatives by the Country: And in regard that, from the Experience of all Ages, it is manifest no Nation can be great or happy without Union, they hope no Pretence whatsoever shall be able to create a Misunderstanding among ourselves, or the least Distrust of his Majesty, whose great Actions for this Nation are writ in the Hearts of his Subjects, and can never, without the blackest Ingratitude, be forgot: And praying, That this House will have Regard to the Voice of the People; that our Religion and Safety may be effectually provided for; that loyal Addresses of this House may be turned into Bills of Supply; and that his Majesty may be enabled powerfully to assist his Allies, before it is too late.

Resolved, That the said Petition is scandalous, insolent, and seditious; tending to destroy the Constitution of Parliaments, and to subvert the established Government of this Realm.

Resolved, That Mr *William Colepeper* is guilty of promoting the said Petition . . .

[Similar resolutions on each of the others.]

Ordered, That the said Mr *William Colepeper* be, for the said Offence, taken into the Custody of the Serjeant at Arms attending this House . . .

[Similar orders on each of the others.]

C.J., XIII, 518.

254. *Dammaree's Case:* Parker's directions to the jury, 1710.

[AT THE SESSIONS-HOUSE IN THE OLD-BAILEY. 1710]

L.C.J. PARKER. Gentlemen of the Jury; Daniel Dammaree, the prisoner at the bar, stands indicted for high treason; for that he, on the first of March last, in the parish of St. Clement Danes, did, with a great multitude of persons, to the number of five hundred, armed with swords and clubs, raise and levy public war against the queen. . . .

This being then the matter of fact on both sides, and what there is in fact, and in presumption; give me leave to take notice what the law is in this case. For it has been insisted on by the counsel for the prisoner (and I must do them right, they have taken into consideration all the cases that relate to this matter)—They insist that this is not levying war; and on this ground, that he was not proved to be at the meeting-house in Drury-Lane, but only at the fire at Dr. Burgess's; and if he was only at one place, one instance would not make it levying war. If, say they, there had been a general intention, it would have gone hard with him; there was an intention the night before, and Mr. Burgess's was only mentioned; and it is not certain that there was a general design to pull down the rest. Nay, he was not there, and it was by accident he came to Lincoln's-inn-fields, and he was but at that one place; and they take notice of some cases, especially that about the bawdy-houses, and that the lord-chief-justice Hale differed from the rest of the judges.

This is a matter that has been often under consideration: the act of the 25th Edward the 3rd, which is the great law for declarations of treason, declares what shall be adjudged treason: compassing or imagining the death of the king, and levying war against the king, are two distinct species of treason. Now they say, that, nothing was designed against the queen. If the levying of war against the queen, was there meant only of a war against the queen's person, it would have been idle to mention it in that act, because they had before made the compassing her death to be treason.

Now he that levies war, does more than compass or imagine the king's death; therefore it has been always ruled, that where there is an actual levying of war, which concerns the person of the king, they lay the treason to be the compassing the death of the king, and give a proof of it by levying war. But there is another levying of war, which is not immediately against the person of the king, but only between some particular persons. There is a vast difference between a man's going to remove an annoyance to himself, and going to remove a public nuisance, as the case of the bawdy-houses: and the general intention to pull them all down is the treason: for if those that were concerned for them would defend them, and the others would pull them down, there would be a war immediately.

In the case of inclosures, where the people of a town have had a part of their common inclosed, though they have come with a great force to throw down that inclosure, yet that is not levying of war; but if any will go to pull down all inclosures, and make it a general thing to reform that which they think a nuisance, that necessarily makes a war between all the lords and the tenants. A bawdy-house is a nuisance, and may be punished as such; and if it be a particular prejudice to any one, if he himself should go in an unlawful manner to redress that prejudice, it might be only a riot; but if he will set up to pull them all down in general, he has taken the queen's right out of her hand: he has made it a general thing, and when they are once up, they may call every man's house a bawdy-house; and this is a general thing, it affects the whole nation.

Now to come to this instance. If you believe the evidence, Dammaree was concerned in pulling down two meeting-houses: he was not present at Drury-lane, that is, he was not proved to be there: but if he set others on to do it, it is his doing, and he as much pulled down that meeting-house in Drury-lane, as if he had pulled it down with his own hands. Besides, they tell you his declaration, that he would have all of them down. Again, these gentlemen do not seem to deny, but if the intention were general, it would be levying war: if it were general, where would it end? And it is taking on them the royal authority; nay, more, for the queen cannot pull them down till the law is altered: therefore he has here taken on him not only the royal authority, but a power that no person in England has. It concerns all that are against the meeting-houses on one side, and all that are for them on the other, and therefore, is levying war.

They said, they would desire this point to be reserved to them on the account of the opinion of the lord chief justice Hale; But I believe this matter has been so often settled, that it would be strange for us to depart from such a settled rule of law; for these are only the same arguments that were offered by the lord-chief-justice; and he offered the same arguments that were used in queen Elizabeth's reign? but it was then held to be treason, and has been held so ever since. His objection made them consider it then, and they did so; and I suppose they will not expect that it should have more weight out of their mouths than out of his. It was then settled, and has been taken for law at all times since, so that it is not a matter now to be called in question. And as to the statute of 13 Eliz. the intention to levy war surely is not an intention to do a thing, which when it is done, is not levying war.

Thus the matter stands in point of law: I take it to be clear that it is levying war, if you take him to be guilty of being at one of the meeting-places, and leading them, and tempting them to another. Whether that is true, or not, is what must be left to your consideration. You have heard what has been said, and what difficulties arise in point of time, and on the other proofs: If you are of opinion, that he was present at Lincoln's-inn-fields, and did encourage them, and acted any otherwise than by force; if you believe he led, or invited them to another place, and pulled down that, then you will find him guilty of high treason. If you think he was not there, or was under a compulsion, then he will not be guilty. As for being drunk, whether he was or not, ought not to influence one way or other.

S.T., xv, 596–7, 605–10.

255. The Riot Act, 1715.

An act for preventing tumults and riotous assemblies, and for the more speedy and effectual punishing the rioters.

1. WHEREAS *of late many rebellious riots and tumults have been in divers parts of this kingdom, to the disturbance of the publick peace, and the endangering of his Majesty's person and government, and the same are yet continued and fomented by persons disaffected to his Majesty, presuming so to do, for that the punishments provided by the laws now in being are not adequate to such heinous offences; and by such rioters his Majesty and his administration have been most maliciously and falsely traduced, with an intent to raise divisions, and to alienate the affections of the people from his Majesty: therefore for the preventing and suppressing of such riots and tumults, and for the more speedy and effectual punishing the offenders therein*; be it enacted . . . That if any persons to the number of twelve or more, being unlawfully, riotously, and tumultuously assembled together, to the disturbance of the publick peace, at any time after the last day of *July* in the year of our Lord one thousand seven hundred and fifteen, and being required or commanded by any one or more justice or justices of the peace, or by the sheriff of the county, or his under-sheriff, or by the mayor, bailiff or bailiffs, or other head-officer, or justice of the peace of any city or town corporate, where such assembly shall be, by proclamation to be made in the King's name, in the form herein after directed, to disperse themselves, and peaceably to depart to their habitations, or to their lawful business, shall, to the number of twelve or more (notwithstanding such proclamation made) unlawfully, riotously, and tumultuously, remain or continue together by the space of one hour after such command or request made by proclamation, that then such continuing together . . . shall be adjudged felony without benefit of clergy, and the offenders therein shall be adjudged felons, and shall suffer death as in case of felony without benefit of clergy.

414

II. And be it further enacted by the authority aforesaid, That the order and form of the proclamation that shall be made by the authority of this act, shall be as hereafter followeth (that is to say) the justice of the peace, or other person authorized by this act to make the said proclamation shall, among the said rioters, or as near to them as he can safely come, with a loud voice command, or cause to be commanded silence to be, while proclamation is making, and after that, shall openly and with loud voice make or cause to be made proclamation in these words, or like in effect:

Our sovereign Lord the King chargeth and commandeth all persons, being assembled, immediately to disperse themselves, and peaceably to depart to their habitations, or to their lawful business, upon the pains contained in the act made in the first year of King George, *for preventing tumults and riotous assemblies.*

God save the King.

And every such justice and justices of the peace, sheriff, under-sheriff, mayor, bailiff, and other head-officer, aforesaid, within the limits of their respective jurisdictions, are hereby authorized, impowered and required, on notice or knowledge of any such unlawful, riotous and tumultuous assembly, to resort to the place where such unlawful, riotous and tumultuous assemblies shall be, of persons to the number of twelve or more, and there to make or cause to be made proclamation in manner aforesaid.

III. And be it further enacted . . . That if such persons so unlawfully, riotously, and tumultuously assembled, or twelve or more of them, after proclamation made in manner aforesaid, shall continue together and not disperse themselves within one hour, That then it shall and may be lawful to and for every justice of the peace, sheriff, or under-sheriff of the county where such assembly shall be, and also to and for every high or petty constable, and other peace-officer within such county, and also to and for every mayor, justice of the peace, sheriff, bailiff, and other head-officer, high or petty constable, and other peace-officer of any city or town corporate where such assembly shall be, and to and for such other person and persons as shall be commanded to be assisting unto any such justice of the peace, sheriff, or under-sheriff, mayor, bailiff, or other head-officer aforesaid (who are hereby authorized and impowered to command all his Majesty's subjects of age and ability to be assisting to them therein) to seize and apprehend,

415

and they are hereby required to seize and apprehend such persons so unlawfully, riotously and tumultuously continuing together after proclamation made, as aforesaid, and forthwith to carry the persons so apprehended before one or more of his Majesty's justices of the peace of the county or place where such persons shall be so apprehended, in order to their being proceeded against for such their offences according to law; and that if the persons so unlawfully, riotously and tumultuously assembled, or any of them, shall happen to be killed, maimed or hurt, in the dispersing, seizing or apprehending, or endeavouring to disperse, seize or apprehend them, by reason of their resisting the persons so dispersing, seizing or apprehending, or endeavouring to disperse, seize or apprehend them, that then every such justice of the peace, sheriff . . . [etc.] and all and singular persons, being aiding and assisting to them, or any of them, shall be free, discharged and indemnified, as well against the King's Majesty, his heirs and successors, as against all and every other person and persons, of, for, or concerning the killing, maiming, or hurting of any such person or persons so unlawfully, riotously and tumultuously assembled, that shall happen to be so killed, maimed or hurt, as aforesaid.

IV. And be it further enacted by the authority aforesaid, That if any persons unlawfully, riotously, tumultuously assembled together, to the disturbance of the publick peace, shall unlawfully, and with force demolish or pull down, or begin to demolish or pull down any church or chapel, or any building for religious worship certified or registred according to the [Toleration Act] . . . or any dwelling-house, barn, stable or other out-house, that then every such demolishing, or pulling down, or beginning to demolish, or pull down, shall be adjudged felony without benefit of clergy, and the offenders therein shall be adjudged felons, and shall suffer death as in the case of felony, without benefit of clergy.

V. Provided always, and be it further enacted by the authority aforesaid, That if any person or persons do, or shall, with force and arms, wilfully and knowingly lett, hinder, or hurt any person or persons that shall begin to proclaim, or go to proclaim according to the proclamation hereby directed to be made, whereby such proclamation shall not be made, that then every such opposing, obstructing, letting, hindering or hurting such person or persons, so beginning or going to make such proclamation, as aforesaid, shall be adjudged felony without benefit of clergy, and the offenders therein shall be adjudged felons, and shall suffer death as in case of felony, without benefit of clergy; and that also every such person or persons so being unlawfully riotously and tumultuously assembled, to the number of twelve, as aforesaid, or more, to whom proclamation should or ought to have been made if the same had not been hindered, as aforesaid, shall likewise, in case they or any of them, to the number of twelve or more, shall continue together, and not disperse themselves within one hour after such lett or hindrance so made, having knowledge of such lett or hindrance so made, shall be adjudged felons, and shall suffer death as in case of felony, without benefit of clergy.

VI. [How the damages shall be made good, if any church, etc., be demolished, etc.]

VII. And be it further enacted by the authority aforesaid, That this act shall be openly read at every quarter-session, and at every leet or law-day.

VIII. Provided always, That no person or persons shall be prosecuted by virtue of this act, for any offence or offences committed contrary to the same, unless such prosecution be commenced within twelve months after the offence committed.

IX & X. [Arrangements for Scotland.]

1 Geo. I, stat. 2, c. 5: *S.L.*, XIII, 142.

256. Mansfield on the use of the military in the Gordon Riots, 1780.

LORD MANSFIELD . . . It has been taken for granted, my lords, and I wish sincerely the task had fallen upon some other noble lord, that his Majesty, in the orders he gave respecting the riots, acted merely upon his prerogative, as being entrusted with the protection and preservation of the state, in cases arising from necessity, and not provided for in the ordinary contemplation and execution of law. This, I take it, is a point that ought to be fully explained. I take the case to be exactly the reverse, and that his Majesty, with the advice of his ministers, acted perfectly and strictly agreeable to law, and the principles of the constitution; and I will give you my reasons within as short a compass as possible. I have not consulted books;—Indeed, I have no books to consult![1]—but as well as my memory serves me, let us see, my lords, how the facts and the law stands, and reflect a light upon each other.

1 They were destroyed in the Gordon Riots.

The noble duke who spoke last observes, that constructive treason is a dangerous thing; but constructive treason is here totally out of the question. The crime, as applied to the fact, is palpable and direct; pulling down all inclosures, demolishing all brothels or bawdy-houses, or chapels,[1] making insurrections, in order to redress grievances, real or pretended, is levying war within the realm, and against the King, though they have no design against his person; because they invade his prerogative by attempting to do that by private authority which he by his office is bound to do; to lower the price of victuals contrary to law; to reform the law or religion of the state, &c. these, with all their several species, are deemed levying war within the realm, and of course against the King, because they all tend to usurp upon the power of the King, who is the acting representative of the whole legislature.

Besides those overt-acts of treason now recounted, the most or all of which the insurgents were guilty of, they were guilty of several acts of felony, such as burning private property, and demolishing private houses, and committing several acts of robbery and open violence.

Here, then, my lords, we shall find the true ground upon which his Majesty, by the advice of his ministers, I presume, proceeded. I do not pretend to speak from any previous knowledge or communication, for I never heard, was present, nor consulted upon the measures adopted by his Majesty's confidential servants; but it appears most clearly to me, that not only every man may legally interfere to suppress a riot, much more prevent acts of felony, treason, and rebellion, in his private capacity, but he is bound to do it as an act of duty; and if called upon by a magistrate, is punishable in case of refusal. What any single individual may lawfully do, so may any number assembled, for a lawful purpose; which the suppression of riots, tumults, and insurrections certainly is. It would be needless to endeavour to prove, that what a private man may undertake to perform may be performed by a magistrate, who is specially authorised by law for the purpose of keeping the peace. It is the peculiar business of all constables to apprehend rioters, and to endeavour to disperse all unlawful assemblies; to apprehend the persons so offending, and in case of resistance, to attack, wound, nay kill those who shall continue to resist. The very act of apprehending in arms the person, with every necessary power for the effectual performance of the duty prescribed

---

[1] See No. 254.

by the law; and consequently every person acting in support of the law is justifiable respecting such acts as may arise in consequence of a faithful and proper discharge of the duties annexed to his office, if he does not abuse the power legally vested in him, which may in that case, according to the circumstances accompanying the transaction, degenerate into an illegal act, though professedly committed under the colour or pretext of law. These several positions I take to be incontrovertible. A private man, if he sees a person committing an unlawful act, more particularly an act amounting to a violent breach of the peace, felony, or treason, may apprehend the offender, and in his attempt to apprehend him may use force to compel him, not to submit to him, but to the law. What a private man may do, a magistrate or peace officer may clearly undertake; and according to the necessity of the case, arising from the danger to be apprehended, any number of men assembled or called together for the purpose are justified to perform. This doctrine I take to be clear and indisputable, with all the possible consequences which can flow from it, and to be true foundation for calling in the military power to assist in quelling the late riots.

The persons who assisted in the suppression of those riots and tumults, in contemplation of law, are to be considered as mere private individuals, acting according to law, and upon any abuse of the legal power with which they were invested, are amenable to the laws of their country. For instance, supposing a soldier, or any other military person, who acted in the course of the late riots, had exceeded the powers with which he was invested, I have not a single doubt but he is liable to be tried and punished, not by martial law, but by the common and statute law of the realm; consequently, the false idea that we are living under a military government, or that the military have any more power, or other power, since the commencement of the riots, is the point which I rose to refute, and on that ground to remove those idle and ill-founded apprehensions, that any part of the laws or the constitution are either suspended or have been dispensed with.

I believe this great mistake has chiefly arisen from the general understanding of the 1st of Geo. the 1st, [Riot Act] a law specially enacted for preventing riots in the first instance, and by consequences for preventing in the end felonious or treasonable insurrections. . . .

. . .

On the whole, my lords, while I deprecate and sincerely lament the cause which rendered it indispensibly necessary to call out the military to assist in the suppression of the late disturbances, I am clearly of opinion, that no steps have been taken which were not strictly legal, as well as fully justifiable in point of policy. Certainly the civil power, whether through native imbecility, through neglect, or the very formidable force they would have been obliged to contend with, were unequal to the task of suppressing the riots, and putting an end to the insurrection. The rabble had augmented their numbers by setting the felons at liberty. If the military had not been called in, none of your lordships can hesitate to agree with me, that within a very few hours the capital would have been in flames, and shortly reduced to an heap of rubbish.

The King's prerogative is clearly out of the question. His Majesty and those who have advised him, have acted strictly conformable to law. The military have been called in, and very wisely called in, not as soldiers, but as citizens: no matter whether their coats be red or brown, they have been called in aid of the laws, not to subvert them, or overturn the constitution, but to preserve both.

P.H., xxi, 694.

257. *Grant* v. *Gould:* **Loughborough's judgement, 1792.**

LORD LOUGHBOROUGH. . . . In the preliminary observations upon the case, my brother *Marshall* went at length into the history of those abuses of martial law, which prevailed in ancient times. This leads me to an observation, that martial law, such as it is described by *Hale*, and such also as it is marked by Mr. Justice *Blackstone*, does not exist in *England* at all. Where martial law is established and prevails in any country, it is of a totally different nature from that, which is inaccurately called martial law, merely because the decision is by a court martial, but which bears no affinity to that which was formerly attempted to be exercised in this kingdom; which was contrary to the constitution, and which has been for a century totally exploded. Where martial law prevails, the authority under which it is exercised, claims a jurisdiction over all military persons, in all circumstances. Even their debts are subject to enquiry by a military authority: Every species of offence, committed by any person who appertains to the army, is tried, not by a civil judicature, but by the judicature of the regiment or corps to which he belongs. It extends also to a great variety of cases, not relating to the discipline of the army, in those states which subsist by military power. Plots against the sovereign, intelligence to the enemy, and the like, are all considered as cases within the cognizance of military authority.

In the reign of King *William*, there was a conspiracy against his person in *Holland*, and the persons guilty of that conspiracy were tried by a council of officers. There was also a conspiracy against him in *England*, but the conspirators were tried by the common law. And within a very recent period, the incendiaries who attempted to set fire to the docks at *Portsmouth*, were tried by the common law. In this country, all the delinquences of soldiers are not triable, as in most countries in *Europe*, by martial law; but where they are ordinary offences against the civil law; they are tried by the common law courts. Therefore it is totally inaccurate, to state martial law as having any place whatever within the realm of *Great Britain*. But there is by the providence and wisdom of the legislature, an army established in this country, of which it is necessary to keep up the establishment. The army being established by the authority of the legislature, it is an indispensable requisite of that establishment, that there should be order and discipline kept up in it, and that the persons who compose the army, for all offences in their military capacity, should be subject to a trial by their officers. That has induced the absolute necessity of a mutiny act, accompanying the army. . . . It is one object of that act to provide for the army; but there is a much greater cause for the existence of a mutiny act,[1] and that is, the preservation of the peace and safety of the kingdom: for there is nothing so dangerous to the civil establishment of a state, as the licentious and undisciplined army; and every country which has a standing army in it, is guarded and protected by a mutiny act. An undisciplined soldiery are apt to be too many for the civil power; but under the command of officers, those officers are answerable to the civil power, that they are kept in good order and discipline. All history and all experience, particularly the experience of the present moment, give the strongest testimony to this. The object of the mutiny act, therefore, is to create a court invested with authority to try those who are a part of the army, in all their different descriptions of officers, and soldiers; and the object of the trial is limited to breaches of military duty. Even by that extensive power granted by the legislature to his majesty, to make articles of war, those articles are

[1] See No. 12.

to be for the better government of his forces, and can extend no further, than they are thought necessary to the regularity and due discipline of the army. . . .

This court being established in this country by positive law, the proceedings of it, and the relation in which it will stand to the courts of *Westminster Hall*, must depend upon the same rules, with all other courts, which are instituted, and have particular powers given them, and whose acts therefore, may become the subject of applications to the courts of *Westminster Hall*, for a prohibition. Naval courts-martial, military courts-martial, courts of admiralty, courts of prize, are all liable to the controuling authority, which the courts of *Westminster Hall* have, from time to time, exercised, for the purpose of preventing them from exceeding the jurisdiction given to them: the general ground of prohibition, being an excess of jurisdiction, when they assume a power to act in matters not within their cognizance.

I have stated these observations generally, upon the nature of an application for a prohibition. The foundation of it must be that the inferior court is acting without jurisdiction. It cannot be a foundation for a prohibition, that in the exercise of their jurisdiction the Court has acted erroneously. That may be a matter of appeal, where there is an appeal, or a matter of review: though the sentence of a court-martial is not subject to a review, there are instances no doubt, where, upon application to the crown, there have been orders to review the proceedings of courts-martial.

My brother *Adair* justly and correctly said, that a prohibition to prevent the proceedings of a court-martial, is not to be granted without very sufficient ground and due consideration. Not that it is not to be granted, because it would be dangerous in all cases to grant prohibitions; for it would be undoubtedly dangerous, if there was a facility in applying for prohibitions, and the sentence were to be stopped, for asking it to be further enquired into. But in such cases it is the duty of the Court to consider the matter fully and deliberately, upon the motion to prohibit, and the Court not without great danger, take the course in such a case which they have done in others, where there is no danger in the delay, to put the matter in prohibition, and determine it, upon the record.

In this case, there are four grounds stated of prohibition. [He reviews and rejects them] . . .

With respect to the sentence itself, and the supposed severity of it,

I observe that the severe part is by the Court deposited where it ought only to be, in the breast of his majesty. I have no doubt but that the intention of that was, to leave room for one application for mercy to his majesty, from the goodness and clemency of whose disposition, applications of this nature are always sure to be duly considered, and to have all the weight they can possibly deserve.

Rule discharged.

H. Blackstone, *Report of Cases in the Courts of Common Pleas and Exchequer Chamber* (5th ed., 1837), vol. II, p. 96.

IV. RESTRICTIONS ON LIBERTY

We have seen how the supremacy of the law was made to reign over all the institutions of the eighteenth century, and how the most substantial bulwarks of liberty were constructed not so much by the legislature as by the judges in individual court cases. However, the liberty of the subject could not always be guaranteed by the rule of law: it could not withstand the combined onslaught of executive, legislature and judiciary to which it was subjected during the French Revolutionary and Napoleonic Wars. Political agitation and economic distress combined once more to produce the most violent outbreaks so far of petitioning, public meetings, political associations, conspiracies and riots, which revealed the pitiful inadequacy of the existing machinery for maintaining public order. Prosecution under the existing law failed to find its mark, for Thomas Hardy, Horne Tooke, John Thelwall and other leaders of the London Corresponding Society and the Society for Constitutional Information, were acquitted of treason by juries amidst scenes of enthusiastic popular rejoicing. In view of this, Pitt's government fell back on adding to the severity of the law, and most of the rights of the subject we have so far covered were seriously curtailed by temporary legislation, a few examples of which will be found in the documents.

The Habeas Corpus Act was suspended in 1794, and annually until 1801, though the word 'suspended' is too strong. The Act (258) allowed any person arrested for treason or suspicion of treason, by a warrant signed by six members of the Privy Council or by a Secretary of State, to be held without bail or mainprize. The Treasonable and Seditious Practices Act of 1795 (259) gave legislative force to some (though not all) of the judicial constructions that had been placed on that part of the Statute of Treasons of Edward III which concerned compassing or imagining the king's death. (It was not concerned with the other two chief aspects, i.e. adhering to the king's enemies, or levying war on the king, the latter of which we referred to in the case of *Dammaree*.[1]) It now became treason, firstly, to compass, not

[1] No. 254.

merely the king's death, but also his injury, restraint or deposition; secondly, to compass the levying of war on him in order to force him to change his measures or in order to intimidate parliament; and, thirdly, to compass the encouragement of any foreigner to invade his dominions. Evidence of this could be the publication of any printing or writing, or any overt act or deed. Moreover, the use of written or spoken words calculated to incite disaffection could be treated as a high misdemeanour.

The right of public meeting was limited by the Seditious Meetings Act of 1795 (260). No meeting of over fifty persons for preparing a petition to the king or parliament for the 'alteration of matters established in church or state,' or for 'deliberating upon any grievance in church or state', could be held unless the time, place and purpose had been previously advertised in the press. Otherwise it became an 'unlawful assembly', and could be dispersed by one or more magistrates. Should twelve or more remain assembled for one hour after the order to disperse, they could be treated as felons. An otherwise lawful meeting could be similarly dispersed if propositions were advanced which suggested that any aspect of the established order should be altered otherwise than by king, lords and commons, or which incited contempt of the king, his government or the constitution.[1] In addition, every 'house, room, field or other place' where political debates or lectures were held would be deemed a disorderly house unless it had previously been licensed by two or more magistrates (universities and schools excepted).

Hardy's society, the London Corresponding Society, and some others were specifically prohibited in the Act against Unlawful Combinations and Confederacies of 1799 (261). Similarly prohibited were societies which imposed unlawful oaths, or which kept the names of certain members secret from the rest, or which had a secret committee, or which consisted of a number of distinct branches.

258. Habeas Corpus Act 'suspended', 1794.

An act to impower his Majesty to secure and detain such persons as his Majesty shall suspect are conspiring against his person and government.

Whereas a traitorous and detestable conspiracy has been formed for subverting the existing laws and constitution, and for introducing the system of anarchy and confusion which has so fatally prevailed in France: *therefore, for the better preservation of his Majesty's sacred person, and for securing the peace and the laws and liberties of this kingdom;* be it enacted . . . That every person or persons that are or shall be in prison within the kingdom of

[1] Certain meetings, like county meetings, and borough meetings called by the mayor, and so on, were excepted.

Great Britain at or upon the day on which this act shall receive his Majesty's royal assent, or after, by warrant of his said Majesty's most honourable privy council, signed by six of the said privy council, for high treason, suspicion of high treason, or treasonable practices, or by warrant, signed by any of his Majesty's secretaries of state, for such causes as aforesaid, may be detained in safe custody, without bail or main-prize, until the first day of *February* one thousand seven hundred and ninety-five; and that no judge or justice of the peace shall bail or try any such person or persons so committed, without order from his said Majesty's privy council signed by six of the said privy council, till the said first day of February one thousand seven hundred and ninety-five; any law or statute to the contrary notwithstanding. . . .

34 Geo. III, c. 54: S.L., xxxix, 556.

259. Treasonable and Seditious Practices Act, 1795.

An act for the safety and preservation of his Majesty's person and government against treasonable and seditious practices and attempts.

. . . be it enacted . . . that if any person or persons whatsoever, after the day of the passing of this act, during the natural life of our most gracious sovereign lord the King, . . . and until the end of the next session of parliament after a demise of the crown, shall, within the realm or without, compass, imagine, invent, devise, or intend death or destruction, or any bodily harm tending to death or destruction, maim or wounding, imprisonment or restraint, of the person of the same our sovereign lord the King, his heirs and successors, or to deprive or depose him or them from the style, honour, or kingly name, of the imperial crown of this realm, or of any other of his Majesty's dominions or countries; or to levy war against his Majesty, his heirs and successors, within this realm, in order, by force or constraint, to compel him or them to change his or their measures or counsels, or in order to put any force or constraint upon, or to intimidate, or overawe, both houses, or either house of parliament; or to move or stir any foreigner or stranger with force to invade this realm, or any other his Majesty's dominions or countries, under the obeisance of his Majesty, his heirs and successors; and such compassings, imaginations, inventions, devices, or intentions, or any of them, shall express, utter, or declare, by publishing any printing or writing, or by any overt act or deed; being legally convicted thereof, upon the oaths of two lawful and credible witnesses, upon trial, or otherwise convicted or attainted by due course of law, then every such person and persons, ... shall be deemed, declared and adjudged, to be a traitor and traitors, and shall suffer pains of death, and also lose and forfeit as in cases of high treason.

II. And be it further enacted, ... That if any person or persons within that part of *Great Britain* called *England*, at any time from and after the day of the passing of this act, during three years from the day of passing this act, and until the end of the then next session of parliament, shall maliciously and advisedly, by writing, printing, preaching, or other speaking, express, publish, utter, or declare any words or sentences to excite or stir up the people to hatred or contempt of the person of his Majesty, his heirs or successors, or the government and constitution of this realm, as by law established, then every such person or persons, being thereof legally convicted, shall be liable to such punishment as may by law be inflicted in cases of high misdemeanors; ... [and for a second offence may either be punished as for high misdemeanor, or banished, or transported for seven years.] ...

36 Geo. III, c. 7: S.L., XL, 561.

260. Seditious Meetings Act, 1795.

An act for the more effectually preventing seditious meetings and assemblies.

Whereas assemblies of divers persons, collected for the purpose or under the pretext of deliberating on public grievances, and of agreeing on petitions, complaints, remonstrances, declarations, or other addresses, to the King, or to both houses, or either house of parliament, have of late been made use of to serve the ends of factious and seditious persons, to the great danger of the public peace, and may become the means of producing confusion and calamities in the nation: Be it enacted ... That no meeting, of any description of persons, exceeding the number of fifty persons, (other than and except any meeting of any county, riding, or division, called by the lord lieutenant, custos rotulorum, or sheriff, of such county; or a meeting called by the convener of any county or stewartry in that part of *Great Britain* called *Scotland*; or any meeting called by two or more justices of the peace of the county or place where such meeting shall be holden; ... or any meeting called by the major part of the grand jury of the county, or of the division of the county, where such meeting shall be holden, at their general assizes or general quarter sessions of the peace; or any meeting of any city, or borough, or town corporate, called by the mayor or other head officer . . . or any meeting of any ward or division of any city or town corporate, called by the alderman or other head officer of such ward or division; or any meeting of any corporate body), shall be holden, for the purpose or on the pretext of considering of or preparing any petition, complaint, remonstrance, or declaration, or other address to the King, or to both houses, or either house of parliament, for alteration of matters established in church or state, or for the purpose or on the pretext of deliberating upon any grievance in church or state, unless notice of the intention to hold such meeting, and of the time and place when and where the same shall be proposed to be holden, and of the purpose for which the same shall be proposed to be holden, shall be given, in the names of seven persons at the least, being householders resident within the county, city, or place where such meeting shall be proposed to be holden, whose places of abode and description shall be inserted in such notice, and which notice . . . [must not be inserted without the authority signed by seven persons and written at the foot of the notice. The notice and authority must be preserved and produced to a justice if required. Penalty of £50 for insertion without authority or failure to produce it.]

II. [Instead of advertising, notice may be given to the clerk of the peace who shall forthwith send a copy to three justices.]

III. [Meetings without notice to be deemed unlawful assemblies.]

IV. And be it enacted, . . . That if any persons, exceeding the number of fifty, being assembled contrary to the provisions herein before contained, and being required or commanded by any one or more justice or justices of the peace, or by the sheriff of the county or his under sheriff, or by the mayor or other head officer or justice of the peace of any city or town corporate, . . . by proclamation to be made in the king's name, . . . to disperse themselves, and peaceably to depart to their habitations, or to their lawful business, shall, to the number of twelve, or more, notwithstanding such proclamation made, remain or continue together by the space of one hour after such command or request made by proclamation, that then such continuing together to the number of twelve or more, . . . shall be adjudged felony without benefit of clergy, and the offenders therein shall be adjudged felons, and shall suffer death, as in case of felony without benefit of clergy.

V. [Proclamation to be made in the following form.] 'Our sovereign lord the King chargeth and commandeth all persons being assembled immediately to disperse themselves, and peaceably to depart to their habitations or to their lawful business, upon the pains contained in the act, made in the thirty-sixth year of King *George* the *Third, for the more effectually preventing seditious meetings and assemblies.*

GOD save the KING.'

VI. And be it further enacted, . . . That in case any meeting shall be holden, in pursuance of any such notice as aforesaid, and the purpose for which the same shall in such notice have been declared to be holden, or any matter which shall be in such notice proposed to be propounded or deliberated upon as such meeting, shall purport that any matter or thing by law established may be altered otherwise than by the authority of the king, lords, and commons, in parliament assembled, or shall tend to incite or stir up the people to hatred or contempt of the person of his majesty, his heirs or successors, or of the government and constitution of this realm, as by law established, it shall be lawful for one or more justice or justices, or sheriff . . . [etc] by proclamation, to require or command the persons there assembled to disperse themselves; . . . [if twelve or more continue for an hour thereafter, they shall suffer death as felons.]

VII. And be it further enacted, . . . That if any one or more justice or justices of the peace, present at any meeting requiring such notice as aforesaid, shall think fit to order any person or persons who shall at such meeting proceed to propound or maintain any proposition for altering any thing by law established, otherwise than by the authority of the king, lords, and commons, in parliament assembled, . . . [or incite contempt of king and constitution], . . . to be taken into custody, to be dealt with according to law; and in case the said justice or justices, or any of them, or any peace officer acting under their or any of their orders, shall be obstructed in taking into custody, any person or persons so ordered to be taken into custody, then and in such case it shall be lawful for any such justice or justices thereupon to make, or cause to be made, such proclamation as aforesaid, in manner aforesaid; . . . [twelve or more disobeying shall suffer death as felons] . . .

XII. *And whereas certain houses, rooms, or places, within the cities of* London *and* Westminster, . . . *and in other places, have of late been frequently used for the purpose of delivering lectures and discourses on and concerning supposed public grievances, . . . to stir up hatred and contempt*

428

of his Majesty's royal person, and of the government and constitution of this realm as by law established: Be it therefore enacted . . . That every house, room, field, or other place where lectures or discourses shall be delivered, or public debates shall be had on or concerning any supposed public grievance, or any matters relating to the laws, constitution, government or policy of these kingdoms, for the purpose of raising or collecting money, or any other valuable thing, from the persons admitted, . . . unless the opening or using of such house, room, field, or place, shall have been previously licensed in manner hereinafter mentioned shall be deemed a disorderly house or place, and the person by whom such house, room, field, or place, shall be opened or used for the purpose aforesaid, shall forfeit the sum of one hundred pounds for every day or time that such house, room, field, or place, shall be opened or used as aforesaid, to such person as will sue for the same, and be otherwise punished as the law directs in cases of disorderly houses; and every person managing or conducting the proceedings, . . . [or lecturing, or debating, or paying or receiving money or tickets] . . . shall for every such offence forfeit the sum of one hundred pounds to such person as will sue for the same.

XVI. [Justices may license places for delivering lectures; and may revoke them.]

XVIII. [Act not to extend to universities]

XIX. [nor to instructors of youth.]

36 Geo. III, c. 8: *S.L.*, XL, 564.

261. Act against Unlawful Combinations and Confederacies, 1799.

An act for the more efficient suppression of societies established for seditious and treasonable purposes; and for better preventing treasonable and seditious practices.

Whereas a traitorous conspiracy has long been carried on, in conjunction with the persons from time to time exercising the powers of government in France, to overturn the laws, constitution, and government, and every existing establishment, civil and ecclesiastical, both in Great Britain and Ireland, and to dissolve the connection between the two kingdoms, so necessary to the security and prosperity of both: and whereas, in pursuance of such design, and in order to carry the same into effect, divers societies have been of late years instituted in this kingdom, and in the kingdom of Ireland, of a new and dangerous nature, inconsistent with publick tranquillity, and with the existence of regular government, particularly certain societies calling themselves, Societies of United Englishmen, United Scotsmen, United Britons, United Irishmen, *and* The London Corresponding Society: *And whereas the members of many such societies have taken unlawful oaths and engagements of fidelity and secrecy, and used secret signs, and appointed committees, secretaries, and other officers, in a secret manner; and many of such societies are composed of different divisions, branches, or parts, which communicate with each other by secretaries, delegates, or otherwise, and by means thereof maintain an influence over large bodies of men, and delude many ignorant and unwary persons into the commission of acts highly criminal: And whereas it is expedient and necessary that all such societies as aforesaid, and all societies of the like nature, should be utterly suppressed and prohibited, as unlawful combinations and confederacies, highly dangerous to the peace and tranquillity of these kingdoms and to the constitution of the government thereof, as by law established:* Be it enacted . . . That from and after the passing of this Act, all the said Societies of *United Irishmen* . . . [etc] are hereby utterly suppressed and prohibited, as being unlawful combinations and confederacies against the government of our sovereign lord the King, and against the peace and security of his Majesty's liege and subjects.

II. And be it further enacted, . . . That . . . societies, now established, or hereafter to be established, the Members whereof shall, according to the rules thereof, or to any provision or agreement for that purpose, be required or admitted to take any oath . . . not required or authorized by law . . . and every society, of which the names of the members or of any of them, shall be kept secret from the society at large, or which shall have any committee or select body so chosen or appointed, that the members constituting the same shall not be known by the society at large to be members of such committee or select body, . . . and every society which shall be composed of different divisions or branches, or of different parts, acting in any manner separately or distinct from each other, or of which any part shall have any separate or distinct president, . . . [etc] . . . shall be deemed and taken to be unlawful combinations and confederacies; . . .

III. Provided always nevertheless, and be it enacted, That nothing herein contained shall extend to any declaration to be taken, subscribed, or assented to by the members of any society, in case the form of such declaration shall have been first approved and subscribed by two or more of his Majesty's justices of the peace for the county, stewartry, riding, division, or place, where such society shall ordinarily assemble, and shall have been registered with the clerk of the peace, or his deputy, for such county . . .

V. *And whereas certain societies have been long accustomed to be holden in this kingdom under the denomination of* Lodges of Free Masons, *the meetings whereof have been in great measure directed to charitable purposes;* be it therefore enacted, That nothing in this act shall extend to the meetings of any such society or lodge which shall, before the passing of this act, have been usually holden under the said denomination and in conformity to the rules prevailing among the said societies of free masons. . . .

39 Geo. III, c. 79: S.L., XLII, pt. I, 309.

BIBLIOGRAPHY

(For abbreviations, see p. xvi)

GENERAL WORKS

Constitutional History

ANSON, Sir W. R. *The law and custom of the constitution:* vol. I, *Parliament* (5th ed. by Sir M. L. Gwyer), Oxford, 1922; vol. II, *The Crown* (4th ed. by A. B. Keith), Oxford, 1935.

CHRIMES, S. B. *English constitutional history* (2nd ed.), Oxford, 1953.

HOLDSWORTH, Sir W. S. *A history of English law* (14 vols.), 1903—[Vols VI, X, XIII are especially valuable for this period.]

KEIR, Sir D. L. *The constitutional history of modern Britain, 1485–1951* (5th ed.), 1953.

MAITLAND, F. W. *The constitutional history of England*, Cambridge, 1908.

THOMSON, M. A. *A constitutional history of England, 1642–1801*, 1938.

Other Collections of Documents

ASPINALL, A. and SMITH, E. Anthony (eds.). *English historical documents*, vol. XI, *1783–1832*, 1959.

BROWNING, A. (ed.). *English historical documents*, vol. VIII, *1660–1714*, 1953.

COSTIN, W. C. and WATSON, J. Steven. *The law and working of the constitution: Documents, 1660–1914* (2 vols.), 1952.

HORN, D. B. and RANSOME, M. *English historical documents*, vol. X, *1714–1783*, 1957.

General History

BRIGGS, A. *The age of improvement (1783–1867)*, 1959.

CLARK, Sir George. *The later Stuarts* (2nd ed.), Oxford, 1956.

GREEN, V. H. H. *The Hanoverians*, 1948.

HALEVY, E. *A History of the English people in the nineteenth century* (6 vols.), 1949–52. [Vol. I is on this period.]

LECKY, W. E. H. *History of England in the eighteenth century* (8 vols.), 1878–1890.

MACAULAY, T. B., Lord. *Critical and historical essays contributed to the Edinburgh Review*, ed. by F. C. Montague (3 vols.), 1903.

—— *History of England from the accession of James II*, ed. by T. F. Henderson, 1907.

MARSHALL, D. *English People in the eighteenth century*, 1956.

MICHAEL, W. *England under George I* (2 vols.), 1936, 1939.

OGG, D. *England in the reigns of James II and William III*, Oxford, 1956.

PLUMB, J. H. *England in the eighteenth century*, 1950.

TREVELYAN, G. M. *England under Queen Anne* (3 vols.), 1930–34.

—— *England under the Stuarts* (19th ed.), 1947.

WILLIAMS, Basil. *The whig supremacy, 1714–60*, Oxford, 1939.

Biographies

KENYON, J. P. *The Stuarts*, 1958.

—— *Robert Spencer, Earl of Sunderland, 1641–1702*, 1958.

BROWNING, A. *Thomas Osborne, Earl of Danby and Duke of Leeds, 1632–1712* (3 vols), Glasgow, 1944–51.

CHURCHILL, Winston, S. *Marlborough: his life and times* (2 vols), 1947.

FOXCROFT, H. C. *The life and letters of Sir George Savile, first Marquis of Halifax* (2 vols.), 1898.

—— *A character of the trimmer: being a short life of the first Marquis of Halifax,* Cambridge, 1946.

NICHOLSON, T. C. and TURBERVILLE, A. S. *Charles Talbot, Duke of Shrewsbury,* Cambridge, 1930.

TURNER, F. C. *James II*, 1948.

PLUMB, J. H. *The first four Georges*, 1956.

—— *Sir Robert Walpole*, vol. I, *The making of a statesman*, 1956.

REALEY, C. B. *The early opposition to Sir Robert Walpole 1720–1727*, Kansas, 1931.

VAUCHER, P. *Robert Walpole et la politique de Fleury, 1731–42*, Paris, 1924.

—— *La crise du ministère Walpole en 1733–4*, Paris, 1924.

SICHEL, W. *Bolingbroke and his times* (2 vols.), 1901–2.

FIELDHOUSE, H. N. 'Bolingbroke's share in the Jacobite intrigue of 1710–14', *E.H.R.*, LII (1937), 443.

WILLIAMS, Basil. *Stanhope*, 1932.

NULLE, S. H. *Thomas Pelham-Holles, Duke of Newcastle: his early political career, 1693–1724*, Philadelphia, 1931.

EYCK, E. *Pitt versus Fox, father and son, 1737–1806*, 1950.

FIFOOT, C. H. S. *Lord Mansfield*, Oxford, 1936.

ILCHESTER, Lord. *Henry Fox, first Lord Holland* (2 vols.), 1920.

YORKE, P. C. *Life and correspondence of Philip Yorke, Earl of Hardwicke, Lord High Chancellor of Great Britain* (3 vols.), Cambridge, 1913.

TUNSTALL, W. C. B. *William Pitt, Earl of Chatham*, 1938.

WILLIAMS, Basil. *Life of William Pitt, Earl of Chatham* (2 vols.), 1913.

WHITWORTH, R. *Field Marshal Lord Ligonier: a story of the British Army, 1702–1770*, Oxford, 1958.

FITZMAURICE, Lord. *Life of William, Earl of Shelburne* (2 vols., 2nd ed.), 1912.

HOBHOUSE, C. *Fox* (2nd ed.), 1947.

MAGNUS, Sir P. M. *Edmund Burke, a life*, 1939.

SHERRARD, O. A. *Life of John Wilkes*, 1930.

ROSE, J. Holland. *William Pitt and National Revival*, 1911.

—— *William Pitt and the great war*, 1911.

THE REVOLUTION (CH. 1)

GEORGE, R. H. 'The charters granted to English parliamentary corporations in 1688', *E.H.R.* LV, 1940, 47.

—— 'A Note on the Bill of Rights: municipal liberties and freedom of parliamentary election', *A.H.R.* XLII, 1937, 670.

KENYON, J. P. 'The Earl of Sunderland and the Revolution of 1688', *C.H.J.* XI, 1955, 272.

KENYON, J. P. 'The Earl of Sunderland and the King's administration, 1693–1695', *E.H.R.* LXXI, 1956, 576.

LASLETT, P. 'The English Revolution and Locke's *Two Treatises of Government'*, *C.H.J.* XII, 1956, 40.

PLUMB, J. H. 'The elections to the Convention Parliament of 1689', *C.H.J.* V, 1937, 235.

THOMSON, M. A. 'The safeguarding of the Protestant Succession 1702–18', *History*, n.s. XXXIX, 1954, 39.

—— 'Parliament and foreign policy, 1689–1714', *History*, n.s. XXXVIII, 1953, 234.

TREVELYAN, G. M. *The English Revolution, 1688–1689*, 1938.

THE CENTRAL GOVERNMENT (CH. 2)

Crown, Ministers and Parliament

BARNES, D. G. *George III and William Pitt, 1783–1806*, Stanford University, 1939.

BROOKE, J. *The Chatham administration, 1766–1768*, 1956.

BUTTERFIELD, H. 'Lord North and Mr Robinson, 1779', *C.H.J.* V, 1937, 255.

—— 'George III and the constitution', *History*, n.s. XLIII, 1958, 14.

—— *George III and the historians*, 1957.

CHRISTIE, I. R. *The end of North's ministry, 1780–1782*, 1958.

DAVIES, Godfrey. 'The fall of Harley in 1708', *E.H.R.* LXVI, 1951, 246.

FOORD, A. S. 'The waning of "The Influence of the Crown"', *E.H.R.* LXII, 1947, 484.

FRYER, W. R. 'The study of British politics between the Revolution and the Reform Act', *Renaissance and Modern Studies*, University of Nottingham, I, 1957, 91.

KEMP, B. *King and Commons 1660–1832*, 1957.

NAMIER, Sir Lewis. *The structure of politics at the accession of George III* (2nd ed.), 1957.

—— *England in the age of the American revolution*, 1930.

—— 'Monarchy and the party system', Essay in *Personalities and powers*, 1955.

—— 'King George III, a study of personality', Essay in *Personalities and power*, 1955.

OWEN, J. B. *The rise of the Pelhams*, 1957.

PARES, R. *King George III and the politicians*, Oxford, 1953.

—— *Limited monarchy in Great Britain in the eighteenth century*, Historical Association: General Series, No. 35, 1957.

—— 'George III and politicians', *T.R.H.S.*, 5th series, I, 1951, 127.

ROBERTS, Clayton 'The growth of ministerial responsibility to parliament in later Stuart England', *J.M.H.* XXVII, 1956, 215.

SEDGWICK, R. *Letters from William Pitt to Lord Bute: 1755–1758. Essays Presented to Sir Lewis Namier* (ed. by R. Pares and A. J. P. Taylor), 1956.

—— *Letters from George III to Lord Bute, 1756–1766*, 1940.

SUTHERLAND, L. S. 'The East India Company in eighteenth century politics', *Econ. H.R.* XVII, 1947, 15.

—— *The East India Company in eighteenth century politics*, Oxford, 1952.

TYLER, J. E. 'John Roberts, M.P. and the first Rockingham administration', *E.H.R.* LXVII, 1952, 547.

WALCOTT, R. *English politics in the early eighteenth century*, Oxford, 1956. (Controversial: see review by J. H. Plumb in *E.H.R.* LXXII, 1957, 126.)

WINSTANLEY, D. A. *Personal and party government: a chapter in the political history of the early years of the reign of George III, 1760–1766*, Cambridge, 1910.

—— *Lord Chatham and the Whig opposition (1766–1772)*, Cambridge, 1912.

Privy Council and Cabinet

ANSON, Sir William R. 'The cabinet in the seventeenth and eighteenth centuries', *E.H.R.* XXIX, 1914, 56.

—— 'The development of the cabinet, 1688–1760', *E.H.R.* XXIX, 1914, 325.

ASPINALL, A. 'The cabinet council, 1783–1835', *Proc. of the British Academy*, XXXVIII, 1952, 145.

CHRISTIE, I. R. 'The cabinet during the Grenville administration, 1763–1765', *E.H.R.* LXXIII, 1958, 86.

NAMIER, Sir Lewis. 'The end of the nominal cabinet', Essay in *In the margin of history*, 1939.

PLUMB, J. H. 'The organisation of the cabinet in the reign of Queen Anne', *T.R.H.S.* 5th series, VII, 1957, 137.

ROBERTS, Clayton. 'Privy Council schemes and ministerial responsibility in later Stuart England', *A.H.R.* LXIV, 1959, 564.

SEDGWICK, R. 'The inner cabinet from 1739 to 1741', *E.H.R.* XXXIV, 1919, 290.

TEMPERLEY, H. W. V. 'Inner and outer cabinet and Privy Council, 1679–1783', *E.H.R.* XXVII, 1912, 682.

—— 'Documents illustrative of the powers of the Privy Council in the seventeenth century', *E.H.R.* XXVIII, 1913, 127.

—— 'A note on inner and outer cabinets; their development and relations in the eighteenth century', *E.H.R.* XXXI, 1916, 291.

TURNER, E. R. *The Privy Council of England in the seventeenth and eighteenth centuries, 1603–1784* (2 vols.), Baltimore, 1927–8.

—— *The Cabinet council of England in the seventeenth and eighteenth centuries, 1622–1784* (2 vols.), Baltimore, 1930–2.

—— 'The development of the cabinet 1688–1760', *A.H.R.* XVIII, 1913, 751.

—— 'The Lords Justices of England', *E.H.R.* XXIX, 1914, 453.

—— 'Committees of the Privy Council, 1688–1760', *E.H.R.* XXXI, 1916, 545.

—— 'The cabinet in the eighteenth century', *E.H.R.* XXXII, 1917, 192.

—— and MEGARO, G. 'The King's Closet in the eighteenth century', *A.H.R.* XLV, 1939–40, 761.

WILLIAMS, Trevor. 'The cabinet in the eighteenth century', *History*, n.s. XXII, 1937–8, 240 and 332.

WINSTANLEY, D. A. 'George III and his first cabinet', *E.H.R.* XVII, 1902, 678.

Administration: (A) Treasury and Revenue Departments

BAXTER, S. B. *The development of the Treasury, 1660–1702*, 1957.

BINNEY, J. E. D. *British public finance and administration 1774–92*, Oxford, 1958.

CLARK, D. M. 'The office of Secretary to the Treasury in the eighteenth century', *A.H.R.* XLII, 1936–7, 22.

GILL, D. M. 'The Treasury, 1660–1714', *E.H.R.* XLVI, 1931, 600.

—— 'The relationship between the Treasury and the Excise and Customs Commissioners, 1660–1714', *C.H.J.* IV, 1932, 94.

HALL, H. *History of the Custom-revenue in England from the earliest times to the year 1827* (2 vols.), 1885.

HOON, E. E. *The organisation of the English Customs system 1696–1786*, New York, 1938.

HUGHES, E. *Studies in administration and finance 1558–1825, with special reference to the history of salt taxation in England*, Manchester, 1934.

—— 'The English Stamp Duties, 1664–1764', *E.H.R.* LVI, 1941, 234.

LEADAM, I. S. 'The finance of Lord Treasurer Godolphin', *T.R.H.S.*, 3rd series, IV, 1910, 21.

LEFTWICH, B. R. 'The later history and administration of the Customs revenue in England (1671–1814)', *T.R.H.S.*, 4th series, XIII, 1930, 187.

TURNER, E. R. 'The Excise scheme of 1733', *E.H.R.* XLII, 1927, 34.

WARD, W. R. *The English Land Tax in the eighteenth century*, Oxford, 1953.

—— 'The administration of the Window and Assessed Taxes, 1696–1798', *E.H.R.* LXVII, 1952, 522.

—— 'The Office for Taxes, 1665–1798' *Bulletin*, XXV, 1952, 204.

—— 'Some eighteenth century civil servants: the English revenue commissioners, 1754–98', *E.H.R.* LXX, 1955, 25.

Administration: (B) The Secretaries of State

BASYE, A. H. 'The Secretary of State for the Colonies, 1768–1782', *A.H.R.* XXVIII, 1922–3, 13.

HORN, D. B. 'The diplomatic experience of Secretaries of State, 1660–1852', *History*, n.s. XLI, 1956, 88.

JONES-PARRY, E. 'Under-Secretaries of State for Foreign Affairs, 1782–1855', *E.H.R.* XLIX, 1934, 308.

SPECTOR, M. M. *The American department of the British government 1768–1782*, New York, 1940.

THOMSON, M. A. *The Secretaries of State 1681–1782*, Oxford, 1932.

Administration: (C) Trade and Colonies

BASYE, A. H. *Lords Commissioners of Trade and Plantations, 1748–1782*, New Haven, Conn., 1925.

CLARKE, M. P. 'The Board of Trade at work', *A.H.R.* XVII, 1911–12, 17.

DICKERSON, O. M. *American colonial government 1696–1765. A study of the British Board of Trade in its relation to the American colonies, political, industrial, administrative*, Cleveland, Ohio, 1912.

HORN, D. B. 'The Board of Trade and consular reports 1696–1782', *E.H.R.* LIV, 1939, 476.

ROOT, W. T. 'The Lords of Trade and Plantations, 1675–96', *A.H.R.* XXIII, 1918, 20.
See also Basye, A. H. (1922–3), p. 436, and Spector, M. M. (1940), p. 436.

Administration: (D) Post Office

ELLIS, K. *The Post Office in the eighteenth century, a study in administrative history,* Oxford, 1958.

Administration: (E) Navy

EHRMAN, J. *The navy in the war of William III, 1689–1697,* Cambridge, 1953.

JAMES, G. F. 'Josiah Burchett, Secretary to the Lords Commissioners of the Admiralty 1695–1742', *Mariner's Mirror,* XXIII, 1937, 477.

—— and SUTHERLAND SHAW, J. J. 'Admiralty administration and personnel, 1619–1714', *Bulletin,* XIV, 1936–7, 10 and 166.

—— 'The Admiralty establishment, 1759', *Bulletin,* XVI, 1938–9, 24.

Administration: (F) Army

CLODE, C. M. *The military forces of the crown* (2 vols.), 1869.

GEE, O. 'The British War Office in the later years of the American War of Independence', *J.M.H.* XXVI, 1954, 123.

JACOBSEN, G. A. *William Blathwayt, a late 17th century English administrator,* New Haven, Conn., 1932.

ROBSON, E. 'Purchase and promotion in the British Army in the eighteenth century', *History,* n.s. XXXVI, 1951, 57.

SUTHERLAND, L. S. and BINNEY, J. 'Henry Fox as Paymaster-General of the Forces', *E.H.R.* LXX, 1955, 229.

WARD, S. G. P. *Wellington's Headquarters: a study of the administrative problems in the Peninsular, 1809–1814,* Oxford, 1957.

See also Whitworth, R. (1958), p. 443.

Administration: (G) Agriculture

MITCHISON, R. 'The Old Board of Agriculture (1793–1822)', *E.H.R.* LXXIV, 1959, 41.

Administration: (H) Civil Servants

CHRISTIE, I. R. 'The political allegiance of John Robinson, 1770–1784', *Bulletin,* XXIX, 1956, 108.

CLARK, G. Kitson. '"Statesmen in Disguise": Reflexions on the history of the neutrality of the Civil Service', *H.J.* II, 1959, 19.

COHEN, E. W. *The growth of the British Civil Service, 1780–1939,* 1941.

FINER, S. E. 'Patronage and the public service', *Public Administration,* XXX, 1952, 329.

JUDGES, A. V. 'Government personnel in the eighteenth century', *Bulletin,* XVII, 1939–40, 67.

See also Jucker, N. S. (1949), p. 438, and Laprade, W. T. (1922), p. 438.

PARLIAMENT (Ch. 3)

House of Lords

HOLDSWORTH, Sir William S. 'The House of Lords, 1689–1783', *L.Q.R.* XLV, 1929, 307 and 432.

RICHARDS, G. C. 'The creation of peers recommended by the younger Pitt', *A.H.R.* XXXIV, 1929, 47.

TURBERVILLE, A. S. *The House of Lords in the reign of William III*, Oxford, 1913.

—— *The House of Lords in the eighteenth century*, Oxford, 1927.

—— *The House of Lords in the age of reform 1784–1837* (ed. by R. J. White), 1958.

—— 'The House of Lords as a court of law, 1784–1837', *L.Q.R.* LII, 1936, 189.

—— 'The younger Pitt and the House of Lords', *History*, n.s. XXI, 1937, 350.

TURNER, E. R. 'The Peerage Bill of 1719', *E.H.R.* XXVIII, 1913, 243.

House of Commons

(A) GENERAL

PORRITT, E. and A. G. *The unreformed House of Commons, parliamentary representation before 1832* (2 vols.), Cambridge, 1903.

See also all entries listed under "Crown, Ministers and Parliament", pp. 434–5.

(B) MEMBERS

JUDD, G. P. *Members of Parliament, 1734–1832*, 1955. (To be read with caution: see review by R. R. Sedgwick in *E.H.R.* LXXI, 1956, 298.)

NAMIER, Sir Lewis. 'Three eighteenth-century politicians', *E.H.R.* XLII, 1927, 408.

—— 'Bruce Fisher, M.P.: a mid-eighteenth century merchant and his connexions', *E.H.R.* XLII, 1927, 514.

—— 'Daniel Pulteney, M.P.', *Bulletin*, XXVIII, 1955, 160.

UNDERDOWN, P. T. 'Edmund Burke, the commissary of his Bristol constituents, 1774–1780', LXXIII, 1958, 252.

(C) ELECTIONS

CHERRY, G. L. 'Influence of irregularities in contested elections upon election policy during the reign of William III', *J.H.M.* XXVII, 1955, 109.

JUCKER, N. S. (ed.). *The Jenkinson papers 1760–1766*, 1949.

LAPRADE, W. T. (ed.). *The Parliamentary papers of John Robinson 1774–1784*, Camden Society, 3rd series, vol. 33, 1922.

SYKES, N. 'The Cathedral Chapter of Exeter and the general election of 1705', *E.H.R.* XLV, 1930, 260.

MORGAN, W. T. 'An eighteenth-century election in England (1710)', *Political Science Quarterly*, XXXVII, 1922, 585.

RANSOME, M. 'Church and Dissent in the election of 1710', *E.H.R.* LVI, 1941, 76.

—— 'The press in the general election of 1710', *C.H.J.* VI, 1939, 209.

MORGAN, W. T. 'Some sidelights upon the general election of 1715', *Essays in modern English history in honor of Wilbur Cortez Abbott*, Cambridge, Mass., 1941.

NULLE, S. H. 'The Duke of Newcastle and the Election of 1727', *J.M.H.* IX, 1937, I.

WILLIAMS, Basil. 'The Duke of Newcastle and the election of 1734' *E.H.R.* XII, 1897, 448.

FRYER, C. E. 'The general election of 1784', *History*, n.s. IX, 1924–5, 221.

GEORGE, D. M. 'Fox's Martyrs: the general election of 1784', *T.R.H.S.*, 4th Series, XXI, 1939, 133.

LAPRADE, W. T. 'Public opinion and the general election of 1784', *E.H.R.* XXXI, 1916, 224.

(D) CONSTITUENCIES

CHRISTIE, I. R. 'Private patronage versus government influence: John Buller and the contest for control of parliamentary elections at Saltash, 1780–1790', *E.H.R.* LXXI, 1956, 249.

FORRESTER, E. G. *Northamptonshire County elections and electioneering, 1695–1832*, Oxford, 1941.

JASPER, R. C. 'Edward Eliot and the acquisition of Grampound', *E.H.R.* LVIII, 1943, 475.

LAPRADE, W. T. 'William Pitt and Westminster elections', *A.H.R.* XVIII, 1912–13, 253.

ROBSON, R. J. *The Oxfordshire election of 1754: a study in the interplay of city, county and university politics*, Oxford, 1949.

(E) RELATIONS WITH THE EXECUTIVE

LEES, R. M. 'The constitutional importance of the "Commissioners for Wool" of 1689. An administrative experiment of the reign of William III', *Economica*, XIII, 1933, 147 and 264.

—— 'Parliament and the proposal for a Council of Trade, 1695–6', *E.H.R.* LIV, 1939, 38.

THOMSON, M. A. 'Parliament and foreign policy, 1689–1714', *History*, n.s. XXXVIII, 1953, 234.

TURNER, E. R. 'Parliament and foreign affairs, 1603–1760', *E.H.R.* XXXIV, 1919, 172.

(F) PARTIES

BURN, W. L. 'The eighteenth century', Essay in *The British Party System* (2nd ed. by S. D. Bailey), 1953.

BUTTERFIELD, H. *The Englishman and his history*, Cambridge, 1944.

—— *The Whig interpretation of history*, 1931.

—— 'Charles James Fox and the Whig opposition in 1792', *C.H.J.* IX, 1949, 293.

CARSWELL, J. P. *The Old Cause. Three biographical studies in Whiggism*, 1955. (On Thomas Wharton, George Bubb Dodington and C. J. Fox.)

CHRISTIE, I. R. 'The Marquis of Rockingham and Lord North's offer of a coalition, June–July, 1780', *E.H.R.* LXIX, 1954, 388.

FEILING, Sir Keith. *A history of the Tory Party, 1640–1714*, Oxford, 1924.

—— *The second Tory Party, 1714–1832*, 1938.

FIELDHOUSE, H. N. 'Bolingbroke and the idea of non-party government', *History*, n.s. XXIII, 1938–9, 41.

GUTTRIDGE, G. H. 'The Whig opposition in England during the American Revolution', *J.M.H.* VI, 1934, 1.

GUTTRIDGE, G. H. *English Whiggism and the American Revolution*, Berkeley, 1942.

MORGAN, W. T. *English political parties and leaders in the reign of Queen Anne, 1702–1710*, 1920.

—— 'The ministerial revolution of 1710 in England', *Political Science Quarterly*, XXXVI, 1921, 184.

NAMIER, Sir Lewis. 'Country Gentlemen in Parliament, 1750–1784', *Personalities and Powers*, 1955.

NEWMAN, A. N. 'The political patronage of Frederick Lewis, Prince of Wales', *H.J.* I, 1958, 68.

SUTHERLAND, L. S. 'The City of London in eighteenth century politics', *Essays presented to Sir Lewis Namier* (ed. by R. Pares and A. J. P. Taylor), 1956.

—— 'Edmund Burke and the first Rockingham Ministry', *E.H.R.* XLVII, 1932, 46.

—— 'Lord Shelburne and East India Company politics 1766–9', *E.H.R.* XLIX, 1934, 450.

WALCOTT, R. 'The East India interest in the general election of 1700–1701', *E.H.R.* LXXII, 1956, 223.

(G) ECONOMICAL REFORM

CHRISTIE, I. R. 'Economical reform and the "Influence of the Crown", 1780', *C.H.J.* XII, 1956, 144.

KEIR, Sir David, 'Economical reform, 1779–87', *L.Q.R.* L, 1934, 368.

KEMP, B. 'Crewe's Act 1782', *E.H.R.* LXVIII, 1953, 258.

(H) POPULAR MOVEMENTS AND PARLIAMENTARY REFORM

BUTTERFIELD, H. *George III, Lord North and the People, 1779–80*, 1949.

—— 'The Yorkshire Association and the crisis of 1779–80', *T.R.H.S.*, 4th series, XXIX, 1947, 69.

EMDEN, C. S. *The people and the constitution: being a history of the development of the people's influence in British government*, Oxford, 1956.

GREAVES, R. W. 'A scheme for the counties', *E.H.R.* XLVIII, 1933, 630.

KEITH-LUCAS, B. 'County meetings', *L.Q.R.* LXX, 1954, 109.

MACCOBY, S. *English Radicalism, 1762–1785. The origins.* 1955.

—— *English Radicalism, 1786–1832. From Paine to Cobbett.* 1955.

RUDE, G. F. E. 'The Gordon Riots: a study of the rioters and their victims', *T.R.H.S.*, 5th series, VI, 1956, 93.

—— '"Wilkes and Liberty", 1768–1769', *The Guildhall Miscellany*, No. 8, 1957, 13.

—— 'The London "Mob" of the eighteenth century', *H.J.* II, 1959, 1.

VEITCH, G. S. *The genesis of Parliamentary Reform*, 1913.

WHALE, G. 'The influence of the Industrial Revolution (1760–1790) on the demand for Parliamentary Reform', *T.R.H.S.*, 4th series, V, 1922, 101.

(I) PRIVILEGES

ASPINALL, A. 'The reporting and publishing of the House of Commons debates, 1771–1834', *Essays presented to Sir Lewis Namier* (ed. by R. Pares and A. J. P. Taylor), 1956.

WITTKE, C. F. *The history of English parliamentary privilege*, Ohio, 1921.

See also Thomas, P. D. G. (1959), p. 443.

THE CHURCH

(J) PROCEDURE

REDLICH, J. *The procedure of the House of Commons: a study of its history and present form* (3 vols.), 1908.

WILLIAMS, O. C. *The clerical organisation of the House of Commons, 1661–1950*, Oxford, 1954.

LOCAL GOVERNMENT (CH. 4)

HISTORICAL ASSOCIATION. *English local history handlist*, S. 2 (revised), 1952.

BELOFF, M. *Public order and popular disturbances, 1660–1714*, Oxford, 1938.

DOWDELL, E. G. *A hundred years of Quarter Sessions: the government of Middlesex from 1660 to 1760*, Cambridge, 1932.

GEORGE, M. D. *London life in the XVIIIth century*, 1925.

HAMILTON, A. H. A. *Quarter Sessions from Queen Elizabeth to Queen Anne: illustrations of local government and history drawn from original records (chiefly . . . of Devon)*, 1878.

HENDERSON, A. J. *London and the national government, 1721–1742. A study of City politics and the Walpole administration*, Durham, N. Carolina, 1945.

HUGHES, E. *North country life in the eighteenth century*, Oxford, 1952.

MARSHALL, D. *The English poor in the 18th century*, 1926.

MELVILLE, A. R. Leslie. *The life and work of Sir John Fielding*, 1935.

PRINGLE, P. *Hue and Cry: the birth of the British police*, 1955.

RADZINOWICZ, L. *History of the English criminal law and its administration from 1750* (5 vols.), 1948– .

REDLICH, J. *Local government in England* (ed. by F. W. Hirst, 2 vols.), 1903.

REITH, C. *The police idea: its history and evolution in England in the 18th century and after*, 1938.

SPENCER, F. H. *Municipal origins: an account of English private bill legislation relating to local government, 1740–1835*, 1911.

WEBB, S. and B. *English local government from the Revolution to the Municipal Corporations Act* (9 vols.), 1906–29.

THE CHURCH (CH. 5)

(A) The Church of England

ABBEY, C. J. and OVERTON, J. H. *The English church in the eighteenth century* (2 vols.), 1878.

ABBEY, C. J. *The English church and its bishops 1700–1800* (2 vols.), 1887.

BAHLMAN, D. W. R. *The moral revolution of 1688*, Oxford, 1957.

BATESON, M. 'Clerical preferment under the Duke of Newcastle', *E.H.R.* VII, 1892, 685.

BENNETT, G. V. *White Kennett, 1660–1728, Bishop of Peterborough*, 1957.

CARPENTER, E. F. *Thomas Sherlock, 1678–1761*, 1936.

—— *The Protestant Bishop: being the life of Henry Compton, 1632–1713, Bishop of London*, 1956.

441

CARPENTER, E. F. *Thomas Tenison, Archbishop of Canterbury, his life and times*, 1948.

CRAGG, G. R. *From Puritanism to the Age of Reason: a study of changes in religious thought within the Church of England, 1660–1700*, Cambridge, 1950.

DUNN, P. J. 'The political and ecclesiastical activities of William Nicholson, Bishop of Carlisle, 1702–18', *Bulletin*, IX, 1931–2, 196.

EVERY, G. *The High Church party, 1688–1718*, 1956.

GEE, H. and HARDY, W. J. *Documents illustrative of English church history*, 1896.

GWATKIN, H. M. *Church and state in England to the death of Queen Anne*, 1917.

HART, A. Tindal. *The life and times of John Sharp, Archbishop of York*, 1949.

—— *The eighteenth century country parson, c. 1689–1830*, Shrewsbury, 1955.

JAMES, F. G. *North country bishop: a biography of William Nicholson*, Oxford, 1957.

LEGG, J. Wickham. *English church life from the Restoration to the Tractarian movement*, 1914.

MAKOWER, F. *The constitutional history and constitution of the Church of England*, 1895.

SAVIDGE, A. *The foundation and early years of Queen Anne's Bounty*, 1955.

STROMBERG, R. N. *Religious liberalism in 18th century England*, Oxford, 1954.

SYKES, N. *Edmund Gibson, Bishop of London*, Oxford, 1926.

—— *Church and state in England in the 18th century*, Cambridge, 1934.

—— *William Wake, Archbishop of Canterbury, 1657–1737* (2 vols.), Cambridge, 1957.

—— *From Shelden to Secker*, Cambridge, 1959.

—— 'The Duke of Newcastle as Ecclesiastical minister', *E.H.R.* LVII, 1942, 59.

—— 'Archbishop Wake and the Whig Party, 1716–23; a study in incompatibility of temperament', *C.H.J.* VIII, 1945, 93.

WHITING, C. E. *Nathaniel Lord Crewe, Bishop of Durham, 1674–1721, and his diocese*, 1940.

See also Sykes, N. (1930), p. 438, and Ransome, M. (1941), p. 438.

(B) The Nonjurors

HAWKINS, L. M. *Allegiance in church and state, the problem of the nonjurors in the English Revolution*, 1928.

OVERTON, J. H. *The nonjurors. Their lives, principles and writings*, 1902.

WAND, J. W. C. *The High Church schism: four lectures on the nonjurors*, 1951.

(C) The Evangelicals

BALLEINE, G. R. *A history of the Evangelical party in the Church of England* (3rd ed.), 1951.

DAVIES, G. C. B. *The early Cornish Evangelicals, 1735–60: a study of Walker of Truro and others*, 1951.

ELLIOTT-BINNS, L. E. *The early Evangelicals: a religious and social study*, 1953.

OVERTON, J. H. *The Evangelical revival in the eighteenth century* (4th ed.), 1898.

SMYTH, C. H. E. *Simeon and church order: a study of the origin of the evangelical revival in Cambridge in the eighteenth century*, Cambridge, 1940.

—— 'The Evangelical movement in perspective', *C.H.J.* VII, 1943, 160.

WOOD, A. Skevington. *Thomas Haweis, 1734–1820*, 1957.

(D) *The Methodists*

PIETTE, M. *John Wesley and the evolution of Protestantism*, 1937.
SIMON, J. S. *The revival of religion in England in the eighteenth century*, 1907.
—— *John Wesley and the religious societies*, 1921.
—— *John Wesley and the Methodist Societies*, 1923.
—— *John Wesley and the advance of Methodism*, 1925.
—— *John Wesley the master builder*, 1927.
—— *John Wesley, the last phase*, 1934.

(E) *The Dissenters*

BENNETT, T. 'Hallam and the Indemnity Acts', *L.Q.R.* XXVI, 1910, 400.
CLARK, H. W. *History of English nonconformity from Wiclif to the close of the nineteenth century* (2 vols.), 1911–13.
COOMER, D. *Dissent under the early Hanoverians*, 1946.
LINCOLN, A. H. *Some political and social ideas of English Dissent, 1763–1800*, Cambridge, 1938.
MANNING, B. L. *The Protestant Dissenting Deputies* (ed. by O. Greenwood), Cambridge, 1952.

(F) *Roman Catholics*

HEXTER, J. H. 'The Protestant revival and the Catholic question in England, 1778–1829', *J.M.H.* VIII, 1936, 297.
HUGHES, P. *The Catholic question, 1688–1829*, 1929.
MATHEW, D. *Catholicism in England 1535–1935. Portrait of a minority: its culture and tradition* (2nd ed.), 1949.
PURCELL, P. 'The Jacobite rising of 1715 and the English Catholics', *E.H.R.* XLIV, 1929, 418.
WARD, B. *The dawn of the Catholic revival in England 1781–1803* (2 vols.), 1909.
WILTON, R. C. 'Early 18th century Catholics in England', *Catholic Historical Review*, n.s. IV, 1925, 367.

LIBERTIES OF THE SUBJECT (CH. 6)

DICEY, A. V. *Introduction to the study of the law of the constitution* (9th ed. by E. C. S. Wade), 1939.

(A) *The Press*

ASPINALL, A. *Politics and the press c. 1780–1850*, 1949.
—— 'Statistical accounts of the London newspapers in the eighteenth century', *E.H.R.* LXIII, 1948, 201.
BURTON, K. G. *The early newspaper press in Berkshire (1723–1855)*, Reading, 1954.
FORD, D. M. 'The growth of the freedom of the press', *E.H.R.* IV, 1889, 1.
HANSON, L. W. *Government and the press, 1695–1763*, Oxford, 1936.
THOMAS, P. D. G. 'The beginning of parliamentary reporting in newspapers, 1768–1774', *E.H.R.* LXXIV, 1959, 623.
WEBB, R. K. *The British working class reader, 1790–1848: literary and social tension*, 1955.

(B) Personal Liberty

CRAWFORD, C. C. 'The writ of Habeas Corpus', *American Law Review*, XLII, 1908, 481.
—— 'The suspension of the Habeas Corpus Act and the Revolution of 1689', *E.H.R.* XXX, 1915, 613.

FIDDES, E. 'Lord Mansfield and the Sommersett Case', *L.Q.R.* L, 1934, 499.

REZNECK, S. 'The statute of 1696: a pioneer measure in the reform of judicial procedure in England', *J.M.H.* II, 1930, 5.

INDEX

2 G